SYLLOGE OF COINS
OF THE BRITISH ISLES

59

SYLLOGE OF COINS OF THE BRITISH ISLES

A British Academy Research Project

The British Sylloge project was first promoted in the early 1950s by Christopher Blunt and other members of the British and Royal Numismatic Societies. An informal committee was formed under the chairmanship of Sir Frank Stenton, who in 1956 secured its admission as a Committee of the British Academy. The first volume, on Anglo-Saxon coins in the Fitzwilliam Museum, Cambridge, was published by the British Academy in 1958.
The aim of the series is to publish detailed and fully illustrated catalogues of coins of the British Isles in British and foreign collections. The volumes range in scope from Ancient British coins to seventeenth-century tokens, with most detailed coverage of the Anglo-Saxon coinage. The collections recorded include those in more than two hundred national, university and provincial museums in Britain and Ireland and of museums in Scandinavia, Germany, Poland, Latvia, Estonia, Russia and the United States of America.

A full listing of the series is printed at the end of this volume. The SCBI Database can be consulted on the Internet via www.britac.ac.uk or www.medievalcoins.org.

This volume is dedicated to the memory of
Mrs Elizabeth G. Norweb
5 February 1917—1 June 2007

The Sultaness Coffee-house, Sweeting's Rents (as 7711),
Museum of London specimen 96.66/1131,
x 2½

SYLLOGE OF COINS OF THE BRITISH ISLES

59

THE NORWEB COLLECTION

CLEVELAND, OHIO, U.S.A.

TOKENS OF THE BRITISH ISLES 1575–1750

PART VII

CITY OF LONDON

BY

R. H. THOMPSON and M. J. DICKINSON

LONDON
PUBLISHED BY SPINK & SON LIMITED
2007

PUBLISHED BY SPINK & SON LIMITED
LONDON 2007

ISBN-10 1-902040-80-5

ISBN-13 978-1-902040-80-6

Production of this volume has been financed
through foundation grants made available
to the American Numismatic Society
in memory of Mrs R. Henry Norweb

Typeset from the authors' disk by Quorum Print Services, Unit 3, Lansdown Industrial Estate,
Gloucester Road, Cheltenham, Gloucestershire GL51 8PL
Printed in Great Britain on acid-free paper at the Cromwell Press, Trowbridge, Wiltshire

CONTENTS

PREFACE

PROCEDURES for Part VII have continued as before. Mrs Elizabeth Norweb and family have supported the project in memory of her mother-in-law. Dr Mark Blackburn has been our editor. Mrs May Sinclair, and Messrs Douglas Saville and Philip Skingley, attended to matters at Spink's. Mr (now Dr) Matthew Weait weighed the tokens long ago. Mr John Spink or his Brighton firm took the photographs, with replacements made by Mr Steve Wakeham. The photographs were cut out by Mr Tim Everson. We are grateful to all.

We have continued in spite of difficulties. One of us (MD) moved house. The other (RT) was struck by lightning through his computer, was merely shocked, but his modem was 'fried'. However, the major difficulty has been the size and complexity of the City of London, with extensive documentation which we have certainly not winnowed completely (Prerogative Court of Canterbury wills hardly at all). We have supplied map references to Ogilby & Morgan (1676), conveniently re-published by the London Topographical Society, who have permitted us to reproduce the Key Map. Thus readers may position the tokens in the City's close-built and pullulating streets.

Actually that adjective is too rude. The obscurity of token-issuers is often a measure of our own ignorance, and we have found many issuers (not all) in manuscripts at the Society of Genealogists compiled by the energetic Percival Boyd (1868-1955), in particular his 'Inhabitants of London' in 238 volumes. That Society is helpfully publishing the *London Livery Company Apprenticeship Registers*, including Vol. 43 *Vintners' Company*, 2006. In that year we proved from another of these registers that the so-called 'Weavers' Arms' on the halfpenny of Edmond Wratten **(6939)** is the first known example of the arms of the Painter-Stainers. The publications of Kenneth Rogers M.D. have been very helpful. Every reference to Woodhead 1966 identifies a Common Councilman or Alderman of the City of London. The Fire Court calendar, and the Mills & Oliver *Survey of Building Sites* after the Great Fire, document many issuers, even with ground plans of some of their houses.

It may cause surprise that corporate issuers are represented, Bridewell Hospital and Christ's Hospital, and even the Corporation of the Poor, which was housed not in the King's but in the Queen's Wardrobe **(7783)**. The City is also represented on a token issued by the 'Clerk of Newgate Market'. The types of **7587** relate it to St Lawrence Jewry, perhaps as a communion token. Private token-issuers include the father of Sir Thomas Rawlinson 1647-1708 **(6907)**, and the father of Sir Francis Dashwood Bt., ancestor of the notorious Dashwoods of West Wycombe **(6610)**. The issuer of **7363** was not himself distinguished, but a decade earlier his house seems to have been a meeting-place for the Ranter sect; though most token-issuers doubtless led steady and dependable lives like Defoe's 'Complete English Tradesman', engaging in a surprising variety of trades.

It has been satisfying to locate the tokens of a wax-chandler bearing the mysterious letters SMCLATCH **(7617-18)**, and to identify him as Grace [*sic*] Hardwin, Master of the Wax Chandlers in 1650-2. The issuer of **6991** has been identified with a Weigher and Teller at the Mint. Thomas Rooks made ink at the East End of St Paul's Cathedral 'near the school'. The rare surname Blumsum enabled us to attribute the issuer to Blackhorse Alley in St Bride's, as distinct from others spelled Black Horse, but too late to place the alley in strict alphabetical order. That surname may come from Bluntisham, Cambs., and others show local origins ranging from the Danelaw (Gilstrape, Snesby) to Sussex (Skarvill, Strudwick), and beyond (Waggoner, Clarveato?). 'Heares Street' is now confirmed as Hart Street, and the new location Smithers Lane is recorded from a non-Williamson token.

Over 230 of the 1,443 types in this volume are not in Williamson, most being fully published for the first time. Many readings and duplicate recordings have been corrected, and several tokens have been reattributed from an Uncertain category, from Middlesex, and even from Ireland **(7616, 7634, 7654, 7178)**. Dickinson 21A, 31A and 395A can be deleted (see **6434, 7597, 6695**). There is a very rare leather piece **(7562)**, and a goodly scattering of pennies, many of them associated with coffee-houses. Coffee was a new import, and since there is much to say about the earliest such token, difficult to describe from any other example, we have been permitted to illustrate a Museum of London specimen in our Frontispiece, and we include an introductory essay on coffee-house tokens. This may form some sort of substitute for the book which Mr R. Henry Norweb III hoped we might write.

CONTEMPORARY REFERENCES TO TOKENS, THE DOWNFALL OF COFFEE-PENCE, AND THE SULTANESS

R. H. Thompson

THE present volume includes what are believed to be the earliest, and the latest, of the main series of seventeenth-century tokens. The source of that belief is Browne Willis, 'An Alphabetical Series of the Traders Pennys, Half Pennys and Farthings set out by Private Persons inter 1648 and 1673, collected by B. W. from 1732 to 1742' (Ashmolean Museum, MS Willis 63). Browne Willis, antiquary, was born only ten years after the first royal proclamation against the tokens, and his antiquarian interests were awakened at Westminster School (1696-1700), so that his annotations in this catalogue were virtually those of a contemporary.[1] The annotations relevant to the history of London tokens are given below under 1648 and 1672, in date order with other contemporary references since these are so rare.

1648. Tower Street: King's Head: S., P. (Norweb **7770-1**):

'*N.B.—This is the first ever coined*'.

Significantly, this token was issued on a street leading west from Tower Hill, where the Tower of London housed the moneyers, now known to have minted the tokens.[2]

1663. Poultry: Exchange tavern: K[ing], W[illiam] (Norweb **7482**):

'*it was so early in the morning, five a Clock, that there was no body stirring elsewhere, only here by mishap Mr King himself was up and standing at the Bar, telling of Brass farthings*'[3].

The counting of the variety of tokens received in change appears to have been a morning chore, unless the vintner was taking an interest in what others had issued. The farthings that he had issued himself were dated 1651.

1665. Temple Bar neighbourhood: Cock ale-house: C., H. (Norweb **7713**):

'*This is to certify that the Master of the* Cock and Bottle, *commonly called the* Cock *alehouse, at Temple Bar, hath dismissed his servants and shut up his house for this long vacation, intending (God willing) to return at Michaelmass* [sic] *next so that all persons*

1 *ODNB* s.v. Willis, Browne (1682-1760); History of Parliament Trust, *The House of Commons 1690-1715*, [by] Eveline Cruickshanks… [et al.] (Cambridge, 2002, 5 vols.), v. 880-2.

2 Ambrose Heal, *A XVII century ms. list of tokens* ([s.l.], 1928, reprinted from *Notes & Queries*), p. 2; J. G. Milne, 'Seventeenth-century tokens: the Browne Willis cabinet', *BNJ* 26 (1951), 333-8 (p. 334); R. H. Thompson, 'Central or local production of seventeenth-century tokens', *BNJ* 59 (1989), 198-211, pl. 16.

3 [Francis Kirkman], *The Counterfeit Lady unveiled* (London, 1673), p. 28; *ODNB* s.v. Carleton [*née* Moders (?)], Mary [*nicknamed* the German Princess] (1634x42-1673), impostor.

who have any accounts or farthings belonging to the said house are desired to repair thither before the 8th of this instant July and they shall receive satisfaction.'[4]

Unstated in this advertisement is the presence of the plague.

1672. Fleet Street, St Dunstan in the West neighbourhood: Seven Stars: Markham, Robert (Norweb **7572**):

'*This is the last Trader, they being this year cryed down*'[5].

Curiously, *Trader* meaning 'A tradesman's token' (as this appears to do) is not recorded by *OED* before 1775, and then refers back to Ireland in 1727.

1672. A quarto pamphlet with the title *The Downfall of Coffee-pence* was in the library of Edward Harley, second earl of Oxford and Mortimer (1689-1741). After his death the Harleian manuscripts were purchased for the British Museum, but it was then too late for the printed books to be acquired. They had been sold by 4 October 1742 to the bookseller Thomas Osborne, who dispersed them gradually during the seventeen-forties, the English historical pamphlets by auction in 1747-48.[6] The pamphlet in question does not appear in the five-volume *Catalogus Bibliothecæ Harleianæ* by Samuel Johnson and others (1743-45), nor is it named amongst the quartos in numbers 1-5 of T. Osborne, *Catalogue of some tracts and pamphlets collected by the late Earl of Oxford* [1747-48]. It was not reprinted in the *Harleian Miscellany, or, A collection of scarce, curious, and entertaining tracts...found in the late Earl of Oxford's library.*[7]

It was, however, described in *A copious and exact catalogue of pamphlets in the Harleian Library, &c.* [1747?].[8] An exact transcription of the title (apart from long *s*), which may be the closest to the original now available, runs as follows:

The *Downfall* of *Coffee-Pence* : Or a true and perfect Account of the short Life, deserved Death, and desired Burial of Coffee-Pence and Half-pence. With the sad Lamentation of their Owners, on their Changing them for Silver; in pursuance of his Majesties Gracious Proclamation, published the 19th of this Instant *August,* 1672. Printed for *Phil. Brooksby,* &c. (In one Sheet) *Quarto* 1672

4 *The Intelligencer,* cit. Jacob Larwood and John Camden Hotten, *The History of Signboards* (London, [pref. 1866]), p. 208.

5 Heal (as note 2), p. 2; Milne, p. 334.

6 Arundell Esdaile, *The British Museum library* (London, 1946), pp. 33-4; *The Diary of Humfrey Wanley 1715-1726*, ed. C. E. Wright and Ruth C. Wright (London, 1966, 2 vols.), i. lxxix.

7 *Harleian miscellany*, ed. W. Oldys (London, 1744-46, 8 vols.).

8 Edward Harley, second Earl of Oxford, *A copious and exact catalogue of pamphlets in the Harleian Library, &c.* [London]: [T. Osborne], [1747?], p. 131, no. 428.

Philip Brooksby was made free of the Stationers' Company by Elizabeth Andrews in 1670, and was a prolific publisher of all kinds of cheap literature until 1697. During the years 1672-83 he was at the Golden Ball near the Hospital Gate, West Smithfield.[9]

This copious catalogue, at the time anonymous, was so highly valued by collectors and scholars that it was reprinted in Thomas Park's edition of the *Harleian Miscellany*, where its author was acknowledged to be William Oldys (1696-1761), herald and antiquary. It may provide the only first-hand record of the pamphlet, which is not recorded by Wing in any library. Dr Christian Dekesel and Yvette Dekesel De Ruyck have also searched their records of anonymous works in European and other libraries, but in vain. From Park's edition of the *Harleian Miscellany* the description and the annotation, with a more modern use of capitals, italics and punctuation, are given below, the only spelling differences in 1747 being *Inconveniencies* for 'Inconveniences', and *Pedegree* for 'pedigree'.[10]

The Downfall of Coffee-Pence: or, a true and perfect account of the short life, deserved death, and desired burial of coffee-pence and half-pence. With the sad lamentation of their owners, on their changing them for silver; in pursuance of his majesties gracious proclamation, published the 19th of this instant August, 1672. Printed for Phil. Brooksby, &c. 1672. (Quarto in one sheet.)

'In this discourse, the author treats, 1. Of a penny in general; its etymology, ancient form, value, &c. 2. Of the first occasion of private persons stamping half-pence and pence. 3. The mischiefs and Inconveniences thence arising. 4. The advantages accruing by a general farthing; and the lamentation of the owners of the prohibited pence and half-pence. He has this observation upon our ancient penny, (p. 4) "From the Saxon's time, unto the reign of King Edward III. our English penny, like a Good Fryday bun, had a cross struck so deep into the midst of it, that you might break out any part of four, to buy what you had occasion for, which was in those times their farthing; so called from High Dutch, whence our English Tongue derives its pedigree, *Ein Viertding*; that is, a fourth thing, or part" '.

The 1747 catalogue entry was copied by the Revd. William Robert Hay (1761-1839)[11] into his copy of Charles Pye's *Provincial Copper Coins or Tokens,* a copy subsequently owned by Dr D. W. Dykes, to whom I am grateful for scanning the

9 Henry R. Plomer, *A dictionary of the printers and booksellers who were at work in England...* [etc.] *from 1668 to 1725* ([London], 1922), p. 52; Donald Wing, *Short-title catalogue of books printed in England...* [etc.], *1641-1700*, 2nd edn. (New York, 1998, 4 vols.), iv. 140-4.

10 Edward Harley, second Earl of Oxford, *A copious and exact catalogue of pamphlets in the Harleian Library*, arranged by William Oldys, Esq. In: *Harleian Miscellany*, ed. T. Park (London, 1808-13, 10 vols.), x. 357-468 (p. 441, no. 428).

11 On Hay see Canon [F. R.] Raines, *The Vicars of Rochdale*, 1883 (Chetham Society, *Remains Historical and Literary connected with the Palatine Counties of Lancaster and Chester*, new series), ii. 284-325; D. W. Dykes, 'Who was "R.Y."?: searching for an identity', *BNJ* 67 (1997), 115-22.

relevant page.[12] Amongst smaller inaccuracies Hay omitted from the title '...Death, and desired...'. In the interim that Pye volume had been owned by Samuel Henry Hamer (1859-1930), who introduced a few more inaccuracies when printing Hay's notes in 1903, and inserted the misleading heading CATALOGUES OF PAMPHLETS IN THE HARLEIAN LIBRARY.[13] There is no cause to think that Hamer or Hay had seen the original pamphlet, even though Hay's paternal grandmother, Abigail, Countess of Kinnoull (d. 1750), was the younger daughter of Robert Harley, the founder of the Harleian Library.

In the Norweb Collection coffee-men or coffee-house keepers have appeared near New College, Oxford, in the two Southwark localities of Borough High Street in 1669 and Tooley Street in 1666 (v. **4852, 5134**), in Beverley in 1671, Leeds and York in 1669, and Dublin in 1664. To judge from the presence of coffee-pots on their tokens, coffee-house keepers were also present in Trumpington Street, Cambridge, and in Exeter, in 1669-70. The presence of a turbaned bust, or Turk's head, may indicate a concern with coffee in Norwich in 1660, and is assumed to do so on tokens not in the collection for Burges in Aylesbury, 1670, Neyld in Derby, 1667, and Corney in Sedbergh, 1672.[14]

Traditionally, the first English coffee-house was opened in Oxford in 1650, as stated by the Oxford antiquary Anthony (à) Wood (1632-1695).[15] However, Prof. Markman Ellis has pointed out that Wood did not make this claim until 1671. In the earliest version of his diary, written up to the end of 1659, he merely claimed that coffee was consumed in private in 1650, and at an unspecified date between 10 August 1654 and 25 April 1655 added that coffee was 'publickly solde'. This addition was conjecturally dated 'March 1651' by Wood's nineteenth-century editor Andrew Clark, but there is no evidence for such an early date.

On the other hand, in 1651 Thomas Hodges, Grocer of London and Turkey merchant, welcomed into his house in Walbrook the young Draper and Levant merchant Daniel Edwards with the prospect of marrying Hodges' daughter Mary (a marriage which took place on 31 March 1652). Daniel Edwards had returned from Izmir = Smyrna with his Greek man-servant Pasqua Rosee, bringing some characteristic habits of Levantine merchants: hard work, Puritan politics, and coffee drinking. Unfortunately, the novelty

12 Charles Pye, *Provincial Copper Coins or Tokens issued between the years 1787 and 1796* (London; Birmingham, [1795]).

13 S. H. Hamer, 'Notes on some interesting token books and their original owner', *Spink Numismatic Circular* 11 (1903), cols. 6048-56 (col. 6054).

14 George Berry and Peter Morley, 'A revised survey of the seventeenth-century tokens of Buckinghamshire', *BNJ* 43 (1973), 96-125, pls. iii-iv (Nos. 9-10 and fig. 10); BW Derbyshire 86, also 88; BW Yorkshire 302.

15 Anthony Wood, *The Life and Times of Anthony Wood*; ed. A. Clark (Oxford, 1891-1900, 5 vols.), i. 168-9; Percy Manning, 'Sport and pastime in Stuart Oxford', in *Surveys and Tokens*, ed. H. E. Salter (Oxford, 1923), 83-135 (pp. 128-9); Samuel Pepys, *The Diary*; ed. Robert Latham and William Matthews (London, 1970-83, 10 vols.), x. 70-2; Brian Cowan, *The Social Life of Coffee* (New Haven & London, 2005), pp. 25, 90-4.

of coffee at Hodges' house drew 'too much company to him' and impeded the family's work, so Hodges and Edwards set up Pasqua Rosee in a stall in St Michael's churchyard to sell coffee to the public, certainly before 1654, and perhaps as early as 1652. This was the first coffee-house in Christendom.[16]

According to the life of Sir Henry Blount by John Aubrey (1626-1697):[17]

'The first coffee-house in London was in St Michael's Alley in Cornhill, opposite to the church; which was set up by one Bowman (coachman to Mr Hodges, a Turkey merchant, who suggested it) in or about the year 1652. 'Twas about four years before any other was set up, and that was by Mr Farr.'

Christopher Bowman, son of a yeoman of South Mimms, Middlesex, was living at Thomas Hodges' house by 1641, and was formally bound apprentice to him in 1644. He became free of the Grocers on 22 February 1654, and as such he was brought in as a partner for Pasqua Rosee when local ale-sellers queried the latter's right, as a foreigner, to trade in the City. Their partnership moved across St Michael's Alley to better premises in 1656, with a new lease signed on 14 August 1657, though Pasqua Rosee's name by then had disappeared. Bowman's coffee-house was a prodigious success until he died in October 1662.[18]

His coffee-house was run after the Great Fire by George Backler and Stephen Hayward, whose undated halfpenny, issued *At the ould Coffee house, formerly Bomans*, is in this volume (**7615**). The earliest dated coffee-house token is from the Solyman, Ivy Lane in 1663 (**7164**), followed by the Hart's Horns, West Smithfield in 1664 (**7810**). The 1666 token of James Farr at the Rainbow is included here (**6951**), and many others may be found through the indexes. James Farr's building also accommodated the bookseller Daniel Pakeman in 1657, and from 1663 to 1669 the printer and bookseller Samuel Speed, who crept into the old *DNB* only so that he could be distinguished from his cousin of the same name, both being grandsons of the historian John Speed. In the *ODNB* he has his own entry, and his 1667 penny token, new to Williamson, appears here (**7158**).[19]

Most coffee-house tokens probably post-date the Restoration, but there is one exception. The most famous coffee-house keeper was Thomas Garraway, whose establishment flourished in Exchange Alley, in the parish of St Mary Woolnoth, from 1668/70 until the late nineteenth century. It began, however, in Sweeting's Rents in the

16 Markman Ellis, *The Coffee-house: a cultural history* (London, 2004), pp. 26-36.

17 John Aubrey, *Brief Lives*; ed. Andrew Clark (Oxford, 1898, 2 vols.), i. 110; ed. Richard Barber (Woodbridge, 1975), pp. 42-3.

18 Ellis (as note 16), pp. 34-41; Harleian Society, *The Parish Registers of St Michael, Cornhill...*, ed. Joseph Lemuel Chester (London, 1882), p. 252. Brian Cowan incorrectly dates Bowman's death to 1663 (*ODNB*, accessed 7 Oct. 2006, s.v. Rosee, Pasqua (fl. 1651-1656)).

19 Ellis (as note 16), p. 133; *ODNB* s.v. Speed, Samuel (bap. 1633, d. 1679?).

parish of St Bartholomew by the Exchange, where Thomas *Garway* and his wife Elizabeth (d. 1674) were living by early 1658, when their son Philip was baptized. Thomas appears from a 1658 notice in *Mercurius Politicus*[20] to have been the first retailer of leaf tea in England:

'That Excellent, and by all Physitians approved, *China* Drink, called by the *Chineans*, *Teha*, by other Nations *Tay alias Tee*, is sold at the *Sultaness-head*, a *Cophee-house* in *Sweetings* Rents by the Royal Exchange, *London*.'

Dr Kenneth Rogers drew strong support from this advertisement for his suggestion that Garraway was the issuer of the anonymous token published here as **7711**:

Obv. THE SVLTANESS A COFFEE HOVSE around female bust to left

Rev. IN SWEETINGS RENTS CORNHIL around arms

Dr Rogers' suggestion can now be confirmed. The arms have been consistently described[21] as 'a cross with a full face in each quarter', but there is no cross as such, and in each quarter there is not a human face (as Burn specifically states and the other cataloguers imply), but a lion's face affronté and cut off closely behind the ears, anciently called a leopard's face. The true identity of what has been described as a cross is clearest on the Museum of London specimen (see Frontispiece). The vertical tapers towards the base, and represents the wedge-shaped figure known as a pile. With tinctures the blazon becomes *Argent a pile between four leopards' heads Gules and over all a fess Gules*, which were the arms of Garraway otherwise Garway, and in particular of Sir Henry Garway, of the parish of St Peter le Poer, lord mayor of London in 1639-40.[22] Use of the arms must show that the token-issuer was a member of the same family. The arms were also quartered (see opposite) by Sir Henry's cousin John Garway of London, merchant, whose fourth son was called Thomas.[23]

For the *ODNB* Brian Cowan found no evidence on Thomas Garraway's parentage.[24] In 1675, however, in order to suppress debate about government actions, a Proclamation for the Suppression of Coffee-houses was proposed. All licences granted for the selling of coffee, chocolate, sherbet or tea would be recalled, and any persons who then traded

20 Kenneth Rogers, *Old London: Cornhill, Threadneedle Street and Lombard Street: old houses and signs* (London and Tonbridge, 1935), p. 76; *ODNB* s.v. Garraway, Thomas (d. 1692?).

21 Jacob Henry Burn, *A descriptive Catalogue of the London Traders, Tavern and Coffee-house Tokens* (London, 1853), no. 989n. and 2nd edn. (London, 1855), no. 1131n.; William Boyne, *Tokens issued in the Seventeenth Century* (London, 1858), London 2418; BW London 3029.

22 John W. Papworth, *An alphabetical Dictionary of Coats of Arms... forming an extensive Ordinary of British Armorials* (London, 1874), p. 1023; *The Visitation of London...1633...1635, made by Sr Henry St George;* ed. Joseph Jackson Howard and Joseph Lemuel Chester (London, 1880-83, 2 vols.), i. 304; *ODNB* s.v. Garway, Sir Henry (bap. 1575, d. 1646).

23 *Vis. Lond. 1633-5* (as note 22), i. 305. Both branches of Garway are depicted with arms quartering *Gules two bars Argent each charged with three mascles Gules a canton Or*, apparently for Gery etc. with a leopard's face *Azure* on the canton (*DBAMO*, i. 56; Papworth 1874, pp. 35-6).

24 *ODNB* s.v. Garraway, Thomas (d. 1692?), coffee-house keeper.

without a licence could be fined £5 a month. This would have ruined the coffee men. They drew up a successful petition under the leadership of Thomas Garraway, whose cousin William Garway (Garraway), MP for Chichester, was influential in opposition circles.[25] William was the eldest son of Sir Henry Garway, the late lord mayor.[26] Therefore the anonymous Sultaness token can be safely attributed to Thomas Garraway otherwise Garway, fourth son of John Garway and of Frances, daughter of Sir Robert *Loret*[27] of Soulbury, Bucks. Thomas's eldest brother Robert was aged eleven in 1634, so the coffee-house keeper will have been the Thomas, son of John Garraway, baptised on 2 December 1632 at Sir Henry Garway's parish church of St Peter le Poer.[28]

Auctions of ships, bulk goods, rare books and (from 1679) wine were held at Garraway's Coffee-house, which in addition to a meeting-place for London's social élite thus became one of the birthplaces of the London stock exchange. It was assessed in poll taxes of the sixteen-nineties, but in that for 1692 Thomas Garraway's name was replaced by another.[29]

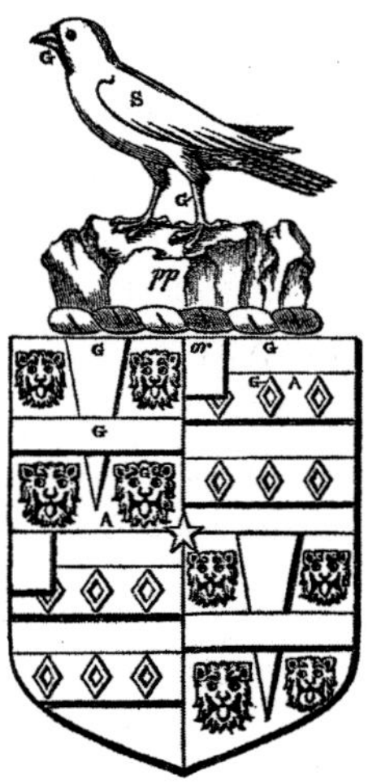

25 Ellis (as note 16), pp. 86-100.

26 Basil Duke Henning, *The House of Commons 1660-1690* (London, 1983, 3 vols.), ii. 373; *ODNB* s.v. Garway, William (bap. 1617, d. 1701), baptized like his father at St Peter le Poer.

27 i.e. Sir Robert Lovett of Liscombe, Bucks. (d. 1643): John Burke, *A genealogical and heraldic History of the extinct and dormant Baronetcies*..., 2nd edn. (London, 1841), p. 324.

28 *Vis. Lond. 1633-5* (as note 22), i. 305; International Genealogical Index.

29 ODNB s.v. Garraway, Thomas (d. 1692?).

ARRANGEMENT

THIS whole volume is confined to the City of London, the 'One Square Mile'. For the inadequacies of Williamson's 'London' chapter, much of which belongs outside the City, see Greenall 1991, pp. 90-2. The City was (and is) administratively distinct from the rest of London, and its tokens are listed in Greenall 1991, pp. 95-107. Here we follow the same arrangement, except that we have transferred the following lanes and courts shared with another administrative area because the portion in the City was minimal:

Field Lane, Field Lane corner, Field Lane neighbourhood, to Metropolitan Middlesex: Holborn;

Golden Lane to Metropolitan Middlesex: Finsbury;

Hartshorn Court to Finsbury likewise;

Red Lion Court, Whitecross Street, also to Finsbury.

Ideally we should have guided users of this volume through the inclusion of a series of street maps, but the size of such an undertaking becomes clear from the twenty large sheets on which John Ogilby and William Morgan printed *A new and accurate map of the City of London, distinct from Westminster and Southwark* in 1676. These sheets were conveniently reprinted by half-sheets in 1992 in book-form, with introduction by Ralph Hyde, and index by John Fisher and Roger Cline, and this has enabled us to give references throughout to the map square in which appears the start of the name of each of the 'streets, lanes, alleys, courts, yards, churches, halls, houses &c'. Thus Fleet Street is followed in square brackets by [31-I2], which refers to double-page map 31, row lettered I, and column numbered 2. Exceptionally, in this case there is just the letter F, the remainder of FLEET STREET being in [32-I3]. This reprinted Ogilby 1676 volume was published by the London Topographical Society, who have kindly permitted us to reproduce the key map by their late chairman, Peter Jackson.

We follow the name of each street (etc.) by the name in full of the ward or wards in which it lay. A few corrections to the Greenall list have been made along the way, most notably to the Wardrobe *otherwise* the King's Wardrobe, which has changed into the Queen's Wardrobe in Tower Royal. The complicated historical geography of the City of London has been a challenge.

The attributions of the tokens have been assessed in the light of published information known to the authors, and those which seem Uncertain have been relegated to the next volume, as have Forgeries. The purpose of the publication, in accordance with Sylloge practice, is to put the tokens in the Norweb Collection at the service of those who would base studies on them, and not itself to publish documentary research (though a considerable amount has been needed simply to publish the tokens). Re-use of Norweb illustrations in such studies of course should be acknowledged.

The tokens in these volumes have been published within an alphabetical sequence of the historic English counties, followed by Ireland, Isle of Man, Sark(?), Scotland, and Wales, in this volume the City of London, with Middlesex (etc.) to follow. A reference has been made where a locality was shared with another administrative area, and where boundaries were altered after the seventeenth century; but no attempt has been made to indicate the local government reorganizations of 1965 and later. The indispensable authority for the names of English parishes, including those in the City, is Youngs 1979 and 1991 (for bibliographical references see Abbreviations, C). Harben 1918 has been followed for the form of a City street-name. Hyphens have been omitted on principle from compound names.

The arrangement is alphabetical by the most specific locality in which tokens were issued, with the addition in brackets of the City of London ward. The intention is to represent every indication of place appearing on the tokens, and separate headings are provided for such subordinate localities as Bear Quay, Bridewell Stairs (not Steps), Hercules' Pillars Alley, Love Lane Post-house, and St Thomas Apostles backside. By logical extension, tokens which name a sign are placed in an alphabetical sequence of 'Named signs', compound signs being spelled with '&' no matter what appears on the token. If an adjective alone is in the legends, a noun is supplied from the device in square brackets and with a query, e.g. *White* [*?Hart*]. Readers accustomed to a single sequence under simple place-names will need to remember to look under any subsequent sub-headings, but a concordance for Williamson's 'London' chapter follows.

Below each heading the various readings for the place-name are given, but for brevity the occurrences of the commonest form may not be enumerated. Incomplete and uncertain readings are spelled out, a point below a character being used to mean that the reading is possible but not certain. A dash indicates a single illegible character, and three dots an indeterminate number of missing characters. The same treatment applies to any readings given in the entries.

The tokens are numbered in a single sequence, continued from Part VI, but now preceded in references by the Part number in small roman numerals. Die-duplicates are distinguished by the addition of a lower-case letter, which coincides with Mrs Norweb's intention to dispose of duplicates, and will avoid five-figure entries. The number alone is used for references to the dies and for indexing; and it is recommended that Norweb references for other specimens should omit the lower-case letters.

Weights were obtained in grams and corrected to the nearest centigram, 0.005 being rounded up in accordance with the 1989 *SCBI Guidance for Authors*. These metric figures have been multiplied by 15.432358 to convert them to grains, and the result corrected to one place of decimals. Metals are described from their appearance on a scraped edge as brass (Br) or copper (Cu); lead or pewter is 'Pb', and **7562** was struck in leather. Between the yellow of high-zinc brass and the brown of 'copper' (low-zinc brass) there is a whole range of tones which are difficult to specify, and the abbreviation 'M' (mixed metal) has been applied to an intermediate tone. Die-axes are expressed in degrees, as recommended by the 1989 *Guidance*.

Under each heading any corporate issue is placed first, and personal issues follow alphabetically, except that two issuers distinguished as senior and junior would be placed in that order. Several entries for one issuer or named sign are arranged chronologically within denomination, with undated tokens normally at the beginning. Tokens which do not name a denomination precede those which do.

The catalogue entries consist of the following elements.

(a) *Issuer statement* Personal issuers, following any sign named on the token, have the surname spelled as on the token, unless family arms or dies represented in the collection recommend another spelling. Forenames are normalized, although either of the following is accepted as they remain alternatives:

Ann or Anne
Edmond or Edmund
Eleanor or Elinor
Geoffrey or Jeffrey
Gervase or Jarvis
Humphrey or Humphry
Laurence or Lawrence
Nathanael or Nathaniel
Rebecca or Rebekah.

As regards abbreviated forms, suspensions such as IO: (which stands for John or Joseph, cf. **7814**, **7816**) and THO: are not extended, except where the full name is documented. Contractions such as SAM^{LL} are silently extended where this can be done with confidence. Readings which differ from the chosen form are added in brackets. To surname and forename is added any trade or other description of the issuer mentioned on the token. Note that a trade description with a capital letter identifies a Livery Company member, who was normally described as 'Citizen and ...', but this is omitted for brevity.

(b) *Issue statement* The date, or 'nd' if the token is not dated; the denomination if named; and any legend such as 'hearty double token'.

(c) *Types* The obverse and reverse fields, separated by a semicolon, are identified by means of a class number (see below), by the transcription of individual letters, or by the word ‘date’. A triangular arrangement of letters is transcribed in two lines separated by ‘|’, the letter at the apex being taken to be one line. Readings not in Williamson are added in brackets, the presence of ornamental stops being indicated, but not their form.

(d) *References* This is normally a number in Williamson (BW), with ‘London’ understood. The reference applies only, of course, to the wording as printed in Williamson, and moreover pays no attention to denominations indicated at the end of his entries (the same goes for denominations in Dickinson). Norweb variations from a published reading are introduced by ‘but . . .’, which is not intended to assert necessarily that the published reading does not exist. Tokens not in Williamson are given as ‘BW —’, followed where possible by the number in Dickinson (see Abbreviations, C). References to other works may be added if they have distinguished varieties, or have simply added information. An asterisked reference means that the published reading is not wholly confirmed by the Norweb specimen(s).

(e) *Provenance* This copies the source recorded on the envelope in which each specimen is stored, and/or on Mrs Norweb’s record cards. A provenance inferred from the accession number, or from an accompanying ticket, is placed in square brackets. From the tickets or other information it has been possible to take the provenance in some cases beyond the immediate source.

(f) *Notes* These cover notes of die-links within the collection (die-links outside the Norweb Collection have not been sought); evidence for attribution; documentation of an issuer which has a direct bearing on the token, dates being in New Style; this includes trade (where none is mentioned on the token), the name of the sign used on the token, and if the token is undated the date of an issuer’s death within the token-issuing period; and any contemporary record of a private token. Also noted are legends starting at irregular positions, by numbers o’clock; 12 o’clock is the norm, but 11 o’clock is not considered irregular.

As regards the plates it was intended originally that, for ease of handling, the photographs should be taken x 1½, to be reduced in printing to 1:1. Subsequently, by measuring tokens and converting the result, it was discovered that different batches of tokens were photographed at varying magnifications around 1½:1. Checks throughout have eliminated extreme examples, but it remains possible that illustrations in this volume are 2% too small, or 2.5% too large. A letter added to the catalogue number identifies which of any die-duplicates has been illustrated.

CONCORDANCE

Below is a concordance between Williamson numbers from his 'London' chapter, or additions to these from *Dickinson* (numbers followed by a large capital A, B, etc.), and the Sylloge number or numbers. A small capital 'N' is added to numbers in the first column to mean 'Nb: variant reading in the Norweb entry', where details should be sought. At the end of the 'London' list are numbers published here from other Williamson chapters, and Sylloge numbers not in *BW* or *Dickinson*.

BW or Dickinson	*Norweb*
London 1	6428
3	6429
4N	6425
5	6427
8	6426
10	6430
11	6431
12C	6433
13N	6432
16N	6456
17N	6457
18	6460-1
20	6435
21	6434
23	6455
24	6436
24A	6437
27N	6454
27A	6454
31A	7597
32N	6465
33	6438
33C	6439
34N	6440
35N	6458
36N	6463
37N	6462
38N	6459
40	6441
44	6442
46	6464
47	6443
48	7377
50	6444
53N	6445
54N	6446
55N	6453
56	6447
59N	6448
60	6449
61	6450
63N	6451
64	6452
66N	6470
67	6466
68N	6497
69N	6496
71	6471
73N	6467
73A	6475
74N	6469
77N	6473
80	6468
81	6472
82	6474
83	6476
84A	6490
86	6491
87N	6492
88	6494
89	6477
90	6478
90A	6479
91	6493
92	6480
94N	6481
95N	6482
96	6483
97N	6484
98	6485

[*continued overleaf*]

BW or Dickinson	*Norweb*
98AN	6486
99	6495
100	6489
101	6487
102N	6488
104N	6502
106B	6504
107N	6505
108	6506
111	6507-8
114	6518
116N	6516
116A	6509
116B	6510
118	6511
121	6517
121A	6512
122	6513
123	6520
124N	6519
125N	6514
126	6515
127	6498
128A	6523
129N	6521
130N	6522
131A	6524
133	6525
134N	6534
136N	6537
137N	6536
139N	6538
140A	6535
141	6531
142	6530
143N	6526
145	6527
147	6528-9
148	6532
148A	6533
151N	6540
162	6541
165	7013
166N	6542
168	6543
170	6545
171N	6546
172N	6549
173N	6547
174	6548
175	6550
176	6551
179	7434
180	7426
181	7427
182N	7433
184N	7428
186N	7432
188	7422
189	7429
190A	7430
191	7431
193	7435
196N	6558
197	6559
198N	6552
199N	6553
200	6557
201	6560
202N	6561
204N	6556
205N	6554
206	6555
208	6564
210	6726
211	6562
212N	6563
216	6565
217N	6566
218	6581
219	6588
220	6568
221	6586
222	6582
223N	6569
224N	6570-1
225	6593
226N	6594

BW or Dickinson	*Norweb*
227	6595
228	6585
229N	6591
229B	6596
231	6597
232	6584
234	6598
235	6572
237	6573
238	6599
242	6567
243	6579-80
244	6587
244A	6574
245N	6602
247N	6592
249	6583
251N	6575
252N	6589
253	6600
254N	6600
254A	6604
256N	6601
259N	6603
262N	6576
263N	6577
264N	6578
265N	6646
268A	6607
270	6605
271	6606
274N	6653
275N	6608
276N	6609
277	6641-2
278	6640
282	6610
283N	6611
283A	6612
284	6613
285A	6499
286N	6614
287	6615
288	6616-17

BW or Dickinson	*Norweb*
289N	6618
290	6652
291N	6619
292	6655
294	6647-8
296	6620
297N	6621
299	6643
300N	6645
301N	6651
302	6624
303N	6623
304	6622
305N	6625
306N	7530
309	6626
310N	6627
311	7062-3
312	7061
313	6628
315	6629
316N	6654
316AN	6630
318N	6631
319	6650
321	6644
321AN	6632
322N	6500
323	6649
325	6633
328N	6876
329N	6634
331	6635
332N	6637
333N	6636
334N	6638-9
339	6658
340N	6659
342N	6660
344N	6661
347	6662
348	6663
348AN	6664
349N	6667

[*continued overleaf*]

BW or Dickinson	*Norweb*	*BW or Dickinson*	*Norweb*
352	6665	428N	6706
353N	6666	429	6715-17
354N	6656	429A	6718
368N	6668	432N	6720
370	6671	433N	6712
372	6672	434B	6713
374	6673	435	6714
375N	6686	436	6722
376N	6687-8	437N	6723
378	6674	439	6724
379N	6685	439A	6725
380	6675	440N	6727
381	6684	459	6729
382	6676	460N	6730
382A	6687-8	461	7289
383N	6679	462N	6732
384	6677-8	464	6731
385	6680	465	6733
386	6681-2	470	6734
387A	6683	476N	6736
394	6699	482N	6743
395N	6689	484N	6744
396A	6690	485N	6745
397N	6691	488A	6746
398	6695	489N	6747
398A	6700	510	6749
399	6697	514	6751
400N	6692	524	6748
403N	6693	571N	6753
404	6698	573	6760
405	6694	574	6752
407N	6696	575	6762
408N	7704	575A	6769
415	6701	576	6728
416	6705	577	7027
417	6702	578N	7254
418N	6703	579	6767
419N	6704	580	7612
422N	6711	583	7028
423	6709	583A	6754
423A	6709	585N	6763
424	6708	586	6761
425	6707	591	6766
426N	6710	593N	6764

BW or Dickinson	*Norweb*
593AN	6755
594	6756
595A	6770
596N	6768
598	7779
599	6765
601	6759
601A	6758
602	6757
607N	6772
607A	6771
607B	6773
608N	6774
608AN	6775
611N	6776
612A	6781
613	6777
615N	6778
616N	6779
617A	6782
619	6780
633	6783
670	6784
671	6785
672	6786
673	6793
674	6787
676B	6790
678N	6788
683N	6791
685	6792
690	6789
701N	6794
702	6795
703-4N	6796
706	6797
707	6801
709N	6798
712A	6800
713N	7709
714	6799
715	6802
716A	6810
717	6812

BW or Dickinson	*Norweb*
719	6806
722	6804
724A	6805
726	6807
729N	6808
730	6809
732N	6803
732A	6811
733N	6813
734N	6814
735	6815
764	6818
765N	6816
765A	6823
766N	6820
767	6817
771	6819
772	6821
773	6822
774	6824
775	6669
778	6825
779N	6828
780N	7585
781N	7586
782	7582
782A	7583
783N	6827
784	6826
784A	6830
786	6829
787N	7578
788	6832
788A	6982
789N	7581
789A	6835
790	7579
792	6831
794N	6833
795	6836
797N	6837
798N	6834
800N	7580
801	6838

[*continued overleaf*]

BW or Dickinson	*Norweb*
804	7323
809	6844
810	6841
810A	6842
811A	6847
813	6845
813A	6846
815	6843
817	6849
823N	6856
825N	6851
825A	6854
826N	6855
829N	6857
830	6858
832	6863
833	6859
835	6861
836N	6864
837	6860
839	6865
840	6872
842N	6867
846	6871
848N	6868
853	6869
855N	6870
856	6873
893N	6875
894	6874
958	7561
960A	7565
961N	7527
962N	6880
963	7563
963A	7564
965N	6882
966N	6883
967N	6884
968N	6881
974	6906
976	6900
977N	6885
978	6886
979	6887
980	6908
981N	6888
982N	6889
983N	6890
984	6909
985	6891
988N	6903
989	6904
990	6892
990AN	6901
991	6902
992	7575-6
993N	7574
994	6907
995	6893
997	6894
998	6896-7
999	6895
1000	6898
1001	6899
1001AN	6910
1003	6911
1003C	6930
1006N	6912
1007N	6913-15
1010	6925
1011	6916
1011A	6928
1011B	6917
1012	6918
1013AN	6946
1014N	6931
1015N	7314
1016	6919
1018	6920
1019	6926
1021N	6921
1022	6922-3
1023	6927
1024N	6924
1025	6929
1033	6933
1035	6932

BW or Dickinson	*Norweb*
1045	6940
1046	6934
1046A	6935
1051N	6941
1052N	6936
1053	6937
1054	6938
1055N	6939
1057N	6947
1058N	6948
1061	6945
1062	6943
1063N	6944
1064	6949
1066	6960
1069	6950
1070N	7528
1072N	7070
1073N	6973
1074N	6951
1075	6952
1077N	6967
1078	6953
1078A	6964
1079N	6963
1080	6972
1081N	6954
1082	6955
1083N	7071
1084N	6970
1085N	7572
1087N	6956
1087A	6751
1087B	6971
1088N	7073
1090	6966
1091	6965
1092	6968
1094N	7156
1095	7072
1096	7570
1097A	6957
1097B	7817
1097CN	7158

BW or Dickinson	*Norweb*
1097D	6961
1098N	6962
1099N	6958
1100	6959
1102	6750
1102A	7529
1103N	7375
1104	6969
1104A	7571
1105N	6974
1108A	6981
1109A	6980
1109B	6976
1110	6977
1110A	6983
1111N	6975
1112N	6978
1113N	6979
1116	6984
1117N	6992
1118	6985
1120	6986
1121N	6994
1122	6993
1123	6987
1124	6988
1125N	6989
1125A	6990
1128	6991
1130	6998
1131N	7000
1132N	7004
1133N	7003
1133B	7001
1134N	7002
1135	6999
1142	7006
1143	7005
1144N	7007
1150N	7009
1151	7010
1154	7011-12
1197	7019
1198N	7025

[*continued overleaf*]

BW or Dickinson	*Norweb*
1201	7020
1203	7023
1204	7014
1205N	7021
1205AN	7015
1207N	7016
1207A	7017
1209	7018
1210	7024
1211	7022
1213N	7026
1228	7043
1230	7044
1232	7045
1256	7031
1257N	7029
1259N	7032
1260N	7030
1269N	7034
1270	7037
1274	7038
1275N	7039
1278N	7040
1279N	7041
1281A	7046
1281B	7047
1282	7048
1285	7049
1287	7050
1290	7052
1293	7054
1294N	7055
1294A	7051
1299N	7056
1301N	7057
1304N	7058
1305N	7059
1308A	7060
1309	7064
1311N	7065
1311A	7066
1312N	7067
1313N	7068
1337A	7069

BW or Dickinson	*Norweb*
1350	7074
1357	7101
1359	7098
1360	7125
1361	7115
1366N	7127
1366A	7121
1368N	7105
1374	6737
1375	7107
1379AN	7075
1381	7092
1382N	7076
1385	7747
1386N	7566
1388N	7117
1389	7093
1392A	6742
1393N	7123
1396N	7097
1399	7112
1403N	7077
1404	7103
1408	7078
1409	7118
1412	7096
1413	7126
1414	7091
1415N	7095
1418	7119
1419	7120
1423	7088
1424	7087
1427N	7122
1428	7116
1430N	6739
1435N	7099
1444	7094
1445	7113-14
1450N	7108
1456N	7128
1457	7090
1459	7008
1461N	7079

BW or Dickinson	*Norweb*
1464N	7080
1465	7081
1466	7109
1467N	7110-11
1468A	7104
1469	7102
1471	7082
1473	7083
1474A	7100
1476N	7089
1482	7084-5
1497A	7129
1499N	7130
1500N	7131
1502	7132
1505	7133
1507N	7134
1510	7143
1511	7135
1512N	7152
1513N	7154
1514	7136
1515N	7150
1517-18	7146
1517-18N	7144-5
1519	7137
1520	7138
1523N	7153
1524	7140
1526	7141
1527	7142
1528N	7147
1529N	7148
1530	7151
1531N	7149
1534N	7155
1535N	7157
1536N	7159
1551N	7162
1554	7160-1
1557	7163
1560N	7164
1562	7166
1566N	7165
1568N	7175
1569N	7173-4
1571N	7167
1573N	7169
1574N	7176
1574A	7168
1574B	7169
1575	7170
1576	7171
1578	7172
1627	7177
1628A	7179
1628B	7181
1629	7180
1632N	7184
1633	7183
1634	7182
1637N	7185
1639N	7186
1640N	7188
1640A	7187
1641N	7229
1643N	7196-7
1644	7231
1645N	7219
1649N	7198
1650N	7199
1651	7200
1652N	7235
1656N	7191
1657	7201
1658N	7190
1659N	7202
1660	7220
1660A	7237
1664N	7203
1665N	7204
1668N	7205
1670N	6878
1671N	7206
1672B	7216
1673	7224
1673N	7222-3
1674N	6879

[*continued overleaf*]

BW or Dickinson	*Norweb*
1675A	7207
1675CN	7225
1676N	7230
1677N	7236
1680N	7208
1681	7193
1682N	7226
1683N	7232
1684	7209
1685N	7234
1688N	7210
1689N	7227
1690N	7195
1691N	7221
1691A	7194
1692N	7211
1693	7212
1694N	7213
1696	7233
1699N	7218
1700N	7214
1700B	7584
1701	7215
1702N	7192
1703	7217
1705	7238
1706AN	7239-40
1708N	7245
1709	7244
1712N	7246
1716	7247
1718B	7248
1720N	7249
1723	7250
1725N	7251
1726N	7252
1727N	7253
1728	7255
1729	7258
1731	7257
1732	7256
1734	7259
1735A	7270
1738N	7271
1752N	7280
1753	7284
1754N	7283
1755	7281
1757	7282
1758	6866
1759A	7286
1760	7287
1761N	7288
1762	7285
1763A	7292
1764N	7816
1764A	7291
1767N	6719
1768	6721
1772	7290
1817N	7297
1825	7293
1826	7295
1827	7294
1831	7296
1832	7298
1833A	7303
1837N	7304
1838N	7302
1839A	7299
1840	7300-1
1841N	7306
1842A	7305
1843	7310
1843A	7307
1844	7308
1845	7313
1846	7309
1847N	7312
1848	7311
1866	7315
1867N	7321-2
1869AN	7316
1871N	7317
1872	7318
1873N	7319
1874	7320
1900A	7324

BW or Dickinson	*Norweb*
1901	7325
1902	7327-8
1903N	7326
1904	7329
1910	7358
1910B	7353
1915	7330
1916N	7331
1917	7359
1918	7333
1921	7349
1922	7334
1922A	7335
1923	7336
1924N	7355
1927N	7350
1928	7337
1929N	7354
1931	7351
1932A	7338
1933N	7360
1935	7339-40
1938	7352
1940	7342
1941N	7343
1942A	7344
1946	7347
1947	7356-7
1952	7361
1954N	7260
1957	7424
1958	7423
1964N	7425
1965N	7867
1966	7365
1967	7368
1968N	7367
1970	7366
1971N	7364
1976A	7370
2010N	7372
2012	7373
2014	7371
2015N	7374
2017N	7384
2018N	7385
2019N	7395
2020N	7389
2021	7394
2023N	7392
2025A	7396
2029	7387
2029A	7393
2030	7390
2031	7388
2033N	7397-8
2036N	7382
2038	7399-7400
2039	7401
2040	7383
2064A	6982
2064B	7378
2064C	7379
2065N	7380
2066	7381
2078	7402
2079N	7406
2081	7405
2082	7403-4
2095	7268-9
2096	7421
2098	7265
2099N	7407
2100	7411
2101N	7261
2103	7266-7
2104	7412
2106	7262
2109	7420
2110	7413
2111	7414
2112	7409
2113	7415-16
2115	7410
2119	7263
2120	7418
2121N	7419
2122N	7417

[*continued overleaf*]

BW or Dickinson	*Norweb*
2123	7264
2125N	7437
2127	7444
2129	7438
2131	7439
2132	7440
2132A	7441
2132B	7442
2134	7443
2135N	7449
2136	7454
2137N	7445
2138N	7448
2139	7446
2141	7451-2
2142-3	7450
2145A	7447
2147N	7453
2149N	7587
2151	7456
2181	7458
2182	7457
2188N	7459
2189N	7461
2190	7460
2192	7462
2193	7463
2194	7464
2196	7467
2197N	7466
2200	6544
2210	7468
2212	7472
2215B	7469
2216A	7471
2217	7470
2229N	7473
2231N	7369
2232N	7474
2233N	7475
2250	7503-4
2251N	7502
2252N	7505
2253N	7506

BW or Dickinson	*Norweb*
2256N	7476
2257N	7477
2267N	7478
2268N	7479
2271	7480
2273	7484
2276	7483
2277	7482
2278	7481
2282N	7489
2283N	7487-8
2284	7485
2285	7486
2285A	7490
2287N	7491
2291N	7493
2292	7501
2293N	7494
2295	7495
2296N	7500
2297B	7499
2298N	7512
2299	7513
2300	7514
2300AN	7515
2301N	7523
2302N	7522
2303	7524
2306	7517
2308N	7518
2309N	7519
2310	7521
2311	7614
2312	7520
2314N	7525
2315	7507
2317	7508
2318	7511
2319N	7509
2374	7531
2376	7532
2379N	7536
2385N	7533
2387C	7535

BW or Dickinson	*Norweb*	*BW or Dickinson*	*Norweb*
2388	7534	2663N	7596
2391	7537	2685	7602
2392	7538	2686N	7610
2395	7539-40	2687N	7603
2396N	7541	2689N	7609
2397	7543	2690	7607
2398	7542	2691	7604-6
2399	7544	2692	7608
2399A	7555	2694	7611
2400N	7560	2694A	6503
2403N	7559	2694B	6660
2404N	7545	2695N	7615
2405	7546	2696	7619
2406N	7556	2697	7621
2407	7548	2698	7620
2407A	7547	2700N	7650
2408	7558	2700A	7651
2411	7549	2701	7657
2412	7551	2702	7660
2413	7552	2703	7658
2416	7553	2706	7661-3
2417N	7557	2707	7653
2419	7554	2708N	7652
2450N	7567	2709	7659
2451N	7568	2710	7656
2478	7569	2713	7655
2479	7573	2716	7628
2480N	7577	2718	7627
2515N	7033	2720N	7626
2636N	7588	2723A	7625
2642N	7597	2724N	7613
2644N	7598	2725	7624
2646	7589	2727N	7629
2647N	7590	2730N	7623
2649N	7600	2731	7633
2650A	7591	2732	7630
2652N	7377	2733N	7631
2654N	7592	2733B	7632
2656N	7601	2736N	7635
2657N	7376	2738	7636
2658N	7599	2739N	7637
2659N	7593	2750A	7639
2660N	7594	2751	7638
2660B	7595	2755	7640

[*continued overleaf*]

BW or Dickinson	*Norweb*
2756A	7644
2757	7641-2
2758N	7643
2758A	7645
2759N	7648
2760	7649
2761	7646
2762	7647
2791N	7673
2792A	7674
2793A	7677
2793B	7664
2794	7665
2796	7678
2797	7667
2797A	7676
2798N	7675
2799	7668
2801	7669
2802N	7666
2807	7670
2808	7671
2809N	7672
2837N	7681
2838	7680
2839N	7806
2841N	7808
2845	7804
2846N	7812
2847	7810
2848N	7807
2849B	7814
2850	7794
2851N	7796
2852N	7795
2853	7813
2856N	7797
2859N	7809
2860N	7798
2862	7692
2863	7799
2863B	7815
2870A	7800
2871N	7801
2878N	7811
2878B	7690
2879	7802
2880N	7691
2884N	7805
2885A	7803
2886	7683
2888	7687
2891N	7684
2892N	7686
2893N	7688-9
2898N	7685
2900N	7701
2901	7693
2902N	7694
2904AN	7035
2905N	7699
2905A	7700
2905B	7702
2906N	7702
2908N	7696
2910N	7695
2910A	7697
2911	7698
2917N	7272
2918N	7274
2919N	7273
2920N	6670
2941N	7703
2949N	7705
3028N	7710
3029N	7711
3037	7713
3041	7712
3054N	6547
3063N	7714
3071N	7715
3072	7716-17
3075	7745
3076	7742
3077N	7740
3078	7727
3079	7736
3080	7718

BW or Dickinson	*Norweb*
3081	7734
3082N	6657
3083N	7719
3084	7743
3084AN	7735
3085A	7746
3091N	7720
3095N	7516
3096AN	6700
3097	7527
3098N	7731
3099N	6868
3100N	7242
3101	7721
3102N	7526
3105N	6852
3106N	6877
3107N	7741
3108	7730
3109	7722
3111	7723
3114	7728
3116A	7744
3118	7243
3119	7739
3121N	7737
3122N	7724
3124	6501
3126	7732
3127N	7738
3129N	7729
3130N	7725
3131	7726
3132N	7733
3135N	7749
3137N	7750
3138N	6995-7
3140N	7751
3142A	7752
3145N	7755
3146N	7753
3147	7754
3148	7756
3204N	7773

BW or Dickinson	*Norweb*
3205N	7759
3206	7760
3211	7761
3212N	7762
3213N	7766
3213A	7767
3213BN	7774
3215	7775
3218N	7776
3219	7763
3220	7770
3220BN	7764
3223	7765
3224N	7275
3224AN	7768
3226	7772
3227N	7758
3228N	7757
3230N	7777
3232	7276
3233	7778
3236N	7780
3270AN	7708
3271N	7782
3271A	7781
3357	7783
3361	7787
3362A	7785
3368	6853
3369	7789
3371N	7791
3371A	7790
3376B	7792
3376C	7793
3432N	7818
3435N	7819-20
3436	7833
3439AN	7838
3440A	7821
3442	7837
3443	7822
3443A	7841
3448A	7835-6
3448BN	7843

[*continued overleaf*]

BW or Dickinson	*Norweb*
3451N	7823
3453N	7825
3454N	7824
3455N	7826
3462	7827
3467	7834
3468	7840
3470N	7828
3471A	7829
3473N	7830
3473BN	7831
3473C	7831
3474	7832
3475	7844
3477N	7788
3478N	7845
3479	7846
3480	7847
3485	7848
3486N	7849
3500	7850
3509	7860
3510N	7277
3513N	7866
3514N	7851
3514A	7852
3517AN	7854
3518N	7855
3519	7861
3523	7278
3524N	7856
3526N	7862
3527	7864
3527N	7865
3528N	7863
3529N	7857-8
3530N	7279
3532	7859
3535N	7706
3536N	7707
Appendix A.14	7562
Middlesex 186A	7654
Southwark 152	6539
Southwark 202B	6738

BW or Dickinson	*Norweb*
Southwark 206	6740
Southwark 207N	6741
Southwark 399N	7726
Ireland 718A	7178
Uncertain 13N	7617-18
Uncertain 57	6475
Uncertain 62DN	7616
Uncertain 88N	7617-18
Uncertain 115N	7634

Not in BW or Dickinson	
—	6590
—	6735
—	6839
—	6840
—	6848
—	6850
—	6862
—	6905
—	6942
—	7036
—	7042
—	7053
—	7086
—	7106
—	7124
—	7139
—	7189
—	7228
—	7241
—	7332
—	7341
—	7345
—	7346
—	7348
—	7362
—	7363
—	7386
—	7391
—	7408
—	7436
—	7455
—	7465

Not in BW or Dickinson	*Norweb*
—	7492
—	7496
—	7497
—	7498
—	7510
—	7550
—	7622
—	7679
—	7682

Not in BW or Dickinson	*Norweb*
—	7748
—	7769
—	7771
—	7784
—	7786
—	7839
—	7842
—	7853

CLASSIFIED INDEX OF TYPES

OBVERSE and reverse types are described by means of a class number, except in the case of letters (which are transcribed) and dates (for which see 5.77). The class numbers identify the types according to their appearance, and so avoid the imprecision and the often unwarranted certainty involved in putting a name to them. Their explanations can encompass both description and a possible name or names, both the modern wording and a contemporary name such as 'Flower-de-Luce'. The classified arrangement can relate types of uncertain identity to others which may have a contemporary name, and relax the grip of earlier identifications which are not certainly right but which cannot be disproved. Above all, the class number in the catalogue briefly identifies a type which can be elaborated below. These advantages outweigh the slight complication of having to refer from the catalogue to the classification for more information about a token illustrated on a facing plate.

The classification employed is that of Neubecker 1974, in which Rentzmann's numismatic material (alphabetical by the German) has been re-arranged into an ordinary of arms with a systematic notation. For a few types there is no provision, but generally the tokens fit in well; and the differences hold out the opportunity for comparing the devices chosen for tokens with more formally heraldic representations.

There are five main categories, here numbered 1 to 5:

GEOMETRICAL

UNIVERSE

LIVING BEINGS

PLANTS

INANIMATE OBJECTS

Neubecker's numbered classes within these five categories have been adopted in their entirety, with occasional modifications of his English wording. The following classes have been added to Neubecker's: 4.15, and 5.82 to 5.89. This notation has been extended to specify subdivisions of the classes which, though sometimes present in Neubecker, are not there numbered. For example, 1.33.10 is a subdivision of 1.33, Checky, which falls within category 1, Geometrical. Related devices are brought together so far as possible within each class.

Except for charges on shields (5.14, 5.15), numismatic left and right are used and not heraldic dexter and sinister. Heraldic conventions are, however, often assumed, for example that a Lion rampant faces to left.

0.1	Blank — 7562
0.4	An uncertain shape giving the impression of a Fleur-de-lis, or a Bird — 6437
0.5	An uncertain shape giving the impression of Three rams' heads, cf. the Glovers' arms — 6439
0.6	An uncertain shape — 6690
0.7	An uncertain shape, possibly a Cheese — 7270
1 GEOMETRICAL	
1.33	Checky
1.33.10	Checky of twenty-five, five by five — 6911, 7163
1.33.12	Checky of twenty-five, five by five, accompanied by an inscription incorporating letters ( ) — 7455
1.33.22	Checky of forty-two, seven by six — 6477, 6690
1.40.3	Roundle. Ball — 6432, 6504, 6530, 6934, 7075, 7696, 7733
1.41	Annulet. Hoop — 7225
1.41.1/ 1.41.6	Annulet accompanied
1.41.1	Within a hoop a cock — 6912, 6916
1.41.2	Within a hoop a bunch of grapes — 6868
1.41.4	Within a hoop three tuns one and two and in base a bunch of grapes. Hoop & Three Tuns — 6782
1.41.5	Within a hoop one or more letters ( ) — 7226, 7724
1.41.6	Within a hoop an inscription — 7227
1.42	Crosslet couped
1.42.4	Within a lozenge fleurdelisée a crosslet formy and around it a date — 7634
1.43	Cross couped — 6822
1.44	Cross formy or paty — 6641-2, 7470, 7643, 7660
1.50	Cross pommé
1.50.4	Double-headed shot between two pieces of round shot (Lavery 1984, p. 159, MS of c.1660), perhaps intended for two pieces of double-headed shot in saltire. Cross Bullets — 7732
1.55	Cross accompanied
1.55.37	A cross formy or paty and in chief the sun. Sun & Red Cross — 7175
1.60	Cross on steps — 7535, 7840
1.61	Cross couped charged
1.61.1	On a cross formy or paty an escutcheon charged with the arms *Quarterly France Modern and England*. Golden Cross — 6807
1.69	Saltire couped
1.69.1	A saltire couped — 6928
1.69.8	Three saltires couped, accompanied by an inscription — 7218
1.70	Saltire

3 LIVING BEINGS

3.1	One person
3.1.2	A person erect without attribute, naked or not obviously clothed, affronté, legs apart, arms embowed, left hand on hip. ?Black Boy — 6610, 7054
3.1.4	A person erect without attribute, naked or not obviously clothed, affronté, legs apart, arms embowed, between two pillars. Hercules — 7072-3, 7305
3.1.5	A person erect without attribute, dressed in a long habit, perhaps with a hood. Friar — 7042, 7045
3.1.6	A person erect without attribute, dressed in flat cap and gown. Blue-coat Boy — 6535
3.1.11	A standing figure accompanied by the body of a lion. Samson — 7627
3.1.12/ 3.1.24	Person holding a rod, spear, club or similar
3.1.13	A person holding a crucifix, accompanied by an inscription — 6667
3.1.19	A person holding in his right hand a club vertical on the ground and in his left a tobacco-pipe to his mouth — 7109
3.1.21	A person, left, holding a club over his shoulder, and right, a post with a trestle base and from the chief a short attachment descending at an angle: ?a quintain to tilt at for military exercise or sport, ?or, A whipping-post = 'Pillar' *sb.* 1.b. (*OED*), in which case the device might be Hercules' Pillars — 6731
3.1.23	A person holding a match to fire a cannon, an inscription in chief and in base. Cannoneer — 7070
3.1.25	A woman holding a plunger shaft in a churn, perhaps pats of butter behind. Dairymaid — 7209, 7385, 7831
3.1.27	A person supported on two crutches — 6783
3.1.32	A naked boy holding a pineapple in his right hand, probably a roll of tobacco under his left arm — 7518, 7522
3.1.34	A person holding an arrow, spear or dart — 6511, 7000
3.1.37	A person holding a bow and arrow — 6955
3.1.40	A person in doublet and hose wearing a sword. Jack of Newbury — 7239-40
3.1.53	A person holding a wool-comb — 6534
3.1.54	A person, perhaps crowned, holding a harp. King David (& Harp). See also 3.1.120 — 7406
3.1.58	A person in a feathered headdress holding a tobacco-pipe — 7438
3.1.59	A person holding a tobacco-pipe in his right hand (away from the mouth), a [tobacco] roll beneath his left arm. Black Boy — 6503, 7084-5
3.1.64	A person in a short cloak holding in his left hand a spear and in his right a handle with head at right angle. Roman soldier with scourge? — 6816
3.1.66	A child holding a truss (surgical appliance) — 7755

3.1.67	A person holding a coffee-pot, perhaps pouring contents into a dish — 6522, 7044
3.1.73	A naked boy holding up his left foot in both hands. ?Spinario (the thorn-puller), an antique bronze of which a copy was made for Charles I; his head is bent over his foot, though a Rubens drawing possibly inspired by a live model has his face towards the spectator as here (Presicce 2005; cf. Larwood 1866, p. 468) — 7577
3.1.75	A person standing on a crescent. Man in the Moon — 6765, 7589
3.1.77/ 3.1.85	Person seated
3.1.79	A woman seated at a spinning wheel of horizontal type — ?7214, 7338
3.1.84	A person astride a barrel, cup in hand, accompanied by letters ( ) — 6444
3.1.89	A person in robe and bishop's mitre holding a devil's nose by tongs in his left hand, and in his right hand a covered cup from working as a goldsmith. St Dunstan and the Devil. AT THE D. AND DUNSTANS — 7715
3.1.90/ 3.1.98	Body and body-shaped clothing
3.1.90	A dress or gown with leading-strings, presumably for a child (Cunnington 1972, pp. 194-5). Coat. Child's Coat. 'Such Coats as these are often painted on signs, and on cloths, to shew where Taylors, Salesmen, and Brokers live, or keep their Shops' (Holme 1688, 3.2.26) — 7834
3.1.91	A dress or gown with leading-strings, presumably for a child (Cunnington 1972, pp. 194-5), accompanied by letters ( ). Coat. Child's Coat — 7046
3.1.96	A stomacher (ornamental covering for the chest worn under the lacing of the bodice), cf. Cunnington 1972, p. 100, fig. 40.(a) — 7818
3.1.105	A person wearing a smock and hat, holding a crook, before him a hound sejant. Shepherd & Dog — 7630
3.1.119	A standing figure facing, holding in his left hand an arrow or dart, in his right a ?tobacco-pipe. Indian — 7015
3.1.120	A person, crowned, holding a harp, dividing a date. King (David) & Harp. See also 3.1.54 — 7363
3.1.121	A person in hat with feather and ankle-length gown, holding in his right hand a horn, accompanied by an inscription. Will Somers, i.e. William Somer (d. 1559), court fool (*ODNB*) — 7453
3.1.122	A person right, perhaps with bellows, beside a still armed left with a receiver — 6778
3.1.123	A man in armour standing facing, his left arm akimbo, his right arm supporting a staff or pike. Pikeman — 7634
3.1.124	A person dressed in a long habit, perhaps with hood, seated. Friar — 7042-3
3.2	Rider. Horseman
3.2.2	A rider, unarmed, blowing a trumpet. ?Postboy — 7779

3.2.3 A rider, unarmed, blowing a horn, accompanied by an inscription. ?Postboy — 7755

3.2.8 A horseman killing a dragon, a sword over his shoulder. St George and the Dragon — 6471, 6536, 7014, 7027, 7121, 7413, 7848

3.2.9 A horseman killing a dragon, a sword or scimitar above his head. St George and the Dragon — 6870, 7332, 7494, 7785

3.2.11 A horseman killing a dragon with a spear or lance. St George and the Dragon — 7674

3.2.12 A horseman killing a dragon with a spear or lance, facing right. St George and the Dragon — 6763

3.2.14 A horseman killing a dragon with a sword beside his head (?). St George and the Dragon — 6464, 7835-6

3.2.16 A horseman killing a dragon with a sword or scimitar above his head and in chief a cock. St George and the Dragon (Cox's?) — 7333

3.3 Person issuant

3.3.13 A person issuant from the further side of a mould or dipping-trough, holding a rod or broach fesswise with candles suspended. Candlemaker. Chandler. Tallow-chandler — 6563, 6658, 6674, 6677-8, 6686, 6859, 6898, 6918, 6931, 7014, 7137, 7212, 7318-19, 7339-40, 7359, 7378, 7551, 7647, 7655, 7714, 7765, 7800, 7857-8

3.4 Several persons

3.4.2 Two persons saluting each other, perhaps hat in hand. Salutation — 6560, 7207, 7284, 7773

3.4.5 Two persons each wearing a hat and supporting a staff — 7107

3.4.6 Two persons supporting on their shoulders a pole from which a barrel is suspended. Two Brewers — 6793

3.4.9 Two persons wielding hammers, an anvil between. Two Smiths — 7360

3.4.17 A person seated left [the Virgin Mary] and an angel kneeling right [Gabriel], between them a dove [the Holy Ghost]. Annunciation. Angelic Salutation — 7096

3.4.20 Two women holding a [black] boy between them in a washtub. Labour in Vain — 7454

3.4.21 Three persons facing, crowned and holding sceptres (etc.). Three Kings. Three Queens — 6949, 7743

3.4.22 Three persons dressed in long habits. Three Nuns — 6486, 6972, 6987, 7009, 7011-12, 7753-4

3.4.24 Three persons standing, the middle one holding aloft a cross-staff. Three Mariners — 6671, 6998

3.4.27 Three persons dancing. Three Morris Dancers — 7443

3.4.29 Three persons and a boat, accompanied by an inscription, perhaps adjacent to a building — 7467

3.4.31 Several persons seated in a boat, oars at work, accompanied by an inscription — 7272

3.4.32	Two persons standing affronté, each wearing a hat and bandolier and holding a staff, between them a flower — 7108
3.4.35	Two men confronté, the one on the right wearing a hat and holding the other by the wrists, who with shoulder-length hair appears to resist being held and kicks hatted figure on the shins. ?Two Wrestlers — 7593
3.5	Human head, bust
3.5.1/ 3.5.19	A facing head, uncrowned
3.5.1	A skull three-quarters left. Death's-head — 6863
3.5.2	A head with a large mouth wide open. Mouth — 6649
3.5.8	A female bust with bushy hair, apparently uncrowned but probably intended for Catherine, Queen of Charles II — 7507
3.5.12	A half-length figure accompanied by an inscription. St Hugh — 7369
3.5.20/ 3.5.29	Head in profile
3.5.21	Bust with receding hair, moustache and beard. Old Man. Grave Maurice, i.e. Maurice, Count of Nassau — 7221
3.5.23	A bust with shoulder-length hair between the letters D Y. James, Duke of York, afterwards King James II — 7008
3.5.24	Bust with hair in pigtail. Roxalana, a character in *The Siege of Rhodes*, played by Hester Davenport — 6745
3.5.27	Within a crescent a face in profile, accompanied by an inscription. Man in the Moon? — 6774
3.5.30/ 3.5.39	Head wreathed about the temples
3.5.33	A head wreathed about the temples turned three-quarters right. Ben Jonson, poet laureate — 7671
3.5.35	A facing bust bearded and wreathed about the temples. Saracen's Head — 7170
3.5.37	A blackamoor's head in profile, left — 7597, 7789
3.5.38	A blackamoor's head in profile, left, accompanied by letters ( ) — 6737
3.5.39	A blackamoor's head in profile, left, accompanied by an inscription — 7805
3.5.40/ 3.5.49	Turbaned head. Turk's Head
3.5.40	A bust with turban, three-quarters left — 6516, 6730, 6878-9, 6995-7, 7185, 7458, 7568, 7758, 7810
3.5.41	A bust with turban, three-quarters left, accompanied by letters ( ) — 6521, 6548
3.5.42	A turbaned bust three-quarters left, accompanied by an inscription — 6696, 6736, 6881, 7164
3.5.43	A turbaned bust in profile, perhaps holding a cup — 6883-4, 7623
3.5.44	A turbaned bust in profile accompanied by letters ( ) — 7342
3.5.45	A turbaned bust in profile holding a cup, accompanied by an inscription — 7639
3.5.46	A turbaned bust three-quarters right — 6882

3.5.88	A crowned facing bust with long hair, and indication of a bosom. Queen's Head — 6576, 7533
3.5.89	Crowned facing bust with a chain about the shoulders holding an orb and sceptre. King's Head — 7306
3.5.90	Crowned female bust facing in ruff and high stiff collar. Queen's Head (Elizabeth I) — 6558-9, 6855, 7126, 7739
3.5.94	Crowned female bust facing with line of dress across her shoulders, perhaps a narrow waist. Queen's Head — 6578, 7274
3.5.96	Crowned female bust facing. Maiden. Maidenhead. Virgin, from the arms of the Worshipful Company of Mercers of London — 6746, 6780, 7487-9
3.5.105/ 3.5.119	Head in profile, crowned
3.5.105	A crowned profile bust to left, apparently Charles II. King's Head — 6638-9, 7038, 7082, 7468, 7544
3.5.109	A crowned profile bust of Charles I to left — 6603
3.5.110	A crowned profile bust to left, apparently female. Queen's Head — 6488
3.5.120/ 3.5.126	Human head accompanied
3.5.123	Head with open mouth accompanied by a hand holding a piece of cloth embowed, the ends pendant: ?a napkin for wiping the mouth cf. Holme 1688, 3.6.30; ?a handkerchief against a sneeze. The Hand and Mouth — 7307
3.5.125	Female bust with long hair, facing, holding in her arms a small quadruped. If a lamb she may be St Agnes, though its right ear seems attached to its forehead. ?A unicorn, as in Raphael's *Lady with a Unicorn* (Rome: Museo Borghese) — 7747
3.6	Hand and arm
3.6.8	Two hands or gloves palewise in fess accompanied by an inscription — 7202
3.6.9/ 3.6.14	Open hand accompanied
3.6.9	An open hand accompanied by a cock — 7846
3.6.14	A dexter hand appaumé in a cuff and in chief a hat with high crown, straight convergent sides, and wide brim, trimmed with a band, perhaps a hatband nowed on right; from the Feltmakers' arms — 7155
3.6.21	A hand holding a feather or quill. Hand & Pen — 7136, 7148, 7351
3.6.22	A right hand fesswise perhaps gloved grasping a bird. Bird in Hand — 6849, 7591
3.6.24	From the base a hand, perhaps gloved, holding a bird. Bird in Hand — 7216
3.6.33	Hand holding an anchor, crowned — 7247
3.6.39	Hand holding a halberd — 6890
3.6.50	A hand holding a coffee-pot — 7316, 7675

3.6.51	A hand grasping the handle of a coffee-pot bendwise accompanied by a bowl [into which coffee is being poured] — 6761, 6999, 7002, 7304, 7433, 7615, 7704, 7757
3.6.52	A hand grasping the handle of a coffee-pot bendwise and on a table bowls [into which coffee is being poured] — 7180
3.6.60/ 3.6.65	Hands joined
3.6.60	Two hands clasped — 6787
3.6.62	A hand holding a glove — 6512, 7281
3.7	Leg, foot, and clothing so shaped
3.7.4	Leg accompanied by a star. Leg and Star — 6465
3.7.7	Leg accompanied by an inscription — 7843
3.7.18	Three legs or stockings palewise in fess. Three Legs — 6971
3.7.24	A boot with turned-down top, internal structure not visible — 7080
3.7.25	A boot with turned-down top, internal structure standing proud, perhaps spurred — 7824-5
3.7.33	A shoe accompanied by an inscription — 7252
3.7.34	A last shaped like a foot — 7428, 7596, 7665
3.7.40	Sole of shoe, sole-shaped last — 6875
3.7.43	?Three tongues, ?Three sole-shaped lasts, palewise in fess — 6941
3.7.45	A patten fesswise — 7426
3.7.48	Three pattens two and one, from the Pattenmakers' arms — 7428
3.9	Heart
3.9.1	A heart, unaccompanied — 7192, 7520, 7795-6
3.10	Mythological beings with a human face
3.10.0/ 3.10.11	Angel
3.10.0	Winged figure standing, details uncertain — 6850
3.10.1	An angel with hands clasped in prayer — 6501, 6593, 6597, 6901, 6963, 7069, 7423-4, 7595, 7688-9
3.10.2	An angel with hands clasped in prayer accompanied by letters ( ) — 7686
3.10.4	An angel with hands extended — 7193
3.10.6	An angel holding in both hands a scroll — 6478, 6500, 6564, 6900, 7683
3.10.9	An angel facing and on the extended right hand a crown — 7410
3.10.16/ 3.10.21	Mermaid
3.10.17	A mermaid holding a mirror in her right hand and perhaps a hair-comb in her left — 6434, 6452, 6510, 6552, 6557, 6687-8, 6695, 6766, 6808, 6835, 6922-3, 7308, 7460-1, 7735
3.10.20	A mermaid holding a comb in her right hand and a mirror in her left — 6798
3.10.21	A mermaid holding a mirror in her right hand and a hair-comb in her left, accompanied by an inscription — 7531

3.11 Lion rampant — 6487, 6572, 6591, 6602, 6640, 6725, 6926, 6977, 6980, 6994, 7020-1, 7024-5, 7055-6, 7147, 7168, 7176, 7234, 7259, 7350, 7354, 7380, 7469, 7472, 7530, 7541, 7620, 7658, 7697, 7710, 7775

3.31 Lion rampant with other charges
3.31.2 A lion accompanied by candles on a rod or broach — 6609, 6633
3.31.5 A lion accompanied by a still and an inscription — 6553
3.31.6 A lion accompanied by a sugarloaf — 7343
3.31.9 A lion holding a key — 7242-3

3.32 Lion rampant accompanied by letters ( ) — 6495

3.35 Lion's head. (For lion's face see 3.44)
3.35.2 A lion's head erased, accompanied by letters ( ) — 7839

3.39 Lion . . . guardant
3.39.1 A lion passant guardant — 6428, 6561, 6713, 6871, 6959, 6993
3.39.2 A lion passant guardant holding a roundle. Lion and Ball — 7415-16
3.39.7 A lion passant guardant and [a lamb?] confronté. Lion and Lamb — 7698
3.39.20 A lion rampant guardant — 6524

3.41 Three lions passant
3.41.1 Three lions passant guardant — 6743, 6810

3.44 Lion's face. (For lion's head see 3.35)
3.44.7 Three leopards' heads, one and two — 7040

3.45 Lions sejant and couchant
3.45.7 A lion couchant accompanied by a lamb — 7202
3.45.9 A lion with nimbus couchant guardant holding a book. (There are no wings to make this the lion of St Mark) — 6776

3.49 Bear
3.49.2 A bear rampant, collared and chained, supporting a staff raguly. Bear & Ragged Staff — 7722, 7833
3.49.5 A bear passant or statant, collared and chained — 6429, 6469, 6475, 6539, 6812, 6917, 7745, 7804
3.49.6 A bear passant or statant, collared and chained, accompanied by letters ( ) — 6960
3.49.7 A bear passant or statant, collared and chained, accompanied by an inscription — 6705
3.49.8 A bear passant or statant unchained — 6703-4
3.49.12 A bear passant, chained, and in base a bull and a horse passant in fess — 7631

3.51 Elephant
3.51.1 An elephant statant and on his back a castle. Elephant & Castle — 7379
3.51.2 An elephant statant and on his back a castle, accompanied by letters ( ). Elephant & Castle — 7384

3.52	Horned cattle
3.52.1/ 3.52.19	Bull
3.52.1	A bull passant — 6513, 6707, 7486, 7521
3.52.2	A bull passant accompanied by a small animal (a dog?) — 7432
3.52.4	A bull passant accompanied by letters ( ) — 7566
3.52.6	A bull statant — 6877, 7039, 7286
3.52.20	Horned cattle with udder passant. Cow — 7127
3.52.21	Horned cattle with udder statant. Cow — 7329
3.52.25	A bull's head couped — 6756, 6760, 6817-19, 6950, 7190-1, 7571, 7585-6, 7731
3.52.26	A bull's head couped accompanied by letters ( ) — 7687
3.52.35	Bull's or cow's head caboshed. Cow's Face — 7617-18
3.53	Deer and kindred animals
3.53.1	A stag or hart trippant, also reindeer, roebuck etc. — 6675, 7311, 7813
3.53.6	A stag or hart courant — 6733
3.53.13	Three stags trippant two and one — 7122, 7545
3.53.15	A deer to right with two nearly straight tapering horns. Antelope, 'and thus depicted by modern heralds' (Berry 1828-40, i. sig. B4a) — 7798
3.53.16	A hind statant
3.53.20	A stag or hart lodged — 6581, 6653, 6697, 6800, 7186, 7237, 7422, 7584, 7817
3.53.21	A stag or hart lodged, accompanied by letters ( ) — 7480
3.53.25	A stag's head couped — 6899
3.53.30/ 3.53.35	Stag's attires. Antlers. Hart's Horns
3.53.30	Antlers, unaccompanied — 6492, 6876, 7506
3.53.31	Antlers accompanied by two [brewers] supporting a pole from which a barrel is suspended — 6795
3.53.32	Stag's attires, antlers, horns, and between them an unidentified charge — 7780
3.53.33	Antlers accompanied by a horseshoe. The Horns & Horseshoe — 7059
3.54	Goat, ram
3.54.1	A goat passant — 7808
3.55	Sheep
3.55.4	A ewe or lamb statant, accompanied by an inscription, perhaps incorporating letters ( ) — 6739
3.56	Paschal lamb
3.56.1	A lamb couchant with nimbus about its head — 6427, 6520, 6726
3.56.2	A lamb passant, perhaps with nimbus, supporting on the dexter shoulder a cross-staff from which flies a pennon charged with a cross. Lamb & Flag — 7376
3.57	Head of goat, ram etc.
3.57.3	Head of a ram or horned sheep couped — 6893

3.57.5 Three goats' heads erased, one and two — 7742

3.58 Fleece

3.58.1 A fleece (so-called): 'a Sheep hung by the middle in a Chain' (Holme 1688, 2.9.29) — 6666, 6744, 6857, 7089-90

3.59 Camel and kindred animals

3.59.2 A camel passant accompanied by a small human figure — 7204

3.60 Horse, donkey

3.60.1 A horse passant. Trotter — 6448, 7162, 7290, 7816

3.60.4 A horse passant, bridled and saddled — 6426, 6628, 6654, 6851, 7004, 7105-6, 7249

3.60.5 A horse passant, bridled and saddled, accompanied by letters ( ) — 6715-18

3.60.20 A horse courant. Colt — 6532-3, 6538, 6620, 6698, 7003, 7152, 7217

3.60.21 A horse courant accompanied by letters ( ) — 7153

3.60.25 Three horses courant. Three Colts — 6702

3.60.30 A horse's head couped, perhaps bridled. Nag's head — 6537, 6550, 6757, 6985, 6989, 7037, 7213, 7230, 7736, 7756

3.61 Unicorn — ?7445

3.61.1 A unicorn passant — 6729, 7375

3.61.2 A unicorn passant gorged with a coronet and chained — 7030

3.62 Pegasus. Winged horse

3.62.1 A winged horse soaring or volant. Flying Horse — 7657

3.62.5 A winged horse and on its wing or above its rump a fleur-de-lis. Flying Horse — 7053

3.63 Beasts not otherwise specified

3.63.1 A cat statant to right. At the Cat — 7637

3.63.5 A rat passant charged with pellets — 6753

3.64 Griffin

3.64.1 A griffin segreant — 6719

3.64.4 A griffin passant — 7094

3.65 Boar

3.65.1 A boar passant or statant — 6641-2, 6741, 6759, 7368, 7529

3.65.2 A boar passant or statant accompanied by a sugarloaf — 7365

3.65.3 A boar accompanied by three horseshoes — 7718

3.65.10 A boar's head couped close, perhaps an apple in its mouth — 6954, 7019, 7031-2, 7166, 7327-8, 7575-6, 7685

3.65.12 A boar's head couped close accompanied by letters ( ) — 7110-11

3.66 Wolf, fox

3.66.1 A fox passant — 6595, 7389, 7446, 7448

3.66.3 A fox courant holding in its mouth a bird. Fox and Goose — 7321-2, 7390

3.66.10 Three foxes courant in pale — 7752

3.92.7	A bird of prey close, belled and jessed — 6975, 7093
3.95	Two-headed eagle
3.95.1	A two-headed eagle displayed — 6613, 6936, 7261, 7409, 7411
3.99	Stilt-bird
3.99.4	Three stilt-birds rising, wings displayed and inverted. Three Cranes — 7481
3.100	Peacock & peahen
3.100.10	A peahen close. At the Peahen — 6604
3.101	Cock & hen
3.101.1/ 3.101.11	A cock, also gamecock (fighting cock), moorcock (heathcock)
3.101.1	A cock close — 6454, 6612, 6680-2, 6834, 6842, 6961, 7144-6, 7271, 7332, 7583, 7701-2, 7713, 7860
3.101.3	Three cocks two and one — 6946
3.101.6	A cock accompanied by a unicorn — 7203
3.101.10	A cock accompanied by a bell — 6565
3.101.11	A cock accompanied by a magpie — 7720
3.101.21	A hen couchant accompanied by smaller birds. Hen and Chickens — 6764, 7064-6, 7124-5, 7862
3.102	Swan, goose
3.102.0	Swan or goose, details uncertain — 7842
3.102.1/ 3.102.6	Swan close
3.102.1	A swan close, perhaps water or reeds in base — 7165, 7331, 7355, 7450-2, 7650, 7653, 7661-3, 7786, 7867
3.102.3	A swan close accompanied by a sugarloaf. The Swan and Sugarloaf — 6459
3.102.4	A swan close accompanied by a shuttle — 7500
3.102.10	A swan rising, wings elevated and addorsed, ducally gorged and chained — 6660, 7729, 7763, 7776
3.102.11	A swan rising, wings elevated and addorsed, unchained or apparently so, perhaps rushes in base — 7776
3.102.12	A swan rising, wings elevated and addorsed, accompanied by letters ( ) — 6435
3.102.16	A swan rising, wings addorsed and inverted, ducally gorged but unchained — 6839
3.102.17	A swan with two necks, close — 6670
3.102.19	Three swans close, two and one. Selby Abbey arms — 7280
3.102.30	A goose close. Gander — 6632
3.102.33	Three birds with long necks volant. Three goslings — 7762
3.103	Duck, martlet
3.103.4	Duck or drake passant. At the Drake — 6549
3.107	Feathers. Plume
3.107.1	Three ostrich feathers in fess. At the Feathers — 6962, 7777
3.107.2	Out of a crest-coronet a plume of three feathers. The Feathers. Prince of Wales' Feathers — 6683, 6712, 7256, 7491

3.115.3 A shoulder of mutton, cf. Larwood 1951, pl. 41 (Shoulder of Mutton and Cucumbers, Yapton, W. Sussex) — 6774

3.116 Insect

3.116.1 A grasshopper — 7293, 7578, 7838

4 PLANTS

4.1 Tree (unaccompanied)

4.1.1 A single tree issuant from a mount. Cherry. Fig tree. Oak. Olive tree. Willow tree — 6517, 6784-5, 7215, 7444, 7678, 7703

4.1.4 A single tree, perhaps acorned, charged with three royal crowns. Royal Oak — 7282

4.1.5 Within a garter a single tree, perhaps acorned, charged with three royal crowns. Royal Oak — 6509

4.2 Tree accompanied

4.2.1 On a mount a tree environed with a serpent between a male and a female figure both naked; from the arms of the Worshipful Company of Fruiterers of the City of London. Adam and Eve — 6668, 7508, 7552, 7727

4.2.5 A tree accompanied by an inscription, perhaps incorporating letters ( ) — 6931, 6978

4.2.11 A mount, thereon a grove of trees, a lion issuing from the grove; the crest of the Woodmongers' Company — 6723

4.3 Trunk, branch, crooked billet

4.3.10 A crooked billet — 6562, 7141

4.3.11 A crooked billet accompanied by letters ( ) — 7590

4.3.12 A crooked billet accompanied by an inscription — 7381

4.3.13 A crooked billet accompanied by a mullet of five points — 6867

4.4 Twigs

4.4.10 A faggot (bundle of twigs) fesswise, in chief and in base a mullet of five points — 6723

4.8 Fruit

4.8.10 An acorn leaved and slipped — 6579-80, 7295, 7457

4.9 Vine

4.9.1 A vine — 7099

4.9.5 A bunch of grapes pendent — 7149, 7246, 7299, 7559

4.9.8 A bunch of grapes, stalk in base — 6478

4.10 Grain and stalked plants

4.10.1 A garb. Wheatsheaf. Oatsheaf — 6614, 6828, 6909, 6983, 7278, 7526, 7560, 7609, 7640, 7761, 7778, 7847

4.10.2/ 4.10.13 Garb accompanied

4.10.2 A garb accompanied by three birds. Wheatsheaf and Three Pigeons — 7060, 7345-6, 7395

4.10.4 A garb accompanied by two stalked flowers — 6445

4.10.6 A garb accompanied by letters ( ) — 6860, 7049, 7633

4.10.12 On a garb three birds — 7473, 7505

5.3.20 A fountain (water not flowing). The Fountain — 6894, 6905, 7401

5.3.21 A fountain with water flowing — 6904, 7199

5.3.23 A fountain between two persons, perhaps intended for Jacob's Well (see also 5.3.53) — 7334

5.3.25 A fountain and in chief a statuette holding out cups — 6462-3

5.3.28 On a circular base a dome supported by columns. At the sign of the Temple — 6970

5.3.30 A masoned still armed left with a receiver, perhaps flammant to right. At the Golden Still — 7123, 7425, 7479, 7542, 7549, 7794

5.3.32 A masoned still armed right with a receiver, perhaps flammant to right — 6447

5.3.41 A pavilion between two mantles and in chief a lion passant guardant; cf. 5.14 Merchant Taylors — 7830

5.3.53 A well with raised bucket between two persons, left with container for water and apparently female, right apparently male with halo. Jacob's Well (John 4: 6-26), between a woman of Samaria and Jesus Christ. See also 5.3.23 — 7348

5.3.75 On a table with a framed base a tobacco stand(?) and pipes, and in chief an arm fesswise from right holding a dish [of coffee] — 6736

5.3.90/ 5.3.97 Vintner's bush and similar structures with a hooped base

5.3.91 A structure with hooped base but no fesswise bars. Stirrup(?) — 6484

5.4 Gateway

5.4.1 An arched opening outlined in part with [stone] blocks. Inner Temple Gate — 7157

5.4.4 A battlemented gatehouse with two windows above two arched passageways, the arch on the right taller and the window above it square, in base a date, and letters around ( ). 'Moorgate' — 7366

5.5 Tower. Castle. (For several castles see 5.12)

5.5.1 A tower battlemented of two embrasures — 6483, 6622, 6804, 7459

5.5.4 A tower battlemented of three embrasures — 6752

5.5.12 A single tower perhaps with flagpole and other towers behind — 6805, 7464

5.7 Masonry with towers

5.7.1 Masonry with a port, roofed, and one lateral battlemented tower with windows. Church — ?7550

5.7.20 Masonry with a port, perhaps with a portcullis, and two battlemented towers, perhaps with loopholes, and a central tower behind. Castle, triple-towered — 6446, 6453, 7447

5.7.25 Masonry with a port and two battlemented towers a central tower behind accompanied by an inscription — 6740

5.7.27 Masonry with a port and two battlemented towers a central tower behind and within the port a standing figure in a knee-length garment holding a staff — 6623

5.7.44 Masonry with loopholes etc. and two battlemented towers a central tower behind and in base between further fortification a port, perhaps a gatehouse — 7650

5.8 Masonry without essential towers

5.8.1 An arcaded building around an angular courtyard filled with a throng of heads surmounted by a tower. Royal Exchange (see Thompson 1993, p. 78) — 7482, 7719

5.8.2 An arcaded building around an angular courtyard filled with a throng of heads surmounted by a tower also grasshoppers. Royal Exchange (see Thompson 1993, p. 78) — 7483

5.8.4 An arcaded building surmounted by a tower also grasshoppers. Royal Exchange (see Thompson 1993, p. 78) — 6902

5.8.5 Through two arches a view of an arcaded building surmounted by a tower. Royal Exchange (see Thompson 1993, p. 78) — 6880

5.8.12 Building of one storey with arched entrance and windows and at each corner of the roof a turret. 'Guildhall' — 7791

5.9 Building with a charge issuant laterally

5.9.10 A windmill of post-mill type with common sails, ladder, and curved quarter-bars — 7850

5.9.11 A windmill of post-mill type with common sails and straight quarter-bars — 6634

5.12 Several buildings

5.12.1 Three towers, two and one — 7602

5.12.10 Several buildings with gables and perhaps flagpole, spires, weathercock. At the Jerusalem — 6966-7

5.12.11 Several buildings with gables and perhaps flagpole, spires, weathercock, accompanied by an inscription. At the City of Norwich — 6643

5.13 Ship, boat

5.13.15 A three-masted ship square-rigged with an oar — 6554, 6844, 7737

5.13.18 A three-masted ship square-rigged without oars. Royal Sovereign — 6584-5, 6945, 7022, 7029, 7324, 7330, 7515, 7608

5.13.23 A three-masted ship square-rigged without oars sailing to right — 7594

5.13.26 A three-masted ship with sails furled — 6525

5.14 Shield. Arms

5.14 Apothecaries On a shield a person, perhaps with head radiant, holding in his left hand an arrow and in his right hand a bow, astride a type of monster with two legs, long neck and long tail nowed; for the arms of the Worshipful Society of Apothecaries of the City of London *Azure, Apollo, the inventor of physic, proper with his head radiant holding in his left hand a bow and in his right hand an arrow Or, supplanting a serpent Argent* (Bromley 1960, p. 1); the bow and arrow are each in the wrong hand, as they are also in Holme 1905, 3.19.8 — 7463

5.14 Bakers — On a shield three garbs, a chief barry wavy of six, over all issuant from a cloud in chief a cubit arm descending therefrom, the hand holding a balance; for the arms of the Worshipful Company of Bakers of the City of London *Gules three garbs Or on a chief barry wavy of six Argent and Azure two anchors Or cabled Gules over all issuant from a cloud proper radiated in chief Or a cubit arm descending therefrom vested Argent cuffed Sable the hand proper holding a balance Or* (Bromley 1960, p. 9); the anchors and rays are omitted — 6542, 6546, 6577, 6669, 6779, 6848, 7335, 7492

5.14 Blacksmiths — On a shield a chevron between three crowned hammers; the arms of the Worshipful Company of Blacksmiths of the City of London *Sable a chevron Or between three hammers Argent handled and crowned Or* (Bromley 1960, p. 22) — 6721, 7431, 7641-2

5.14 Brewers — A shield: on a chevron perhaps engrailed, between six barley-sheaves in saltire, three kilderkins; the arms of the Worshipful Company of Brewers of London *Gules on a chevron engrailed Argent, between six barley sheaves in saltire Or, three kilderkins sable hooped Or* (Bromley 1960, p. 28) — 6843

5.14 Broderers — A shield paly of six on a fess between three lions passant guardant two broaches in saltire between as many quills; for the arms of the Worshipful Company of Broderers of the City of London *Paly of six Argent and Azure on a fess Gules between three lions passant guardant Or langued and armed Gules two broaches in saltire between as many quills Or* (Bromley 1960, p. 31) — 7326

5.14 Butchers — On a shield two poleaxes addorsed in saltire, between three bulls' heads couped, two in fess and one in base, on a chief a boar's head couped between two bunches of broom; for the arms of the Worshipful Company of Butchers of the City of London *Azure two poleaxes in saltire Or, blades inwards, between two bulls' heads couped in fess Argent, on a chief Argent a boar's head couped Gules, tusked Or, langued Azure, between two bunches of holly Vert, banded Or* (Bromley 1960, p. 34); the placing of the poleaxes and the number of bulls' heads differ, but agree with Stow 1633, sig. 3H2a = p. 627, Wallis 1677, pl. 32, and Berry 1828-40, i, sig. U1a — 6543

5.14 Butchers 2 — On a shield two poleaxes addorsed in saltire, in base one bull's head, on a chief a boar's head couped between two bunches of broom; for the arms of the Worshipful Company of Butchers of the City of London (see above); the placing of the poleaxes and the single bull's head differ — 7656

5.14 Clothworkers — On a shield a chevron ermine between in chief two havettes and in base a teasel cob; the arms of the Worshipful Company of Clothworkers of the City of London *Sable a chevron ermine between in chief two havettes Argent and in base a teasel cob Or* (Bromley 1960, p. 46) — 7320, 7427, 7638

5.14 Cooks — On a shield a chevron between three plant forms; for the arms of the Worshipful Company of Cooks of the City of London *Argent a chevron engrailed Sable between three columbine flowers Azure* (Bromley 1960, p. 52) — 7005

5.14 Coopers — A shield gyronny of eight, on a chevron between three annulets a royne between two broad axes, on a chief three lilies; the arms of the Worshipful Company of Coopers of London *Gyronny of eight Gules and Sable, on a chevron between three annulets Or a royne between two broad axes Azure, a chief Vert thereon three lilies Argent* (Bromley 1960, p. 55) — 7289, 7514

5.14 Drapers — On a shield [three clouds] perhaps with sunbeams issuing crowned with imperial crowns; the arms of the Worshipful Company of Drapers of the City of London *Azure three clouds with sunbeams issuing proper crowned with imperial crowns Or* (Bromley 1960, p. 72) — 6727, 6734, 6797, 7238, 7601

5.14 Dyers — On a shield a chevron between three bags, perhaps corded; for the arms of the Worshipful Company of Dyers of the City of London *Sable a chevron engrailed Argent between three bags of madder Argent corded Or* (Bromley 1960, p. 79) — 6796, 7254

5.14 Fishmongers — On a shield three dolphins naiant embowed in pale, perhaps crowned, between two pairs of stockfishes in saltire, over the mouth of each fish perhaps a crown, on a chief three pairs of keys in saltire; for the arms of the Worshipful Company of Fishmongers of the City of London *Azure three dolphins naiant embowed in pale Argent finned toothed and crowned Or between two pairs of stockfishes in saltire Argent over the mouth of each fish a crown Or; on a chief Gules three pairs of keys of St Peter in saltire Or* (Bromley 1960, p. 90) — 7513, 7604-7

5.14 Fishmongers 2 — Similar but stockfishes omitted — 7101

5.14 Fletchers — On a shield a chevron between three broad arrows; for the arms of the Worshipful Company of Fletchers of the City of London *Sable a chevron Or between three broad arrows also Or headed and feathered Argent* (Bromley 1960, p. 96) — 7517

5.14 Grocers — On a shield a chevron between nine cloves; the arms of the Worshipful Company of Grocers of the City of London *Argent a chevron Gules between nine cloves Sable* (Bromley 1960, p.

130) — 6466, 6496-7, 6621, 6636, 6732, 6953, 6973, 7010, 7172, 7222-4, 7391, 7625, 7646, 7659, 7693, 7740, 7774, 7815

5.14 Haberdashers — A shield barry wavy of six, on a bend a lion passant guardant; the arms of the Worshipful Company of Haberdashers of the City of London *Barry wavy of six Argent and Azure on a bend Gules a lion passant guardant Or* (Bromley 1960, p. 137) — ?6526

5.14 Innholders 2 — On a shield a chevron perhaps party per pale and per chevron between three garbs; for the arms of the Worshipful Company of Innholders of the City of London *c.*1530-1634 *Azure a chevron per pale and per chevron Argent and Gules between three oatsheaves Or* (Bromley 1960, pp. 144-6) — 6794, 7616

5.14 Ironmongers — A shield: on a chevron between three gads of steel three swivels; the arms of the Worshipful Company of Ironmongers of the City of London *Argent on a chevron Gules between three gads of steel Azure three swivels Or* (Bromley 1960, p. 148) — 6692, 7521

5.14 Leathersellers — On a shield three roebucks passant reguardant; the arms of the Worshipful Company of Leathersellers of London (Bromley 1960, p. 156) — 7139, 7248, 7837

5.14 London City 1 — On a shield a cross, in the first quarter a sword erect point upwards; for the arms of the City of London *Argent a cross Gules in the first quarter a sword in pale point upwards of the last* (Briggs 1971, p. 240) — 6706, 7386

5.14 Mercers — On a shield, perhaps issuant from a bank of clouds, a figure of the Virgin couped at the shoulders, the neck perhaps encircled by a jewelled necklace and perhaps wreathed about the temples with a chaplet of roses and crowned with a celestial crown, the whole perhaps within a bordure of clouds; the arms of the Worshipful Company of Mercers of the City of London *Gules issuant from a bank of clouds a figure of the Virgin couped at the shoulders proper vested in a crimson robe adorned with gold, the neck encircled by a jewelled necklace, crined Or and wreathed about the temples with a chaplet of roses alternately Argent and of the first, and crowned with a celestial crown, the whole within a bordure of clouds also proper* (Bromley 1960, pp. 168-9); see also 5.14 Pin Makers

5.14 Merchant Taylors — On a shield a pavilion between two mantles, on a chief a lion passant guardant; the arms of the Worshipful Company of Merchant Taylors of the City of London *Argent a pavilion imperial purple garnished Or lined ermine between two mantles also imperial purple lined ermine, on a chief Azure a lion passant guardant Or* (Bromley 1960, p. 174) — 6937, 7344, 7399-7400, 7439, 7668, 7748

5.14 Pewterers — A shield: on a chevron between three strikes as many roses; the arms of the Worshipful Company of Pewterers of London (Bromley 1960, p. 197) — 7245

5.14 Pin Makers — On a shield a figure of the Virgin couped at the shoulders and crowned; for arms ascribed to the Worshipful Company of Pin Makers of the City of London *Vert a demi-virgin couped at the waist proper, mantled Gules turned down ermine, her hair dishevelled, on her head an eastern crown Or* (Berry 1828-40, i. sig. U3b; Welch 1914, p. 23). The same as some versions of 5.14 Mercers — 6607

5.14 Salters — On a shield party per chevron three covered salts, the salt shedding on both sides of the salts; the arms of the Worshipful Company of Salters of the City of London *Party per chevron Azure and Gules three covered salts Argent garnished Or, the salt shedding on both sides of the salts Argent* (Bromley 1960, p. 215) — 6515

5.14 Tallow Chandlers — A shield: on a field of six pieces three doves, each holding in its beak an olive branch; the arms of the Worshipful Company of Tallow Chandlers of the City of London *On a field of six pieces Azure and Argent three doves Argent membered Gules, each holding in its beak an olive branch Or* (Bromley 1960, p. 237) — 6629, 7501, 7636, 7792, 7797

5.14 Tallow Chandlers 2 — The arms of the Worshipful Company of Tallow Chandlers of London, as above, but the divisions of the field omitted — 7509

5.14 Tylers & Bricklayers 2 — On a shield a chevron between three brick-axes palewise; for the arms of the Worshipful Company of Tylers and Bricklayers of the City of London *Azure a chevron Or in chief a fleur-de-lis Argent between two brick-axes palewise Or in base a 'brush' also Or* (Bromley 1960, p. 247). The 'brush' (bundle of laths) is replaced by a third brick-axe — 6935

5.14 Weavers — A shield: on a chevron between three leopards' heads each holding in the mouth a shuttle, three roses; the arms of the Worshipful Company of Weavers of the City of London (Bromley 1960, p. 263) — 6514, 6652, 6773, 7041

5.14 Woodmongers 2 — On a shield a chevron between three faggots; for arms *Argent a chevron Sable between three faggots Vert* (Welch 1914, p. 32, citing Harleian MS 1098, f. 59) — 7845

5.14.1 Grocers — A shield as at 5.14 Grocers, accompanied by letters ( ) — 6693

5.14.1 Mercers — A shield as at 5.14 Mercers, accompanied by letters ( ) — 6456

5.14.1 Tallow Chandlers — A shield as at 5.14 Tallow Chandlers accompanied by letters ( ) — 7208

5.14.2 Mercers — A shield as at 5.14 Mercers, accompanied by an inscription — 6456

5.14.5 — A shield quarterly, the 1st and 4th grand quarters France Modern and England quarterly, the 2nd Scotland, the 3rd Ireland; the Royal Arms of 1603-88. King's Arms — 6747, 6840, 6852, 7610, 7811, 7859

5.14.185 — On a shield a chevron between three escallops; for the arms of Michell *Sable a chevron Or between three escallops Argent* (DBAMO 1992-, ii. 334) — 6676

5.14.186	On a shield ten torteaux four three two and one in chief a label of three points; for the arms of Babington *Argent ten torteaux four three two and one in chief a label of three points Azure* (Papworth 1874, p. 1055; Vis. Lond. 1633-5, i. 36) — 6982
5.14.187	On a shield a lion rampant [in patterned border?]; perhaps for the arms of Wallis etc. (unlocated) *Gules a lion rampant Argent within a bordure gobony Argent and Azure* (Berry 1828-40, ii. sig. 5X3v.; Papworth 1874, p. 119) — 6991
5.14.188	On a shield three stags or harts trippant; possibly in error for three roebucks passant reguardant, see 5.14 Leathersellers — 7474
5.14.189	On a shield a fess dancetty in chief three crescents — 7538
5.14.190	On a shield three chevrons between (?), in base a lion's head? — 7644
5.14.191	On a shield a pile between four leopards' heads and over all a fess; for the arms of Garway, Garroway *Argent a pile between four leopards' heads Gules and over all a fess Gules* (Papworth 1874, p. 1023; Vis. Lond. 1633-5, i. 304-5) — 7711
5.14.192	On a shield three escutcheons, two and one; from the arms of the Worshipful Company of Painter-Stainers, *Quarterly first and fourth Azure three escutcheons Argent, second and third Azure a chevron between three phoenix heads erased Or beaked Gules* (Bromley 1960, p. 184) — 6939
5.15	Complete achievement of arms
5.15 Blacksmiths	A shield as at 5.14 Blacksmiths; crest, a phoenix firing herself with the sun's beams; and perhaps mantling, the armorial bearings of the Worshipful Company of Blacksmiths of the City of London (Bromley 1960, p. 22) — 7539-40
5.15.4	A shield quarterly France Modern and England, the Royal Arms of *c.*1400-1603; ensigned with a royal crown — 7135
5.15.39	On a shield two swords in saltire within a bordure engrailed; the arms of Brand, of Holborn or of Gray's Inn and Suffolk, *Azure two swords Argent hilts Or in saltire, a bordure engrailed Or;* crest perhaps *Out of a ducal coronet Or a leopard's head proper* (Burke 1884, p. 116; Vis. Essex 1552-1634, i. 357) — 7235
5.16	Helmet, crest
5.16.1	A close helm in profile — 6635, 6720, 7726, 7766
5.17	Portcullis and similar
5.17.1	A portcullis furnished with rings and chains — 6551
5.17.5	A portcullis or similar (without rings or chains), the verticals pointed in base. At the Red [Lattice?] — 7751
5.17.10	Transverse bars, the verticals projecting in chief and in base. Harrow — 6627, 7372
5.17.13	Transverse bars forming a square frame with none projecting. Harrow — 6480, 7462, 7599

5.42 Sword, dagger
5.42.1 A sword or dagger erect point in chief. The Dagger — 7377
5.42.2 A sword or dagger erect point in chief piercing a roundle. At the Sword and Ball — 7118
5.42.4 A sword or dagger erect and in chief a magpie. At the Dagger and Pie — 6992
5.42.6 A sword or dagger erect and in chief a crown; from the arms of the Company of Woodmongers *Gules a sword erect Argent hilt and pommel Or enfiled with a ducal coronet of the last, between two flanches Argent charged with a faggot proper* (Welch 1914, p. 32) — 6708-9
5.42.7 A sword erect, enfiled with a crown, between two faggots; from the arms of the Company of Woodmongers, as at 5.42.6 — 6710
5.42.22 A sword or dagger point in base and an anchor — 6748
5.42.30 Two swords or daggers in saltire points in chief — 7341, 7723, 7803

5.43 Knife, scissors, shears
5.43.8 Three pruning-knives palewise in fess — 6885
5.43.11 A cheese-knife, blade in base, accompanied by letters ( ) — 6829
5.43.20 Open scissors blades in chief — 7133
5.43.30 A pair of shears blades in base. At the Shears — 6722, 7151
5.43.31 A pair of shears blades in base accompanied by letters ( ). At the Shears — 7866
5.43.35 A pair of shears blades in chief — 7159

5.45 Axe, hatchet
5.45.1 An axe fesswise head to left blade in base. At the Hatchet — 6906
5.45.11 A battleaxe palewise head to left — 7519

5.47 Gonfalon
5.47.11 A rectangular signboard hanging from a bar in chief charged with a bell — 7852
5.47.20 A rectangular signboard and a curved support in chief, perhaps a lateral support to right — 7853

5.49 Armillary sphere, globe
5.49.1 A globe (unsupported) — 6605, 7091, 7257, 7564-5, 7782
5.49.5 A globe on a stand. At the Globe (tavern) — 7092, 7312

5.50 Other circular charges
5.50.1 A roundle suspended, perhaps on a chain. At the (Golden) Ball — 7133, 7220, 7291, 7296
5.50.5 A roundle (without support or suspender) — 6467
5.50.12 A roundle pierced with a square hole. Millstone — 6814
5.50.18 Within a dial marked with roman numerals one or two pointers. Clock face — 6608
5.50.30 An annulet-headed staff. Frying-pan — 6691
5.50.33 A staff attached in chief to a large annulet and in base to a small annulet [for suspension]. At the Gilt Frying-pan — 7219

5.64.16	Three sugarloaves in fess and braced. (At) the 3 Sugar-loaves — 7128, 7356-7, 7485
5.64.19	Three sugarloaves in fess and in chief a tobacco roll(?) fesswise — 7784
5.64.22	Three sugarloaves one and two — 6714, 7760, 7812
5.64.30/ 5.64.49	Tun, barrel, cask
5.64.30	A tun, barrel, or cask fesswise. At the Tun — 6460-1, 6892, 7402, 7652
5.64.33	Three tuns one and two. (At) the Three Tuns (tavern), the Three Tun tavern — 7023, 7028, 7119-20, 7309, 7353, 7558, 7628
5.64.34	Three tuns one and two accompanied by letters ( ) — 7640
5.64.40	Three tuns two and one. At [the 3?] Tuns — 6792, 6811, 6846-7, 7226, 7317, 7744
5.64.42	Three tuns two and one accompanied by an inscription — 7227
5.64.43	Three tuns in pale. At the 3 Tuns — 6845
5.64.45	A tun surmounting a stalked flower — 6631
5.64.46	A tun surmounting three arrows palewise in fess points in base. The Tun and 3 Arrows — 6589-90
5.64.50/ 5.64.64	Woolpack, woolsack
5.64.50	A woolpack/woolsack fesswise. At Woolsack — 6895, 6984, 7154
5.64.52	A woolpack/woolsack fesswise accompanied by an inscription — 6625
5.64.55	A woolpack/woolsack fesswise (or similar) charged with a letter or monogram — 6896-7
5.64.65/ 5.64.74	Still/distillatory armed left or right
5.64.65	A still on a masoned base armed left — 6474
5.64.69	A still on a masoned base armed right with receiver — 7355
5.64.72	A still on legs armed left and in base three tuns(?) — 6777
5.64.75/ 5.64.79	Still, double-armed
5.64.75	A double-armed still on a masoned base — 6527
5.64.76	A double-armed still on a masoned base flammant — 7273
5.64.77	A double-armed still on legs with two receivers — 6689
5.64.79	A double-armed still in chief of a masoned base — 7244
5.64.80/ 5.64.84	Mortar
5.64.80	From a mortar two pestles issuant — 7156
5.64.85/ 5.64.89	Jug/pitcher/black-jack with curved sides
5.64.89	Jug etc. handled left accompanied by a cock in chief a crown. Cock and Bottle — 6451
5.64.100/ 5.64.109	Covered cup, salt
5.64.104	Three covered cups two and one, perhaps shedding salt; from the arms of the Worshipful Company of Salters of the City of London — 6694, 7098
5.64.150/ 5.64.158	Lamp, lantern

5.64.150	A lantern enclosing a candle, in chief a ring [for suspension] — 6523
5.64.153	A framework above a thick base (probably too heavy for a birdcage). Lamp(?) — 6664
5.64.158	From a vertical container pointed in chief two pipes on either side flammant. Oil lamp of four lights — 7781
5.64.160/ 5.64.161	Drum (musical instrument)
5.64.160	A drum fesswise: a cylinder with a head at either end lapped over the open end of the shell and secured by a counter-hoop, the heads being tensioned by ropes which tie them together diagonally across the shell — 6662
5.64.173	A container of fesswise construction rising from wider base to two short handles(?), see better Boyne 1858, pl. 22.12. Soapbox, as named on BW 473, and in 1660 (*OED*) — 7279
5.64.174	A soapbox, as at 5.64.173, accompanied by initials ( ) — 7826
5.64.205	Out of a container with a foot and convex sides six or seven longitudinal charges. Case of Knives, see Thompson 2002a (p. 168) — 7440
5.65	Balance, pair of scales
5.65.5	A balance in equilibrium, pans uncharged, and in base a garb; cf. 5.14 Bakers — 7442
5.65.30	A balance weighed down on the right perhaps to denote that the inequality of justice was against the issuer and to the advantage of the buyer — 7403-4
5.66	Key
5.66.3	A key palewise bow in chief bit to left accompanied by an inscription. At the Golden Key — 6732
5.66.4	A key palewise bow in chief bit to left accompanied by a cock — 6825
5.66.13	A key palewise bow in chief bit to right between two dice — 6858
5.66.17	A key palewise bow in base bit to left accompanied by an inscription — 7210
5.66.20	Two keys in saltire bows in base bits outwards. At the Cross Keys — 6841, 7187, 7598
5.66.30	Two keys in saltire bows in chief bits outwards. At the Cross Keys — 7188, 7672, 7759
5.67	Lock, padlock
5.67.7	A padlock between two pairs of shears. The Lock and Shears — 7569
5.68	Horseshoe
5.68.1	A horseshoe points in chief. At the Horseshoe — 6933, 7007, 7573
5.68.10	A horseshoe points in base. At the Horseshoe — 6472, 6505, 6673, 6755, 7018, 7112, 7198, 7537, 7734
5.68.11	A horseshoe points in base accompanied by letters ( ) — 6575

5.76.153 A monogram of T and a smaller B between two pellets and in chief a cinquefoil — 7251
5.76.154 A monogram of R, H — 7309
5.76.155 A monogram of C, H, R, I, S, T, O, P, E, K, A, N — 7337
5.76.156 A merchant's mark incorporating the conjoined letters M, F — 7395
5.76.157 A merchant's mark incorporating H, H, as Oddie 127 (2001-4, p. 433) — 7746
5.76.158 A monogram of T and a smaller D — 7536
5.76.159 A monogram of the letters *S, B* and perhaps *E, I, L, M, N, P, T, V, W* — 7623
5.76.160 A monogram (letters uncertain) — 7694
5.76.161 A monogram: on a letter T a letter L to right — 7700

5.77 Inscription in roman capitals, or numerals, perhaps accompanied by letters ( ). (Where an inscription consists solely of a date, or letters and a date, this word replaces the class number, except that date figures in an irregular arrangement are transcribed in full) — 6429 . . . 7867 (many instances)
5.77.1 Inscription in italic letters, perhaps accompanied by letters ( ) — 6425, 6446, 6516, 6553, 6609, 6621, 6633, 6646, 6659, 6661, 6696, 6852, 6870, 6881-4, 6910, 6924, 6930, 7033, 7050, 7055, 7070-1, 7164, 7253, 7362, 7615, 7639, 7692, 7758, 7763

5.79 Knot, lace, strap
5.79.9 Three knots palewise in fess — 6944

5.82 Tobacco roll and similar with square ends
5.82.1 An oblong figure fesswise divided palewise, perhaps showing a circular cross-section at one end, palewise divisions correspondingly curved (no projections). Roll of cloth? Roll of tobacco (formed from coils of spun or twist tobacco). The Tobacco Roll — 7629, 7695
5.82.28 An oblong figure fesswise divided palewise, from one end a thick projection, and in chief a crescent — 7050

5.83 Shuttle and similar with pointed ends
5.83.43 A charge with curved sides, ends pointing in opposite directions, and long wide piercing fesswise. Shuttle? Bread roll? — 6624

5.84 Tobacco-pipe
5.84.14 Two tobacco-pipes in saltire bowls in chief and outwards and in base a tobacco roll fesswise — 7543
5.84.30 Three tobacco-pipes fesswise in pale, bowls of first and third in chief to left, bowl of second in chief to right — 7074
5.84.36 Three tobacco-pipes palewise in fess, bowls of first and third in base to left, bowl of second in chief to right. At the Three Tobacco-pipes — 7394

5.85 Book. Bible
5.85.1 A closed book with clasps, the binding decorated — 7532

5.85.5	Three closed books two and one. At the Three Bibles — 7288
5.89	Weight
5.89.2	A weight(?) accompanied by letters ( ) — 6440

INDEX TO CLASSIFICATION

ABBREVIATIONS

A. GENERAL

In addition to the usual abbreviations for counties etc., the following are used:

*	(before a reference) Published reading not wholly confirmed by specimen
appr.	Apprenticed
Archd. L.	Archdeaconry of London
b.	Born
bap.	Baptised
bd.	Buried
Br	Brass, or any yellowish alloy of copper
Cu	Copper, or an alloy of similar colour
d.	Died
f.	Feminine
fl.	Flourished
g	Grams
gr	Grains
i.m.	Initial mark
M	A metal intermediate in colour between copper and brass; mixed metal
m.	Masculine
md.	Married
nd	Not dated
obv.	Obverse
Pb	Lead or pewter
PCC	Prerogative Court of Canterbury
rev.	Reverse
var.	Variety

B. COLLECTORS, DEALERS, AND COLLECTIONS CITED IN THE TEXT

Baldwin	Albert Henry Frederick Baldwin (1889-1970), of Messrs A. H. Baldwin & Sons Ltd, London coin dealers since *c*.1880 [6428 . . . 7865, at least 324 specimens]
Baldwin's Auction 38	Baldwin's Auctions Ltd, Auction no. 38, 4 October 2004 [cf. 6761, 7374, 7764]
Bird	Dr Brian Bird (1913-1993), psychiatrist, of Cleveland Heights, Ohio, U.S.A., a member of the British Numismatic Society 1965-85 (Pagan 2003, p. 218), who sold his Anglo-Saxon and Norman coins through Glendining on 20 November 1974, and his seventeenth-century tokens (all ex Norweb) through Spink Sale 35, 11 April 1984, lots 255-97 [cf. 6895, 6945]

BM	See British Museum
Brand	Virgil Michael Brand (1862-1926), of Chicago, brewer, who built up a collection of more than 350,000 coins. In London he was buying from Spink at least as early as 1895. At his death the collection was divided between his two brothers, and portions have since been dispersed through dealers, auction rooms, and privately. See Bowers 1983, who includes comments by Mrs Norweb [6960, 6997, 7181, 7358b, 7371c, 7404, ?7425b, 7427, 7718a]
British Museum	The British Museum collection of seventeenth-century tokens was briefly described by Boyne 1858, pp. x-xi, by Keary 1885, and by Cook 2001. Subsequent acquisitions have included the Fletcher Irish cabinet (for which see *SCBI* 49, p. lvii), Udal's Dorset cabinet, and Walker's Essex cabinet (for which see *SCBI* 38, p. lxxii). By March 1975 the Museum held 10,201 seventeenth-century tokens, to which at least 1,250 have since been added, 1,218 of them from the Norweb Collection [cf. 6426 . . . 7865, many instances]
C.B.	See Crowther-Beynon
Carlyon-Britton, R.	Raymond Carlyon Carlyon-Britton, FSA (1893-1960), a member of the British Numismatic Society from 1911 (Pagan 2003, p. 221). Portions of his collection of coins were acquired by Seaby from 1949 (Manville 1986, pp. 375-6) [7323]
Carthew	Col. Ranulphus John Carthew, JP, Royal Field Artillery (1863-1943), of Woodbridge Abbey, who became a Fellow of the Royal Numismatic Society in 1905 (Pagan 1986, p. 89), and was a member of the British Numismatic Society 1906-20 (Pagan 2003, p. 221). His 'magnificent' collection of seventeenth-century tokens was offered in *SCMB*, March 1946 and May 1953. Inexplicably he is named as Col. Thomas Carthew in Preston-Morley 1981, p. 136, in Spink Sale 28, and thence in Manville 1986, p. 376 [6433 . . . 7867, at least 276 specimens]
Clark	Nigel A. Clark, a coin collector, and dealer since 1976, first in Brentwood (Essex), then East Grinstead (West Sussex), and subsequently in Blackheath in the London Borough of Greenwich. He was a member of the British Numismatic Society 1974-91 (Pagan 2003, p. 222) [6462, 6547b, 7097, 7207]
Coins & Antiquities	Coins & Antiquities Ltd, successors to D. J. Crowther Ltd (established 1966), were London dealers in coins, medals and classical antiquities from *c.*1968 to 1979 [6515, 6864]
Crowther-Beynon	'C.B.', a source for Nott, was probably Vernon Bryan Crowther-Beynon MBE FSA (1865-1941), cf. *SCBI* 31, p. xiv, and *BNJ* 24 (1941-4), 57 [7415b, 7416b, 7452, 7662c]
Daniels	James Herbert Daniels (1864-1936), of Brighton, a coin dealer whose stock was auctioned after his death by Glendining, 25-26 March and 17-18 June 1936. He was an original member of the British Numismatic Society (Pagan 2003, p. 224) [7056, 7163, 7273b, 7606, 7655b, 7687b, 7689, 7761b, 7806c, 7858]
Day	G. Day, a source for Gilbert; unidentified [7616]

Deane — Patrick Deane, a coin dealer since 1973, first in London, subsequently in Orpington in the London Borough of Bromley. He was a member of the British Numismatic Society 1973-8 (Pagan 2003, p. 225) [6705, 7464]

Faulkner — William James Faulkner (1862-1939), of Endon, Staffs., a member of the British Numismatic Society from 1915, and a Fellow of the Royal Numismatic Society from 1921 (Pagan 1986, p. 93). His seventeenth-century tokens, meticulously described on envelopes ruled in pencil, were sold through Glendining, 21-23 May 1940; his duplicates are in commerce [6608, 6755, 7366b]

Gilbert — William Gilbert, LRIBA (*c.*1878-1944), a Fellow of the Royal Numismatic Society from 1913 (Pagan 1986, p. 93) [6646, 6736, ?7059, 7225, 7272a, 7616]

Glendining 25-26 Sep. 1907 — Glendining, 25-26 September 1907: including an extensive collection of seventeenth-century tokens, the property of an unidentified collector, lots 1-67 [cf. 7100]

Greenall 1997 — Philip Dalton Greenall, MSc (1915-1991), of Hampstead, a Fellow of the Royal Numismatic Society from 1966 and a member of the British Numismatic Society from 1971. His collection of tokens was sold by Baldwin's Auctions Ltd as Auction no. 16, 30 October 1997 [cf. 6449, 6463, 6484, 6662, 6717, 6723, 6882, 6935-6, 7083, 7101, 7124, 7326, 7449, 7467, 7516, 7580, 7624, 7665, 7706, 7743, 7769, 7791, 7850, 7859]

Harris 2002 — Mrs Dora Harris (d. *c.*2000). Her collection of [Greater] London seventeenth-century tokens was sold as lots 492-568 in Dix Noonan Webb's Auction no. 56, 11 December 2002 [cf. 6562, 6642, 6804, 7157, 7379, 7590]

Hodgkin 1914 — John Eliot Hodgkin, FSA, published on London tokens in *NC* 1885, and on his acquisitions in *Rariora* 1900-2. His son Gerard (d. 1900) was Williamson's sub-editor for London. The J. E. Hodgkin collection of 17c tokens and medals was auctioned by Sotheby 22-23 April 1914 (Manville 1986, p. 225) [?7562, 7746, 7831; cf. 7713]

Hunter, M. O. — Pseudonym of Prof. T. O. Mabbott, q.v.

Johnson, B. G. — Burdett G. Johnson (1885-1947), coin dealer, of St Louis, Missouri, U.S.A. [7199b]

Longman 1958 — William Longman, FSA (1882-1967), a member of the publishing family of that name, was a Fellow of the Royal Numismatic Society 1911-33 (Pagan 1986, p. 99), and a member of the British Numismatic Society 1915-60 (Pagan 2003, p. 239). See also *SCBI* 43, p. xliii. He published in 1916 *Tokens of the Eighteenth Century connected with Booksellers & Bookmakers*, and sold a related collection through Glendining on 12-13 March 1958 [7288, 7532, 7622]

Mabbott — Prof. Thomas Ollive Mabbott (1898-1968), a US member of the British Numismatic Society from 1930 and a Fellow of the Royal Numismatic Society from 1934 (Pagan 1986, p. 128). He published notes on some rare or unpublished seventeenth-century tokens in *NC*

	1931, and edited manuscripts by Thomas Chatterton, sometimes using the pseudonym M. O. Hunter [7625]
Macfadyen	Frank Edward Macfadyen (1871-1939), of Newcastle upon Tyne, a Fellow of the Royal Numismatic Society from 1901 and original member of the British Numismatic Society, who sold his collection of English and Irish copper coins, seventeenth-century tokens etc., through Sotheby, 15-16 July 1907 [6607, 6664, 6770, 6775, 6823, 6964, 6976, 7046, 7069, 7239, 7324b, 7335, 7370, 7393, 7396, 7465, 7471, 7490, 7571, 7645, 7677, 7697b, 7800, 7814b, 7843]
MoL	See Museum of London
Museum of London	Opened 1976 to incorporate the Guildhall Museum (1826) and the London Museum (1911); see Sheppard 1991 [cf. 6439 . . . 7867, many instances]
Nott	Ralph Augustus Nott (1883-1960): see *SCBI* 31, pp. xii-xv, and also Abbreviations, C, section (a) [6425a . . . 7867, at least 1,444 specimens]
Parkes Weber	Frederic Parkes Weber (1863-1962), MD FRCP FSA, was a member of the Numismatic Society of London from 1885, FRNS 1904, hon. 1954, and a member of the British Numismatic Society from 1955 (Pagan 1986, p. 74, 2003, p. 256). He published *Aspects of Death in Art*, including tokens, and contributed to *NC* on medals, etc. He was a benefactor to the British Museum, and in 1954 founded the Parkes Weber Essay Prize for young numismatists [cf. 6496]
Pridmore	Major Fred S. Pridmore, RAPC (1914-1980), the authority on British colonial coins and tokens, was elected a member of the Yorkshire Numismatic Society 1938, and was a member of the British Numismatic Society 1944-71, hon. 1976 (Pagan 2003, p. 246) [6494, 6640, 6743, ?6760a, 6844, 7037b, 7133a, ?7173, 7186, ?7223, 7317a, 7619, 7827]
S&B No. 80	S&B's Coin and Medal Bulletin, No. 80, January-March 2005 [cf. 6840]
S. Museum	A source for Nott on 12 July 1956; unidentified [6512]
Schwer	Siegfried Ernest (Fred) Schwer (1936-2006), a coin dealer in Woodbridge 1966-86, then in Felixstowe, both Suffolk. He traded as The Token Specialist until 1991. His remaining stock of tokens, tickets, passes etc., and his library, were offered as lots 220-380 through Glendining, 4 June 1992. See also Dix Noonan Webb, Auction no. 72, 13 December 2006, p. [5], for his life as a professional golfer. He published price guides to 18th-century tokens [pref. 1983], and to unofficial farthings 1986, also Sara Payne, *The Gurteens of Haverhill* 1984, and R. C. Bell, *Political and Commemorative Pieces* 1987. He was a member of the British Numismatic Society 1976-95 (Pagan 2003, p. 249) [6608, 6755]
Seaby	B. A. Seaby Ltd, London coin dealers from 1926 until 1991 [6625, 6667, 6674a, 6682b, 6702a, 6711a, 6717, 6745, 6793, 6857, 6956, 7007, 7048, 7084, 7150, 7154, 7167, 7193a, 7206b, 7249, 7262, 7287b, 7299, 7313, 7318b, 7323, 7331a, 7333, 7346, 7365, 7392c,

	7479, 7534a, 7560, 7612, 7679, 7718d, 7720b-c, 7777, 7781, 7825b, 7832]
Sedgwick 1986	Frank Sedgwick, a City of London architect, inherited a general token collection in 1959, then concentrated on 18c City of London buildings and 17c London and Southwark. His collection of [Greater] London seventeenth-century tokens was sold as lots 1-69 in Spink Sale 51, 16 April 1986; many were not in Williamson [cf. 6490, 6976, 7393, 7430, 7632]
Shuttlewood 2001	Roger Alan Shuttlewood (1941-2000), stockbroker, was a member of the British Numismatic Society from 1969 (Pagan 2003, p. 250). His collection of sixteenth- and seventeenth-century tokens was sold as lots 616-715 in Spink Sale 151, 15 March 2001. See p. 6 of the catalogue for details of his collection of Tudor silver coins; in the same sale was his extensive collection of farthings of James I and Charles I [cf. 6433, 7076, 7568, 7666]
Snell	A. B. Snell, a source for Baldwin in 1922; not identified [7691b]
Sotheby 25 July 1938	Sotheby, 25 July 1938: lot 88, containing 23 tokens, part of the property of an unnamed consignor, was purchased by Nott for £4/10/- [6486, 7651, 7675c]
Sotheby 24 January 1979	Sotheby, 24 January 1979: including 'a small collection of seventeenth-century tokens', lots 146-51, most specimens of which were ex Faulkner (q.v.) [6608, 6755]
Spink	Spink & Son Ltd, London coin dealers since 1666 [?6449, ?6455, 6508, ?6660, 6685, 6691, 6712, 6737, 6740-1, 6798, 6810, 6815, 6860, 6866c, 6871, 6874, 6882, 6896, 6902, 6912, 6927, 6995, 6999, 7014, 7030, 7064, 7087, 7093, ?7107b, 7125, 7130b, 7131a, 7132, 7138b, 7151c, ?7161, 7162, 7188a, 7202, 7209, 7213, 7251b, 7252, 7253b, 7255, 7256a, 7258, 7265, 7279, 7297, 7329, 7372, 7378, 7383, 7388a, 7389-90, 7438, 7446b, 7448, 7475a, 7499, 7516b, 7555, 7559, 7586, 7588, 7593, 7601b, 7625, 7633, 7640b, 7646, 7653, 7676b, 7678, 7687c, 7691a, 7694-5, 7704, 7708, 7718e, 7722b, 7731a, 7753, 7756, 7770b, 7778, 7799, 7808, ?7844a, ?7846a]
Spink Sale 28	Spink Coin Auctions, Sale no. 28, 28 April 1983
Stevens [i.e. Stephens]	'Homer Stevens' presumably refers to Homer R. Stephens, who published a *Check List of Conder Tokens* in 1937, and various notes in *The Numismatist* and the *Coin Collector's Journal* of 1936-42 such as 'English tokens relating to America' and 'Sightseeing in the British Isles via Condor [!] tokens' [6781]
Symonds	Henry Symonds, FSA (1859-1933), barrister, was a member of the Numismatic Society of London 1885-1900, FRNS from 1909, also a member of the British Numismatic Society 1909-19, Vice-President 1914, 1917 (Pagan 1986, p. 73, 2003, p. 253), and editor of the Dorset Natural History and Antiquarian Field Club *Proceedings*, etc. He published articles on Dorset and Somerset seventeenth-century tokens [cf. 7342]
Taffs	Herbert William Taffs, MVO, MBE (1870-1955), a member of the Numismatic Society of London from 1896, a founder member of the

	British Numismatic Society, hon. 1950, and President 1938-45 (Pagan 1986, p. 73, 2003, p. 253). His collection was auctioned by Glendining, 21-23 Nov. 1956; tokens from it were identified by Nott on the back of his own tickets, by the abbreviation 'T'. [6425a . . . 7861a, at least 468 specimens]
Wetton 1989	John Lancaster Wetton, FRICS, MTPI (1911-1988), of Woking, planning inspector, was collecting tokens from 1930, following a gift from George C. Williamson. His seventeenth-century tokens from Greater London were auctioned as Part 2 of his collection, lots 132-269 in Spink Sale 74, 29 November 1989; Part 1 – those from elsewhere in England – had been offered as lots 426-51 in Spink Sale 67, 16 November 1988. His retained Surrey collection was eventually sold to the Surrey Archaeological Society [cf. 6572, 6578, 6631, 6634, 6917, 6981, 7029, 7382, 7395, 7500, 7588, 7738]

C. BIBLIOGRAPHICAL

(a) MANUSCRIPT SOURCES

Boyd	Percival Boyd, [Inhabitants of London]. Society of Genealogists, MS. (238 vols. plus index, 27 vols.). Formerly known as 'Citizens of London'
Nightingale MS	Benjamin Nightingale, Manuscript notes in his large-paper copy of Akerman 1849 (q.v.), the property of R. H. Thompson
Nott	Ralph Nott, Manuscript notes in his copy of Williamson (q.v.), the property of R. H. Thompson
PROB 11	National Archives/Public Record Office. Prerogative Court of Canterbury: Registered copy wills 1383-1858

(b) PRINTED SOURCES

BNJ =	*The British Numismatic Journal*
CCNB Newsletter =	*Newsletter –Coordinating Committee for Numismatics in Britain*
NC =	The Numismatic Chronicle
NCirc =	*The Numismatic Circular* subsequently *Spink Numismatic Circular*
S&B =	*S&B's Coin & Medal Bulletin*
SCMB =	*Seaby's Coin and Medal Bulletin* subsequently *Seaby Coin & Medal Bulletin*
TCSB =	*Bulletin –Token Corresponding Society*
Akerman 1849	John Yonge Akerman, *Tradesmen's Tokens current in London and its Vicinity between the Years 1648 and 1672, described from the Originals in the British Museum, and in several Private Collections* (London, 1849)
Aubrey 1898	John Aubrey, *Brief Lives*; ed. Andrew Clark (Oxford, 1898). 2 vols.
Aubrey 1982	John Aubrey, *Brief Lives*; a modern English version edited by Richard Barber (Woodbridge, 1982)

Bagust 1937	F. Bagust, *Some Notes on the small Post Offices of London in the Seventeenth and Eighteenth Centuries* ([Bournemouth], 1937). British Library gives Bournemouth as the place of publication, but 'Copies of this book can be obtained from me . . . 8 Downs Road, Clapton, London E.5'; Florence Bagust was a teacher at Clapton & Stamford Hill School of Art, and local historian
Baldwin's Auction 38	See Abbreviations, B
Bardsley 1901	Charles Wareing Bardsley, *A Dictionary of English and Welsh Surnames, with special American Instances*; revised for the press by his widow (London, 1901)
Bartholomew 1972	John Bartholomew & Son Ltd, *Gazetteer of the British Isles*, 9th edn., reprinted with . . . Supplement . . . (Edinburgh, 1972)
Bedloe 1679	William Bedloe, *A Narrative and Impartial Discovery of the Horrid Popish Plot* . . . (London, 1679)
Berry 1828-40	William Berry, *Encyclopædia Heraldica, or, Complete Dictionary of Heraldry* (London, [1828-40]). 4 vols.
Berry 1978	George Berry, *Taverns and Tokens of Pepys' London* (London, 1978)
Berry 1990	George Berry, 'The forty favoured taverns permitted to trade in Tudor London', *Coin News*, 27 no. 3 (May 1990), 36-40
Biddle 2005	Martin Biddle, *Nonsuch Palace, [2]: the material culture of a noble Restoration household;* with contributions by . . . [others] (Oxford, 2005)
Bowers 1983	Q. David Bowers, *Virgil Brand, the Man and his Era: profile of a numismatist* (Wolfeboro, New Hampshire, 1983)
Boyd 1934	Percival Boyd, *Roll of the Drapers' Company of London* (Croydon, 1934)
Boyne 1858	William Boyne, *Tokens issued in the Seventeenth Century* (London, 1858)
Briggs 1971	Geoffrey Briggs, *Civic & Corporate Heraldry* (Ramsbury, 1971)
Bromley 1960	John Bromley, *The Armorial Bearings of the Guilds of London: a record of the heraldry of the surviving companies with historical notes*; with . . . [illustrations] by Heather Child . . . (London, 1960)
Burke 1884	Sir Bernard Burke, *The General Armory of England, Scotland, Ireland and Wales* . . .; with a Supplement (London, 1884)
Burke 2003	*Burke's Peerage, Baronetage & Knightage*, 107th edn., editor-in-chief Charles Mosley (Wilmington, Del., 2003). 3 vols.
Burn 1855	Jacob Henry Burn, *A Descriptive Catalogue of the London Traders, Tavern, and Coffee-house Tokens current in the Seventeenth Century, presented to the Corporation Library by Henry Benjamin Hanbury Beaufoy*, 2nd edn. (London, 1855)
BW	See Williamson
Cal. S.P. Dom.	National Archives/Public Record Office, *Calendar of State Papers, Domestic Series, 1547-* (London, 1856-)
Caldecott 1907	J. B. Caldecott and G. C. Yates, 'Leaden tokens', *BNJ* 4 (1907), 317-26, pl.

Challis 1989	C. E. Challis, 'Mint officials and moneyers of the Stuart period', *BNJ* 59 (1989), 157-97
Cockett 1928	C. Bernard Cockett, *John Bunyan's England: a tour with a camera . . .*; photographs by J. Dixon-Scott (London: Homeland Association, 1928)
Cook 2001	Barrie Cook, 'Seventeenth-century tokens in the British Museum', *CCNB Newsletter*, no. 27 (April 2001), 3
Cotterell 1929	Howard Herschel Cotterell, *Old Pewter, its Makers and Marks in England, Scotland and Ireland* (London, 1929)
Cottle 1978	Basil Cottle, *The Penguin Dictionary of Surnames*, 2nd edn. (Harmondsworth, 1978)
Cowan 2005	Brian Cowan, *The Social Life of Coffee* (New Haven and London, 2005)
Cunnington 1972	C. Willett Cunnington and Phillis Cunnington, *Handbook of English Costume in the Seventeenth Century . . .*, 3rd edn. (London, 1972)
Dale 1931	Society of Genealogists (Great Britain), *The Inhabitants of London in 1638*; edited from MS 272 in Lambeth Palace Library by T. C. Dale (London, 1931). 2 vols.
Dale 1934	*The Hearth Tax of 1663 (apparently corrected to 1666/7)*: the Wards of Farringdon Within and Without, transcribed from MS E.179/147/627 at the [Public] Record Office by the Rev. T. C. Dale (London: Society of Genealogists, 1934). Reproduced from typewriting; cover and half-title 'London Hearth Tax 1663: Wards of Farringdon Within and Without, from a transcription by Rev. T. C. Dale (1934)'
DBAMO 1992-	*Dictionary of British Arms: Medieval Ordinary*, Vol. 1–, ed. D. H. B. Chesshyre, T. Woodcock . . . [et al.] (London, 1992-)
Dickinson	Michael Dickinson, *Seventeenth-century Tokens of the British Isles and their Values* (London, 1986)
Dickinson 1989	M. J. Dickinson and R. H. Thompson, 'Three seventeenth-century tokens overstruck on others', *NCirc* 97 (1989), 325-6
Dickinson 2001	Michael Dickinson, 'Unpublished Tokens from the Shuttlewood Collection', *NCirc* 109 (2001), 369-71
Dickinson forthcoming	M. J. Dickinson, 'Letter punches used in the legends of tokens by David Ramage', forthcoming
DNB	*Dictionary of National Biography* (London, 1885-1996)
Dummelow 1973	John Dummelow, *The Wax Chandlers of London* (Chichester, 1973)
Ekwall 1954	Eilert Ekwall, *Street-names of the City of London* (Oxford, 1954)
Ekwall 1960	Eilert Ekwall, *The Concise Oxford Dictionary of English Place-Names*, 4th edn. (Oxford, 1960)
Elrington 1970	C. R. Elrington, *The Victoria History of the Counties of England: Handbook for Editors and Authors* (London, 1970)
Eveleigh 1985	David J. Eveleigh, *Candle Lighting* (Aylesbury, 1985). Shire album 132
Fairbairn 1905	*Fairbairn's Book of Crests of the Families of Great Britain and Ireland*, 4th edn., revised and enlarged (London, 1905). 2 vols.

Fire Court 1966- *The Fire Court: Calendar to the Judgments and Decrees of the Court of Judicature appointed to determine Differences between Landlords and Tenants as to rebuilding after the Great Fire*, ed. Philip E. Jones (London, 1966-)

Fitch 1992-8 Church of England. Diocese of London. Commissary Court. London Division. *Index to Testamentary Records in the Commissary Court of London (London Division) now preserved in Guildhall Library, London*, Vol. 4: 1626-1649 and 1661-1700, ed. Marc Fitch (London, 1992-98). 3 vols. The Index library

Flecknoe 1658 Richard Flecknoe, *Enigmaticall Characters* ([London?], 1658)

Fleet 2000 R. J. Fleet, 'Statistical methods for identifying possible issuers' names for London seventeenth century tokens displaying only initials', *BNJ* 70 (2000), 150-2

Franks 1859-61 A. W. Franks, 'A London token of the 17th century', *Proceedings of the Society of Antiquaries of London*, 2nd series, 1 (1859-61), 97-9

Franks 1862 Augustus W. Franks, 'London tokens of the seventeenth century: additions to the list published in . . . [Boyne] 1858', *NC* new series 2 (1862), 81-103

GEC 1910-98 G. E. C[okayne], *The Complete Peerage...*, (London; Stroud, 1910-98). 14 vols. in 15

Gerritsen 1998 *A Dictionary of Medieval Heroes*, ed. Willem P. Gerritsen and Anthony G. van Melle; translated from the Dutch by Tanis Guest (Woodbridge, 1998)

Gilbert 1927 W. Gilbert, 'Unpublished seventeenth-century tokens in the collection of William Gilbert', *NC* 5th series 7 (1927), 121-55, 342-69, pls. vi-vii, xv

Gilbert 1987 John R. Gilbert, 'Seventeenth-century trade tokens from the Thames 1981-86', *SCMB* (1987), 191-9

Greenall 1991 Philip D. Greenall, 'Dividing seventeenth-century tokens between London and Middlesex', *BNJ* 61 (1991), 90-123, pl. 12. 'Appendix: list of places in each division', [by] Stella Greenall, with contributions by Michael Dickinson and Robert Thompson, pp. 94-123

Greenall 1997 See Abbreviations, B

Hanks 1988 Patrick Hanks and Flavia Hodges, *A Dictionary of Surnames*; special consultant for Jewish Names David L. Gold (Oxford, 1988)

Harben 1918 Henry A. Harben, *A Dictionary of London* (London, 1918)

Harl. 26 (1887) Harleian Society, *Allegations for Marriage Licences issued by the Bishop of London 1611 to 1828*, extracted by Joseph Lemuel Chester, Vol. II (London, 1887). The Publications of the Harleian Society, Vol. XXVI

Harl. 33 (1892) Harleian Society, *Allegations for Marriage Licences issued by the Vicar-General of the Archbishop of Canterbury, 1660 to 1668*, ed. George J. Armytage (London, 1892). The Publications of the Harleian Society, Vol. XXXIII

Harl. Reg. 3, 1878 Harleian Society, *The Rejester Booke of Saynte De'nis Backchurch Parishe (City of London) for Maryages, Christenynges, and Buryalles*

	begynnynge in the Yeare of o^{r} *Lord God 1538*, ed. Joseph Lemuel Chester (London, 1878). The publications of the Harleian Society, Register section, Vol. III
Harl. Reg. 4, 1879	Harleian Society, *A Register of all the Christninges, Burialles & Weddinges within the Parish of Saint Peeters upon Cornhill...*, Part II..., ed. Granville W. G. Leveson Gower (London, 1879). The Publications of the Harleian Society, Register section, Vol. IV
Harl. Reg. 30, 1903	Harleian Society, *The Registers of St Vedast, Foster Lane, and of St Michael le Quern, London*, Vol. II, ed. Willoughby A. Littledale (London, 1903). The Publications of the Harleian Society, Register section, Vol. XXX
Harl. Reg. 31, 1904	Harleian Society, *The Registers of St Helen's, Bishopsgate, London*, ed. W. Bruce Bannerman (London, 1904). The Publications of the Harleian Society, Register section, Vol. XXXI
Hatton 1708	[Edward Hatton], *A New View of London* (London, 1708). 2 vols.
Heal 1928	Ambrose Heal, *A XVII Century MS List of Tokens* ([s.l.], 1928). Reprinted from *Notes and Queries*, 154 (January-June 1928), with Addenda
Heal 1931	Ambrose Heal, *The English Writing Masters and their Copy Books* (Cambridge, 1931)
Heal 1972	Sir Ambrose Heal, *The London Goldsmiths 1200-1800* [1st edn. reprinted]. (Newton Abbot, 1972)
Hodgkin 1914	See Abbreviations, B
Holme 1688	Randle Holme, *The Academy of Armory* . . . (Chester, 1688). Contains Book I, chapter 1 to Book III, chapter 13, only
Holme 1905	Randle Holme, *The Academy of Armory* . . ., Second volume . . ., ed. I. H. Jeayes (London, 1905). Contains Book III, chapter 14 to Book IV, chapter 13
Hulbert 1972	Joan Hulbert, 'Down at the Old Cock and Bottle: a pub crawl round 17th-century London with Samuel Pepys and a pocketful of tavern tokens', *Coin Collecting Weekly* 1(2), 5 Feb. 1972, 5
Hume 1956	Ivor Noel Hume, *Treasure in the Thames* (London, 1956)
Hume 1974	Ivor Noel Hume, *All the best Rubbish* (London, 1974)
Hunnisett 1972	R. F. Hunnisett, *Indexing for Editors* (London, 1972). Archives and the User, no. 2
Hyde 1992	See Ogilby 1676
IGI	*International Genealogical Index*, v.2.5.0 (1999-2005) <http://www.familysearch.org>
Johnson 1914-22	A. H. Johnson, *The History of the Worshipful Company of Drapers of London* (Oxford, 1914-22). 5 vols.
Jones 1966	*London Inhabitants within the Walls 1695*; [assessments preserved in the Corporation of London Records Office; this index . . . prepared . . . by various hands, under the direction of Mr P. E. Jones]; introduction by D. V. Glass (London, 1966)

Jowett 2005	Judy Jowett, *The Warning Carriers: how messengers of the Goldsmiths' Company warned the luxury trades of criminal activities in eighteenth-century London* (London, 2005)
Keary 1885	C. F. Keary and Warwick Wroth, *The Seventeenth-century Tokens in the British Museum not described in Boyne* (London, 1885). Reprinted from *NC* 3rd series 4 (1884), 281-342
Kent 2005	John Kent, *Coinage and Currency in London from the London and Middlesex Records and other Sources* (London, 2005)
Kirkman 1673	[Francis Kirkman], *The Counterfeit Lady Unveiled* (London, 1673)
Larwood 1866	Jacob Larwood [i.e. Herman Diederik Johan van Schevichaven] and John Camden Hotten, *The History of Signboards . . .* (London, [pref. 1866]). The 'fifth edition' (etc.) was really a reissue of the 1st edn.
Larwood 1951	*English Inn Signs*, being a revised and modernized version of 'History of Signboards' by Jacob Larwood and John Camden Hotten; [revised by W. E. Tate]; with a chapter on the modern inn sign by Gerald Millar (London, 1951)
Lavery 1984	Brian Lavery, *The Ship of the Line, Vol. 2* (London, 1984)
LCC 1914	London County Council, *Survey of London, Vol. 5: The Parish of St Giles-in-the-Fields, Part II* (London, 1914)
Le Neve 1873	Peter Le Neve, *Le Neve's Pedigrees of the Knights made by King Charles II ... Queen Anne*, ed. George W. Marshall (London, 1873)
Leake 1666	*An exact Surveigh of the Streets, Lanes and Churches contained within the Ruines of the City of London*, first described in six Plats by John Leake... [et al.] in Dec^{ber} A^{o} 1666; reduced here into one intire plat by John Leake. Wenceslas Hollar fecit, 1667. 2 sheets
Leeds 1933	E. T. Leeds, 'Three stoneware flagons found in Oxford', *Antiquaries Journal*, 13 (1933), 470-73, pl.
Lillywhite 1963	Bryant Lillywhite, *London Coffee houses* (London, 1963)
Lillywhite 1972	Bryant Lillywhite, *London Signs* (London, 1972). [Numbers 1-2034 are also in Lillywhite 1963, but the 1972 form of name is followed]
Lindsay 1970	J. Seymour Lindsay, *Iron and Brass Implements of the English House*. Revised and enlarged [edn.] (London, 1970)
Linecar 1955	Howard W. A. Linecar, *Coins* (London, 1955)
Macfadyen	See Abbreviations, B
McKinley 1988	Richard McKinley, *The Surnames of Sussex* (Oxford, 1988). English Surnames series, V
MacLysaght 1985	Edward MacLysaght, *The Surnames of Ireland*, 6th edn. (Dublin, 1985)
Manville 1986	Harrington E. Manville [and] Terence J. Robertson, *British Numismatic Auction Catalogues, 1710-1984* (London, 1986). Encyclopaedia of British numismatics, Vol. 1
Masters 1974	Betty R. Masters, *The Public Markets of the City of London surveyed by William Leybourn in 1677* (London, 1974)
Matar 1998	Nabil Matar, *Islam in Britain 1558-1685* (Cambridge, 1998)
Mills 1962-7	Peter Mills and John Oliver, *The Survey of Building Sites in the City of London after the Great Fire of 1666* (London, 1962-7). 5 vols.

Mills 2001	A. D. Mills, *A Dictionary of London Place Names* (Oxford, 2001)
Milne 1951	J. Grafton Milne, 'Seventeenth-century tokens: the Browne Willis cabinet', *BNJ* 26 (1949-51), 333-8
Murdoch 1985	Tessa Murdoch, *The Quiet Conquest: the Huguenots 1685 to 1985*: [catalogue of] a Museum of London exhibition . . . (London, 1985)
Neubecker 1974	Ottfried Neubecker, Wilhelm Rentzmann, *Wappen-Bilder-Lexikon = Dictionnaire héraldique = Encyclopaedia of heraldry* (München [=Munich], 1974)
Newcourt 1658	Richard Newcourt, *London: an exact Delineation of the Cities of London and Westminster and the Suburbs thereof, . . . Southwark [etc.]*; Willm Faithorne sculpsit ([London], 1658)
Oddie 2001-4	Gary Oddie, 'Merchants' Marks', *TCSB* 7 (2001-4), 207-19, 304, 433
ODNB	*Oxford Dictionary of National Biography* (Oxford, 2004). 60 vols. and online
OED	*Oxford English Dictionary*
Ogilby 1676	John Ogilby and William Morgan, [*A new and accurate Map of the City of London*]. *The A to Z of Restoration London (the City of London, 1676)*; introductory notes by Ralph Hyde; index compiled by John Fisher and Roger Cline (London, 1992)
Ogilby 1677	John Ogilby & William Morgan, *London survey'd, or, An Explanation of the large Map of London* . . . (London, 1677)
Ordnance Survey 1989	Ordnance Survey, *Gazetteer of Great Britain*, 2nd edn. (Southampton, 1989)
Pagan 1986	H. E. Pagan, 'Record of members and Fellows', in *A History of the Royal Numismatic Society, 1836-1986*, by R. A. G. Carson . . . (London, 1986), pp. 51-143
Pagan 2003	Hugh Pagan [and] Charles Farthing, 'Members of the British Numismatic Society 1903-2003', *BNJ* 73 (2003), 213-67
Papworth 1874	John W. Papworth, *An Alphabetical Dictionary of Coats of Arms . . . forming an extensive Ordinary of British Armorials*, ed. Alfred W. Morant (London, 1874)
Pearl 1978	Valerie Pearl, 'Puritans and poor relief: the London Workhouse, 1649-1660', in *Puritans and Revolutionaries*, ed. Donald Pennington and Keith Thomas (Oxford, 1978), pp. 206-32
Pepys 1970-83	*The Diary of Samuel Pepys: a new and complete transcription*; ed. Robert Latham and William Matthews (London, 1970-83). 11 vols.
Percival 2003	Geoff Percival, 'John Yates of Albrough', *TCSB* 7 (2001-4), 238
Plomer 1907	Henry R. Plomer, *A Dictionary of the Booksellers and Printers who were at Work in England, Scotland and Ireland from 1641 to 1667* (London, 1907)
Presicce 2005	Claudio Parisi Presicce, *The Spinario: [catalogue of an exhibition], London, The British Museum, 15 March-14 April 2005* (Bologna, 2005)
Preston-Morley 1981	Peter Preston-Morley & Harry Pegg, *A Revised Survey of the Seventeenth-century Tokens of Nottinghamshire* ([London], 1983). Reprinted from *BNJ* 51 (1981), 134-96, pls. xvi-xxiii

Preston-Morley 1994 — Peter Preston-Morley, [The Lamb and Ink Bottle token], *S&B* no. 20 (Sep./Oct. 1994), 6 (Correspondence to the editor)

Price 1906 — F. G. Hilton Price, 'Signs of old London [2]', *London Topographical Record*, 3 (1906), 110-65

Prockter 1979 — Adrian Prockter and Robert Taylor, *The A-Z of Elizabethan London* (London, 1979)

Pugh 1973 — Ralph B. Pugh, 'A gaol's changing face: Newgate Prison', *Country Life*, 154 (1973), 1014-16

Reaney 1995 — P. H. Reaney, *A Dictionary of English Surnames*, 3rd edn., with corrections and additions by R. M. Wilson (Oxford, 1995)

Redmonds 1973 — George Redmonds, [*The Surnames of*] *Yorkshire, West Riding* (Chichester, 1973). English Surnames series, I

Redmonds 2004 — George Redmonds, *Christian Names in Local and Family History* (Kew, 2004)

Ricketts 2001 — Carl Ricketts, *Pewterers of London, 1600-1900* ([London], 2001)

Roberts 1803 — E. S. S. [i.e. Barré Charles Roberts], [The Profession of Jeremy Busher at Shoe-lane end, Smoaker], *Gentleman's Magazine*, 73 (1803), 510-11

Rocque 1747 — John Rocque, [*A Plan of the Cities of London and Westminster and Borough of Southwark*, 1747], *The A-Z of Georgian London*; introductory notes by Ralph Hyde (Lympne, 1981)

Rogers 1928a — Kenneth Rogers, 'On some issuers of seventeenth-century London tokens whose names were not known to Boyne and Williamson', *NC*, 5th series 8 (1928), 61-97, Addenda 338

Rogers 1928b — Kenneth Rogers, *The Boar's Head Tavern in Eastcheap, with some Account of the Parish of St Michael's Crooked Lane* (London, 1928)

Rogers 1928c — Kenneth Rogers, *The Mermaid and Mitre Taverns in Old London* (London, 1928)

Rogers 1928d — Kenneth Rogers, 'The King's Head Tavern, Leadenhall Street', *London Topographical Record*, 14 (1928), 36-48, plan

Rogers 1931 — Kenneth Rogers, *Old Cheapside and Poultry: Ancient Houses and Signs* (London, 1931)

Rogers 1935 — Kenneth Rogers, *Old London: Cornhill, Threadneedle Street and Lombard Street: old houses and signs* (London and Tonbridge, 1935)

Rogers 1937 — Kenneth Rogers, *Signs and Taverns round about Old London Bridge, including Gracechurch Street, Fenchurch Street and Leadenhall Street* (London, 1937)

Rogers 1991 — K. H. Rogers, *Vikings & Surnames* (York, 1991)

Routing 1650 — *The Routing of the Ranters* ([London], [1650]), Wing 1972-88, R2055

SCBI 31 — *SCBI 31: The Norweb Collection, Cleveland, Ohio, U.S.A.: Tokens of the British Isles, 1575-1750. Part I: England: Bedfordshire to Devon*, by R. H. Thompson (London, 1984)

SCBI 38 — *SCBI 38: The Norweb Collection, Cleveland, Ohio, U.S.A.: Tokens of the British Isles, 1575-1750. Part II: Dorset, Durham, Essex and Gloucestershire*, by R. H. Thompson (London, 1988)

SCBI 43	*SCBI 43: The Norweb Collection, Cleveland, Ohio, U.S.A.: Tokens of the British Isles, 1575-1750. Part III: Hampshire to Lincolnshire*, by R. H. Thompson and M. J. Dickinson (London, 1992)
SCBI 49	*SCBI 49: The Norweb Collection, Cleveland, Ohio, U.S.A.: Tokens of the British Isles, 1575-1750. Part VI: Wiltshire to Yorkshire, Ireland to Wales*, by R. H. Thompson and M. J. Dickinson (London, 1999)
Seaby 1949	Herbert Allen Seaby and Peter John Seaby, *A Catalogue of the Copper Coins and Tokens of the British Isles* (London, 1949)
Seaby 1970	Peter Seaby, *Seaby's Standard Catalogue, Part 3: Coins and Tokens of Ireland* (London, 1970)
Searle 1902	W. G. Searle, 'Some unpublished seventeenth-century tokens', *NC* 4th series 2 (1902), 378-84
Sharman 1983	Robert Sharman, 'Unpublished seventeenth-century tokens recovered from the Thames', *SCMB* (1983), 122-5
Sharman 1984	Robert Sharman, 'More unpublished seventeenth-century tokens recovered from the Thames', *TCSB* 4 no.1 (winter 1984), 22-3
Sharman 1986	Robert Sharman, 'Unpublished leaden tokens of the mid-seventeenth century', *TCSB* 4 no. 5 (1986), 6-7
Sharman 1994	Robert Sharman, 'An unpublished 17th-century token of St Paul's Churchyard', *S&B* no. 19 (July/August 1994), 6-7
Sheppard 1991	Francis Sheppard, *The Treasury of London's Past: an historical account of the Museum of London and its predecessors, the Guildhall Museum and the London Museum* (London, 1991)
Smith 1980	John Smith, b. 1567, [*The Names and Surnames of all the able and sufficient Men in Body fit for His Majesty's Service in the Wars, within the County of Gloucester*] *Men & Armour for Gloucestershire in 1608* (Gloucester, 1980). First published 1902
Smyth 1849	*The Obituary of Richard Smyth, Secondary of the Poultry Compter, London, being a Catalogue of all such Persons as he knew in their Life, extending from A.D. 1627 to A.D. 1674*, ed. Sir Henry Ellis (London, 1849). Camden Society, old series, XLIV
Spink Sales	See Abbreviations, B
Spufford 1985	Margaret Spufford, *Small Books and Pleasant Histories: popular fiction and its readership in seventeenth-century England* (Cambridge, 1985)
Stow 1603	John Stow, *A Survey of London*; reprinted from the text of 1603, with introduction and notes by Charles Lethbridge Kingsford (Oxford, 1971). 2 vols.; first published 1908; reprinted (with amendments and additions). References are to the original 1603 pagination, as printed in the margins
Stow 1633	John Stow, *The Survey of London*; afterwards inlarged by . . . A. M[unday] . . . and now completely finished by . . . A. M[unday], H. D[yson] and others (London, 1633)
Stow 1720	*A Survey of the Cities of London and Westminster . . .*, written at first . . . by John Stow; now lastly, corrected, improved, and very much enlarged . . . by John Strype (London, 1720). 2 vols.

Taffs 1933	H. W. Taffs, 'Exhibitions', *BNJ* 21 (1931-3), 215-16
Thompson 1891	Corrie Leonard Thompson, 'Boyne's "Trade Tokens"', *Notes and Queries*, 7th series 12 (July-December 1891), 301-2
Thompson 1989	R. H. Thompson, 'Central or local production of seventeenth-century tokens', *BNJ* 59 (1989), 198-211, pl. 16
Thompson 1993	R. H. Thompson, 'The Royal Exchange on seventeenth-century tokens', *NCirc* 101 (1993), 78-80
Thompson 1997b	Robert H. Thompson, 'Tokens of the Royal Exchange', in *The Royal Exchange*, ed. Ann Saunders (London, 1997), pp. 239-49
Thompson 2000	R. H. Thompson, 'Edward Nourse and a farthing's worth of copper', *BNJ* 70 (2000), 147-50
Thompson 2002a	Robert Thompson, 'The Case of Knives: an unrecognised sign on seventeenth-century tokens', *TCSB* 7 (2001-4), 165-8
Thompson 2002b	Robert Thompson, 'The Radulphus Olliffus tokens', *TCSB* 7 (2001-4), 174-7
Thompson 2005a	Robert Thompson and Michael Dickinson, 'Mistress Tisbery's lament: monograms in Ambrose Heal's manuscript', *TCSB* 8 (2004-6), 109-11
Thompson 2005b	R. H. Thompson, 'A Token of the London baker whose oven sparked the Great Fire', *NCirc* 113 (2005), 315-16
Thompson 2005c	Robert H. Thompson, 'Un monogramme: qu'est-ce que c'est?', *Le Livre des Mereils (Centre National de Recherche sur les Jetons et les Méreaux du Moyen Âge)*, no. 52-54 (2004-5), 73-5
Vis. Essex 1552-1634	*The Visitations of Essex by Hawley 1552, Hervey 1558, Cooke 1570, Raven 1612, and Owen and Lilly 1634; to which are added miscellaneous Essex Pedigrees from various Harleian Manuscripts, and an Appendix containing Berry's Essex Pedigrees*; ed. Walter C. Metcalfe (London, 1878-9). 2 vols. The Publications of the Harleian Society, Vol. XIII-XIV
Vis. Lond. 1633-5	*The Visitation of London, Anno Domini 1633, 1634 and 1635, made by Sr Henry St George*; ed. Joseph Jackson Howard and Joseph Lemuel Chester (London, 1880, 1883). 2 vols. The Publications of the Harleian Society, Vol. XV, XVII
Vis. Som. 1672	*The Visitation of Somerset and the City of Bristol, 1672, made by Sir Edward Bysshe*; ed. G. D. Squibb (London, 1992). The Publications of the Harleian Society, new series Vol. 11
Wallis 1677	*Londons Armory . . ., printed for the author Rich. Wallis* (London, 1677). References are to the reproduction in Welch 1914
Ward 1715	[Edward Ward], *A Vade-Mecum for Malt-Worms, the second part* (London, [c.1715]). So dated in *The Cambridge Bibliography of English Literature*, ed. F. W. Bateson (Cambridge, 1940-57), ii. 598; there were other editions
Watts 2004	*The Cambridge Dictionary of English Place-names*, ed. Victor Watts (Cambridge, 2004)
Webb 1915	Percy H. Webb, [An unpublished halfpenny token], *NC* 4th series 15 (1915), Proc. 6

Webb 1996- — Cliff Webb, *London Livery Company Apprenticeship Registers* (London, 1996-).
Vol. 5: Glass-sellers' Company 1664-1812, [and], Woolmen's Company 1665-1828. 1997
Vol. 8: Gunmakers' Company 1656-1800. 1997
Vol. 11: Distillers' Company 1659-1811. 1997
Vol. 15: Gold and Silver Wyre Drawers' Company 1693-1837. 1998
Vol. 17: Innholders' Company 1642-1643, 1654-1670, 1673-1800. 1998
Vol. 18: Poulters' Company 1691-1729, 1754-1800. 1998
Vol. 21: Founders' Company 1643-1800. 1998
Vol. 22: Armourers' and Brasiers' Company c.1610-1800. 1998
Vol. 24: Ironmongers' Company 1655-1800. 1999
Vol. 26: Cooks' Company 1654-1800. 1999
Vol. 28: Farriers' Company 1619-1800. 1999
Vol. 31: Wax Chandlers' Company 1666-1800, [and], Brown Bakers' Company 1615-1646. 2000
Vol. 35: Cutlers' Company 1442-1498, 1565-1800. 2001
Vol. 36: Brewers' Company 1531-1685. 2001
Vol. 38: Painter-Stainers' Company 1655, 1666-1800. 2003
Vol. 39: Tallow Chandlers' Company 1633-1800. 2003
Vol. 40: Pewterers' Company 1611-1800. 2003
Vol. 41: Blacksmiths' Company 1605-1800. 2004
Vol. 42: Society of Apothecaries 1670-1800, with, Masons' Company 1619-1639. 2006
Vol. 43: Vintners' Company 1609-1800. 2006
Vol. 44: Fishmongers' Company 1614-1800. 2006

Weinreb 1993 — Ben Weinreb and Christopher Hibbert, *The London Encyclopaedia*, revised edn. (London and Basingstoke, 1993)

Welch 1914 — Charles Welch, *Coat-Armour of the London Livery Companies* (London, 1914)

Wheatley 1891 — Henry B. Wheatley, *London Past and Present* (London, 1891). 3 vols.

Whittet 1983 — T. D. Whittet, 'A survey of apothecaries' tokens, including some previously unrecognised specimens, Part 2: London and Southwark', *Pharmaceutical Journal*, 230 (1983), 133-40

Willcocks 1975 — R. M. Willcocks, *England's Postal History to 1840* (London, 1975)

Williamson — George C. Williamson, *Trade Tokens issued in the Seventeenth Century; a new and revised edition of William Boyne's work* (London, 1889-91). 2 vols.

Wing 1972-88 — Donald Wing, *Short-title Catalogue of Books printed in England, Scotland, Ireland, Wales and British America and of English Books printed in other Countries, 1641-1700*, 2nd edn. (New York, 1972-88)

Withycombe 1977 — E. G. Withycombe, *The Oxford Dictionary of English Christian Names*, 3rd edn. (Oxford, 1977)

Woodhead 1966 — J. R. Woodhead, *The Rulers of London 1660-1689* (London, [1966]). References to Woodhead identify an Alderman or Common

	Councilman of the City of London, but these have not been separately noticed or indexed
Youngs 1979	Frederic A. Youngs, *Guide to the Local Administrative Units of England*, Vol. I: Southern England (London, 1979)
Youngs 1991	Frederic A. Youngs, *Guide to the Local Administrative Units of England*, Vol. II: Northern England (London, 1991)

CORRECTIONS TO PART VI (*SCBI* 49)

<table>
<tr><td>Page xxix</td><td>Delete class 3.64.4</td></tr>
<tr><td>Page xxxi</td><td>Class 3.114.1 A dragon passant: add 6169</td></tr>
<tr><td>Page xxxii</td><td>Class 4.2.8: delete accompanied by an inscription</td></tr>
<tr><td>Page xli</td><td>Class 5.14.163: add perhaps accompanied by an inscription</td></tr>
<tr><td>Page xlviii</td><td>Class 5.77: for full read full)</td></tr>
<tr><td>Page lii</td><td>Leeds: for City read Borough</td></tr>
<tr><td>5586a (preceding)</td><td>Readings: for CROSS read CROSE</td></tr>
<tr><td>5782</td><td>For attribution see Percival 2003</td></tr>
<tr><td>5790</td><td>For nd read I668; for [no date], read |I668, rev.</td></tr>
<tr><td>6093</td><td>Add Evidence of (?original) tinning on obv.</td></tr>
<tr><td>6158</td><td>A specimen in Sotheby's sale L00570, 25 May 2000, lot 74, completes GLOBE and confirms BRAY and HIS</td></tr>
<tr><td>6168</td><td>A specimen in the same lot reads WILL·</td></tr>
<tr><td>6169</td><td>For 3.64.4 read 3.114.1</td></tr>
<tr><td>6283</td><td>On Plate 37 the obv. should have been turned clockwise by about 25°</td></tr>
<tr><td>6349 (following)</td><td>For Uncertain III read 7178 (Knightrider Street)</td></tr>
<tr><td>Page 240</td><td>Add Salisbury (Wilts.), St Edmund churchyard, 5588 n.</td></tr>
</table>

MISSING TOKENS IN PART VII

The following were recorded but are now missing:

BW 1200, two specimens, both axis 180°, ex Nott, one of larger diameter, on thick flan
BW 1480, 0°, ex Nott
*BW 1484 (HOLḄ– –NE, Ạ W) but FLEC^{E}, 0°, ex Nott
*BW 1486 (M E Ẉ) but MICHAELL, 180°, ex Baldwin
BW 1488 but CROWNE&̣TOBACKO, 180°, ex Nott
*Dickinson 1664A = Gilbert 1927, 153 but C̣LOVFER = ···|I67I|···, rev. = POVL|TERER|···, 270°, ex Baldwin
BW 1849 but A swan close and beneath its head a suspended ball (?), LVDGATE, 180°, ex Nott
BW 1851, 180°, ex Nott
BW 1853 but BELL|·SAVIG·GAT·LVD·GATE·HILL· = Portcullis(?), 180°, ex Nott
BW 1854 but THOMAS, [probably I^{D}], possibly LVDGAT^{E}, 180°, ex Baldwin
*BW 1855 (SYLVẸ. . .Ṛ, LVDGA. . .ṬREET), two specimens, both 90°, ex Nott
BW 1856, 0°, ex Nott
BW 2249, two specimens, both 90°, ex Nott

PLATES

CITY OF LONDON

The City occurs as LONDON on 6433, 7515, 7521, 7623; LONDO^{N} on 6706; LON on 7516, 7634. The City's Bridewell hospital was the issuer of 6706, Christ's Hospital of 6783 (John Bannister at the Matron's Cellar), the arms of the City appear on 7386 issued by a City tenant (Richard Robinson) who styled himself clerk of Newgate Market, and the Corporation of the Poor was the unnamed authority for 7783 at the Wardrobe. The City arms on 7497-8 almost suggest a municipal brew-house at Puddle Dock, but more likely they refer to its name, cf. Pearl 1978, p. 229. There is no specimen here of the Newgate Prison token (BW 2043), with the building illustrated from the BM specimen by Pugh 1973

ABCHURCH LANE (Langbourn & Candlewick & Walbrook wards) [37-I13]

The reading is ABCHVRCH LANE throughout

	Weight g	*Weight* gr		*Die axis*	
6425a	1.16	17.9	Cu	0°	*Milett,* John. 1664. 5.77.1; M|IS. BW 4 but *1664*. Nott [ex Taffs]. ?John Millet of St Nicholas Acons, Clothworker; md. Sarah Wright 1655 (Boyd 40202)
6425b	0.81	12.5	Cu	0°	Same dies. [Nott]

Named signs

6426	0.80	12.3	M	180°	*Black Horse* (AT THE): ?T—, W—. nd. 3.60.4; T|WA. BW 8. Nott [ex Taffs]. Reading completed from BM specimen
6427a	1.01	15.5	M	180°	*Lamb* (AT THE LAMBE): ?P—, R—. 1649. 3.56.1; P|RS. BW 5. [Nott]
6427b	0.98	15.1	M	180°	Same dies. Nott [ex Taffs]
6428	1.11	17.2	M	180°	*Lion* (AT THE): C[hubb?], T[homas]. 1649. 3.39.1; C|TA. BW 1. Baldwin. See also 7710. Identity of issuer suggested from a specimen overstruck by THO:CHVBBE COOKE IN SWEETINGS RENTS (Dickinson 1989, p. 325)
6429a	1.80	27.7	Br	270°	*White [?Bear]* (AT THE WHIT): Lucas, Ralph. 1665 ½d. 3.49.5; 5.77. BW 3. Nott. White Bear tavern destroyed September 1666 (Burn 1855, 76 n.)
6429b	1.75	27.0	Br	270°	Same dies. [Baldwin]
					White Hart see 6733 (Cannon Street: *White Hart*)

ADDLE HILL (Castle Baynard ward) [34-I8]

See also ADDLE STREET. The reading is ON ADDLE HILL, cf. *Addlehill* 1649 (*Cal. S.P. Dom.* 1649-50, 523)

6430a	1.02	15.8	M	180°	*Stedman,* Thomas. 1656. 2.1; S|TD. BW 10. Nott
6430b	0.99	15.3	M	180°	Same dies. Nott [ex Taffs]

ADDLE STREET *subsequently* BASINGHALL STREET (Cripplegate ward Within) [25-F10]

The reading is ADDELL STREET; disregarded is an alternative attribution to Addle Hill, which occurs as *Adlestreete* 1603 (Stow 1603, ii. 12)

Named signs

6431a	1.17	18.1	Cu	180°	*Sugarloaf* (AT THE SVGER LOFE): ?K—, A—. nd. 5.64.3 (A K); A K. BW 11. Nott
6431b	0.99	15.3	Cu	180°	Same dies. [Nott ex Taffs]

ALDERMANBURY (Cripplegate ward Within) [26-F11]

The reading is ALDERMAN BARY on 6432, BVRY LONDON on 6433

6432	0.58	9.0	Br	180°	*Hilton,* Robert. nd. 1.40.3; H|RM. *BW 13 but ALDERMAN•BARY. Nott [ex Taffs]. ?Robert Hilton of St Mary Aldermanbury, chandler, md. Mary Randall 1658, d. 1665 (Boyd 10872)

Named signs

6433	3.74	57.7	Br	0°	*Alderman* (AT Y͞ SIGNE OF Y^{E}): Hartley, Lowe. 1670 1d. 3.5.48 (•LOWE•HARTLEY•AT•Y͞ SIGNE•OF•Y^{E} around); 5.77 (LONDON|•I^{D}•|1670; •ALDERMAN•IN•ALDERMAN•BVRY around). BW —; *Dickinson 12C (YE). Nott [ex Carthew]. Reading largely completed from Shuttlewood 2001, lot 640. Cf. 7362

ALDERSGATE neighbourhood (Aldersgate ward) [25-F9]

See also NEW RENTS. The reading is ALDERSG on 7597; ALDERSGATE on 7598; ALLDERSGATE on 7377; AT ALDERS GATE on 6434; NEERE ALDERSGATE on 7589; NERE ALLDERS GATE on 7600; cf. 6462-5

Named signs

6434	0.89	13.8	M	180°	*Mermaid tavern* (THE MERMAYDE TAVERN): ?B—, I/J—. 1651. 3.10.17; I B. BW 21. Nott. For John Bradway at the Mermaid on the Back see ii. 1595c (Glos.: Bristol. The Back). A report of this specimen, ex Carthew, was the source of Dickinson's London 21A, which should be deleted

[*continued overleaf*]

PLATE 1

6425a 6426 6427b 6428 6429b 6430a

6431a 6432 6433 6434 6435 6436

6437 6438 6439 6440 6441 6442

6443 6444 6445 6446 6447 6448

Plate 1 (*cont.*)

ALDERSGATE STREET (Aldersgate ward) [14-C8]

See also HORN ALLEY; HOUNDSDITCH. The reading is ALDERSGATE STREET on 6435-8, 6440, 6442-3, 6446-7, 6449, 6451, 6453, 6460 (SṬṚ–ET), 6461, 7129, STREETE on 6444, 6452, STRET on 6450, STRETE on 6458; ALDERSGATESTREETE on 6445; ẠḶDERS:GATE ṢTREET on 6439; ALDERS GATE STREET on 6448, 6459; ALDERSGAT STREET on 6456; ALDERSGA^{T} STREET on 6441; ALDERSGATSTREETE on 6454; ALDERGATE STREET on 6455; ALLDERS GATE STREET on 6457

	Weight *g*	*gr*		*Die axis*	
6435	4.00	61.7	Br	270°	*Awnsham,* Richard. 1667 ½d. 3.102.12; 5.77. BW 20. Nott [ex Taffs]
6436	1.04 (chipped)	16.1	Br	180°	*Bookham* (BOOKḤAM), William. 1667 ½d. 5.62.1; 5.77. *BW 24. Nott [ex Baldwin]. Reading largely confirmed from BM specimen
6437	1.23	19.0	Cu	270°	*Bourne* (ḄOVṚNE), Thomas. nd. 0.4 (THOMAS•ḄOVṚNE•AT•THẸ around); B|TM (.B.|T[?plant]M; IN•ALDERSGATE•STREET around). BW —; Dickinson 24A, from a report of this specimen. Baldwin
6438	1.29	19.9	Cu	180°	*Fish,* John. nd ½d. 3.109.1; 5.38.1. BW 33. Nott [ex Carthew]. Reading confirmed from BM specimen. John Fish, oilman, at The Dolphin and Anchor (Woodhead 1966, p. 69)
6439	1.30	20.1	M	180°	*Glover,* Ri—, ironmonger (IRONMONỌẸṚ). nd ½d. 0.5 (•RI:GLOVER•IRONMONỌẸṚ around); 5.77 (HIS|HALF|PENY|•••; •IN•ẠḶDERS:GATE•ṢTREET around). BW —; Dickinson 33C, from a report of this specimen. Nott. Reading largely completed from MoL specimen
6440	1.84	28.4	Br	270°	*Grove,* Tho—, chees[e]monger. 1668 ½d. 5.89.2 (G|TE); 5.77. BW 34 but THO:. Nott [ex Taffs]
6441	2.90	44.8	Br	270°	*Jones,* Walter. nd ½d. 2.4.7; 5.76.139. BW 40. Nott. See also 6457
6442	1.20	18.6	Br	0°	*Mace,* Thomason. nd ½d. 5.77; 4.12.5. BW 44. Nott. Sign-names probably indicated by Deputies Court or Rose and Rainbow Court 1720 (Harben 1918, p. 511)
6443	1.93	29.8	Br	90°	*Norton,* John. 1667 ½d. (HAḶFE). 3.108.2 (N|II); 5.77. *BW 47. Nott [ex Taffs]
6444	1.80	27.8	Br	180°	*Ruddle,* Henry. 1666 ½d. 3.1.84 (R|HB); 5.77. BW 50. Nott. ?Henry Ruddle of St Botolph without Aldersgate, Glazier, md. Bridget Seagrave 1666 (Boyd 34351)
6445	0.35 (chipped)	5.4	Cu	180°	*Singleton,* Thomas. nd. 4.10.4; S|TI. BW 53 but ALDERSGATESTREETE. Nott
6446	1.81	27.9	Cu	0°	*Stancliffe,* Michael (*Michaell*), hosier. 1667 ½d. 5.77.1; 5.7.20. BW 54 but I6 ½ 67. Nott [ex Taffs]. ?Michael Stancliff of All Hallows, Bread Street, Haberdasher, hosier, d. 1680 (Boyd 31625)
6447	1.70	26.2	Cu	0°	*Symonds,* Michael (MICHAELL). nd ½d. 5.3.32; 5.77. BW 56. Nott [ex Taffs]. Michael Simons of St Botolph without Aldersgate, b. 1636, Distiller, fl. 1700 (Boyd 34511). He bound apprentices 1661-94 (Webb 1996-, xi. 3, 26 etc.)
6448	2.85	44.0	Br	0°	*Wallman,* Roger. [16]66 ½d. 3.60.1; 5.77. BW 59 but ALDERS•GATE. Nott [ex Taffs]. There was a Black Horse in Aldersgate Street, 1677 etc. (Lillywhite 1972, no. 3283)

	Weight g	Weight gr		Die axis	
6449	2.32	35.8	Cu	270°	*Warner,* John. 1668 ½d. 5.70.4; 5.77 (W|IA). BW 60. Nott [ex Taffs or Spink]. Mullet i.m. on obv. semi-pierced, like Greenall 1997, lot 85. John Warner, apothecary, paid hearth tax in St Botolph without Aldersgate 1666 (Whittet 1983, p. 136). A John Warner bound apprentices 1670-1717 (Webb 1996-, xlii. 114)
6450	0.96	14.8	Br	270°	*Warrin,* Nicholas. nd. 3.68.1; W|NI. BW 61. Nott
6451	1.85	28.6	Br	270°	*White,* Matthew (MATHEW). nd ½d. 5.64.89; 5.77 (W|MA). BW 63 but HALFE|PENNY. Nott [ex Taffs]. 'Mr White's house at the Cock and Bottle' 1668 (BW 63 n.), which suggests that the device as represented was read from right to left
6452	1.85 (chipped)	28.6	Br	180°	*Wickins,* John. 1667 ½d. 3.10.17; 5.77. BW 64. Nott [ex Carthew]. Reading confirmed from MoL specimen

Named signs

6453	1.01	15.5	Cu	90°	*Castle* (AT Y^{E}): Stone, Tho—. nd. 5.7.20; T S. BW 55 but THO:. Nott [ex Carthew]
6454	2.27 (chipped)	35.0	Br	180°	*Cock* (AT Y^{E}): Cooke, Nicholas (ṆICHOLAS), grocer. 1668 1d. (PẸNNY). 3.101.1; 5.77. *BW 27 but ALDERSGATSTREETE, I668; *Dickinson 27A. Nott [ex Taffs]. Reading partly confirmed from MoL specimen, but Burn's recording of its date as 1666 (1855, 91) is now seen to be erroneous. Nicholas Cook of St Giles without Cripplegate, b. 1639, Grocer (Boyd 20227)
6455	1.01	15.6	M	180°	[*?Feathers*] *& Sugarloaf:* ?B—, T—. 1656. 3.107.5; T B. BW 23. Spink [1972+, or Nott]
6456	2.02	31.2	Br	0°	*Maidenhead* (THE MAIDENHEAD): ?A—, E—. [16]68 ½d. 5.14.1 Mercers (E A); 5.14.2 Mercers. BW 16 but MAIDENHEAD. Nott
6457	1.31	20.2	M	180°	*Seven Stars* (AT THE 7 STARS): ?A—, R—. nd. 2.4.7; A|RD. BW 17 but ALLDERS•GATE. Nott [ex Taffs]. Edge hammered up. See also 6441
6458	1.08	16.7	Br	180°	*Sun tavern* (AT THE SONN TAVERN): H[utchinson], R[alph]. nd. 2.1; H|RS. BW 35 but STRETE. Nott [ex Carthew]. Ralph Hutchinson, b. 1605, Vintner, md. Sarah Row 1655 (Rogers 1928a, p. 62; Boyd 29125). A Ralph Hutchinson appr. 1620, bound apprentices 1630-58 (Webb 1996-, xliii. 159, 364)
6459	1.06	16.4	M	180°	*Swan & Sugar*[*loaf*] (THE): ?I/J—, C—. nd. 3.102.3; I|CS. BW 38 but ALDERS•GATE, •I•|C•S. Nott. Reading confirmed from BM specimen
6460	1.31	20.2	M	180°	*Tun* (AT THE TVNN): ?A—, T—. nd. 5.64.30; A|TE. *BW 18 (STREET). Nott. Same obv. die as 6461
6461	1.30	20.0	Cu	180°	*Tun* (AT THE TVNN): ?A—, T—. nd. 5.64.30; A|TE. BW 18. Nott [ex Taffs]. Same obv. die as 6460

ALDERSGATE within (Aldersgate ward) [25-F9]

See also St MARTIN LE GRAND liberty/street. The reading is WITH IN ALDERS GATE on 7599; WITH:\|IN ALDERSGATE on 6463; W^{TH}:IN ALDERS GATE on 6462

6462	0.58	8.9	Br	180°	*Hutchinson,* Matthew (MATHEW). nd. 5.3.25; H|MA. BW 37 but W^{TH}:IN•ALDERS•GATE, in chief of the fountain a small figure holding cups in outstretched hands. Clark 1977. See also 6463
6463	1.78	27.5	Br	0°	*Hutchinson,* Matthew (MATHEW). nd ½d. 5.3.25; H|MA. BW 36 but WITH:, in chief of the fountain a small figure holding cups in outstretched hands. Nott [ex Carthew]. Matthew Hutchinson fl. 1653-68; wife Anne (Rogers 1928c, pp. 51-5, 65, 67-8). The small figure is clearer on Greenall 1997, pl. 3.86

ALDERSGATE without (Aldersgate ward) [25-F9]

The reading is WITHOVT ALDERSGATE on both

6464	0.96	14.8	Br	90°	*Mynn,* John. nd. 3.2.14; M|IM. BW 46. Baldwin. Reading completed from MoL specimen. Mr John Myn, Grocer; wife Mary d. 1670 (Smyth 1849, p. 88). See also Gilbert 1927, 82 (Aldersgate Street)

Named signs

6465	2.68	41.3	Br	0°	*Leg & Star* (AT Y^{E}): Finch, Richard. nd ½d. 3.7.4; 5.77. BW 32 but leg beside star. Nott [ex Carthew]

[*continued overleaf*]

6449 6450 6451 6452 6453 6454

6455 6456 6457 6458 6459 6460

6461 6462 6463 6464 6465 6466

6467 6468 6469 6470 6471 6472

Plate 2 (*cont.*)

ALDGATE neighbourhood (Aldgate ward) [29-G18]

The reading is AT ALGATE; cf. 6467-97

					Turner, Simon *see* 6496-7 (Aldgate without. The Pie neighbourhood)

Named signs

	Weight			*Die*	
	g	*gr*		*axis*	
					Coach & Horses see 6470 (Aldgate within)
6466	1.05	16.2	Br	180°	*Gun* (AT THE): Langham, John. nd. 5.14 Grocers; 5.55.1. BW 67. Nott [ex Taffs]. Perhaps the same sign as the GVNE WITHOVT ALGATE, see 6491. ?John Langham, grocer, fl. St Helen Bishopsgate 1667 (Harl. Reg. 31, 1904, p. 43)

ALDGATE within *subsequently* ALDGATE (*street*) (Aldgate ward) [29-G18]

The reading is WITHIN ALGATE on 6469, 6472-3, 6475, ALDGATE on 6468, ALGAT on 6474, ALL GATE on 6467, ALL GATTE on 6471; AT ALLGATE on 6470

6467	0.86	13.3	Br	180°	*Draper,* Richard. nd. 5.50.5; D|RD. BW 73 but ALL•GATE, circular charge (?Ball) without attributes of a globe. Nott
6468	0.93	14.4	Br	0°	*Tidder,* John. [16]57. 3.108.16; T|IA. BW 80. Nott [ex Taffs]

Named signs

6469	1.10	16.9	Br	270°	*Bear* (AT THE BEARE): Ford, Wil—. nd. 3.49.5; F|WA. BW 74 but FORD. Nott [ex Taffs]
6470	1.43 (chipped)	22.1	Cu	0°	*Coach & Horses* (AT THE): Game, John. nd ½d. 5.53.6; 5.53.6. BW 66 but AT•ALLGATE. Nott [ex Carthew]. It seems probable that this house, for hire of horses or carriages, stood on the south side of Fenchurch Street . . . The name of John Game appears . . . from 1651 (Rogers 1937, p. 149). Samuel Pepys hired horses of Mr Game in 1663 (Pepys 1970-83, iv. 119-20, 218)
6471	0.77	11.9	Br	180°	*George* (AT THE): B[ailey], N[icholas]. 1649. 3.2.8; B|NE. BW 71. Nott. Reading confirmed from BM specimen. Nicholas Bailey leased the *George*; bd. 1654; lease afterwards assigned by Elizabeth Bailey (Rogers 1928a, p. 62)
6472	0.97	14.9	Br	270°	*Horseshoe* (AT Y^{E} HORSHOOE): ?W—, T—. nd. 5.68.10; W|TE. BW 81. Nott [ex Taffs]

ALDGATE within (*cont.*)

Named signs (*cont.*)

	Weight g	Weight gr		Die axis	
6473	0.76	11.7	Br	0°	*Mitre tavern* (AT $\mathrm{Y^E}$MYTER TAVERNE): N[orris], H[enry]. [16]57. 5.59.20; N|HS. BW 77 but TAVERNE, ALGATE•57. Nott [ex Carthew]. Issuer Mr Norris, fl. 1657 (Rogers 1928a, p. 63, 1928c, pp. 119-21); Henry Norris appr. Vintner 1650 (Webb 1996-, xliii. 215). Woodhead 1966, p. 122, had no cause to extend initial H to Hugh
6474	0.68	10.4	Br	180°	*Still* (AT $\mathrm{Y^E}$): Walton, Richard. nd. 5.64.65; W|RT. BW 82. Nott [ex Carthew]. Reading confirmed from BM specimen. Richard Walton, Distiller; will, PCC, 1685, St Katherine Cree (Boyd 30222). Bound apprentices 1669-78 (Webb 1996-, xi. 8-9, 14, 28)

ALDGATE within. Corner shop

The reading is CORNER SHOPE WITHIN ALGATE

6475	1.11	17.1	Br	180°	*?F—*, T—, cheesemonger. nd. 3.49.5 (•CHEESEMONGER•CORNER around); F|TA (.F.|•|T.A; •SHOPE•WITHIN•ALGATE around). BW —; Dickinson 73A. Baldwin. Rev. legend starts at 6 o'clock. BW Uncertain 57 (CHEESMONGER.CORNER) may be an obverse brockage of this issue

ALDGATE without *subsequently* ALDGATE HIGH STREET *etc.* (Aldgate ward) [29-G18]

The reading is WITHOVT ALGATE on 6477, 6483, 6485, 6488, 6491, 6493-4, ALDGATE on 6495, ALGAT on 6476, ALLGAT on 6478, ALLGATE on 6481, 6486, ALL GATE on 6480, 6487, 6489 (GAṬE), 6490, 6492; HIGHSTRET WITHOVT ALGATE on 6482; WITH OVT ALLGAT on 6479, ALLGATE on 6484; AT ALGATE on 6496-7

6476	0.94	14.4	Br	180°	*Atcheson,* Dorothy, cheesemonger (CHES|MONGER). nd. 2.1; 5.62.11 (D A). BW 83. Nott [ex Taffs]
6477	1.78	27.5	Cu	90°	*Gryer,* David. 1667 ½d. 1.33.22; 5.77. BW 89. Nott [ex Taffs]
6478a	1.01	15.6	Br	180°	*Harper,* Gabriel (GABRIELL). [16]59. 3.10.6; 4.9.8. BW 90. Nott [ex Taffs]
6478b	1.01	15.5	Br	180°	Same dies. [Nott]
6479	1.04	16.0	Br	180°	*Hey,* William, grocer (GROSER). nd. 2.4.7 (•WILLIAM•HEY•GROSER around); W H (W•H; •WITH•OVT•ALLGAT around). BW —; Dickinson 90A, from a report of this specimen. Baldwin
6480	1.24	19.1	Br	210°	*Ingrame,* Thomas. nd. 5.17.13; 5.54. BW 92. Nott [ex Taffs]. ?Thomas Ingram of St Botolph without Aldgate, Butcher; will, PCC, 1666 (Boyd 17804)
6481	1.45	22.3	Br	180°	*Kildermore,* Andrew. nd. 5.38.2; K|AE. BW 94 but WITHOVT•ALLGATE. Nott [ex Taffs]
6482	1.49	23.0	Cu	0°	*Quick,* Joh[n]. 1665 ½d. 5.70.1; 5.77. BW 95 but IOH:, HIGHSTRET. Nott [ex Taffs]. Reading completed from BM specimen
6483	1.11	17.1	M	180°	*Slightholme,* Thomas. nd. 5.5.1; 5.5.1. BW 96. Nott [ex Taffs]. Surname from Sleightholme, Co. Durham
6484	0.92	14.1	Br	180°	*Sparke,* Tho—. nd. 5.3.91; S|TM. BW 97 but WITH•OVT, device apparently a stirrup. Nott [ex Taffs or Carthew]. Reading confirmed from Greenall 1997, pl. 3.86, on which the device is clearer though upside down
6485	2.20	33.9	Br	0°	*Thacker,* Thomas. 1668 ½d. 3.115.2; 5.77 (T|TS). BW 98. Nott [ex Taffs]
6486	1.05	16.3	M	180°	*Thorne,* Margaret (MARGERET). nd. 3.4.22 (•MARGERET•THORNE around); M T (•|M•T|•; •WITHOVT•ALLGATE around). BW —; Dickinson 98A, from a report of this specimen, but MARGERET. Nott [ex Sotheby 25 July 1938, lot 88]
6487	1.26	19.4	Br	180°	*Ward,* Robert. nd. 3.11; W|RA. BW 101. Nott [ex Carthew]. Reading confirmed from BM specimen
6488	1.81	28.0	Cu	180°	*Withers,* Tho—. 1666 ½d. 3.5.110; 5.77 (W|TM). BW 102 but THO:. Nott

Named signs

6489	0.89	13.7	Br	180°	*Blue Bell* (AT THE BLEW BELL): ?W—, C—. nd. 5.70.1; C W. *BW 100. Nott. Reading largely confirmed from BM specimen and Wetton 1989, lot 135. In the Bird collection (lot 284) ex Norweb ex Nott the same rev. occurred with a different obv. die, axis 180°
6490	0.91	14.0	M	180°	*Dripping-pan* (AT THE DRIPINPAN): ?B—, E—. nd. 5.64.208 (•AT•THE•DRIPINPAN around); B|EE (•B•|E•E; •WITHOVT•ALL•GATE around). BW —; Dickinson 84A. Nott [ex Carthew]. First forename initial has also been read as F. Reading confirmed from Sedgwick 1986, pl. 1.2
6491	0.86	13.2	Br	90°	*Gun* (AT THE GVNE): ?D—, W—. 1659. 5.55.1; D|WA. BW 86. Nott [ex Taffs]. Rev. struck off-centre. Reading confirmed from BM specimen. See also 6466
6492	1.17	18.1	Br	180°	*Hart's Horns* (AT THE): ?F—, E—. nd. 3.53.30; F|ED. BW 87 but ALL•GATE. Nott [ex Taffs]
6493	1.03	15.8	Br	180°	*Pie* (AT THE PYE): ?I/J—, W—. 1648. 3.108.7; I|WA. BW 91. Nott [or Baldwin]

[*continued overleaf*]

6473 6474 6475 6476 6477 6478a

6479 6480 6481 6482 6483 6484

6485 6486 6487 6488 6489 6490

6491 6492 6493 6494 6495 6496

Plate 3 (*cont.*)

	Weight *g*	*gr*		Die axis	
6494	1.64	25.4	Cu	90°	*Pie* (AT THE): Gillat, David. 1671 ½d. 3.108.7; 5.77 (D G). BW 88. Baldwin [ex Pridmore]. David Gillett of St Botolph without Aldgate, b. 1644, Haberdasher, ?Vintner (Boyd 20875)
6495	1.55	24.0	Br	0°	*Red* [*?Lion*] (AT THE RED): Vertue, John. 1668 ½d. 3.32 (I V); 5.77. BW 99. Nott

A L D G A T E without. The Pie neighbourhood

The reading is NEXT on 6497, NEX^{T} on 6496, THE PIE AT ALGATE

6496	1.20	18.4	Br	0°	*Turner,* Simon. nd. 3.108.7; 5.14 Grocers. BW 69 but NEX^{T}, THE[no stop]PIE. Nott [ex Taffs]. Reading NEX^{T} confirmed from BM specimen ex Parkes Weber. The Pie at Aldgate is taken to be the same sign as the Pie without Aldgate (6493-4)

ALDGATE without. The Pie neighbourhood (*cont.*)

	Weight g	Weight gr		Die axis	
6497a	3.92	60.5	Br	0°	*Turner,* Simon. nd 1d. 5.14 Grocers; 3.108.9. BW 68 but I^{D}. Baldwin. Brass with plug of copper
6497b	3.66	56.5	Br	0°	Same dies. Nott [ex Carthew]. Plug missing; illustrated Thompson 1989, pl. 16.6

ALL HALLOWS BARKING neighbourhood (Tower ward) [39-J17]

The reading is AGINST BARKIN CHVRCH

Named signs

6498 1.03 16.0 M 180° *Crown* (AT THE): ?S—, W—. nd. 5.60.1; S|WM. BW 127. Nott. For attribution cf. Crown Court, across Seething Lane from the church [39-J17, m91]

ANGEL ALLEY (Bishopsgate ward Without) (*lost beneath Liverpool Street Station*) [18-C16, c9]

The reading is ANGELL ALLY WITHOVT BISHOPSGAT on 6499; WITHOVT BISHOP GATE BY ANGELL ALLY on 6500

6499 0.52 (chipped) 8.1 Br 0° *Fish,* John. nd. 3.109.13 (•IOHN•FISH•IN•ANGELL•ALLY: around); F|IA (•F•|I•A|•; •WITHOVT•BISHOPSGAT around). BW —; Dickinson 285A, from a report of this specimen. Baldwin

ANGEL ALLEY neighbourhood (Bishopsgate ward Without)

The reading is WITHOVT BISHOP GATE BY ANGELL ALLY

6500a 0.87 13.4 M 180° *?S—,* E—. nd. 3.10.6; S|EA. BW 322 but obv. and rev. transposed. Baldwin [or Nott ex Taffs]

6500b 0.79 12.2 M 180° Same dies. Nott

ANGEL ALLEY *subsequently* RED BULL WHARF (Dowgate ward) [37-K13, n19]

The reading is ANGELL ALLY IN THAMES STREET

6501a 1.11 17.2 Br 90° *Surridge,* Obadiah. 1668 ½d. 3.10.1; 5.77 (S|OA). BW 3124. Nott [ex Carthew]. ?Obadiah Surridge of St Lawrence Jewry, Weaver, porter, fl. 1681; md. Anne Edwards 1666 (Boyd 32410). Diameter 21 mm

6501b 0.81 (chipped) 12.5 Br 0° Same dies. [Nott ex Taffs]. Diameter 19-20 mm

AVE MARIA LANE (Castle Baynard ward & Farringdon ward Within) [24-H7]

The reading is AVEMARY LANE

6502 1.39 (chipped) 21.4 Br 0° *Robinson,* Godfrey. 1658. 3.92.2; G R|date. BW 104 but AVEMARY. Baldwin. Reading confirmed from Baldwin's Auction 38, lot 785 (illus.)

AXE YARD (Aldgate ward, St Mary Axe) [28-F16, f91]

The reading is S MAREYACṬ–ẠX̣ỴẸARD

Named signs

6503 0.79 12.1 Br 180° *Black Boy* (THE BLACK BOAY): ?H—, – —. nd. 3.1.59 (•THE•BLACK•BOAY•IN around); H|–E (•H•|–•E; •S•MAREYACṬ–ẠX̣ỴẸARD around). BW —; *Gilbert 1927, 237, *Dickinson 2694A (S•MAREY•ACTS•AXYEARD, initial W) but MAREYACṬ... and apparently undated. Nott

'BACON'S INN'

Cotterell, John *see* v. 5280 (Warwickshire: Bacon's End)

BALL ALLEY (Broad Street ward, London Wall) (*lost*) [17-E13, e48]

The reading is BALL ALLY LONDON WALL

6504 0.94 14.4 Br 0° *Tooley,* David. nd. 1.40.3 (•DAVID•TOOLEY•IN:BALL around); T|DI (•T•|DI; •ALLY•LONDON:WALL around). BW —; Dickinson 106B. Nott. David Toolye, of All Hallows, London Wall, md. Jane Bayle, St Michael Cornhill 1631 (Harl. Reg. 7 (1882), p. 26)

BARBICAN (Aldersgate ward & Cripplegate ward Without) [15-C9]

See also WHITE LION COURT. The reading is BARBICAN on 6506, 6509-11, 6515, 6518-20, *Barbican* on 6516; BARBICANN on 6507-8, 6513; BARBACAN on 6512; BARBECAN on 6514; BARBIKN on 6517; BARBYCAN on 6505

6505 0.67 10.3 Br 180° *Alexander,* Edmond. nd. 5.68.10; A|EM. BW 107 but ALEXANDE^{R}. Nott [ex Carthew]

6506 1.33 20.4 M 180° *Babington,* Elizabeth. 1653. E B; date. BW 108. Nott

[*continued overleaf*]

6497a 6498 6499 6500a 6501a 6502

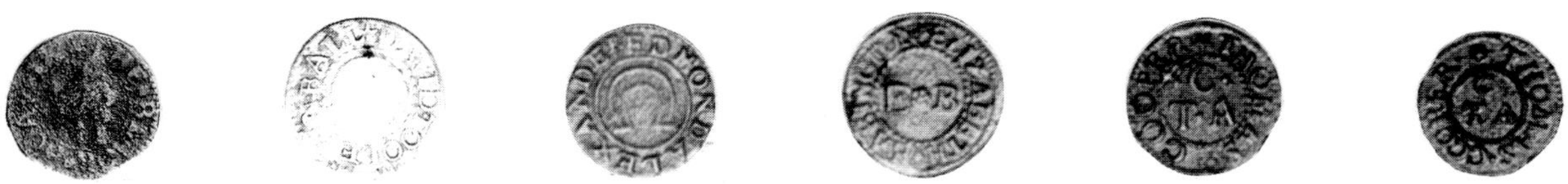

6503 6504 6505 6506 6507 6508

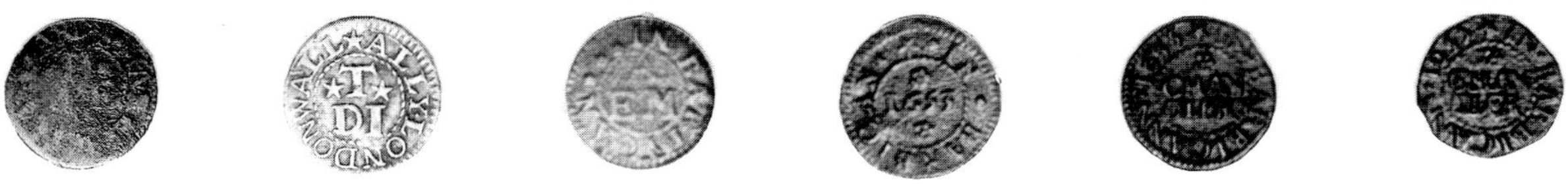

6509 6510 6511 6512 6513 6514

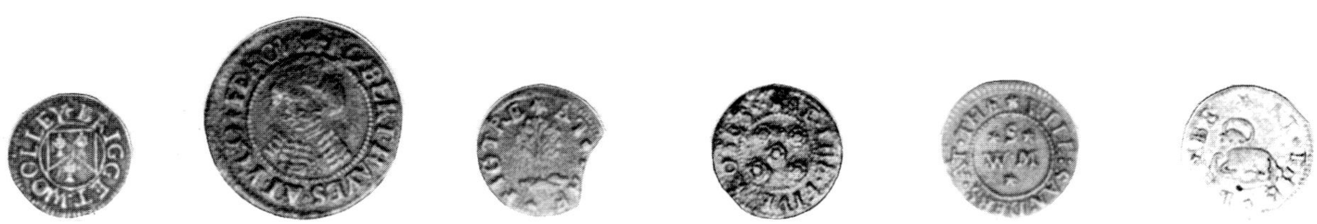

6515 6516 6517 6518 6519 6520

Plate 4 (*cont.*)

<table>
<tr><td></td><td colspan="2">Weight</td><td></td><td>Die</td><td></td></tr>
<tr><td></td><td>g</td><td>gr</td><td></td><td>axis</td><td></td></tr>
<tr><td>6507</td><td>1.43</td><td>22.0</td><td>M</td><td>180°</td><td>Cooper, Thomas, chandler (CHAN|DLER). 1655. C|TA; 5.77. BW 111. Nott. Same rev. die as 6508</td></tr>
<tr><td>6508</td><td>0.63</td><td>9.8</td><td>Br</td><td>180°</td><td>Cooper, Thomas, chandler (CHAN|DLER). 1655. C|TA; 5.77. BW 111. Nott [ex Spink]. Same rev. die as 6507</td></tr>
<tr><td>6509</td><td>1.66</td><td>25.6</td><td>Br</td><td>0°</td><td>Kitchinman, Thomas. 1666 ½d. 4.1.5 (•THOMAS•KITCHINMAN•AT•Y^{E} around); 5.77 (HIS|HALF|PENY|••:••; IN•BARBICAN•I666 around). BW —; Dickinson 116A. Baldwin</td></tr>
<tr><td>6510</td><td>2.22</td><td>34.3</td><td>Br</td><td>270°</td><td>Lane, Samuel (SAMVELL). 1668 ½d. 3.10.17 (•SAMVELL•LANE•AT•Y^{E} around); 5.77 (HIS|HALF|PENY; •IN•BARBICAN•I668 around). BW —; Dickinson 116B, from a report of this specimen. Baldwin</td></tr>
<tr><td>6511</td><td>1.48</td><td>22.9</td><td>Br</td><td>180°</td><td>Leech, James, bodice-maker (BODIS|MAKE|ER). nd. 5.77; 3.1.34. BW 118. Nott [ex Taffs]</td></tr>
<tr><td>6512</td><td>0.94</td><td>14.4</td><td>Br</td><td>90°</td><td>Revell, John. 1667. 3.6.62 (•IOHN•REVELL•AṬ•THE around); R|IE (•R•|IE|•; •IN•BARBACAN•I667 around). BW —; Dickinson 121A. Nott ex 'S. Museum. 12/7/56'</td></tr>
<tr><td>6513</td><td>0.85
(chipped)</td><td>13.1</td><td>Br</td><td>180°</td><td>Rudd, William. 1655. 3.52.1; R|WA. BW 122. Nott [ex Carthew]</td></tr>
<tr><td>6514</td><td>0.78</td><td>12.0</td><td>Br</td><td>0°</td><td>Shatchwell, Will[iam]. nd. 5.14 Weavers; S|WI. BW 125 but WILL:. Nott [ex Carthew]. William Shatwell, Weaver, St Giles without Cripplegate; will (Satchwell), PCC, 1675; md. Elizabeth Goldsmith 1664 (Boyd 50055)</td></tr>
<tr><td>6515</td><td>0.92</td><td>14.2</td><td>Br</td><td>180°</td><td>Woolley, Bridget (BRIGGET). nd. 5.14 Salters; B W. BW 126. Coins & Antiquities [1977]</td></tr>
<tr><td colspan="6">Named signs</td></tr>
<tr><td>6516</td><td>4.86</td><td>75.0</td><td>Br</td><td>0°</td><td>[Hayes] coffee-house (AT Y^{E}COFFE HOVS), formerly in Panyer Alley (Pannyer Ally): Hayes, Robert. nd. 3.5.40; 5.77.1. BW 116 but COFFE. Nott [ex Carthew]. See also 7458. The Coffee-house is named as in Lillywhite 1972, no. 556. The 24 mm diameter suggests a penny denomination</td></tr>
<tr><td>6517</td><td>0.93</td><td>14.3</td><td>Br</td><td>180°</td><td>Fig-tree (AT THE FIGTRE): ?P—, S—. 1653. 4.1.1; S P. BW 121. Nott [ex Carthew]. Reading confirmed from MoL specimen</td></tr>
<tr><td>6518</td><td>1.00</td><td>15.4</td><td>Br</td><td>180°</td><td>Five Roses (AT THE): ?G—, R—. 1664. 4.12.10; G|RD. BW 114. Nott [ex Taffs]</td></tr>
<tr><td>6519</td><td>0.95</td><td>14.7</td><td>Cu</td><td>180°</td><td>Golden [?Anchor] (AT THE): Sanders, Will—. nd. S|WM; 5.38.8 (W S). BW 124 but WILL:. Nott</td></tr>
<tr><td>6520</td><td>0.79</td><td>12.2</td><td>Br</td><td>180°</td><td>Lamb (AT THE LAMBE): ?S—, R—. nd. 3.56.1; R S. BW 123. Nott</td></tr>
</table>

BARKING CHURCH *see* ALL HALLOWS BARKING neighbourhood

BARTHOLOMEW CLOSE (Farringdon ward Without) [14-E8]

The reading is S BARTHOLOMEWS CLOSE on 6521; ^{T}S BARTHOLOMEWS CLOSE on 6522; S^{T} BATHOLMV;CLOS^{E} on 6523

	Weight g	Weight gr		Die axis	
6521	2.41	37.2	M	0°	*Kempe,* Richard. 1666 ½d. 3.5.41 (R K); 5.77. BW 129 but BARTHOLOMEWS. Nott. 'Kemp's Coffee House' otherwise 'Turks Head' (Lillywhite 1972, nos. 666, 1400)
Named signs					
6522	3.75	57.9	Br	0°	[*Russell's*] *coffee-house* (HIS): Russell, William. 1671. 5.77; 3.1.67. BW 130 but IN.^{T}S.BARTHOLOMEWS [*sic*]. Nott. Reading completed from BM specimens. The Coffee-house is named as in Lillywhite 1972, no. 1113. The 24-24.5 mm diameter suggests a penny denomination
6523	1.46	22.5	Br	225°	*Lantern* (AT Y^{E}LANT|HORN): Adson, Robert (ROBART). nd. 5.64.150 (•ROBART• ADSON•AT•Y^{E}LANT around); A|RS (•A•|R S|•; •HORN•IN•S^{T}BATHOLMV;CLOS^{E} around). BW —; Dickinson 128A, from a report of this specimen. Baldwin. Description virtually completed from a specimen available to the authors

BARTHOLOMEW LANE (Broad Street ward) [27-G13]

The reading is BARTHOLMEW LANE on both

6524	0.67	10.3	Br	270°	*Coast,* Robert (ṚOBẸRT). nd. 3.39.20 (•ṚOBẸRT•COAST•IN•:• around); C|RG (•C•|RG; •BARTHOLMEW•LANE•:• around). BW —; *Dickinson 131A. Nott [ex Taffs]. The lion rampant appears to be *guardant*
6525	0.64	9.8	Br	0°	*Levett,* William. nd. 5.13.26; L|WM. BW 133. Nott. William Levett or Levitt, Cook, wife Mary, fl. 1655 (Rogers 1935, p. 64, Berry 1978, p. 31); bound apprentices 1655-74 (Webb 1996-, xxvi. 68); d. 1679 (Pepys 1970-83, x. 232)

BASING LANE *subsequently* CANNON STREET (part) (Cordwainer & Bread Street wards) [35-I10]

The reading is BASING LANE on 6527-9; BASAN LANE on 6526; BASEN LANE on 6532-3; BASIN LANE on 6531; BASSING LANE on 6530

6526	0.90	14.0	M	180°	*Benet,* John. 1650. 5.14 Haberdashers(?); B|II. BW 143 but ?Haberdashers' Arms. Baldwin. Reading (but not obv. device) completed from BM specimen
6527	0.77	11.9	Br	180°	*Cock,* John. 1666. 5.64.75; C|IE. BW 145. Baldwin [or Nott ex Carthew]. Reading completed from MoL specimen. ?John Cock of St Mary Aldermary, Draper, who md. Eleanor Smith 1660, d. 1670 (Boyd 24877). Two Foundations set out for Mr John Cocke 1669 (Mills 1962-7, i. 9, iv. 138)
6528	1.31	20.2	Cu	270°	*Fletcher,* Vincent. 1666. 2.4.7; F|VF. BW 147. Nott [ex Carthew]. ?Vincent Fletcher (1638-1677), Tallow-chandler, who md. Frances Haffam or Hawthorne 1666, bound apprentices 1671-3 (Boyd 20737, unlocated; Webb 1996-, xxxix. 27, 109)
6529	0.58 (chipped)	9.0	Br	90°	*Fletcher,* Vincent. 1666. 2.4.7; F|VF. BW 147. Nott. See 6528
Named signs					
6530	1.14	17.5	M	180°	*Ball* (AT THE): ?A—, B—. 1659. 1.40.3; B A. BW 142. Nott
6531	0.96 (chipped)	14.8	M	180°	*Seven Stars* (AT THE SEAVEN STARES): ?A—, A—. 1650. 2.4.7; A|AP. BW 141. Nott [ex Taffs]. Reading confirmed from BM specimen
6532	1.32	20.4	M	180°	*White Horse* (AT THE WHIT HORS): ?G—, I/J—. 1652. 3.60.20; I G. BW 148. Nott. Same obv. die as 6533
6533	0.84	12.9	Cu	0°	*White Horse* (AT THE WHIT HORS): ?P—, W—. 1664. 3.60.20 (•AT•THE•WHIT•HORS around); W P (•••|W•P|•••; •IN•BASEN•LANE•I664 around). BW —; Dickinson 148A. Baldwin. Same obv. die as 6532

[*continued overleaf*]

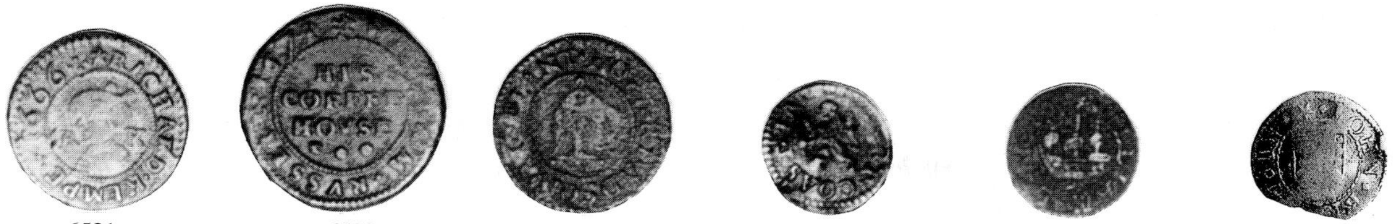

6521 6522 6523 6524 6525 6526

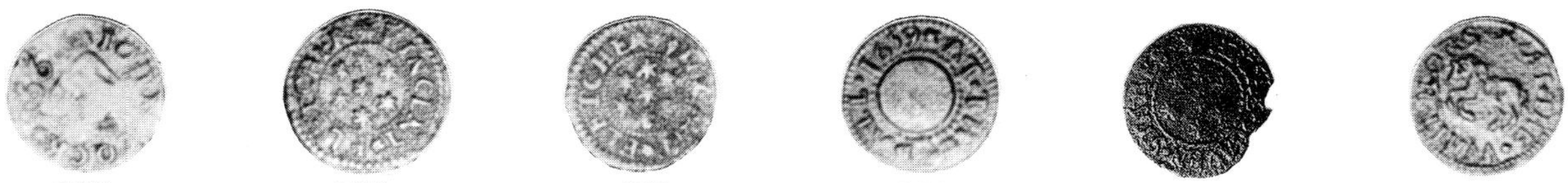

6527 6528 6529 6530 6531 6532

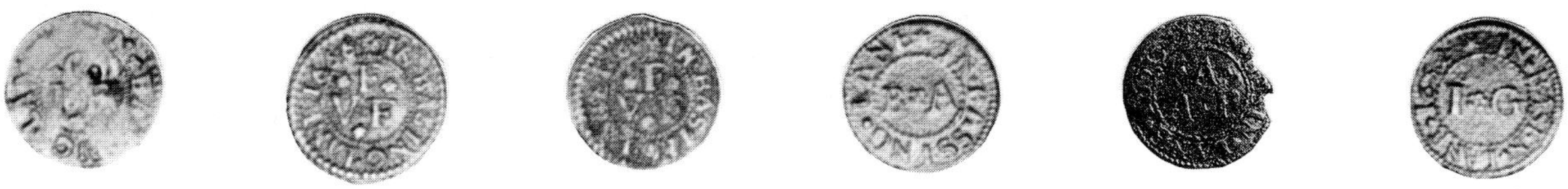

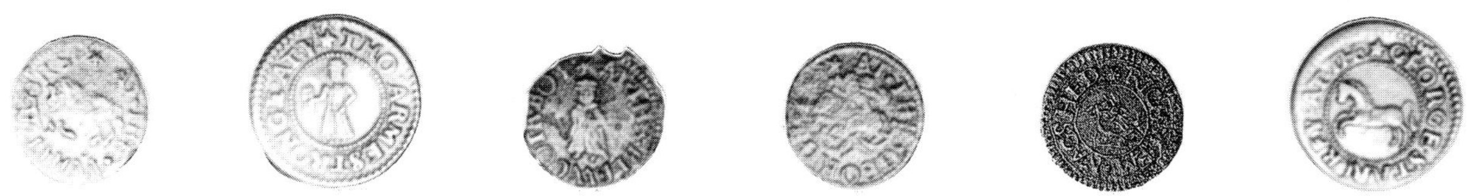

6533 6534 6535 6536 6537 6538a

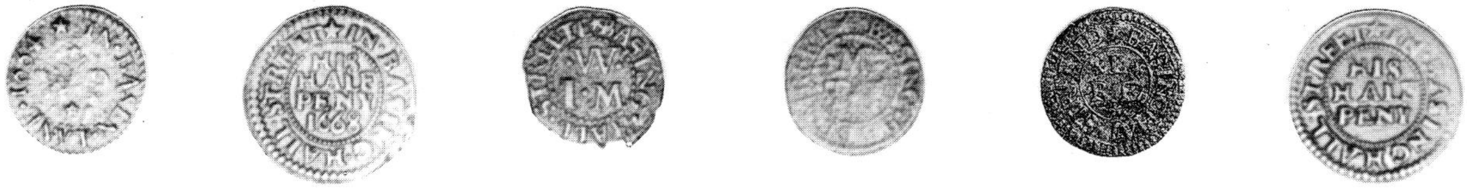

6539a 6540 6541 6542 6543 6544

Plate 5 (*cont.*)

BASINGHALL STREET [*previously* BASSISHAW STREET *etc.*] (Bassishaw & Coleman Street wards) [26-G11]

The reading is BASING HALL STREET on 6534 (dated 1668), 6536, STREETE on 6535; BASINGHALL STREET on 6538; BASINGHAL STR^{T} END on 6537. Yet Harben 1918, p. 53, found *Basinghallstreete* first mentioned 1670-1

	Weight *g*	*gr*		*Die axis*	
6534	1.95	30.1	Br	30°	*Armestronge,* Tho—. 1668 ½d. 3.1.53; 5.77. BW 134 but THO:, man holding a wool-card. Nott. E of Y^{E} either F in error or from a broken punch. For the wool-card cf. iv. 4130. Thomas Armstrong of St Michael Bassishaw, Clothworker, fl. 1673 (Boyd 41140)
Named signs					
6535	0.96 (chipped)	14.8	Br	180°	*Blue-coat Boy* (AT THE BLEWCOTE BOY): ?W—, I/J—. nd. 3.1.6 (•AT•THE•BLEWCOTE•BOY around); W|IM (•W•|I•M; •BASING•HALL•STREETE around). BW —; Dickinson 140A, from a report of this specimen. Baldwin. S of BASING formed partly from, or cancels, ?5
6536	1.03	15.9	Br	180°	*George* (AT THE): ?M—, T—. nd. 3.2.8; M|TI. BW 137 but BASING•HALL. Nott. Reading confirmed from BM specimen; it is assumed that AT THE GEORGE IN . . . does not mean 'At the George Inn . . .'
6537	0.83	12.8	Br	0°	*Nag's Head* (NAGS HED): Lem, Rich[ard]. nd. 3.60.30; L|RE. BW 136 but RICH:, NAGS[no stop]HED, BASINGHAL. Nott [ex Carthew]. Richard Lem of St Olave Jewry, Vintner, md. Sarah as his second wife 1658 (Boyd 39624). Richard Lem appr. 1642, bound apprentices 1656-61 (Webb 1996-, xliii. 183, 367)
6538a	1.84	28.4	Cu	0°	[*White Horse*] (AT THE): Starckey, George. nd ½d. 3.60.20; 5.77. BW 139 but THE. Nott. Sign name from BW 138. George Starkey of St Michael Bassishaw, Draper, free 1650; victualler; will, Archd. L., 1677 (Boyd 38786). Foundation to be staked out 1667 (Mills 1962-7, i. 5)
6538b	1.67	25.8	Cu	0°	Same dies. Nott [ex Baldwin]

BEAR QUAY *subsequently* (new) CUSTOM HOUSE (Tower ward, Thames Street) [38-K16, n43: Great Bear Quay]

The reading is AT BARE KEY

Named signs

6539a	1.19	18.3	Br	0°	*Bear* (AT THE BEARE): Stower, Philip (PHILLIP). nd. 3.49.5; S|PS. BW Southwark 152. [Nott]. Philip Stowers of St Dunstan in the East, Innholder, md. Susan Saywell 1655 (Boyd 16721); bound apprentices 1655/6-74 (Webb 1996-, xvii. 35)
6539b	0.72 (corroded)	11.0	Br	0°	Same dies. [?Baldwin]

BEARBINDER LANE *subsequently* MANSION HOUSE PLACE (Langbourn & Walbrook wards) [27-H13]

The reading is BEAREBINDER LAN^{E}

Named signs

6540	1.63	25.1	Br	0°	*Lobster* (AT THE): ?H—, T—. nd. T H; 3.111.0. BW 151 but LAN^{E}. Nott [ex Taffs]. Obv. reading confirmed from BM specimen with rev. from a different die, reading LANE as BW 151

BEDLAM *see* OLD BETHLEHEM HOSPITAL; OLD BETHLEM

BEECH LANE *subsequently* BEECH STREET (Cripplegate ward Without) [15-C10]

See also GLOVERS' HALL neighbourhood. The reading is BEECH LANE on 6542-3, 7013; BEICH LANE on 6541

6541	0.87	13.4	Br	270°	*Baker,* Peter. 1658. 3.67.35; B|PM. BW 162. Nott [ex Carthew]. For an overstruck specimen see iv. 3221a
6542	0.45 (chipped)	6.9	Br	330°	*Hales,* Robert. [16]59. 5.14 Bakers; H|RE. BW 166 but HALES, THE. Nott [ex Carthew]. Reading completed from MoL specimen
6543	2.14	33.1	Br	180°	*Taylor,* Thomas. 1668 ½d. 5.14 Butchers; 5.77 (T|TS). BW 168. Nott [ex Carthew]

BELL YARD *subsequently* QUEEN VICTORIA STREET *etc.* (Castle Baynard ward, Upper Thames Street) [34-J8, cf. m21]

Near Helmet Court (Harben 1918, p. 65). The reading is BEL YARD BY POWLS WHARF

Named signs

6544	0.74	11.4	M	180°	*Frying-pan* (THE FRIEN PAN): ?T—, D—. nd. 5.50.40; T|DI. BW 2200. Nott [ex Taffs]. Reading completed from BM specimen

BELL YARD (Farringdon ward Without *and* Middlesex: Westminster: Temple Bar neighbourhood) [31-I2]

The reading is BELL YARD on 6545, 6547-51, with NEAR TEMPLE BARR on 6545, NEAR TEMPL BAR on 6550, NEARE TEMPLE BARR on 6548, NEARE TEMPL BAR on 6549, NERE TEMPLE BAR on 6551, WITHIN TEMPLE BARR on 6547; BELL YEAR^{D} NEARE TEMPLE BAR on 6546

	Weight			*Die*	
	g	*gr*		*axis*	
6545	1.71	26.3	Cu	0°	*Drew,* Victor. 1667 ½d. 2.2.2; 5.77. BW 170. Baldwin
6546	2.30	35.5	Br	330°	*Fann,* Matthew (MATHEW). 1667 ½d. 5.14 Bakers; 5.77 (F|ME). BW 171 but YEAR^{D}. Nott [ex Taffs]
6547a	2.62	40.4	Cu	30°	*Lawrance,* Tho—. [16]66 ½d. 5.17.33; 5.77 (L|TA). BW 173 but THO:LAWRANCE, 66; BW 3054 but THO:LAWRANCE•IN•BELL•YARD. Nott
6547b	2.56	39.4	Cu	30°	Same dies. Clark 1977
6548	1.38	21.3	Br	0°	*Lions,* Jacob. 1666 ½d. 3.5.41 (I L); 5.77. BW 174. Nott. Reading completed from BM specimen. 'Lions' Coffee House . . .' (Lillywhite 1972, no. 728)
Named signs					
6549a	2.55	39.3	Br	180°	*Drake* (AT Y^{E}): Jonson, Will[iam]. 1667 ½d. 3.103.4; 5.77. BW 172 but DRAKE•IN. Baldwin. William Johnson, Vintner (Rogers 1928a, p. 67). See also Middlesex I: Holborn: Chancery Lane: *I/J*—, W—. Cf. Webb 1996-, xliii. 166, 365
6549b	1.89	29.1	Cu	0°	Same dies. Nott
6550	1.46	22.6	Br	0°	*Nag['s Head] tavern* (AT Y^{E}): Porter, Stephen. 1667. 3.60.30; 5.77. BW 175. Baldwin. Stephen Porter, appr. Vintner 1650, bound apprentices 1661-3 (Webb 1996-, xliii. 6, 236, 244)
6551	0.89	13.7	M	180°	*Portcullis* (THE PERCVLIS): ?R—, W—. nd. 5.17.1; R|WL. BW 176. Nott [ex Taffs]

BETHLEM [*i.e.* BEDLAM] *see* OLD BETHLEHEM HOSPITAL; OLD BETHLEM

BILLINGSGATE neighbourhood (Billingsgate ward) [38-K15]

See also DICE QUAY; LITTLE SOMER'S KEY. The reading is AT BILLINGS GATE on 6552, 6555, 6558 (BỊḶḶINGS), 6559-60; *at Billings Gate* on 6553; AT BILINGS GATE on 6556; AT BILLIN GATE on 6557; BY BILLINSGAT^{E} on 6561; NEAR BILLINSGATE on 6857; NEAR BILLINGS\|GATE (the Ns retrograde) on 7272; the place is unnamed on 6554

6552	0.95	14.6	Cu	180°	*Cash,* Rob[ert]. 1663. 3.10.17; C|RA. BW 198 but ROB:, BILLINGS•GATE. Nott [ex Carthew]. Robert Cash appr. Vintner 1646 (Webb 1996-, xliii. 55). Francis Heath held a lease of the Mermaid; he sublet 1663 to Johan Hayward, widow (cf. 6557); she leased to Robert Cash, whence the sign name; d. by 1667 and his widow Anne had md. Stephen Locke, cf. BW 2916 (Fire Court 1966-, i. 121-2; Rogers 1928a, p. 63, 1928c, pp. 69-70). See also 6559 and 7735
6553	2.03	31.4	Cu	180°	*Eldridge,* John. nd ½d. 5.77.1; 3.31.5. BW 199 but rev. inscription in chief. Nott [ex Taffs]. John Eldridge, Fishmonger, appr. 1647; by 1682 of St Mary at Hill (Boyd 38468; Woodhead 1966, p. 65); ?the issuer after the Fire of a halfpenny in Drury Lane, Westminster and Holborn (Middlesex I), q.v. He bound apprentices 1655-72 (Webb 1996-, xliv. 157)
6554	0.95	14.7	M	180°	'*Yeomen* (THE 4) *of the Waterside* (WATER SIDE)'. nd 'tokens'. 5.13.15; 3.112.1. BW 205 but WATER•SIDE. Baldwin. Location from 6555
6555	1.92	29.6	M	180°	'*Yeomen* (YEWMEN) *of the Waterside* (WATER|SID)'. nd. 3.111.4; 3.112.1. BW 206. Nott [ex Taffs]
Named signs					
6556	1.26	19.5	Br	180°	*Basket* (AT THE): Wild, Everard. nd ½d. 5.77; W|EB. BW 204 but BILINGS·GATE. Nott [ex Taffs]. Everard Wild of St Mary at Hill, Merchant Taylor, fl. 1700; md. Bridget Inge 1656 (Boyd 58755)
6557	0.80	12.4	Br	180°	*Mermaid tavern* (THE MAIRMEAD TAVERN): H[ayward], V[alentine]. 1650. 3.10.17; H|VI. BW 200. Nott [ex Taffs]. Valentine Hayward jun. was granted a lease of the Mermaid tavern in 1650 (Fire Court 1966-, i. 121 n.); md. Joan Green 1643, Joan Harward 1654; d. 1663 (Boyd 25075). Valentine Hayward, Vintner, bound apprentices 1656-60 (Webb 1996-, xliii. 40, 223). See also 6552
6558	1.05	16.2	M	0°	*Queen's Head* (AT THE): ?B—, S—. nd. 3.5.90; B|SM. BW 196 but BỊḶḶINGS•GATE. Nott [ex Carthew]
6559	1.05	16.2	M	180°	*Queen's Head* (AT THE): ?C—, R—. nd. 3.5.90; C|RA. BW 197. Nott [ex Taffs]. Issuer identified by Rogers 1928a p. 63, 1928c pp. 69-70, as Robert Cash, suggesting that c.1663 he changed his sign from the Mermaid (see 6552)

[*continued overleaf*]

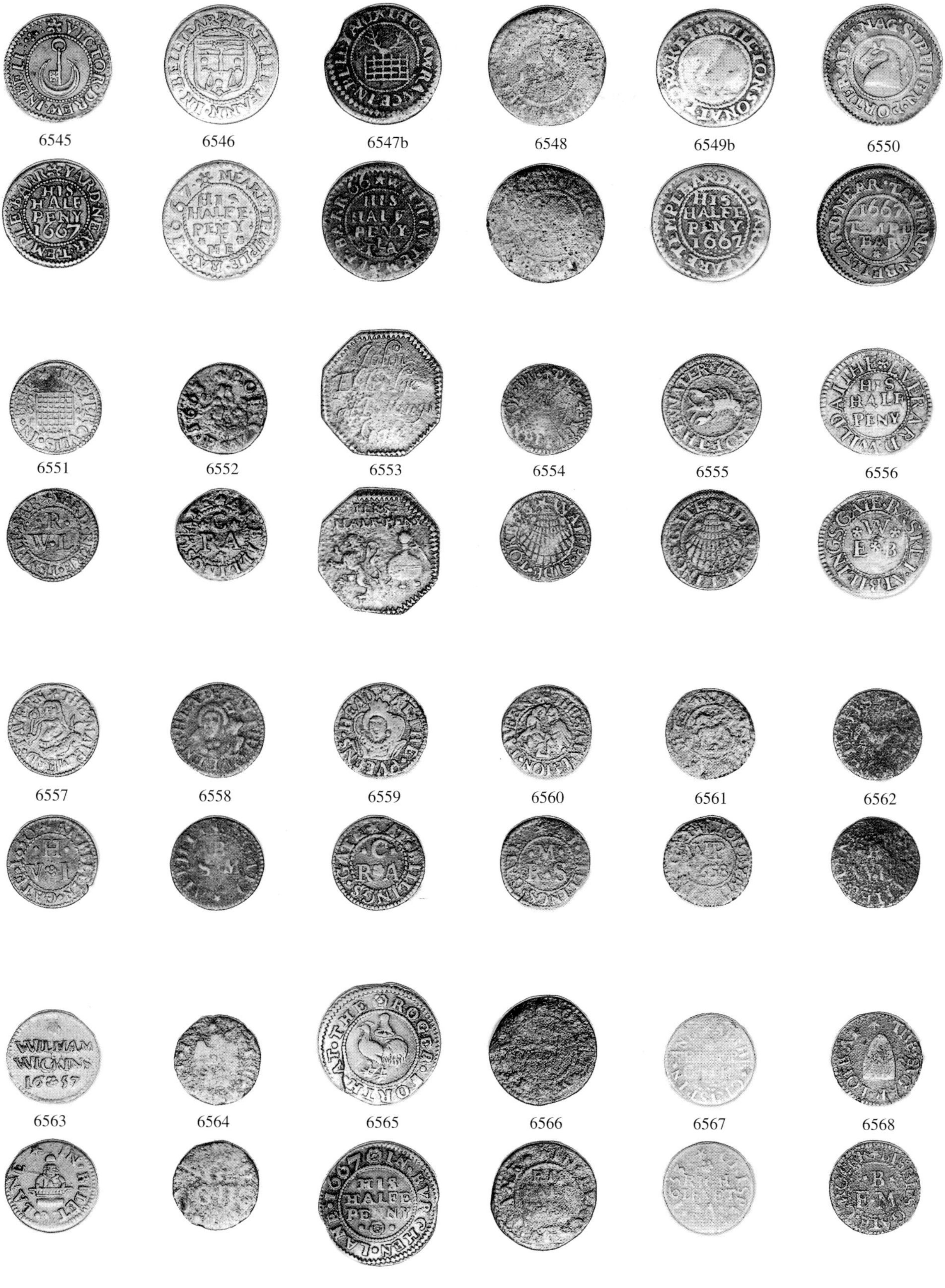

6545 6546 6547b 6548 6549b 6550

6551 6552 6553 6554 6555 6556

6557 6558 6559 6560 6561 6562

6563 6564 6565 6566 6567 6568

Plate 6 (*cont.*)

	Weight			*Die*	
	g	*gr*		*axis*	
6560	0.75	11.6	M	0°	*Salutation tavern* (THE SALVTAION TAVERN): ?M—, R—. nd. 3.4.2; M|RS. BW 201. Nott [ex Taffs]. ?Richard Moss or Morse of St Mary at Hill, d. 1701; md. Sarah Hammond 1650 (Rogers 1928a, p. 63; Boyd 38445). Richard Moss(e) appr. Vintner 1635 (Webb 1996-, xliii. 208, see also 371). Three Foundations to be staked out 1667 (Mills 1962-7, i. 16)
6561	1.02	15.7	Br	0°	*White Lion:* Potter (POTTER), Will[iam]. 1658. 3.39.1; W P|date. *BW 202 but BILLINSGAT^{E}; Woodhead 1966, p. 132. Nott [ex Carthew]. William Potter of St Mary at Hill, Clothworker, d. 1683 (Boyd 25932). Foundation to be set out 1667 (Mills 1962-7, i. 73)

BILLITER LANE *subsequently* BILLITER STREET (Aldgate ward) [29-H17]

See also BROWN'S ALLEY. The reading is BILLITER LANE on 6562; BILETR LANE on 6563; BILETTER LANE on 6564; BILLETER LANE on 6726

6562	0.69	10.6	M	180°	*Phillips,* William. nd. 4.3.10; P|WE. BW 211. Baldwin. Location read as LITEL LANE, 'unp[ublishe]d'. Reading completed from Harris 2002, lot 495 (illus.). Whittet 1983, p. 136, identified the issuer as the apothecary William Phillips; but he was located in the parish of St Dionis Backchurch (which Billiter Lane was not), his only known wife was Mary (Woodhead 1966, p. 130), and Whittet's 'rod of Aesculapius' is the same punch (inverted) as on v. 4972 AT THE CROOKED BILLET
6563	1.37	21.1	Cu	180°	*Wickins,* William. 1657 (I6•57). 5.77; 3.3.13. BW 212 but I6•57. Nott. Reading confirmed from BM specimen

Named signs

6564	0.67	10.3	M	180°	*Angel* (AT THE): ?G—, G—. nd. 3.10.6; G|GH. BW 208. Nott. Reading confirmed from BM specimen

BIRCHIN LANE (Cornhill & Langbourn wards) [27-H14]

The reading is BVRCHEN LANE on both

6565	2.04	31.4	Cu	270°	*Forth,* Roger. 1667 ½d. 3.101.10; 5.77. BW 216. Nott [ex Taffs]. Roger Forth of St Michael Cornhill (1642-82), Innholder (Boyd 17624). Foundation to be staked out 1668 (Mills 1962-7, i. 7)

Named signs

6566	1.68	25.9	Cu	270°	*Bell ordinary* (THE): White, Robert. nd ½d. 5.77; 5.77. BW 217 but BELL. Nott [ex Carthew]. Reading confirmed from BM specimen. A Robert White appr. Vintner 1652 (Webb 1996-, xliii. 317)

BISHOPSGATE neighbourhood (Bishopsgate wards Within & Without) [18-E16]

The reading is BISHOPGATE on 6567; AT BISHIPS GATE on 6568. Cf. 6593-6655

Named signs

6567	1.07	16.6	Br	180°	*Crispin & Crispianus*(AT THE): Levet, Rich[ard]. 1653. 5.77; 5.77 (RICH|LEVET|A). BW 242. Nott. Reading confirmed from BM specimen. Richard Levett, Cordwainer, Master 1663; will, PCC, 1665, St Martin Outwich; wife Anne (Boyd 25175)
6568	1.03	15.8	Br	180°	*Sugarloaf*(THE SVGAR LOFE): ?B—, F—, grocer. nd. 5.64.1; B|FM. BW 220. Nott [ex Taffs]. See also 6587

B I S H O P S G A T E S T R E E T *subsequently* B I S H O P S G A T E (Bishopsgate wards Within & Without, & Cornhill ward) [18-E16]

Stow seems to confine the name to the part within the gate (Harben 1918, p. 76); see also BISHOPSGATE Within. The reading is BISHOP GATE STREETE on 6579-80, 6583, 6585, 6587-8; BISHOP GAT STRET (the letters S retrograde) on 6577; BISHOPGATE STREETE on 6573-4; BISHOPSGATE STREET on 6569, 6576, 6591, STREETE on 6584, STRE^{T} on 6570; ḄISHOPSGAT STREET on 6582; BISHOPS GATE STREET on 6575, 6592, STREETE on 6572, 6586; BISHOPṢ GẠṬ STRE^{T} on 6571; BISSHOPS GAT STREET on 6578; BVSHOPES GATE STREET on 6589-90; BVSHOPSGAT STRET on 6581

	Weight			Die	
	g	*gr*		*axis*	
6569	0.99	15.2	Br	180°	*Bennet,* Will—. 1657. B|WR; 3.5.84. BW 223 but WILL:. Nott [ex Carthew]. See also 6653
6570	0.73	11.2	Br	180°	*Blackborne,* Tho—. nd. 5.64.1; B|TS. BW 224 but STRE^{T}. Nott. ?Thomas Blackborn of St Peter Cornhill, Merchant Taylor; md. Susan Holmes 1653; d. 1665 (Boyd 22948). Same obv. die as 6571
6571	1.31 (corroded)	20.2	Br	0°	*Blackborne,* Tho—. nd. 5.64.1; Ḅ|TS. *BW 224 but BISHOPṢ•GẠṬ•STRE^{T}. Baldwin. Same obv. die as 6570, q.v.
6572	2.16	33.3	Br	0°	*Hearne,* John. 1666 ½d. 3.11; 5.77 (H|IM). BW 235. Nott. Description confirmed from BM (Linecar 1955, pl. 19.84) and MoL specimens, and Wetton 1989, pl. 7.142. Rev. struck off-centre. John Hearne of St Helen Bishopsgate, Cook; md. Mary Page 1658 (Boyd 4391)
6573	1.02	15.8	Br	180°	*Horne,* Hen—, cheesemonger (CHESE MONGER). nd. H|HM; H|HM. BW 237. Nott. Die flaw obliterates E of HEN, the letter confirmed from MoL specimens
6574	0.66	10.1	Br	180°	*Miller,* Richard. nd. R M (•|R•M•|•; •RICHARD•MILLER•IN around); 4.12.1 (•BISHOPGATE STREETE around). BW —; Dickinson 244A. Nott [ex Carthew]
6575	1.37	21.1	Br	0°	*Russell,* Henry. 1667 ½d. 5.68.11 (R|HA); 5.77. BW 251 but BISHOPS•GATE, PENNY. Baldwin
6576	1.23	19.0	Br	90°	*Wilson,* John. nd. 3.5.88; W|IA. BW 262 but STREET. Nott [ex Carthew]. Reading completed from BM specimen. John Wilson of St Ethelburga, Vintner, 'Queen's Head'; md. Anne Briscoe 1661; d. 1687 (Boyd 26880). Cf. Webb 1996-, xliii. 324, 392
6577	0.90	13.9	Br	180°	*Winfield,* Philip (PHILLIP). nd. 5.14 Bakers; W|PE. BW 263 but GAT. Nott. Reading completed from BM specimen. The letters S are in mirror image. Philip Wingfield of St Michael Cornhill, Baker, Master 1663, 1670; md. Elizabeth Hide 1636; bd. St Ethelburga 1680 (Boyd 3970)
6578	2.91	44.9	Cu	225°	[*?*]. [16]66 ½d. 3.5.94; 5.76.140. BW 264 but GAT, 66. Nott [ex Carthew]. Rev. legend starts at 6 o'clock. Reading completed from BM specimen and Wetton 1989, pl. 7.143. Evidence of die-clashing on obv.
Named signs					
6579	1.14	17.6	M	180°	*Acorn* (AT THE ACORNE): ?M—, I/J—. nd. 4.8.10; M|IK. BW 243. Nott. Same rev. die as 6580. For supposed attribution to Joseph Moore see Dickinson forthcoming
6580	1.04	16.1	M	180°	*Acorn* (AT THE ACORNE): ?M—, I/J—. nd. 4.8.10; M|IK. BW 243. Nott. Same rev. die as 6579, q.v.
6581	0.88 (chipped)	13.5	Br	210°	*Black Hart* (AT THE BLACK HEART): ?A—, H—. nd. 3.53.20; A|HA. BW 218. Nott. Reading completed from BM specimen
6582	1.80 (chipped)	27.7	Br	150°	*Flower-pot* (AT Y^{E}FLOWER POTT): Baker, John (IO– –). nd ½d. (HALFE). 4.11.24; 5.77. *BW 222 (IOHN). Nott [ex Carthew]. Although superscript, the E of Y^{E} is no smaller. Cf. 6601
6583	1.11 (edge cuts)	17.1	Br	180°	*Mitre tavern* (AT THE MITER TAVERN): R[obinson], R[ichard]. nd. 5.59.20; R|RM. BW 249. Nott [ex Carthew]. Reading completed from BM specimen. Richard Robinson at the Mitre 1644 (Rogers 1928a p. 65, 1928c p. 122); appr. Vintner 1625, bound apprentices 1639-58 (Webb 1996-, xliii. 251, 379)
6584	0.82	12.7	Br	180°	*Ship tavern* (THE SHIP TAVERNE): H[icks], A[scanius]. nd. 5.13.18; H|AS. BW 232. Nott. Reading confirmed from Berry 1978, p. 34. The Ship otherwise the Great James; issuer Ascanius Hicks (Rogers 1928a p. 64, 1928c pp. 191, 193), Vintner, md. Susan Ellis 1637, fl. 1650 (Boyd 4402); appr. 1624, bound apprentices 1640-9 (Webb 1996-, xliii. 144, 361). Ascanius or Iulus was son of Aeneas; from him the Julian *gens* at Rome claimed descent
6585	1.14	17.5	M	180°	*Ship tavern* (THE): D[rayton], E[dward]. nd. 5.13.18; E D. BW 228. Nott. Issuer Edward Drayton of St Helen Bishopsgate, Vintner, md. 1651, d. 1677 (Rogers 1928a, p. 64; Boyd 4249); appr. 1623, bound apprentices from 1653 (Webb 1996-, xliii. 90, 351)
6586	0.77	11.9	Br	180°	*Star tavern* (THE STARR TAVERNE): B[est], H[ugh]. nd. 2.4.3; B|HI. BW 221. Nott [ex Carthew]. Issuer Hugh Best, wife ?Jane; the Star re-named the White Lion, see 6591 (Rogers 1928a, p. 64). Hugh Best appr. Vintner 1627, bound apprentices 1640-70 (Webb 1996-, xliii. 27, 339)
6587	0.95	14.6	Br	180°	*Sugarloaf* (THE SHVGER LOFE): ?M—, R—. nd. 5.64.1; M|RS. BW 244. Nott. Reading confirmed from BM specimen. See also 6568
6588	0.94	14.4	Br	180°	*Sun* (AT THE SVNN): ?A—, W—. nd. 2.1; A|WI. BW 219. Nott

[*continued overleaf*]

6569 6570 6571 6572 6573 6574

6575 6576 6577 6578 6579 6580

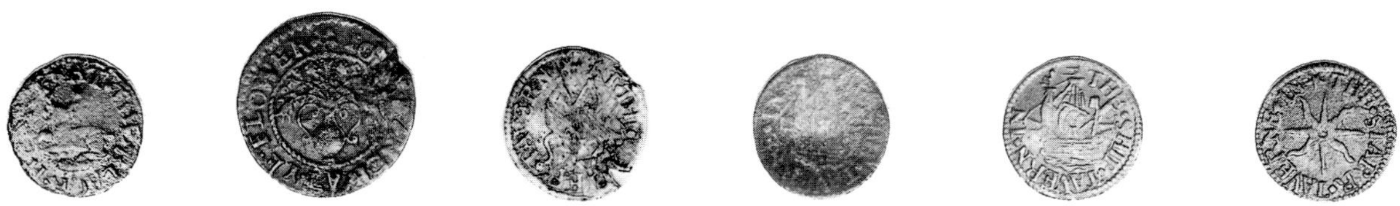

6581 6582 6583 6584 6585 6586

6587 6588 6589 6590 6591 6592

Plate 7 (*cont.*)

	Weight			*Die*	
	g	*gr*		*axis*	
6589	1.16	17.9	Br	180°	*Tun & Three Arrows* (THE TVN AND 3 ARROS): ?S—, I/J—. nd. 5.64.46; S|IH. BW 252 but 3•ARROS. Nott. Same rev. die as 6590, q.v.
6590	0.83	12.8	Br	0°	*Tun & Three Arrows* (THE TVN & 3 ARROS): ?S—, I/J—. nd. 5.64.46 (•THE•TVN•&•3•ARROS•IN around); S|IH (•S•|I•H; •BVSHOPES•GATE•STREET around). BW —, cf. 6589. Nott [ex Taffs]. Same rev. die as 6589. See also BW 272 (Bishopsgate Without)
6591	1.47 (corroded)	22.7	Cu	270°	*White* [*?Lion*] (Y^E WHIT): Dowding, Richard. 1670 ½d. 3.11; 5.77. BW 229 but Y^E WHIT, IN•BISHOPSGATE. Nott [ex Carthew]. Richard Dowding of St Helen Bishopsgate, victualler, fl. 1674 (Boyd 5698). The White Lion formerly the Star, see 6586

BISHOPSGATE STREET. Black Bull inn neighbourhood (St Ethelburga parish) [28-F15, B26]

The reading is NEXT|THE BVLL|IN BISHOPS|GATE|STREET. The Bull Inn or Black Bull Inn (Lillywhite 1972, 4049)

6592	8.78	135.4	Cu	180°	*Nourse,* Edw[ard]. 1666, 'his farthing (FARTHINGE) worth of copper'. 5.77; 5.77. BW 247 but EDW:, FAR=|THINGE. Nott. Edward Nourse (1624-1690), Girdler, md. Mary Wells, St Michael Cornhill 1649, there 1665, 1667 after the Fire, bd. there; trade, brazier; his father responsible for the 1657 Gloucester Farthing (ii. 1649-57). For weight and attribution see Thompson 2000

B I S H O P S G A T E Within *subsequently* B I S H O P S G A T E (Bishopsgate ward Within) [18-E16]

See also BISHOPSGATE STREET. The reading is WITHIN BISHOPSGATE on 6593, 6596, 6604, BISHOPS GATE on 6595, 6597, 6600, BISHOPGATE on 6598, BISHOP GATE on 6594, 6603, B:|GATE on 6602; WITH|IN BISHIPSGATE on 6601, BISHIPGATE on 6599

	Weight *g*	*gr*		*Die axis*	
6593	0.89 (edge cuts)	13.8	Br	0°	*Bond,* John. nd. 3.10.1; B|IM. BW 225. Nott [ex Taffs]
6594	1.35	20.8	Br	270°	*Childe,* Mary. nd. 5.68.30; M C. BW 226 but BISHOP•GATE. Nott [ex Carthew]
6595	0.94 (chipped)	14.5	Br	0°	*Collins,* Charles (CHARLS). 1664. 3.66.1; C|CA. BW 227. Nott [ex Carthew]. Rev. reading confirmed from BM specimen. Charles Collins of St Helen Bishopsgate, Poulter; will, PCC, 1671; wife Anne (Boyd 39473)
6596	0.62	9.6	Br	180°	*Frobysher,* Theophilus. nd. 5.60.1 (•THEOPHILVS•FROBYSHER around); F|TE (•F•|•T•E•|•; •WITHIN•BISHOPSGATE: around). BW —; Dickinson 229B. Nott [ex Taffs]
6597	4.33	66.8	Cu	270°	*Gullifer,* Henry. 1668 1d. 3.10.1; 5.77. BW 231. Nott [ex Taffs]
6598	2.02 (chipped)	31.2	Cu	0°	*Hasell,* James, cook. 1667 ½d. 3.92.2; 5.77. BW 234. Nott. Reading confirmed from BM specimen
6599	1.20	18.5	Br	180°	*Ives,* John. 1657. I|IM; date. BW 238. Nott [ex Carthew]
6600a	1.62	24.9	Br	180°	*Shaller,* Walter. 1666 ½d. 5.77; 2.2. BW 253. Nott [ex Taffs]
6600b	1.61	24.8	Br	180°	Same dies. Nott [ex Carthew]. Overstruck on . . .A– –ṆẸ. . .VM. . .; . . .G̣R. . . Also read as BW 254, for which this specimen could well have been the source
Named signs					
6601	0.85	13.2	Br	180°	*Flower-pot* (THE FLOWERPOT): ?T—, L—. nd. 4.11.20; T|LM. BW 256 but FLOWERPOT. Nott [ex Taffs]. Reading confirmed from BM specimen. Cf. 6582
6602	0.49	7.5	Br	90°	*Golden Lion* (GOVLḌEN LYON): Morris, Edm—. [16]57. 3.11; M|EA. *BW 245 but EDM:, B:. Nott. ?Edmond Morris, Grocer, fl. 1700; md. Anne Brown (Boyd 26823, unlocated)
6603	1.19	18.4	Br	0°	*King's Head tavern* (THE KINGSHED TAVERN): ?W—, G—. nd. W|GM; 3.5.109. BW 259 but KINGSHED, obv. and rev. transposed; Akerman 1849, fig. 55. Nott. Description completed from BM specimen
6604	1.17	18.1	Br	0°	*Peahen* (AT Y^{E}PEHEN): Smith, John. nd. 3.100.10 (•IOHN•SMITH•AT•Y^{E}PEHEN around); I S (•|I•S|•; •WITHIN•BISHOPSGATE around). BW —; Dickinson 254A. Nott [ex Taffs]

B I S H O P S G A T E Without *subsequently* B I S H O P S G A T E (Bishopsgate ward Without) [18-E16]

See also ANGEL ALLEY; DUNNING'S ALLEY; HALF MOON ALLEY; RED LION COURT (Bishopsgate Without). The reading is WITHOVT BISHOPS GATE on 6609-10, 6612, 6615, 6623, 6628, 6635, 6643, 6647-8, 6653, 6654 (–ỊTHOVT), BISHOPSGATE on 6605, 6613-14, 6618, 6621, 6630 (ẈỊTHOVT), 6634, 6652, 6876; *without Bishopsgate* on 6646; WỊ–HOVT BISHOPS:|GATE on 6619; WITHOVT BISHOP GATE on 6500, 6608 (. . .Ọ VT BISHOP̣), 6616-17, 6640-2, 6644-5, 6649, 6651, 6655, BISHOPGA^{T} on 7530, BISHOPGATE on 6620, 6624, 6631, BISHOPPS GATE on 6622 (BIṢHOPPS), 6637, BISHOPSGAT on 6499, 6607 (ẈỊTHOVT), BISHOPS GAT on 6633, BISHIPS GATE on 6606, BISHOS G̣–ṬE on 6611, BISHOPGAT on 6626, B GATE on 7061-3; WITH|OVT BISHOPSGATE on 6625; WITH|OVT BISHOPS GATE on 6627; WITH OVT BISHOPGATE on 6650; WTH|OVT BISHOPSGATE on 6629; WTHOVT BISHOPS GATE on 6638-9; W^{THO} BISHOP^{S} GATE on 6632; WITHOVTH BISHOPGAT on 6636

6605	1.60	24.7	Br	90°	*Barnard,* John. nd ½d. 5.49.1; 5.77. BW 270. Nott [ex Carthew]. Reading completed from MoL specimen
6606	1.11	17.1	M	180°	*Bathurst* (BAT|HVRST), confectioner. nd. 5.77; 5.64.15. BW 271. Nott
6607	1.08	16.6	Br	180°	*Be. . .y* (BẸ. . .Y), John, pin-maker (PEN MAKR). nd. 5.14 Pin Makers (•IOHN•BẸ. . .Y•PEN•MAKR around); B|IA (•B•|I•A; •ẈỊTHOVT•BISHOPSGAT around). BW —; Dickinson 268A (this specimen, as described in Macfadyen, lot 149). Baldwin [ex Macfadyen, lot 149]. Surname read on Macfadyen's ticket as 'Bailey', but perhaps BERR(E)Y
6608	0.71	10.9	Cu	180°	*Burgin* (ḄVṚGỊN), Henry (HENRỴ). nd. 5.50.18; B|HM. *BW 275 (WITHOVT) but BISHOP̣•GATE. [?ex Schwer ex Sotheby 24 Jan. 1979, lot 149] ex? ex Faulkner
6609a	1.56	24.0	Cu	90°	*Butcher,* Ralph. 1666. 5.77.1; 3.31.2. BW 276 but *1666*. Nott. Edge hammered up. Diameter 16-16.5 mm. ?Issuer in Tower Street before the Fire (7760). See also Henry Salter with a similar sign (6633)
6609b	1.12	17.3	Cu	90°	Same dies. Nott. Diameter 17-17.5 mm
6610	1.63	25.2	Cu	0°	*Dashwood,* Francis (FRANCES). nd ½d. 3.1.2; 5.77. BW 282. Nott [ex Taffs]. Reading confirmed from BM specimen. Evidence of die-clashing on obv. ?Francis Dashwood 1603-1683, of St Botolph without Bishopsgate, Saddler, Master 1653; Turkey merchant; Alderman 1658; father of Sir Samuel Dashwood MP and Sir Francis Dashwood Bt. (Boyd 14016; Woodhead 1966, p. 56; Burke 2003 s.v. Dashwood of West Wycombe). Sign may be a Black Boy though no attributes have been observed

[*continued overleaf*]

6593 6594 6595 6596 6597 6598

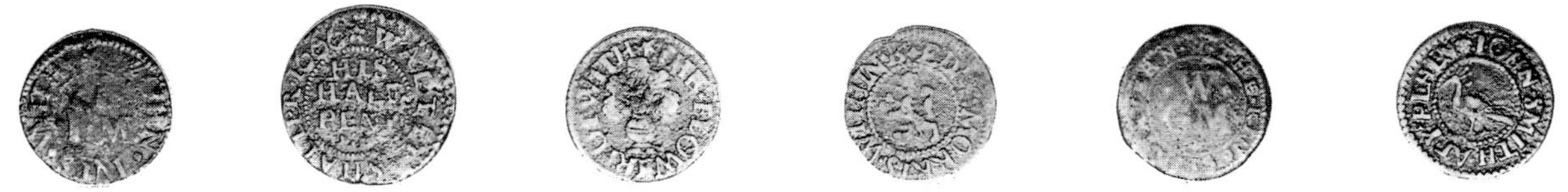

6599 6600a 6601 6602 6603 6604

6605 6606 6607 6608 6609a 6610

6611 6612 6613 6614 6615 6616

Plate 8 (*cont.*)

	Weight g	*Weight gr*		*Die axis*	
6611	1.00	15.4	Br	150°	*Dollison,* Thomas. 1667 ½d. 5.54.1 (T D); 5.77. BW 283 but BISHOS•Ġ̣–ṬE [*sic*]. Nott. Reading largely completed from MoL specimen. Overstruck on: Portsmouth (Hants.), *The Hulk:* Pearse, Edward. •ẸḌWẠRḌ•P̣EARS^{E}ẠṬ•Ỵ^{E}ḤṾLKẸ; IN•P̣ỌṚṬ. . .OVṬH•Ị667. Centres unclear, die axis 180°; cf. Norweb iii. 1980, but both dies different
6612	2.25	34.6	Br	0°	*Duffild,* William. 1666 ½d. 3.101.1 (•WILLIAM•DVFFILD•I666 around); 5.77 (HIS|HALF|PENY|•:•; •WITHOVT•BISHOPS•GATE around). BW —; Dickinson 283A. Nott. William Duffield of St Botolph without Bishopsgate, b. 1635, Vintner (Boyd 42479). William Duffell appr. 1657 (Webb 1996-, xliii. 91)
6613	2.33	35.9	Br	180°	*Eagles,* Peter. 1668 ½d. 3.95.1; 5.77. BW 284. Baldwin. Reading confirmed from BM specimen
6614	2.17	33.5	Br	180°	*Fossey,* Joseph, mealman. 1668 ½d. 4.10.1; 5.77. BW 286 but WITHOVT. Nott
6615	1.68	25.8	Cu	90°	*Fydge,* Thomas. 1666 ½d. 5.77; 5.64.1. BW 287. Nott [ex Taffs]. Reading confirmed from BM specimen. Thomas Fyge, apothecary; physician 1661 (Woodhead 1966, p. 74; Whittet 1983, p. 135)
6616	0.92	14.2	Br	180°	*Goss,* Thomas. 1652. 5.3.10; T G. BW 288. Nott. ?Thomas Goss, Wax Chandler, fl. 1651 (Boyd 25030, unlocated)

BISHOPSGATE Without (*cont.*)

	Weight g	Weight gr		Die axis	
6617	0.95	14.7	Br	180°	*Goss,* Thomas. 1652. 5.3.10; T G. BW 288. Nott [ex Taffs]. See also 6616
6618	1.02	15.7	Br	270°	*Greene,* John, tallow-chandler (TALLO' CH'). nd. 2.2; G|IL. BW 289 but TALLO:CH:. Baldwin. John Greene apprenticed Tallow Chandler 1649, bound apprentices 1664-76 (Webb 1996-, xxxix. 44, 126). John Green of St Botolph without Bishopsgate, Tallow Chandler, md. Lea[h] Dagley 1663 (Boyd 20467)
6619	0.58	8.9	Br	0°	*?H—,* S—, salter. 1658. H|SA; 3.108.7. *BW 291 (WITHOVT) but BISHOPS:. No provenance, 1979
6620	0.89	13.7	Br	180°	*Hampson,* Samuel (SAMVELL). nd. 3.60.20; H|SA. BW 296. Nott [ex Carthew]
6621	0.73	11.3	Cu	180°	*Hardy,* Francis, grocer. 1666. 5.77.1; 5.14 Grocers. BW 297 but *1666*. Nott [ex Taffs]. Francis Hardy of St Botolph without Bishopsgate, Grocer, b. 1623 (Boyd 20642)
6622	1.00	15.5	M	225°	*Jordan,* William. nd. 5.5.1; I|WA. *BW 304 (Y^{E}). Nott [ex Baldwin]. Reading largely confirmed from MoL specimen
6623	2.20	33.9	Br	0°	*Jordan,* William. nd ½d. 5.7.27; 5.77 (I|WA). BW 303 but BISHOPS•GATE:, within the entrance a soldier(?) holding a staff. Nott [ex Taffs]. The standing figure in the archway has the left arm akimbo, with hand on hip, the right arm supporting a pike; he wears a short tunic and has a bandolier across his chest
6624	1.20	18.5	Br	180°	*Jordon,* Henry, victualler (VITLER). nd. 5.83.43; I|HF. BW 302. Nott
6625	0.85	13.2	Br	90°	*Kentish,* John. [16]57. 5.64.52; K|IM. BW 305 but WITH [no hyphen] = A woolpack charged with I657. Seaby, [*SCMB* April 1967]. Date 1657 on obv. might be year the sign was erected
6626	1.40	21.6	Br	180°	*Middleton,* Thomas. nd. M|TK; M|TK. BW 309. Nott
6627	0.91	14.1	Br	270°	*Nicolls,* George. [16]57. 5.17.10; N|GA. BW 310 but WITH . Nott [ex Carthew]
6628	2.95	45.5	Br	270°	*Overton,* Dorothy. nd ½d. 3.60.4; 5.77. BW 313. Nott. Reading confirmed from BM specimen
6629	0.73	11.3	Cu	0°	*Partridge,* Andrew. 1664. 5.14 Tallow Chandlers; P|AI. BW 315. Baldwin. Reading confirmed from BM specimen. Andrew Partridge of St Botolph without Bishopsgate, Tallow Chandler, d. 1667; md. Joan Partridge [*sic*] (Boyd 25258)
					Plowman, Edward *see* 6654 (*White* [*Horse*]: Plowman)
6630	1.25 (chipped)	19.2	Br	180°	*Porramore* (PORRAMOR–), Thomas. nd ½d. 5.77 (HIS|HALF|PENY|•:•; •THOMAS• PORRAMOR–; around); P|TM (•P•|T M|•; •WITHOVT•BISHOPSGATE around). BW —; Dickinson 316A but PORRAMOR–. Baldwin. Surname presumably a version of Paramor etc., i.e. 'paramour'
6631	1.93	29.7	Br	0°	*Quelch,* Hen—, oilman (OYLEMAN). nd ½d. 5.64.45; 5.77. BW 318 but HEN:, stalked flower apparently a rose. Nott [ex Carthew]. Reading completed from Wetton 1989, pl. 7.147. ?Henry Quelch of St Peter Cornhill, Draper, free 1654; oilman, Leadenhall Street; fl. 1696 (Boyd 5815)
6632	1.11	17.2	Br	180°	*?S—,* G—, mealman (MEALE MAN). nd. S|GM (.S.|G M|•; [crown] MEALE[?stop] MAN•W^{THO} around); 3.102.30 ([crown]•BISHOP^{S}•GATE• around). BW —; Dickinson 321A but MEALE MAN. Baldwin
6633	0.63	9.8	Cu	0°	*Salter,* Henry. 1667. 5.77.1; 3.31.2. BW 325. Nott [ex Taffs]. Description completed from BM and MoL specimens. See also Ralph Butcher with a similar sign (6609)
6634	0.99	15.3	Br	0°	*Smaley,* Will—, baker. nd. 5.9.11; S|WA. BW 329 but WILL:. Nott [ex Carthew]. Rev. legend starts between 10 and 11 o'clock. Reading confirmed from Wetton 1989, pl. 7.146
6635	0.90	13.9	M	0°	*Studd,* Robert. nd. 5.16.1; S|RM. BW 331. [Nott]. Robert Studd of St Botolph without Bishopsgate, Armourer; children with wife Alice bap. 1647-9 (Boyd 25421). Apprenticed Armourer 1633, bound apprentice 1658 (Webb 1996-, xxii. 47, 55)
6636	1.06	16.3	M	180°	*Tutchin* (TVCHIN), Tho—, grocer. nd. 5.14 Grocers; 5.64.1. BW 333 but WITHOVTH•BISHOPGAT. Baldwin. Form of surname from 6637, but both a form of Twitchin etc., *Tuchyn* 1577 (Reaney 1995, p. 459). Burn's note (1855, 187), repeated by BW, should be ignored: the Deputy was William Tutchen (Woodhead 1966, p. 166)
6637	1.48	22.8	M	180°	*Tutchin,* Tho—. nd ½d. 5.77; 5.64.1. BW 332 but BISHOPPS•GATE. Nott [ex Carthew]
6638	0.96	14.8	Br	0°	*Tuthill,* John. nd. 3.5.105; T|IE. BW 334 but WTHOVT, a stop below ^{H}. Nott [ex Taffs]. Obv. legend starts at 1 o'clock. Same rev. die as 6639
6639	0.90	13.9	Br	90°	*Tuthill,* John. nd. 3.5.105; T|IE. BW 334 but WTHOVT, a stop below ^{H}. Nott. Obv. legend starts at 1 o'clock. Same rev. die as 6638
Named signs					
6640	0.92	14.2	Br	180°	*Black Lion* (AT THE BLACK LYON): ?C—, G—. nd. 3.11; 5.32.10 (C|GE). BW 278. Baldwin [ex Pridmore]

6617 6618 6619 6620 6621 6622

6623 6624 6625 6626 6627 6628

6629 6630 6631 6632 6633 6634

6635 6636 6637 6638 6639 6640

BISHOPSGATE Without (*cont.*)

Named signs (*cont.*)

	Weight g	gr		Die axis	
6641	0.87	13.4	M	180°	*Blue Boar* (AT THE BLEW BOORE): ?C—, E—. nd. 1.44; 3.65.1. BW 277. Nott. Same obv. die as 6642
6642	0.81 (chipped)	12.4	M	180°	*Blue Boar* (AT THE BLEW BOORE): ?C—, E—. nd. 1.44; 3.65.1. BW 277. Baldwin. Same obv. die as 6641. Reading WITHOVT confirmed from Harris 2002, lot 496 (illus.)
6643	2.40	37.1	Cu	0°	*City of Norwich* (AT Y^{E}CITTY OF NORWICH): Hutton, Samuel (SAMVELL). nd ½d. 5.12.11; 5.77. BW 299. Nott [ex Carthew]
6644	0.85	13.1	Br	180°	*Golden Anchor* (THE GOVLDEN ANCHOR): ?S—, B—. nd. 5.38.1; S|BS. BW 321. Nott. Reading confirmed from MoL specimen
6645	0.89	13.7	M	180°	*Gridiron* (AT THE GRIDEIRON): ?I/J—, H—. nd. 5.17.38; I|HM. BW 300 but GRIDEIRON. Nott. Reading confirmed from Lillywhite 1972, pl. 14.3
6646	2.92	45.0	Br	180°	*Harrow (at the):* Antrobus, Benjamin. nd. 5.17.18; 5.77.1. BW 265 but *at, without.* Baldwin [ex Gilbert]. Benjamin Antrobus (A), Draper, fl. 1634-97; (B), Draper, free 1668, fl. 1713 (Boyd 16258, unlocated; Boyd 1934, p. 5)
6647	2.14	33.1	Cu	180°	*Lord Craven* (A– Y^{E}SINE OF MY LORD CRAVEN): Hall, Arthur (ARTHVṚ). nd ½d. 5.77; 5.77. *BW 294 (AT). Nott. E of CRAVEN either an F with lower horizontal bar weakly added, or a weakly entered E altered unintentionally to F. Same rev. die as 6648, q.v.
6648	2.53	39.0	Cu	180°	*Lord Craven* (AT Y^{E}SINE OF MY LORD CRAVEN): Hall, Arthur. nd ½d. 5.77; 5.77. BW 294. Nott. Reading confirmed from BM specimen; same rev. die as 6647. William Craven (1608-1697), created Baron Craven of Hampsted Marshall 1627, Viscount Craven of Uffington and Earl of Craven 1665; d. unmarried *pace* BW 294 n. (ODNB; GEC 1910-98, iii. 500-1)
6649	0.67	10.3	M	180°	*Mouth tavern* (AT THE): ?S—, R—. nd. 3.5.2; S|RK. BW 323. Nott. V of MOVTH double-punched. Reading confirmed from Berry 1978, p. 35
6650	1.11	17.1	M	180°	*Rainbow* (AT THE RAINEBOWE): ?R—, E—. nd. 2.12.1; R|EG. BW 319. Nott
6651	0.84	13.0	Br	180°	*Rose & Crown* (THE ROSE AND CROVN): ?I/J—, W—. nd. 4.12.2; I|WM. BW 301 but CROVN. Nott. Reading confirmed from BM specimen
6652	1.65	25.5	Cu	0°	*Three Leopards' Heads* (AT THE 3 LIBERTS HEADS): ?H—, M—. nd. 5.14 Weavers; M H. BW 290. Nott. Reading confirmed from BM specimens
6653	0.99 (chipped, corroded)	15.3	Cu	90°	*White* [*?Hart*] (AT Y^{E}): Benet, Will— (WILL:). nd ½d. 3.53.20; 5.77. *BW 274 but WILL:. Nott. Description largely completed from BM specimen. See also 6569
6654	2.01	31.0	Cu	0°	*White* [*?Horse*] (AT WHIṬ): Plowman, Edward. nd ½d. 3.60.4; 5.77. *BW 316 (WITHOVT) but AT•WHIṬ. Baldwin. Restruck after turning over. Edward Plowman of St Botolph without Bishopsgate, b. 1621; wife Jane; children bap. 1648-58 (Boyd 20569)

BISHOPSGATE Without. Sun neighbourhood

The reading is BY THE SVN WITHOVT BISHOP GATE. There was a Sun in Bishopsgate Street [?Within], cf. 6588, and a Sun in Old Bethlem (without Bishopsgate), cf. BW 183

6655	1.19	18.3	Br	180°	*?H—, S—.* nd. 4.12.11; H|SA. BW 292. Nott. Reading confirmed from BM specimen. Initial mark at 10 o'clock, legend starts at 1 o'clock. The device is a Rose on which shine rays from a nearby Sun

BLACK HORSE ALLEY [*i.e.* BLACKHORSE ALLEY] *subsequently* LUDGATE CIRCUS *and* ST BRIDE STREET (Farringdon ward Without, Fleet Street) [23-H5, i17]

The reading is BLACKE HORSE ALLY

Named signs

6656a	1.85	28.6	Cu	180°	*King's Head* (AT Y^{E}KINGES HEAD): Blumsum, Tho—. nd ½d. 5.77; 3.5.81. BW 354 but THO:BLVMSVM•AT•Y^{E}KINGES, BLACKE•HORSE. Nott [ex Taffs]. Thomas Blumsome of St Bride's, Baker, widower, & Jane Lewgar licensed to marry 1661 (Harl. 26 (1887), p. 286); appr. a Brown Baker 1635 (Webb 1996-, xxxi. 4)
6656b	1.17	18.0	Cu	180°	Same dies. [Nott ex Carthew]

[*continued overleaf*]

PLATE 10

6641 6642 6643 6644 6645 6646

6647 6648 6649 6650 6651 6652

6653 6654 6655 6656a 6657 6658

6659 6660 6661 6662 6663 6664

BLACK SWAN ALLEY *subsequently* KENNET WHARF (Vintry ward, Garlick Hill neighbourhood) [36-J11, m50, confirmed from Ogilby 1677, p. 35]

The reading is SWAN ALLY AT Y[E]FOOT OF GAR:|LICK HILL IN THAMS STREET, i.e. *Black Swan Alley* Leake 1666 [pub. 1667] to Strype 1755 (Harben 1918, p. 330)

	Weight			*Die*	
	g	*gr*		*axis*	
6657	3.13	48.3	Cu	90°	*Beech,* James. 1666 ½d. 5.77; 5.77. BW 3082 but GAR:. Nott [ex Carthew]. Reading completed from MoL specimen. James Beach of St James Garlickhithe, Cooper; children bap. 1648-9 (Boyd 49650). ?Issuer after the Fire of a halfpenny at Bow Street, Westminster (Middlesex I), but there is no support for Burn's 'taverner' in [Black] Swan Alley (1855, 1130)

BLACKFRIARS (Farringdon ward Within) [33-I6]

The reading is BLACK FRIERS on 6658-60, 6662-4, FRYERS on 6665-6; BLACKE FRYERS on 6667; BLACKFRYERS on 6661

6658	0.71	10.9	M	180°	*Cranwel,* William. nd. 3.3.13; C|WR. BW 339. Baldwin [or Nott]. Reading confirmed from MoL specimen
6659	0.90	14.0	Cu	0°	*Hooton,* Thomas. 1664. 5.77.1; H|TE. BW 340 but *1664*. Nott. Reading completed from BM specimen
6660	0.81	12.5	Br	180°	*Insley,* Tho—. nd. 3.102.10; I|TS. BW 342 but [heart]THO:INSLEY•AT•THE•, rev. [heart]IN•BLACK•FRIERS:• = •I•|T•S; Dickinson 2694B ('St Mary Friars'), from a report of this specimen. Baldwin [or Nott ex Spink]. Description virtually completed from MoL specimen. The BW listing must have been taken from the present specimen, overstruck on: Kendal (Westmorland): *Adlington,* Edmond. . . .ND•ADLIN. . . = ?Arms; . . .L•I659 = ?, die axis 270°, struck off-centre (cf. woodcut of BW Westmorland 8)
6661	0.79 (corroded, chipped)	12.3	Cu	0°	*Kidder,* William. 1666. 5.77.1; W K. BW 344 but *1666*. Nott [ex Taffs]. Reading completed from BM specimen
6662	0.78 (chipped)	12.1	M	0°	*Simkins,* Charles. 1657. 5.64.160; S|CM. BW 347. Nott [ex Taffs]. Reading confirmed from Greenall 1997, lot 94
6663	0.93	14.3	Br	180°	*Simson,* Nicholas (NICOLAS). 1659. 3.91.1; S|NE. BW 348. Nott [ex Taffs]. The 'wreath' described by Akerman 1849 no. 251, Boyne 1858 London 283, et al., appears to be the base of flames which consume a Phoenix
6664	0.86	13.2	Br	0°	*Smith,* Josiah (IOSIAS). nd. 5.64.153 (•IOSIAS•SMITH• around); S|IS (•S•|I•S; •BLACK•FRIERS around). BW —; Dickinson 348A but description revised. Baldwin [ex Macfadyen, lot 149]. Rev. initial mark at 10 o'clock

	Weight g	Weight gr		Die axis	
6665a	0.85	13.1	Cu	270°	*Wilson,* Thomas. nd. 4.12.1; W|TA. BW 352. Nott [ex Taffs]
6665b	0.79	12.1	Cu	270°	Same dies. [Nott ex Carthew]
6666	0.64	9.8	Br	0°	*Yeo,* Philip (PHILLIP). nd. 3.58.1; Y|PI. BW 353 but PHILLIP. Nott [ex Taffs]

Named signs

6667	5.58	86.1	Br	0°	*Black Friar mum house* (AT Y^{E}BLACKE FRYER *mum hous*): Sutton, Tho—. 1671 (– –7I) 1d. 3.1.13; 5.77. *BW 349 (I67I) but THO:SVTTON, *mum hous*, rev. BLACKE, I^{D}. Seaby, [*SCMB* April 1967]. Reading partially completed from MoL specimen (Lillywhite 1972, pl. 14.7). Mum was a kind of beer originally brewed in Brunswick

BLACKHORSE ALLEY *see* BLACK HORSE ALLEY (above)

BLOW BLADDER STREET *subsequently* NEWGATE STREET (part) (Aldersgate ward & Farringdon ward Within) [25-G9]

The reading is BLOWBLADER ST^{R}

6668	0.96	14.7	Br	0°	*Joyce,* Rich—. nd. 4.2.1; I|RD. BW 368 but RICH:, ST^{R}. Nott [ex Carthew]. Reading confirmed from BM specimen

BORES HEAD COURT (Farringdon ward Without, Cow Lane) (*lost*) [13-E6, d95]

The reading is BOARS HEAD COVRT COW LANE END

6669	2.17	33.5	Cu	180°	*Tarat,* Thomas. nd ½d. 5.14 Bakers; 5.77. BW 775. Nott [ex Carthew]. Reading confirmed from BM specimen

BOSS ALLEY (Billingsgate ward) [*recte* LITTLE SOMER'S KEY]

The reading is AT LITLE SOMERS KEY, mistakenly placed under BOSS ALLEY because BW 2921 has been supposed to read 'BOS ALLE SOMERS KEY'; though we had noted with puzzlement that Boss Alley ran north out of Thames Street, east of St Mary (at) Hill (Harben 1918, p. 92), so 150 feet = 46 metres from Little Somer's Key [38-K15, n33]. In fact, BW 2921 appears to derive from Museum of London specimen NN19223, on which the same dies as BW 2920 are overstruck on a specimen of Robert Bustord in BOSTON (BW Lincs. 18), whence the letters BOS. Consequently BW London 2921 should be deleted

Named signs

6670	0.89 (chipped)	13.8	Br	0°	*Swan with Two Necks* (SWAN WITH 2 NECKS): ?M—. nd. 3.102.17; 5.76.141 (M). BW 2920 but LITLE. Baldwin. Location from BW 2921, see above

BOSS ALLEY (Billingsgate ward) (*lost*) [38-J16: not identified]/BOSS ALLEY *subsequently* TRIG WHARF (Queenhithe ward) [35-J9, m27 but erased]

The reading is BOSS ALLEY, cf. *Boss Alley* (Ogilby 1677, p. 35, m27)

Named signs

6671a	0.98	15.2	Br	180°	*Three Mariners* (AT THE 3 MARRINRS): ?R—, W—. 1653. 3.4.24; R|WC. BW 370. Nott [ex Taffs]. A of MARRINRS double-punched
6671b	0.79	12.2	Br	180°	Same dies. [Nott]

BOTOLPH LANE (Billingsgate ward) [38-J15]

The reading is BVTOLPH LANE

6672	2.49	38.5	Cu	180°	*Crane,* John. 1666 ½d. 5.77; C|IM. BW 372. Nott [ex Taffs]. Reading confirmed from MoL specimen. Foundations to be staked out 1669-73 (Mills 1962-7, i. 11)

BOW CHURCH *see* ST MARY LE BOW neighbourhood

BOW LANE (Cheap & Cordwainer wards) [26-H11]

The reading is BOW LANE on 6673-4, 6676, 6679-83, 6686; BOWE LANE on 6675, 6677-8, 6684-5, 6687-8

6673a	1.06	16.4	Br	180°	*Brailsford,* ?Peter (PRT). nd. 5.68.10; P B. BW 374. Nott [ex Taffs]. Letters PRT unexplained; perhaps 'Peter' or a diminutive such as 'Perote'
6673b	0.71	11.0	Br	180°	Same dies. [Nott ex Carthew]

[*continued overleaf*]

6665a 6666 6667 6668 6669 6670

6671a 6672 6673a 6674b 6675b 6676b

6677 6678 6679a 6680a 6681a 6682a

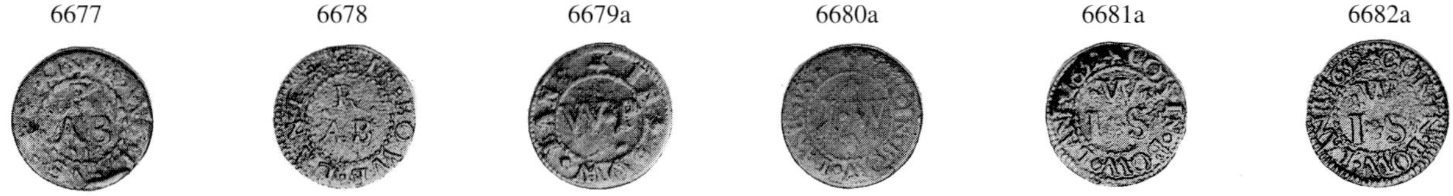

6683 6684b 6685 6686b 6687b 6688

Plate 11 (*cont.*)

	Weight *g*	*gr*		*Die axis*	
6674a	1.12	17.2	Br	270°	*Dix,* John, tallow-chandler. nd ½d. 3.3.13; 5.77 (D|IE). BW 378. [Nott ex Seaby]. The tallow-chandler appears to wear a flat hat as on 6931 (Fetter Lane neighbourhood: Ivye, John), and not the more usual conical cap. Foundation set out for John Dix(e) in [Half Moon] Court in Bow Lane 1669 (Mills 1962-7, i. 9, iv. 180v)
6674b	1.06	16.3	Br	270°	Same dies. Nott
6675a	0.79	12.2	Br	0°	*Hill,* Bartholomew. nd. 3.53.1; H|BM. BW 380. [Nott]. Diameter 15.5-16 mm
6675b	0.67	10.3	Br	180°	Same dies. Nott [ex Taffs]. Diameter 14.5-15 mm
6675c	0.58 (chipped)	8.9	Br	180°	Same dies. No provenance. Diameter 15.5-16 mm
6676a	1.10 (chipped)	17.0	Br	180°	*Michell,* John, apothecary. nd. 5.14.185; M|IC. BW 382. [?Baldwin]. John Michell of St Thomas Apostle, Apothecary, Master 1679; licensed to marry Sisly (Cicely) Orwin 1662 (Harl. 33 (1892), p. 53; Boyd 20164; Whittet 1983, p. 134). John Mitchell bound apprentices 1679-81 (Webb 1996-, xlii. 15, 36)
6676b	1.04	16.0	Br	180°	Same dies. Nott [ex Taffs]
6677	1.14	17.6	Br	180°	*Ragdale,* Andrew. nd. 3.3.13; R|AB. BW 384. Nott [ex Carthew]. Andrew Ragdale of St Thomas Apostle, Cutler, md. Barbara Dikes 1660 (Boyd 51084); bound apprentices 1680-1712 (Webb 1996-, xxxv. 144). Same obv. die as 6678
6678	0.88	13.5	Br	180°	*Ragdale,* Andrew. nd. 3.3.13; R|AB. BW 384. Nott [ex Taffs]. Same obv. die as 6677, q.v., flawed above initial mark
Named signs					
6679a	1.18	18.2	Br	180°	*Bell* (AT THE): ?P—, W—. nd. 5.70.1; W P. BW 383 but AT[no stop]THE. Nott [ex Carthew]
6679b	0.93	14.4	Br	180°	Same dies. [?Baldwin]
6680a	1.04	16.0	Br	180°	*Cock* (AT THE COK): Wolrich, John. 1650. 3.101.1; I W. BW 385. Nott. Same obv. die as 6681 (q.v.), 6682
6680b	0.98	15.1	Br	180°	Same dies. [?Baldwin]
6681a	0.99	15.3	Br	180°	*Cock* (AT THE COK): Wolrich, John. 1652. 3.101.1; W|IS. BW 386. Nott. John Woolrich of St Mary Aldermary, Cook, d. 1668; widow Sarah (Andrews) (Boyd 25546; Webb 1996-, xxvi. 71). Same obv. die as 6680, 6682
6681b	0.97	15.0	Br	180°	Same dies. [Nott]
6682a	1.08	16.7	Br	180°	*Cock* (AT THE COK): Wolrich, John. 1652. 3.101.1; W|IS. BW 386. Nott. Same obv. die as 6680, 6681 (q.v.), slightly flawed above initial mark
6682b	0.93	14.3	Br	180°	Same dies, obv. slightly flawed. [Nott ex Seaby]
6683	0.68	10.5	Br	90°	*Dark House* (AT Y^{E}DARK HOVS): Wormwell, John. nd. 3.107.2 (•IOHN•WORMWELL AT•Y^{E} around); W|IS (•W•|I•S; •DARK HOVS•IN•BOW•LANE around). BW —; Dickinson 387A. Nott. Rev. struck off-centre
6684a	0.89	13.8	M	180°	*Green Dragon* (AT THE GREENE DRAGON): ?K—, I/J—. nd. 3.114.1; K|IC. BW 381. [Nott ex Taffs]. ?James Kendall, chandler at Bow Lane; wife Christabel, children bap. 1647-58 (Boyd 50504)
6684b	0.77	11.9	M	180°	Same dies. Nott
6685	1.12	17.2	Br	180°	*Green [?Dragon]* (ẠṬ GṚEN): Hich. . . (HIC̣H. . .), Michael (MICHELL). nd. 3.114.1; H|MM. *BW 379 but HIC̣H. . .ẠṬ:. Nott [ex Spink]. The BW listing could well have been from this specimen
6686a	1.88	29.0	Cu	180°	*Horseshoe* (AT THE HORS SHOO): ?C—, D—, tallow-chandler (TOLOWCHAND:). nd. 3.3.13; C|DI. BW 375 but TOLOWCHAND:. Nott. The flaws on both dies indicate a later striking than 6686b. Diameter 18 mm; ?intended as a halfpenny
6686b	1.10	17.0	M	180°	Same dies. Baldwin. Diameter 16-16.5 mm
6687a	1.56	24.1	Cu	0°	*Mermaid tavern* (THE MERMAYD TAVERN): P[owell], J[ohn]. 1652. 3.10.17; P|IA. Burn 1855, 219; Boyne 1858, 308; BW 376 but •P•|I•A; Dickinson 382A. [Nott ex Taffs]. John Powell, Vintner; wife Ann(e); both bd. 1661 (Rogers 1928a, p. 65, 1928c, pp. 72-4; Boyd 25287); cf. Webb 1996-, xliii. 237, 377. Same rev. die as 6688
6687b	1.17	18.0	Br	180°	Same dies. Baldwin
6688	0.71	10.9	M	180°	*Mermaid tavern* (THE MERMAYD TAVERN): P[owell], J[ohn]. 1652. 3.10.17; P|IA. Burn 1855, 219; Boyne 1858, 308; BW 376 but •P•|I•A; Dickinson 382A. Nott [ex Carthew]. Same rev. die as 6687, q.v.

BREAD STREET (Bread Street ward) [25-H10]

See also STAR COURT. The reading is BREAD STREET on 6694-5, 6697-8; *Bread Street* on 6696; BREADSTREET on 6689, 6691, 7704; BREADSTREE^{T} on 6693; ḄREDSTRẸET on 6690; LOWER END OF BREDSTREET on 6692

	Weight g	Weight gr		Die axis	
6689a	1.66	25.6	Br	90°	*Barnes,* William, distil[l]er. nd. 5.64.77; B|WḤ. BW 395 but BREADSTREET, B|W[flowerknot]Ḥ. Nott [ex Carthew]. Reading largely confirmed from BM specimen. William Barnes of St Mildred Bread Street, wife Hester; children bap. 1669, 1673 (Boyd 30912; Webb 1996-, xi. 35)
6689b	1.20	18.5	Br	90°	Same dies. Nott [ex Taffs]
6690	0.50 (corroded)	7.8	Br	0°	*Cle. . .* (ÇḶẸ. . .), Joseph (IOṢẸP–). 1666. 0.6 (•IOṢẸP–•̣ÇḶẸ. . . around); Ç|ḶM (•Ç•|Ị• M|•; •IN•ḄREDSTRẸET•I666 around). BW —; Dickinson 396A, from reports of this specimen. Nott. Also read as THOMAS CH. . . (Norweb envelope), and LEO. . ., the first initial as L, and the design an Indian holding a bow (report to B. A. Seaby Ltd by Nott, assuming the die axis to be 180°)
6691	0.67 (chipped)	10.3	Br	0°	*Croft,* Richard. nd. 5.50.30; R C. BW 397 but BREADSTREET, obv. device probably a Frying-pan. Nott [ex Spink]. Richard Croft of All Hallows Bread Street, Draper, free 1654, fl. 1667 (Boyd 31593; 1934, p. 48). By 1624 most Drapers had no connection with the clothing industry (Johnson 1914-22, iii. 93)
6692a	2.67	41.2	Br	0°	*Jennens,* John. nd. 2.1; 5.14 Ironmongers. BW 400 but BREDSTREET. Nott [ex Taffs]. Struck off-centre. Apprentices bound to John Jennen(s), Ironmonger, 1655-6 (Webb 1996-, xxiv. 37, 52)
6692b	2.04	31.5	Br	0°	Same dies. [Nott]
6693a	1.13	17.5	Br	150°	*Noble,* Will, confectioner and grocer. 1668 ½d. 5.77; 5.14.1 Grocers (W N). BW 403 but BREADSTREE^{T}. Nott [ex Carthew]
6693b	1.03	15.9	Br	150°	Same dies. Nott [ex Taffs]
6694	0.77	11.9	M	180°	*Sallowes,* Benjamin. 1656. 5.64.104; S|BM. BW 405. Nott [ex Carthew]. Reading completed from MoL specimen
Named signs					
6695	0.50 (corroded)	7.7	Br	270°	*Mermaid tavern* (Y^{E}MERMAYD TAVERN): ?D—, T— (Ṭ). [16]57. 3.10.17; D|ṬM. *BW 398. Nott. Description largely completed from Rogers 1928c, facing p. 128, fig. 1. Also identified as 'William Barnes, W.395.A. Unpub:', whence Dickinson 395A, which should be deleted. ?Thomas Dodsworth of St Mildred Poultry, b. 1631, Vintner; md. Alice Michell as his 2nd wife 1661; will, PCC, 1662 (Rogers 1928a, p. 65, 1928c, p. 188; Boyd 19704). Thomas Dodsworth appr. 1643, bound apprentices 1656-62 (Webb 1996-, xliii. 88, 351)
6696a	5.62 (pierced)	86.7	Br	270°	*Ward's coffee-house:* Ward, [—]. 1671. 3.5.42; 5.77.1. BW 407 but *Soly*[Turk's head]*man*, no stops on rev. Nott [ex Taffs]. Reading confirmed from BM specimen. Sulayman II 'the Magnificent' ruled 1520-66. The 27 mm diameter suggests a penny denomination
6696b	5.11	78.8	Br	270°	Same dies. Nott [ex Carthew]. Diameter 27-27.5 mm
6697a	0.85	13.1	Br	180°	*White Hart tavern* (Y^{E}WHIT HART TAVERN): ?H—, R—. [16]57. 3.53.20; H|RE. BW 399. Nott [ex Taffs]. H of WHIT cancels ?H
6697b	0.68	10.5	Br	180°	Same dies. Nott [ex Carthew]
6698a	1.01	15.5	Br	180°	*White Horse* (AT THE WHITE HORES): ?R—, R—. 1649. 3.60.20; R|RE. BW 404. Nott
6698b	0.78	12.1	Br	180°	Same dies. [?Baldwin -1968]

BREAD STREET HILL (Queenhithe ward) [35-J10]

The reading is ON BREED STREETE HILL on 6699; BRẸẸD SṬṚ [HILL] on 6700

Named signs

6699	1.03	15.8	M	180°	*Star* (THE): ?B—, G—. 1649. 2.4.3; B|GM. BW 394. Nott [ex Carthew]

BREAD STREET HILL neighbourhood

The reading is [THEA]M[S STR NEARE] BRẸẸD SṬṚ [HILL]

6700	1.78 (chipped)	27.5	Cu	90°	*Goldson* (ĢỌḶḌSON), Robert (RỌḄERT). nd. 3.91.1 (•RỌḄERT•ĢỌḶḌSOṆ. . .M– around); G|RS (·G·|••|R• S|•••; . . .•BRẸẸD•SṬṚ. . . around). BW —; Dickinson 398A, from a report of this specimen, *3096A but BRẸẸD. Baldwin. Dickinson 3096A was recorded from a specimen of which the legends were reported by John Wetton as reading ROBERT GOLDSON IN THEAMS, rev. STR NEARE BREED (not BLEED) STR HILL

[*continued overleaf*]

PLATE 12

6689b 6690 6691 6692b 6693a 6694

6695 6696a 6697a 6698a 6699 6700

6701 6702b 6703a 6704 6705 6706

6707 6708a 6709a 6710 6711a 6712

Plate 12 (*cont.*)

BRIDE LANE (Farringdon ward Without) [33-I6]

See also GREEN'S RENTS. The reading is BRIDE LANE throughout

	Weight *g*	*gr*		*Die axis*	
6701	1.32	20.4	Cu	240°	*Adley,* William. 1663 ½d. 5.77; A|WI. BW 415. Nott [ex Baldwin]. Reading HIS|HALFE|IENY [*sic*] completed and elsewhere confirmed from BM specimen
Named signs					
6702a	0.89 (chipped)	13.7	Br	180°	*Three Colts* (AT THE 3 COLTES): ?C—, R—. 1652. 3.60.25; C|RE. BW 417. [Nott ex Seaby]
6702b	0.66	10.2	Br	180°	Same dies. Nott [ex Taffs]
6703a	0.88 (chipped)	13.6	Cu	90°	*White* [*?Bear*] (A^{T} Y^{E}WHIT): Hearne, Will—. nd. 3.49.8; H|WM. BW 418 but WILL:, A^{T}. Nott [ex Taffs]. Reading WILL: confirmed from BM specimen. Same obv. die as 6704, q.v.
6703b	0.82	12.6	Cu	0°	Same dies. [Nott]
6704	1.40	21.5	Cu	0°	*White* [*?Bear*] (A^{T} Y^{E}WHIT): Hearne, Will—. nd. 3.49.8; W H. BW 419 but WILL:, A^{T}. Nott. Initials appear to cancel other characters. Same obv. die as 6703. Clearer specimens might show the bear to be collared and chained, cf. 6705
6705	2.72	42.0	M	180°	*White Bear* (AT WHITE BEARE): Birtwissell, Daniel (DANIELL). 1666 ½d. 3.49.7; 5.77. BW 416. Deane

The BRIDEWELL (Farringdon ward Without) [33-I5]

The reading is BRIDEWEL LONDO^{N} on 6706; OVLD BRID WELL on 6707; cf. 6708-11

6706	3.31	51.0	Br	0°	*Bridewell hospital* (Y^{E} HOSPITALL OF BRIDEWEL). nd ½d. 5.14 London City 1; 5.14 London City 1. BW 428 but HALF•PENY, LONDO^{N}. Nott [ex Carthew]. Double-struck. Reading completed from BM and MoL specimens. For an overstruck specimen see vi. 5409. Bridewell Palace had been granted to the City in 1552 as a workhouse for the vagrant poor (Harben 1918, pp. 103-4, etc.)
Named signs					
6707	0.99	15.2	M	180°	*Pied Bull* (AT THE PYD BVLL): ?E—, M—. 1652. 3.52.1; E|MA. BW 425. Nott [ex Carthew]

BRIDEWELL DOCK neighbourhood *subsequently* NEW BRIDGE STREET (Farringdon ward Without) [33-J6]

See also FLEET DITCH. The reading is AT BRIDEWELL DOCKE on 6708; AT BRIDE\|WELL DOCK on 6709; AT BRID WELLDOCKE on 6710

6708a	1.21	18.6	M	0°	*Chapman,* Robert. nd. 5.42.6; C|RE. BW 424. Nott. 'Mr Robert Chapman, Woodmonger' 1664 (BW 424 n.)
6708b	1.10	17.0	M	0°	Same dies. [Nott]
6709a	2.10	32.4	Cu	270°	*Chapman,* Robert. nd ½d. 5.42.6; C|RE. BW 423; Dickinson 423A. Baldwin. See 6708
6709b	1.70 (chipped)	26.2	Cu	270°	Same dies. [Nott ex Taffs]
6710	0.88	13.5	M	180°	*Ray,* Giles (GILLS), woodmong[er]. nd. 5.42.7; R|GI. BW 426 but GILLS, WOODMONG:, WELLDOCKE. Nott

BRIDEWELL STAIRS [*i.e.* BLACKFRIARS STAIRS] (Farringdon ward Within, Blackfriars) [33-J6]

The reading is VPON BRIDWELL STERS, cf. *Bridewell Stayers on Blackfryers Side* 1672 (Mills 1962-7, v. 157, also 74v.). Therefore they were the same as Blackfriars Stairs

Named signs					
6711a	1.07	16.5	M	180°	*Sun tavern* (AT THE): ?C—, A—. nd. 2.1; C|AE. BW 422 but STERS. Nott [ex Seaby]. Rev. STERS read as STEPS by Akerman 1849 no. 302, Burn 1853 no. 194 etc., whence 'Bridewell Steps… Perhaps led to Bridewell Dock' in Harben 1918, p. 104. In the Bird collection (lot 287) ex Norweb the same rev. occurred with an earlier obv. die exhibiting narrow Ns as on rev., axis 180°
6711b	1.04	16.1	M	180°	Same dies. [Nott ex Taffs]

BROAD STREET *subsequently* OLD BROAD STREET (Broad Street ward) [27-G14]

The reading is BROAD STREETE on 6715-18, STREET on 6713-14; BROADSTREET on 6712, 6720-1; BROADSTREETE on 6719

6712	2.99	46.1	Br	180°	*Lumbard,* Hugh. 1667 ½d. 3.107.2; 5.77 (L|HI). BW 433 but BROADSTREET. Nott [ex Spink]. See also 7706

BROAD STREET (*cont.*)

	Weight *g*	*gr*		*Die axis*	
6713a	1.49 (pierced)	22.9	Br	270°	*Nethercoate,* Edward. 1669 ½d. 3.39.1 (•EDWARD•NETHERCOATE around); 5.77 (N|EE) (HIS|HALF|PENY|N|E.E; •IN•BROAD•STREET•1669 around). BW —; Dickinson 434B. [Nott]. ?Edward Nethercot of St Michael Cornhill, Currier; md. Elizabeth Twichell 1655 (Boyd 22469)
6713b	1.36	21.0	Br	180°	Same dies. Nott [or Baldwin]
6714	0.96	14.8	Cu	90°	*Slaney,* Stephen. nd. 5.64.22; S S. BW 435. Nott [ex Taffs]. Slane, Slaney, one of the few Irish toponymics

Named signs

6715a	1.22	18.9	M	150°	*White Horse* (AT THE WHITE HORSẸ): ?B—, E—. 1658. 3.60.5 (Ṛ); B|EA|date. *BW 429. Nott
6715b	0.94	14.5	Br	150°	Same dies. [Baldwin]
6716a	1.02	15.8	Br	180°	*White Horse* (AT THE): ?B—, E—. 1658. 3.60.5 (R); B|EA|date. BW 429. Baldwin. Same obv. die as 6717
6716b	0.60	9.2	Br	180°	Same dies. [?Baldwin]
6717	1.18	18.1	Br	180°	*White Horse* (AT THE): ?B—, E—. 1658. 3.60.5 (R); B|EA|date. BW 429. Nott [ex Seaby]. Same obv. die as 6716, the R above the horse and the date confirmed from Greenall 1997, lot 96
6718	0.78	12.0	Br	270°	*White Horse* (AT THE): ?B—, E—. 1670. 3.60.5 (R) (•AT•THE•WHITE•HORSE around); B|EA|date (•B•|E•A|I670; •IN•BROAD•STREETE around). BW —, cf. 6715-17; Dickinson 429A. Nott [or Baldwin]

BROAD STREET neighbourhood [18-E15]

The reading is AT BROADSTREET CORNER on 6720; AT LONDON WALL NEAR BROADSTREET on 6721; AT LONDO^{N} WALL NEARE BROADSTREETE on 6719

6719	1.75	27.0	Br	90°	*Griffin,* Charles. 1668 ½d. 3.64.1; 5.77. *BW 1767 but BROADSTREETE. Nott [ex Carthew]
6720	0.82	12.7	Cu	180°	*How,* John. nd. 5.16.1; H|IM. BW 432 but BROADSTREET. Nott [ex Taffs]. John How apprenticed an armourer 1642 (Webb 1996-, xxii. 30); John How of All Hallows London Wall, Armourer, md. Margery Alkinton as 3rd wife 1662; will, PCC, 1667 (Boyd 20111)
6721	1.07	16.5	Br	180°	*Ithell,* George. nd ½d. 5.14 Blacksmiths; 5.77. BW 1768. Nott [ex Carthew]

BROKEN WHARF (Queenhithe ward, Thames Street) [35-J9]

The reading is AT BROKEN WHARF on 6724, WHARFE on 6725, WHORFE on 6723; AT BROCKEN WHARFE on 6722

6722a	2.20	33.9	Br	0°	*Andrus,* Hugh. 1667 ½d. 5.43.30; 5.77. BW 436. Nott [ex Taffs]
6722b	1.86	28.8	Br	0°	Same dies. [Nott]
6723	0.84	13.0	Br	0°	*Austin,* Robert (ROB^{T}), woodm[onger]. nd. 4.4.10; 4.2.11. BW 437 but ROB^{T}, Lion issuing from grove of trees. Nott. Reading confirmed from Greenall 1997, pl. 3.95. Evidence of die-clashing on obv. Robert Austin of St Mary Somerset, Woodmonger, d. 1661 (Boyd 55793)
6724a	1.44	22.2	M	180°	*North,* Will[iam] and *North,* Elizabeth. nd. 5.37.13; N|WE. BW 439. Nott [ex Taffs]. William North of St Mary Somerset, Merchant Taylor, Cordwainer; md. Elizabeth Cheyney 1625, she d. 1659 (Boyd 52265)
6724b	1.09	16.8	M	180°	Same dies. [Nott ex Carthew]

Named signs

6725	0.96	14.8	Br	90°	*White Lion* (AT THẸ W̤ḤỊṬ LYON): ?P—, R—. nd. 3.11 (•AT•THẸ•W̤ḤỊṬ•LYON around); R P (R•P; •AT•BROKEN•WHARFE around). BW —; Dickinson 439A, from Heal 1928, p. 7. Baldwin. Obv. legend starts at 2 o'clock. Flaw or damage to die at top of initial R, hence the TR monogram reading in Heal and Dickinson

BROWN'S ALLEY *subsequently* ?BROWN'S COURT (Aldgate ward, Billiter Lane) [29-H17: not identified]

The reading is BROVNS ALLY IN BILLETER LANE

6726	0.95	14.6	Br	180°	*?L—,* W—. 1648. 3.56.1; L|WK. BW 210. Nott [ex Carthew]. Reading completed from BM specimen

BUCKLERSBURY (Walbrook & Cheap wards) [26-H12]

The reading is BVCKLERS BVRY

Named signs

6727a	0.76 (chipped)	11.7	Br	180°	*Flower-de-luce* (AT Y^{E}FLOWERDELVCE): ?R—, S—. [16]57. 4.13.7 (S R); 5.14 Drapers. BW 440 but FLOWERDELVCE, BVCKLERS•BVRY. [Baldwin -1968]
6727b	0.67	10.3	Br	0°	Same dies. Nott

[*continued overleaf*]

6713b 6714 6715a 6716a 6717 6718

6719 6720 6721 6722a 6723 6724a

6725 6726 6727b 6728a 6729 6730a

6731 6732b 6733a 6734b 6735 6736

Plate 13 (*cont.*)

BULL HEAD YARD (Cheap ward, Cheapside) [26-H11, i52: not identified]

The reading is BVLL HEAD YARD CHEPSIDE. The relationship of *Bullhead Yard* to Cheapside is shown in Mills 1962-7, iv. 124, and to Trump Alley, iv. 182

	Weight *g*	*gr*		*Die axis*	
6728a	3.06	47.2	Cu	270°	*Clifton,* Joseph. 1663 ½d. 5.77; I C|date. BW 576. Nott [ex Taffs]. Diameter 19-20 mm
6728b	2.02	31.1	Cu	0°	Same dies. Nott. Diameter 18.5-19 mm

BUTCHER ROW *see* Middlesex I: Westminster

CANNON STREET *previously* CANDLEWICK STREET (Walbrook ward) [37-I13]

See also LONDON STONE neighbourhood. The reading is CANNON STREETE on 6729, 6731, 6733, STREET on 6730, STRET on 6732

6729	0.84	12.9	M	180°	*Bagne,* Nathaniel (NATHANIELL). nd. 3.61.1; B|NS. BW 459. Nott [ex Carthew]. Reading confirmed from BM specimen
6730a	3.99	61.6	Br	180°	*Blunt,* Anne. 1672 1d. 3.5.40; 5.77. BW 460 but I^{D}. Nott. Diameter 22-24 mm
6730b	3.59	55.3	Br	180°	Same dies. Nott [ex Carthew]. Diameter 24 mm
6730c	2.44	37.7	Br	180°	Same dies. Nott [ex Taffs]. Diameter 25-26 mm
6731	0.79 (chipped)	12.2	Br	270°	*Heath,* Francis. nd. 3.1.21; H|FI. BW 464. Nott. Reading confirmed from MoL specimen. Appr. Haberdasher 1616; md. Jane Roby 1621; Distiller 1664 (Woodhead 1966, p. 87). Foundations to be set out for Francis Heath (below London Stone), 1668 (Mills 1962-7, i. 20(2)). The obv. description 'Hercules… near a beacon' goes back to Franks 1862, no. 27, but is unsupported
Named signs					
6732a	7.84	120.9	Br	0°	*Golden Key* (AT Y^{E} GOVLDEN KEY): Colcock, Tho—, grocer. nd 1d. 5.14 Grocers; 5.66.3. BW 462 but THO:. Baldwin -1968. Diameter 26-26.5 mm. Although the I of the denomination appears to be arabic 1 the character is probably from a broken punch
6732b	2.57	39.6	Br	0°	Same dies. Nott [ex Carthew]. Diameter 24 mm
6733a	0.89	13.7	Br	90°	*White Hart* (AT Y^{E}): S[pence], B[rian]. nd. 3.53.6; S|BI. BW 465. [Nott]. Double-struck. Diameter 17-17.5 mm. Bryan(t) Spence, bd. 1670, wife Isabel; from the same house as BW 7, AT THE WHIT HART IN ABCHVRCH LANE (Rogers 1928a, pp. 62, 66). Foundation to be staked out 1668 (Mills 1962-7, i. 20)
6733b	0.71	10.9	Br	270°	Same dies. Nott. Diameter 16-16.5 mm
6733c	0.55 (chipped, pierced)	8.5	Br	270°	Same dies. Nott [ex Taffs]. Diameter 16 mm

CAREY LANE (Aldersgate ward & Farringdon ward Within) [25-G9]

The reading is CAREY LANE

6734a	1.08	16.6	Br	0°	*Jackson,* John. nd. 5.14 Drapers; I|IM. BW 470. Nott. ?John Jackson of St Mary Aldermanbury, Cook, translated from Drapers, d. 1664 (Boyd 10901)
6734b	1.02	15.8	Br	270°	Same dies. Nott [ex Taffs]

CARPENTERS' HALL neighbourhood (Broad Street ward, London Wall) [17-E13, A69, identified from Rocque 1747, sheet 1E8 = page 5Bc]

The reading is BY LONDON WAL NEARE CARPENTERS HALL

6735	2.84	43.8	Br	0°	*Tucker,* Rich—. 1666 ½d. (HAḶF̣E PEṆṆY). 5.60.4 (•2^{D}|C R|[crown]•R•T•) (•RICH:TVCKER•BY•LONDON•WAL around); 5.77 (HIS|HAḶF̣E|PEṆṆY|1666; •NEARE•CARPENTERS•HALL around). BW —; cf. BW 1773 (RIC, WALL, crown alone, NEAR, PENY, undated), which is largely confirmed from BM specimen. Nott [ex Carthew]. Obv. •2^{D} is partly between C and R, and presumably means (King Charles) the Second

CARTER LANE (Castle Baynard ward) [34-I7]

Prosser, William *see* Uncertain I

Named signs

Soap Box: Bartholomew, Isaac *see* Uncertain I

CARTER LANE neighbourhood [34-I7]

The reading is AT CARTER LANE END NEAR CREED LANE

	Weight			Die	
	g	*gr*		*axis*	
6736	3.27	50.5	Br	180°	*Outridge,* Tho—. nd 1d. 5.3.75; 3.5.42. BW 476 but THO:, I^{D}. Baldwin [ex Gilbert]. Obv. legend starts at 3 o'clock

Sharpe, Robert *see* Uncertain I

Named signs

Dolphin: ?B—, I/J— *see* Uncertain I

CASTLE LANE *subsequently* ST ANDREW'S WHARF (Castle Baynard ward) [34-J7, m11]

Blake, Thomas *see* Uncertain I

CASTLE YARD *subsequently* FURNIVAL STREET (Farringdon ward Without) [22-G3]

The reading is CASTLE YARD throughout (CAṬLE on 6738), with NEAR HOLBOR^{N} on 6737, NEARE HOLBORN on 6739, NEER HOLBOR^{N} on 6742

	Weight *g*	*gr*		*Die axis*	
6737	1.49	23.0	Br	330°	*Bold,* Elizabeth. 1666 ½d. 3.5.38 (E B); 5.77. BW 1374. Nott [ex Spink]
6738	0.85	13.1	Cu	0°	*Cropper* (CROP̣PER), Arthur. 1657. 5.51.26 (•ARTHVR•CROP̣PER;IN around); C|AS (.C.|AS; •CASṬLE;YARD:I657 around). BW —; *Dickinson, Southwark 202B. Nott
6739	1.38	21.2	Br	270°	*Lambe* (ḶAMBE), John, confectioner. 1667 ½d. (HAḶFE PEṆNY). 3.55.4; 5.77 (L|IṂ). *BW 1430 but lamb statant. Nott. Also read as 'John Eambe, not in Williamson'
6740	1.47	22.6	Br	270°	*Pickfat,* George, tallow-chandler. 1666 ½d. 5.7.25; P̣|GE|date. *BW Southwark 206. Spink. Reading largely completed from BM specimen. 'Pickfatt' occurs 1649 as an alias of 'Pickford' (Reaney 1995, p. 350)
6741	1.88	29.0	Br	180°	*Walker,* John. nd ½d. 3.65.1; W|IE. BW Southwark 207 but PENNY. Spink

Named signs

6742	1.21	18.7	Br	90°	*Blue* [*?Anchor*] (AT BLEW): Cox, John. 1666 ½d. 5.38.22 (C|I M) (•IOHN•COX•AT•BLEW•I666 around); 5.77 (HIS|HALF|PENY|•:•:•; •IN•CASTLE• YARD• NEER•HOLBOR^{N} around). BW —; Dickinson 1392A. Baldwin

CATEATON STREET *subsequently* GRESHAM STREET (Cheap & Coleman Street wards & Cripplegate ward Within) [26-G11]

See also ST LAWRENCE JEWRY. The reading is CATEATEN STREET on 6747, STREETE on 6745; CATEATO^{N} STRET on 6744; CATTEATEN STRET on 6743, CATTEATE^{N} STRET on 6746

6743	1.04	16.0	Cu	180°	*Betton,* Thomas. nd. 3.41.1; T B. BW 482 but IN:CATTEATEN, lions passant guardant. Baldwin [ex Pridmore]. Reading completed from MoL specimen
6744	0.91	14.0	Br	90°	*Hatton,* Partridge (PARTRIDG). nd. 3.58.1; H|PI. BW 484 but HATTO^{N}, CATEATO^{N}. Nott [ex Taffs]. Reading confirmed from BM specimens
6745	1.82	28.0	Cu	0°	*Lacy,* Tho—. nd ½d. (2 below line). 3.5.24 (ROXCEL: LANA around); L|TM. BW 485 but THO:, the 1 of fraction absent, ROXCEL:. Nott [ex Seaby]. Form of denomination confirmed from BM and MoL specimens. Roxalana was a character in *The Siege of Rhodes* 1656-9, the first English opera (Pepys 1970-83, ii. 130, x. 86); Hester Davenport (1642-1717) was known as Roxalana from her most famous role (ODNB)
6746	1.36	21.0	Cu	0°	*Ward,* Thomas. nd. 3.5.96 (•THOMAS•WARD• around); W|TB (.W.|TB; •IN:CATTEATE^{N}STRET around). BW —; Dickinson 488A. Nott [ex Taffs]
6747a	1.75	26.9	Cu	90°	*Ware,* Roger. 1664 ½d. 5.14.5; 5.77. BW 489 but PENY. Nott. ?The King's Arms tavern, as for BW 487 issued by James Ware (Rogers 1928a, p. 67). Roger Ware appr. to James Ware, Vintner, 1650 (Webb 1996-, xliii. 309, see also 390); of St Lawrence Jewry; children bap. 1669-70 (Boyd 26597)
6747b	1.27 (chipped)	19.5	Cu	90°	Same dies. Nott [ex Taffs]

CHANCERY LANE (Farringdon ward Without *and* Middlesex: Holborn *and* Westminster) *see* Middlesex I: Holborn

CHANCERY LANE neighbourhood (Farringdon ward Without, Fleet Street) [32-I3]

The reading is AT CHANCERY LANE END on 6748-9; CHANCEREY LANE END IN FLEET STREET on 6751; FLEETE STREETE on 6750

6748	1.06	16.3	Cu	0°	*Taft,* Humphrey, cutler. 1665. 5.42.22; 5.77. BW 524; Webb 1996-, xxxv. ?42, 49, 78, 109. Nott

Named signs

6749a	1.74	26.8	Cu	0°	*King's Head tavern* (THE): K[ent], T[homas]. nd. 3.5.79; K|TA. BW 510. Nott [ex Taffs]. Obv. flaw more developed than on 6749b and c. Thomas Kent, Vintner, at the King's Head c.1630 to 1660 (Rogers 1928a, p. 68, 1928c, pp. 151-2). A Thomas Kent bound an apprentice 1649 (Webb 1996-, xliii. 262). See also 6750-1
6749b	0.94	14.5	M	180°	Same dies; obv. flawed at HE of HEAD. [Baldwin -1968]
6749c	0.88	13.6	M	180°	Same dies, obv. flawed as 6749b. [?Baldwin]

[*continued overleaf*]

6737 6738 6739 6740 6741 6742

6743 6744 6745 6746 6747a 6748

6749a 6750 6751a 6752 6753 6754

6755 6756 6757 6758 6759 6760a

Plate 14 (*cont.*)

	Weight			Die	
	g	*gr*		*axis*	
6750	1.11	17.1	M	0°	*King's Head [tavern]* (AT THE): W[illson], L[ewis and] M[orris], H[enry]. nd. 3.5.79; L W|H M. BW 1102. Nott [ex Carthew]. In St Dunstan in the West parish lists of 1660 and 1661 Lewis Willson and Henry Morris replaced Thomas Kent (see 6749), whence names and placing to Chancery Lane; Willson alone occurs 1661-2 (Rogers 1928a, pp. 77-8, 1928c, p. 152). Lewis Wilson appr. Vintner 1651, Henry Morris appr. Vintner 1653 (Webb 1996-, xliii. 207, 324, see also 392). For successor William Mart see 6751. For Willson see also 6969 and Middlesex I: Westminster: The Strand
6751a	2.31	35.6	Br	0°	[*King's Head tavern*]: Mart, William. nd ½d. 5.77; 3.5.60 (M|WK). BW 514; Dickinson also 1087A. Nott [ex Carthew]. Issued 1666 or later at the King's Head Tavern (Rogers 1928a, p. 78); see also 6749-50. William Mart appr. Vintner 1650 (Webb 1996-, xliii. 196, see also 370); at the King's Head, Chancery Lane end 1666-82 (Rogers 1928c, p. 152; Woodhead 1966, p. 112). See also 6956
6751b	1.55	23.8	Br	0°	Same dies. [Baldwin]

CHEAPSIDE (Cordwainer & Cheap wards & Cripplegate & Farringdon wards Within & Bread Street ward) [25-H10]

See also BULL HEAD YARD; GREAT CONDUIT neighbourhood; LITTLE CHEAPSIDE; OLD CHANGE; ST MARY LE BOW neighbourhood; TRUMP ALLEY. The reading is CHEAPSIDE on 6752-3, 6764-5, 6768, 7028, 7612, C̣HẸAPSIDE on 6755, CHEAP̣SIDE on 7027; CHEAP\|SIDE on 6759, 6761, 6767; CHEAP SIDE on 6756, 6758, 6760, 7779; CHEAPSIDE MARKETT on 6763; CHEAPESIDE on 6754; CHEAPE SIDE on 6757, 6762, 7441; CHEAPS^{D} on 6769; CHEAPSID on 6770; C̣HEAPSYDE on 6766; CHEPSIDE on 6728

6752	1.15	17.8	Cu	0°	*Browne,* Fabian. nd. 5.5.4; B|FA. BW 574. Nott [ex Taffs]. Fabian Brown of St Matthew Friday Street; md. Anne Dansbury 1647 (Boyd 32123). The Wheatesheafe in Westcheap was leased 1651 to Fabian Browne (Fire Court 1966-, i. 105, Rogers 1928a, p. 69), but *pace* Rogers the device here is a castle. Foundation set out for Mr Fabian Browne in Cheapside at Friday Street end 1667 (Mills 1962-7, i. 27, ii. 49)
6753	4.30	66.4	Br	90°	*Clerke,* Allanson. 1672 1d. 3.63.5 (•ALLANSON•CLERKE• around); 5.77 (•D|•I•|I672; •IN•CHEAPSIDE•[flaw] around). BW 571 but description revised. Baldwin. Allanson Clarke of St Matthew Friday Street and St Vedast Foster Lane, Girdler, d. 1679 (Boyd 32150). The 'cat' (BW 571), also described as a hog, appears to be a rat
6754	0.69	10.6	Br	180°	*Hiller,* Richard. nd. 2.1.5 (•RICHARD:HILLER around); R H (•••|RH|•••; •IN:CHEAPESIDE• around). BW —; Dickinson 583A. Baldwin. Tinned. Richard Hiller of St Mary le Bow, Draper, free 1632, Warden 1668, 1677; bodice-maker at the Falcon, Cheapside, 1633; or rather [explaining the Sun below the Falcon?] his son Richard, apprenticed Draper 1658 (Boyd 26760, cf. 17397)
6755	0.68	10.5	Br	180°	*Mudd* (ṂVDḌ), Thomas (ṬḤ. . .Ṣ), grocer. nd. 5.68.10 (•ṬḤ. . .Ṣ•ṂVDḌ•ỊN around); T M (•••|TM|•••; •C̣HẸAPSIDE•GROCER around). BW —; *Dickinson 593A (THOMAS) but ṂVDḌ. [? ex Schwer ex Sotheby 24 Jan. 1979, lot 149 ex ? ex Baldwin ex Faulkner, lot 154]
6756	0.83	12.8	Cu	0°	*Peirce,* George. 1665. 3.52.25; P|GM. BW 594. Nott [ex Carthew]. No evidence for Peirce as taverner at the Bull Head tavern, cf. 6760 (Rogers 1931, p. 79). ?George Peirce, Vintner, fl. 1670; wife Mary (Boyd 25918, unlocated). George Pearce appr. 1653 (Webb 1996-, xliii. 227, see also 375)
					Ringstead, Fran[cis] *see* 6770
6757	0.67	10.4	Br	180°	*Woodfall,* Mary. nd. 3.60.30; M W. BW 602. Baldwin [or Nott ex Carthew]. Mary Woodfall, widowed 1657, absent from the hearth tax list of 1662 (Berry 1978, p. 50)
Named signs					
6758	0.90	13.8	Br	180°	*Black* [*?Bell*] (–^{E}ḄLA^{K}): Wheatley (WHEATḶẸY), Sam—. 1660. 5.70.1 (•SAM:WHEATḶẸY•–^{E}ḄLA^{K} around); W (•••|S W|•••; •IN•CHEAP•SIDE•I660 around). BW —; Dickinson 601A, from a report of this specimen. Baldwin. Also read as Y^{E}SELA^{R} = Wheatsheaf
6759	1.05	16.3	Cu	0°	*Blue Boar* (AT THE BLEW BOAR): Wallis, Ezekiel (EZEKIELL). nd. 5.77; 3.65.1. BW 601. Nott. Ezekiel Wallis of St Peter Westcheap, Mercer; silkman 1662; will, PCC, 1667, St Botolph Aldersgate (Rogers 1931, p. 16; Boyd 25481)
6760a	0.90 (chipped)	13.9	M	90°	*Bull's Head tavern* (THE BVLL HEAD TAVERNE): B[enson], T[homas]. 1650. 3.52.25; B|TE. BW 573. Baldwin -1968 [ex Pridmore] [or Nott ex Taffs]. Thomas Benson of All Hallows Honey Lane, Vintner, Master 1671, 'Bull head in Cheape' 1641-62 (Boyd 15041; Woodhead 1966, p. 29). Cf. Webb 1996-, xliii. 26, 339
6760b	0.87	13.4	M	180°	Same dies. [Nott ex Carthew]

Named signs (*cont.*)

	Weight g	*Weight* gr		*Die axis*	
6761	4.13	63.7	Br	90°	[*Cheapside*] *coffee-house* (AT THE COFFEE HOVSE): Kiftell, Charles. 1669. 3.6.51; 5.77. BW 586; Rogers 1931, pp. 23-4. Baldwin -1968. Reading confirmed from Baldwin's Auction 38, lot 788 (illus.). Coffee-house named as in Lillywhite 1972, no. 4583; the presence of THE precludes 'Kiftell's Coffee-house' (Lillywhite 1972, no. 670). The 24 mm diameter suggests a penny
6762	1.04	16.0	Br	180°	*Feathers tavern* (THE FEATERS TAVERN): C[oates], T[homas]. 1650. 3.107.5; C|TE. BW 575. Nott [ex Carthew]. Reading completed from BM specimen. Thomas Coates appr. 1636 (Webb 1996-, xliii. 65, see also 347). Col. Thomas Coates of St Pancras Soper Lane, Vintner; wife Elizabeth died 1653 (Boyd 14859; Rogers 1928a, p. 69, 1931, pp. 59-61; Mills 1962-7, v. 44v; Berry 1978, pp. 46-7)
6763	5.25	81.0	Br	270°	*George* (AT THE GEORG): Jarvis, Edward. nd. 3.2.12; 5.76.142. BW 585 but monogram of complete name. Nott [ex Taffs]. ?Same issuer as 6988. The 27 mm diameter suggests a penny
6764	1.29	19.9	Br	90°	*Hen & Chickens* (AT Y^{E}HEN & CHICKINS): Mostyn, Will[iam]. nd ½d. 3.101.21; 5.77 (M|WE). BW 593 but WILL:, HEN•&. Nott [ex Carthew]. William Mostyn, appr. Vintner 1663 (Webb 1996-, xliii. 208); wife Elizabeth (Rogers 1931, p. 38; Boyd 25881)
6765	0.98	15.2	Br	180°	*Man in the Moon tavern* (THE): T[urner], S[amuel]. nd. 3.1.75; T|SS. BW 599. Nott. Reading confirmed from BM specimen. Samuel Turner, Vintner, fl. 1641-60 (Rogers 1928a, p. 71, 1928c, pp. 189, 191). Cf. Webb 1996-, xliii. 388
6766	1.21	18.7	M	180°	*Mermaid tavern* (THE MEARMAD TAVERN): ?M—, R—. 1651. 3.10.17; M|RM. *BW 591. Nott [ex Carthew]. ?Richard Marsh of St Vedast, Vintner; son bap. 1650 (Rogers 1928a, pp. 65-6, 70; Boyd 52234); bound an apprentice 1650 (Webb 1996-, xliii. 50)
6767	1.02	15.7	Br	180°	*Mitre* (AT THE MITR): D[udley], T[homas]. nd, 'forget not'. 5.59.20; T D. BW 579. Baldwin -1968. Thomas Dudley of St Mary Colechurch and St Mary Magdalene Fish Street, Vintner, kept the Mitre 1648-50 (Rogers 1928a, p. 69, 1928c, pp. 86-93; Boyd 9344). Cf. Webb 1996-, xliii. 352
6768a	2.40	37.0	Br	90°	*Raven* (AT Y^{E}): Royle, Richard. nd. 3.108.4; R R. BW 596 but INCHEAPSIDE. Baldwin ex ? 1922
6768b	1.27 (chipped)	19.5	Br	90°	Same dies. Nott
6769	0.47	7.3	Br	270°	*Star* (AT Y^{E}): Clark, Anthony, cook (COOḲ). nd. 2.4.12 (ANTHONY•CLARK•AT•Y^{E} around); C|AA (•C•|AA; STAR•IN•CHEAPS^{D}COOḲ around). BW —; Dickinson 575A. Nott. Ḳ of COOḲ faint, joined to S of STAR. Anthony Clark fl. 1658, md. Anne Cole at St Vedast 1657 (Boyd 51799). See also Middlesex I: Westminster: Drury Lane
6770	0.62	9.6	Br	270°	[*Star*] *tavern* (AT [star] TAVERNE): Ringstead, Fran[cis] (F̣RAN:). nd. 2.4.2 (•F̣RAN:RINGSTEAD•AT around); F R (•|F•R|•; •TAVERNE•IN•CHEAPSID around). BW —; *Dickinson 595A. Baldwin [ex Macfadyen, lot 150]. Francis Ringstead appr. Vintner 1647 (Webb 1996-, xliii. 249, see also 379), at the Star tavern, 1660 (Pepys 1970-83, i. 52, 307, x. 426), in Hearth Tax list 1668 (Rogers 1931, p. 20)

CHICK LANE *subsequently* CHARTERHOUSE STREET (Farringdon ward Without) [13-E6]

The reading is CHICK LANE on 6772-5, 6777-9, 6781-2; CHICKE LANE on 6771, 6780; CHEK LANE on 6776

6771	1.41	21.8	Br	270°	*Cowly,* Thomas. 1666. 2.1 (•THOMAS•COWLY•I666 around); 5.76.143 (•••|[covered cup]TCM or TMC monogram[covered cup]|•••; •IN•CHICKE•LANE•• around). BW —; Dickinson 607A. Baldwin -1968
6772	2.29	35.3	Br	90°	*Cowly,* Thomas. 1666 ½d. 2.1; 5.76.143 (TCM or TMC). BW 607 but a covered cup either side of monogram. Nott
6773	0.56	8.7	Br	0°	*Crouch,* Will—, mealman. 1663. 5.14 Weavers (•WILL:CROVCH•MEALMAN around); C|WM (.C.|WM; •IN•CHICK•LANE•I663• around). BW —; Dickinson 607B. Nott [ex Taffs]
6774	2.27	35.0	Cu	90°	*English,* Peter. 1668 ½d. 3.115.3; 3.5.27. BW 608 but •HIS•HALF•PENY• around double crescent framing face in profile. Nott [ex Taffs]. The rev. device probably represents the Man in the Moon
6775	1.15	17.8	Br	270°	*Fishwick,* John. nd. 5.51.23 (•IOHN•FISHWICK around); F|IF (•F•|I'F|•; •IN•CHICK•LANE around). BW —; Dickinson 608A but 'boat' (Sharman 1984, p. 22) probably a mount or base. Baldwin [ex Macfadyen, lot 150]
6776	1.03	15.8	Br	180°	*Hallet,* Richard. 1659. 3.45.9; H|RA. BW 611 but no wings to make this the lion of St Mark. Nott. Reading confirmed from BM specimen

[*continued overleaf*]

6761 6762 6763 6764 6765 6766

6767 6768a 6769 6770 6771 6772

6773 6774 6775 6776 6777a 6778b

6779 6780 6781 6782 6783 6784

Plate 15 (*cont.*)

	Weight g	*gr*		*Die axis*	
6777a	2.45	37.8	Br	180°	*Knight,* Henry, brewer. 1669 ½d. 5.64.72; 5.77 (K|HE). BW 613; Woodhead 1966, p. 103. Nott [ex Taffs]. Henry Knight, Innholder, fl. 1641, Smithfield precinct (Boyd 58205); Henry Knight, Brewer, Alderman 1667 (Boyd 28211, unlocated)
6777b	1.18	18.2	Br	180°	Same dies. Nott
6778a	0.79	12.2	Br	180°	*Mason,* John. nd. I M; 3.1.122. BW 615 but person beside still. Nott [ex Carthew]. Diameter 17-17.5 mm. Broken in two
6778b	0.49	7.6	Br	0°	Same dies. Nott [ex Taffs]. Diameter 16 mm
6779	1.78	27.5	Br	0°	*Rawllinson,* Richard. 1667 ½d. 5.14 Bakers; 5.77. BW 616 but RAWLLINSON. Nott
6780	2.20	34.0	Cu	270°	*West,* Robert. 1667 ½d. 3.5.96; 5.77 (W|RA). BW 619. Nott [ex Carthew]. Reading confirmed from BM specimen

CHICK LANE neighbourhood

The reading is AT CHICK LANE END on both

6781	1.86	28.7	Br	180°	*Kettle,* Henry, brewer. 1671 ½d. 5.76.144 (HK) (HK|I67I; •HENRY•KETTLE•BREWER around); 5.76.144 (HK) (HK|½; •AT•CHICK•LANE•END around). BW —; Dickinson 612A. Stevens. Henry Kettle, Brewer, bd. St Sepulchre 1671 (Boyd 28683)

Named signs

6782	2.35	36.3	Br	0°	*Hoop & Three Tuns* (AT Y^{E}HOOP AND 3 TVNS): Shaw, Rich—. nd ½d. 1.41.4 (•RICH:SHAW•AT•Y^{E}HOOP•AND•3 around); 5.77 (R S) (•••|R½S|•••; •TVNS•AT•CHICK•LANE•END around). BW —; Dickinson 617A. Baldwin

CHRIST'S HOSPITAL *subsequently* GENERAL POST OFFICE/KING EDWARD BUILDING (Farringdon ward Within, Newgate Street). Matron's Cellar [24-F8]

The site of the Grey Friars monastery was granted to the City 1547, and furnished for the maintenance of poor fatherless children (Harben 1918, p. 141). The reading is AT THE MATRONS SELLER IN THE HOSPITALL

6783	0.71	11.0	Br	270°	*Bannister,* John. nd. 3.1.27; 5.77. BW 633. Nott [ex Spink]. Reading completed from BM specimen

CHURCH LANE (Dowgate ward, Thames Street) [36-K12: Allhollows Lane]/CHURCH LANE (Farringdon ward Within, Carter Lane) [34-I7, k67]/CHURCH LANE (Farringdon ward Without, Snow Hill) (*lost*) [24-F7, f35]/CHURCH LANE (Portsoken ward, Aldgate High Street) [29-F18, g16]/CHURCH LANE (Vintry ward, Thames Street) [36-J11, m54] *see* Uncertain I

CLOAK LANE (Vintry & Dowgate & Walbrook wards) [36-I12]

The reading is CLOAK LANE on 6784; CLOAKE LANE on 6785; Harben 1918, p. 153, found the first mention in Ogilby, and thought it was probably named after the Fire

Named signs

6784	0.74	11.5	M	180°	*Willow Tree* (AT THE): ?B—, N—. nd. 4.1.1; B|NI. BW 670. Nott. Obv. die subsequently used on 7444 (Old Change)

CLOAK LANE (*cont.*)

Named signs (*cont.*)

	Weight g	Weight gr		Die axis	
6785	1.10	17.0	M	180°	*Willow Tree* (AT THE): ?B—, I/J—. nd. 4.1.1; B|IP. BW 671. Nott [ex Baldwin]. The presence of stops between each word both sides confirmed from BM specimen

CLOTH FAIR (Farringdon ward Without) [14-E7]

The reading is CLOATH FAIRE on 6787-9, 6791-3, FAIR on 6786; CLOVTH FAIR on 6790

6786	1.04	16.0	Br	0°	*Ashbourn,* Christo—, chandler. nd ½d. 2.1; 5.77. BW 672. Nott
6787	1.23	18.9	M	180°	*Chandler,* William. nd. 3.6.60; C|WS. BW 674. Nott. William Chandler of St Bartholomew the Great, Baker, fl. 1641; wife Susan; will, PCC, 1658 (Boyd 27787)
6788	1.81	27.9	Br	180°	*Fawson,* William. 1667 ½d. 5.77; W F. BW 678 but I667. Nott
6789	1.13	17.4	M	180°	*Temple,* Michael (MIKHILL). nd. 3.107.5; T|MA. BW 690. Nott [ex Carthew]

Named signs

6790	1.35	20.9	Br	270°	*Dog's Head in the Pot* (AT THE DOGS HEAD ỊṆ ṬHE POT): Dickson (DICḲSON), John. nd ½d. 3.67.14 (•IOHN•DICḲSON•AT•THE•DOGS around); 5.77 (HIS|HALF|PẸNY|•••; •HEAD•ỊṆ ṬHE POT•CLOVTH•FAIR around). BW —; *Dickinson 676B. Baldwin. Rev. struck off-centre
6791	1.31	20.2	Br	0°	*Harrow* (AT Y^E^HARRO): How, William. 1667 ½d. 5.17.16; 5.77 (H|WE). BW 683 but Y^E^. Nott [ex Carthew]
6792	0.94	14.6	Br	180°	[*Three Tuns*]: Ingersoule, Henry. [16]58. 5.64.40; I|HD. BW 685. Nott [ex Taffs]. Sign name from BW 684. Surname from Inkersall, Derbyshire (Reaney 1995 s.v. Ingersoll). Obv. legend starts between 10 and 11 o'clock. Overstruck on another ?token (unidentified)
6793	1.44	22.2	Br	270°	*Two Brewers* (AT THE 2 BREWERS): Bincks, William. 1666 ½d. 3.4.6; 5.77. BW 673. Seaby, [*SCMB* April 1967]

COCK LANE (Farringdon ward Without, Giltspur Street) [23-F6]

Greene, Robert *see* Uncertain I
Norman, Richard *see* Uncertain I
Ward, Joseph *see* Uncertain I

COLCHESTER STREET *subsequently* PEPYS STREET (Aldgate ward) [39-I18]

Peerwyre, Thomas *see* ii. 1248-53 (Essex: Colchester. Wyre Street, Long/Wyre Street, Short: *Peeke*)

COLDHARBOUR *subsequently* CITY OF LONDON BREWERY (Dowgate ward) [37-K13]

The reading is AT COALHARBOR on 6794; AT COLLHARBER on 6796; COLE HARBER THAMS STRET on 6795

Bickford, Thomas *see* Middlesex I: Stepney: Coal Stairs

6794	0.82	12.6	Cu	0°	*Chapman,* Lancelot. nd. 5.14 Innholders 2; C|LM. BW 701 but COALHARBOR. Nott [ex Carthew]. ?Lancelot Chapman of St Magnus the Martyr, 1638 rent £20, wood and coal wharf in St Magnus; md. Mabel Haton 1638, children b. 1639, 1649 (Boyd 49860). Launcellot Chapman, woodmonger, d. 1673 (Woodhead 1966, p. 45)
6795	1.98	30.6	Cu	180°	*Cooper,* Henry. nd ½d. 3.53.31; 5.77. BW 702. Nott [ex Carthew]. Description confirmed from BM specimen

COLDHARBOUR. The Gate

The reading is AT COLLHARBER GAT

6796	0.90	13.9	Br	90°	*Elleis,* Andrew. 1658. 5.14 Dyers (•ANDREW•ELLEIS•I658 around); E|AS (•E•|A•S; •AT•COLLHARBER•GAT around). BW 703-4 but descriptions revised. Nott [ex Carthew]. The MoL has an example from the same dies; the alternative reading EILEIS for BW 703 and the revised description of BW 704 in Dickinson were from reports of the present specimen

COLEMAN STREET (Coleman Street ward) [26-G12]

See also SWAN ALLEY. The reading is COLEMAN STREET on 7709, ÇOLEMAN STREEṬ on 6798; COLLMAN STREETE on 6800; COLMAN STREET on 6799, 6801, STREETE on 6797

6797	1.99	30.7	Br	0°	*Abbutt,* John. 1666 ½d. 5.77; 5.14 Drapers. BW 706. Nott [ex Carthew]. Reading completed from BM specimen. Foundation set out for Mr John Abbott 1668 (Mills 1962-7, i. 21, iv. 13)

[*continued overleaf*]

6785 6786 6787 6788 6789 6790

6791 6792 6793 6794 6795 6796

6797 6798 6799 6800 6801 6802

6803 6804 6805 6806 6807 6808

Plate 16 (*cont.*)

No.	Weight g	Weight gr		Die axis	
6798	0.65 (chipped)	10.1	Br	180°	*Forde* (F̣OṚ–E), Rob—, grocer. nd. 3.10.20; R F. *BW 709 (FORDE) but ROB;. Nott [ex Spink]. Description largely completed from MoL specimen. There may be another character after STREEṬ. 'Mr Ford, grocer of Coleman Street, against London Wall, died *ex peste*', 20 Jan. 1666 (Smyth 1849, p. 71)

Named signs

6799	2.92	45.0	Cu	180°	*Black* [*?Bell*] (AT Y^{E}): Sibley, Joseph. 1663 ½d. 5.70.1; 5.77. BW 714. Nott. Reading confirmed from BM specimen. E of Y^{E} from broken punch, resembling F. Joseph Sibley, Tallow-chandler (Woodhead 1966, p. 149)
6800	1.21	18.6	Br	210°	*White Hart* (AT THE WHIT HART): ?P—, I/J—. nd. 3.53.20 (•AT•THE•WHIT•HART•IN around); P|IG (•P•|I•G; •COLLMAN•STREETE around). BW —; Dickinson 712A. Nott [ex Carthew]

COLEMAN STREET neighbourhood

The reading is (?AT) CORNER COLMAN STREET

6801	0.68	10.5	Cu	180°	*Colman,* Samuel (SAMVELL). nd. 2.2.5; C|SA. BW 707. Nott [ex Taffs]. 'My cozen Coleman's brother, a grocer at ye corner house in Coleman Street, next Beech Lane, blown up wth gunpowder, by a sparke of fire falling into a gunpowder barrell from a pipe of tobacco', 21 Feb. 1666 (Smyth 1849, p. 71); however, Beech Lane [15-C10] does not adjoin this Coleman Street. BW's 'sugar-loaf' appears to be a bell

COLLEGE HILL (Vintry & Cordwainer wards) [36-J11]

See also TOWER ROYAL; The WARDROBE. The reading is ON COLLEDGE HILL

6802	1.10	16.9	M	180°	*Trowell,* Francis. 1664. Date; F T. BW 715. Nott [ex Carthew]

CORNHILL (Cornhill ward) [27-H13]

See also SWEETING'S RENTS. The reading is CORNHILL on 6805, 6807, 6810, 6812, ÇỌRNH. . . on 6811; CORN HILL on 6806, 6808-9; CORNEHILL on 6803; CORNHIL on 7711; CORNE HILL on 6804

6803	1.19	18.3	Br	210°	*Whittaker,* Gama—, grocer (GROSE). nd. 5.64.1; G W. BW 732 but GAMA:, AT Y, GROSE. Nott. No trace of superscript E and R after Y and GROSE respectively. Gamaliel was used as a christian name in the 16th and 17th c. (Withycombe 1977, p. 125; see also Redmonds 2004, pp. 150-2)

Named signs

					Bear tavern see *White Bear tavern*
6804	1.19	18.4	M	180°	*Castle tavern* (AT THE): ?H—, T—. 1651. 5.5.1; T H. BW 722. Nott. Reading CASTLE confirmed from Harris 2002, lot 504. ?Thomas Horsman (Rogers 1928a, p. 72, 1935, pp. 45-7); although the Castle was leased to him 1653-4. Thomas Hors(e)man appr. Vintner 1642, bound an apprentice 1651 (Webb 1996-, xliii. 153, 196)
6805	0.81 (chipped)	12.6	Br	90°	*Castle* (THE): K[insey], R[ichard]. 1657. 5.5.12 (•THE•CASTLE•IN••• around); K|RE (.K.|R·E; •CORNHILL•1657• around). BW —; Dickinson 724A. Baldwin. Richard Kinsey, vintner, at the Castle tavern 1654-71, 'Captain' 1660-1; Elizabeth Kensey fl. 1662 (Rogers 1928a, p. 72, 1935, pp. 45-8). Cf. Webb 1996-, xliii. 365
6806	1.03	15.9	Br	180°	*Dolphin tavern* (AT THE): H[inton], H[umphrey]. nd. 3.109.1; H|HA. BW 719. Nott. Humphrey Hinton, Vintner, appr. 1627 (Webb 1996-, xliii. 147, see also 362); Dolphin tavern demised to him 1654; wife Alice; bd. St Michael Cornhill 1670 (Rogers 1928a, p. 71, 1935, pp. 28-9; Boyd 2679; Woodhead 1966, p. 91)
6807	0.95	14.7	Br	180°	*Golden Cross* (AT THE): R[ea], R[oger]. 1649. 1.61.1; R|RV. BW 726. Nott. Roger Rea the elder, Stationer, at the 'Guilt Cross' in Cornhill 1662 (BW 726 n.); md. Ursula le Neve; d. 1677 (Le Neve 1873, p. 168; Woodhead 1966, p. 136)
6808	1.05	16.2	M	180°	*Mermaid tavern* (THE MERMAYDE TAVERN): T[apping], W[illiam]. 1651. 3.10.17; T|WM. BW 729 but MERMAYDE, CORN•HILL. Nott. William Tapping, Vintner, md. Mary Southerly 1640, bd. St Michael Cornhill 1658 (Rogers 1928a, p. 72, 1928c, pp. 76-9, 192; Boyd 3401). Cf. Webb 1996-, xliii. 386

CORNHILL (*cont.*)

Named signs (*cont.*)

	Weight g	gr		*Die axis*	
6809	1.17	18.0	Br	180°	*Seven Stars* (AT THE): ?W—, M—. 1648. 2.4.11; W|MI. BW 730. Nott [ex Carthew]
6810	1.43	22.1	Br	180°	*Three Golden Lions* (THE 3 GOLDEN LYONS): ?C—, S—. 1660. 3.41.1 (•THE•3•GOLDEN•LYONS around); S C (S•C; •IN•CORNHILL•I660 around). BW —; Dickinson 716A. Nott [ex Spink]. Books were published at this sign 1632-55 (Burn 1855, pp. 75-6; BW 716 n.), but it is not clear that the issuer (fl. 1653-60) was himself a stationer, cf. Rogers 1928a, p. 71, Berry 1978, p. 54
6811	0.73	11.3	Br	270°	*Three Tuns* (AT ... TVNS): Wilkinson, Stephen (STEP̣–EN). 1657. 5.64.40 (•STEP̣–EN•WILKINSON•AT around); I6|SW|57 (I6|SW|57; ...TVNS•IN•C̣ORNH... around). BW —; *Dickinson 732A (STEPHEN, YE 3 TVNS). Baldwin. ?Stephen Wilkinson of St Margaret Lothbury, b. 1631, appr. Vintner 1648, bound an apprentice 1658, fl. 1663 (Boyd 43072; Webb 1996-, xliii. 240)
6812	0.91	14.0	Br	180°	[*White*] *Bear tavern* (AT THE BEARE TAVERN): D[owse], R[obert]. 1656. 3.49.5; D|RW. BW 717. Nott. Date confirmed from Berry 1978, p. 54. Robert Dowse, Vintner, bd. St Michael Cornhill 1661; wife Winifred; sign the White Bear (Rogers 1928a, p. 71, 1935, p. 22). Cf. Webb 1996-, xliii. 351

COUSIN LANE (Dowgate ward, Thames Street) [36-K12]

The reading is COZEN LANE on 6815; CVZEN LANE AT DOWGAT on 6813; CVZEN LANE THAMES STREET on 6814

6813	0.93	14.3	Cu	0°	*Burry,* Dan[iel], woodmonger (WOODMVNGR). nd. 5.17.26; B|DM. BW 733 but DAN:; Woodhead 1966, p. 29 s.v. Berry. Nott [ex Carthew]. Flaw or mark of abbreviation on R of WOODMVNGR. Lease came to Daniell Berry about Sept. 1658; he was to rebuild after the Fire; Foundations to be staked out 1667-8 (Fire Court 1966-, i. 134-5; Mills 1962-7, i. 23)
6814	0.88	13.5	Cu	0°	*Marte,* John. nd. 5.50.12; 5.76.145 (IoM). BW 734 but obv. millstone, rev. monogram. Nott [ex Carthew]
6815	1.02	15.8	Br	0°	*Tull,* Peter, woodmonger (WOODMON|GER). nd. 5.54; T|PA. BW 735. [Nott ex Spink]

COW LANE *subsequently* SMITHFIELD STREET (Farringdon ward Without) [13-E6]

The reading is COW LANE on 6669, 6816, 6818-19, 6821-3; COWLANE on 6820; COWE LANE on 6817, 6824

6816	0.69	10.6	Cu	0°	*Collis,* John. 1657. 3.1.64; C|IA. BW 765 but COW[no stop]LANE[no stop]I657. Nott [ex Taffs]
6817	0.85	13.1	Cu	0°	*Hill,* James. nd. 3.52.25; H|IM. BW 767. Nott [ex Carthew]. Rev. legend starts at 9 o'clock. Cf. 6818-19

Named signs

6818	1.01	15.6	M	180°	*Bull's Head* (AT THE BVLL HEAD): Beard, John. nd. 3.52.25; B|IL. BW 764. Nott
6819	1.72	26.5	Br	180°	*Bull's Head* (AT Y^{E}BVLL HEAD): Stringfellow, William. nd ½d. (HỊS). 5.77; 3.52.25. *BW 771. [Nott ex Taffs]. Reading largely completed from MoL specimen 16746
6820	1.23	19.0	M	0°	*Dragon* (AT THE): Goddard, Eliz—. nd. 3.114.1; E G. BW 766 but COWLANE. Nott
6821	0.93 (chipped)	14.4	M	180°	*Plough* (AT THE PLOW): ?T—, C—. nd. 5.54; T|CA. BW 772. Nott [ex Carthew]
6822	1.23	19.0	Br	0°	*Red Cross* (AT THE RED CROS): T[unman], T[homas]. [16]58. 1.43; T|TA. BW 773. Nott. Forename initial T confirmed from BM specimen. Thomas Tunman of St Sepulchre, Grocer; 1st wife Anne Gray, 2nd Joan Pool 1665, 3rd Anne —(?); will, PCC, 1670 (Boyd 58217; Woodhead 1966, p. 165). Surname Townman occurred as *Tunman* 1598, 1672 (Bardsley 1901, p. 761)

COW LANE neighbourhood

See also BORES HEAD COURT. The reading is AT COW LANE END on 6823; AT COWE LANE END on 6824

Named signs

6823	1.20	18.5	Br	0°	*Crown tavern* (AT Y^{E}): Collins, Richard. nd ½d. 5.60.1 (•RICHARD•COLLINS•AT•Y^{E}CROWN around); 5.77 (C|RA) (HIS|HALFE|PENNY|C|R.A; •TAVERN•AT•COW•LANE•END around). BW —; Dickinson 765A. Baldwin [ex Macfadyen, lot 150]
6824	1.13	17.4	Br	180°	*Sugarloaf* (THE SHVGER LOFE): ?T—, W—. 1652. 5.64.1; T|WM. BW 774. Nott

COX'S QUAY (Billingsgate ward) (*lost*) [38-K15, n29]

The reading is AT COCKES KEY

6825	0.99	15.2	Br	0°	*Bostock,* Christopher. 1669 ½d. 5.66.4; 5.77 (B|CA). BW 778. Nott [ex Carthew]. Reading PENY confirmed from Dickinson, pl. 2

[*continued overleaf*]

6809

6810

6811

6812

6813

6814

6815

6816

6817

6818

6819

6820

6821

6822

6823

6824

6825

6826

6827b

6828

6829

6830

6831

6832

CREECHURCH LANE (Aldgate ward) [29-G17, h54]

See also ST KATHERINE CREE neighbourhood. The reading is CREECHVRCH LANE on 6826-7; CREE:|CHVRCH on 6828

Named signs

	Weight *g*	*gr*		*Die axis*	
6826	3.93	60.6	Cu	0°	*Crown* (AT Y^{E}): Shrawley (SHRAWLY), Edward. [16]66 ½d. 5.60.1; 5.77 (S|EI). BW 784. Nott [ex Taffs]. Reading completed from BM specimen. Form of surname as 6827, *Shrawley* selected as for the place-name (Watts 2004). Edge hammered up
6827a	4.71	72.6	Cu	0°	*Crown* (AT Y^{E}): Shrawley, Edward. 1669 1d. 5.60.1; 5.77 (S|EI). BW 783 but CREECHVRCH, I^{D}. Nott
6827b	4.12	63.6	Cu	0°	Same dies. Nott. Edge hammered up
6827c	3.43	52.9	Cu	0°	Same dies. Nott
6828	1.72	26.5	Cu	30°	*Oatsheaf* (THE OATE SHEAF): ?B—, R—, chandler. nd ½d. 4.10.1; 5.77 (B|RM). BW 779 but CREE:. Nott [ex Taffs]. Reading confirmed from BM specimens

CREED LANE (Castle Baynard ward & Farringdon ward Within) [34-I7]

The reading is CREED LANE on 6736, C̣REED LANE on 6830; Y^{E}LOWER END OF CREEDE LANE on 6829

6829	1.08	16.6	Br	180°	*Newbery,* Tho—, cheesemonger (CHEESMONG^{R}). 1669 ½d. 5.43.11 (N|TS); 5.77. BW 786. Nott [ex Taffs]. Reading confirmed from BM specimen

Named signs

6830	0.95	14.6	M	180°	*Dog's Head in the Pot* (AT THE): ?D—, L— (Ḷ). nd. D|ḶE (.D.|Ḷ•E; •AT•THE•DOGS• HEAD•IN around); 3.67.14 (•THE•POT•IN•C̣REED•LANE around). BW —; Dickinson 784A, from a report of this specimen. Baldwin

CREED LANE neighbourhood *see* CARTER LANE neighbourhood

CRIPPLEGATE neighbourhood (Cripplegate wards Within & Without & Farringdon ward Within) [15-E10]

See also The POSTERN. The reading is AT CREPLE GATE on 6831; CRIP̣LEGAT on 6982; BY CRIPLEGAT̄E on 7479. Cf. 6832-7

Named signs

					Sun tavern: Hodgkin, Isaac *see* 6836 (Cripplegate Without)
6831	1.09	16.8	M	180°	*White Hind brew-house* (AT THE WHIT HYND BRVHOVS): ?F—, G—. nd. 3.53.16; G F. BW 792. Nott. Description confirmed from MoL specimen

CRIPPLEGATE CHURCH *see* ST GILES WITHOUT CRIPPLEGATE neighbourhood

CRIPPLEGATE Within (Cripplegate ward Within) [15-E10]

The reading is WITHIN CRIPLE GATE

6832	2.04	31.5	Cu	270°	*Ashley* [i.e. *?Ashby*], Thomas. 1666 ½d. 5.60.1; 5.77. BW 788. [Nott ex Carthew]. Cf. a similar token but with surname ASHBY (Gilbert 1927, 119). ?Thomas Ashby of St Mary Aldermanbury, b. 1641, Haberdasher, threadman 1679 (Boyd 33306)

C R I P P L E G A T E Without (Cripplegate ward Without) [15-E10]

The reading is AT CRIPPEL GATE on 6836; WITHOVT CRIPLEGAT on 6833, CRIPLEGAṬE on 6837, CRIPPLEGATE on 6835, CRIPPLE GATE on 6834

	Weight *g*	*gr*		*Die axis*	
6833	0.60	9.2	Cu	180°	*Greenhill,* Tho—. nd. 3.108.16; G|TM. BW 794 but THO:, WITHOVT:CRIPLEGAT. Nott. Thomas Greenhill, apothecary; wife Mary d. 1664 (Whittet 1983, p. 135). Thomas Greenhill bound an apprentice 1673 (Webb 1996-, xlii. 54)
6834	1.50	23.2	Cu	180°	*Phipps,* Edward. nd ½d. 3.101.1; 5.77 (P|ES). BW 798 but CRIPPLE•GATE. Nott [ex Taffs]. Reading confirmed from BM specimen
Named signs					
6835	1.42	21.9	Br	0°	*Mermaid* (AT Y^{E}): Benion, Samuel. 1668 ½d. 3.10.17 (•SAMVEL•BENION•AT• Y^{E}MERMAI^{D} around); 5.77 (B|SS) (HIS|HALFE|PENNY|•B•|S.S; •WITHOVT• CRIPPLEGATE•I668 around). BW —; Dickinson 789A, from a report of this specimen. Baldwin
6836	1.25	19.2	M	180°	*Sun tavern* (AT THE SVNNE TAVERN): H[odgkin], I[saac]. nd. 2.1; H|IE. BW 795. Nott [ex Taffs]. Identification of issuer from 6837 and Gilbert 1927, 178. Isaac Hodgkin appr. Vintner 1639 (Webb 1996-, xliii. 148, see also 362), d. 1686; he was elsewhere 1670-84 (Woodhead 1966, p. 91)
6837	2.26 (pierced)	34.9	Br	270°	[*Sun tavern*]: Hodgkin, Isaac. [16]6̣6̣ ½d. (HỊS HAḶF̣E). 2.1; 5.77. *BW 797 but AT•Y^{E}, CRIPLEGAṬE•6̣6̣. Nott [ex Carthew]. Sign name from 6836, q.v.

C R O O K E D L A N E (Candlewick ward & Bridge ward Within) [37-J14]

See also 'MILES CROOKED LANE'; ST MICHAEL'S LANE. The reading is CROOCKED LANE on 6839; CROOKED LANE on 6838

6838	1.63	25.2	Cu	180°	*Cole,* Thomas, tallow-chandler. 1669 ½d. 5.32.9; 5.77. BW 801. Nott [ex Carthew]
Named signs					
6839	0.75	11.6	Br	180°	*Swan* (AT Y^{E}): Hiatt (HỊAṬṬ), Rich—. [16]57. 3.102.16 ([lis]RICH:HỊAṬṬ AT Y^{E}SWAN around); H|RE (.H.|R·E|•; [lis]IN CROOCKED•LANE57 around). BW —. Baldwin. Letter E in rev. field cancels unidentified character

C R U T C H E D F R I A R S (Aldgate ward) [29-H18]

The reading is CRVCHED FRYERS on 6840-1, 6843, FRỊARS on 6845, FRIERS 6844; CROWCHEṬ FRỊERS on 6842; CRVTCHED FRIERS on 6846-7; CRVTCHET FRYERS on 6848

6840	2.16	33.4	Cu	0°	*Garfeild* (GARF̣EỊLD), William. [16]66 ½d. 5.14.5 (•WILLIAM•G̣ARF̣EỊLD•AT: around); 5.77 (G|WE) (HIS|HALF|PENY|G|W.E; •IN•CRVCHED•FRYERS•66 around). BW —. Baldwin. Reading partly confirmed from *S&B* No. 80, T19
6841	1.65	25.5	Br	0°	*Greene,* Tho—. [16]67 ½d. 5.66.20; 5.77 (G|TI). BW 810. Nott
6842	0.76	11.7	M	180°	*Greensmith,* Will (ẈỊḶḶ). nd. 3.101.1 (•ẈỊḶḶ•GREENSMITH• around); G|WD (•G•|W•D; •IN•CROWCHEṬ•FRỊERS around). BW —; *Dickinson 810A. Nott
6843	0.99	15.2	Cu	60°	*Starkey,* Philip. nd. 5.14 Brewers; S|PM. BW 815. Nott. Philip Starky, Brewer; md. Mary Raimond 1661; will, PCC, 1679 (Boyd 26007, unlocated)
Named signs					
6844	0.80 (chipped)	12.3	Br	180°	*Ship* (AT THE SHIPPE): ?B—, W—. nd. 5.13.15; B|WE. BW 809. Baldwin [ex Pridmore]
6845	1.23	19.0	M	180°	*Three Tuns* (AT THE 3 TVNNES): P[ace], T[heophilus]. nd. 5.64.43; P|TM. *BW 813. Baldwin. Issuer identified from 6846
6846	1.86	28.8	M	180°	[*Three Tuns*]: Pace, Theophilus. nd ½d. 5.77 (HIS|HALF|PENY; •THEOPHILVS•PACE around); 5.64.40 (•IN·CRVTCHED·FRIERS around). BW —; Dickinson 813A. Baldwin. Sign name from 6845. V of THEOPHILVS over A or inverted V
6847	1.92	29.6	M	180°	[*Three Tuns tavern*]: Kent, John. nd ½d. 5.77 (HIS|HALF|PENY; •IOHN•KENT•IN around); 5.64.40 (•CRVTCHED·FRIERS around). BW —; Dickinson 811A. Baldwin. Sign name from BW 811 and Pepys 1970-83, viii. 208; see also 7023. Vintner, tavern keeper, fl. 1631-89; in Crutched Friars post-Fire (Rogers 1937, pp. 123-4; Woodhead 1966, p. 102). Cf. Webb 1996-, xliii. 365

[*continued overleaf*]

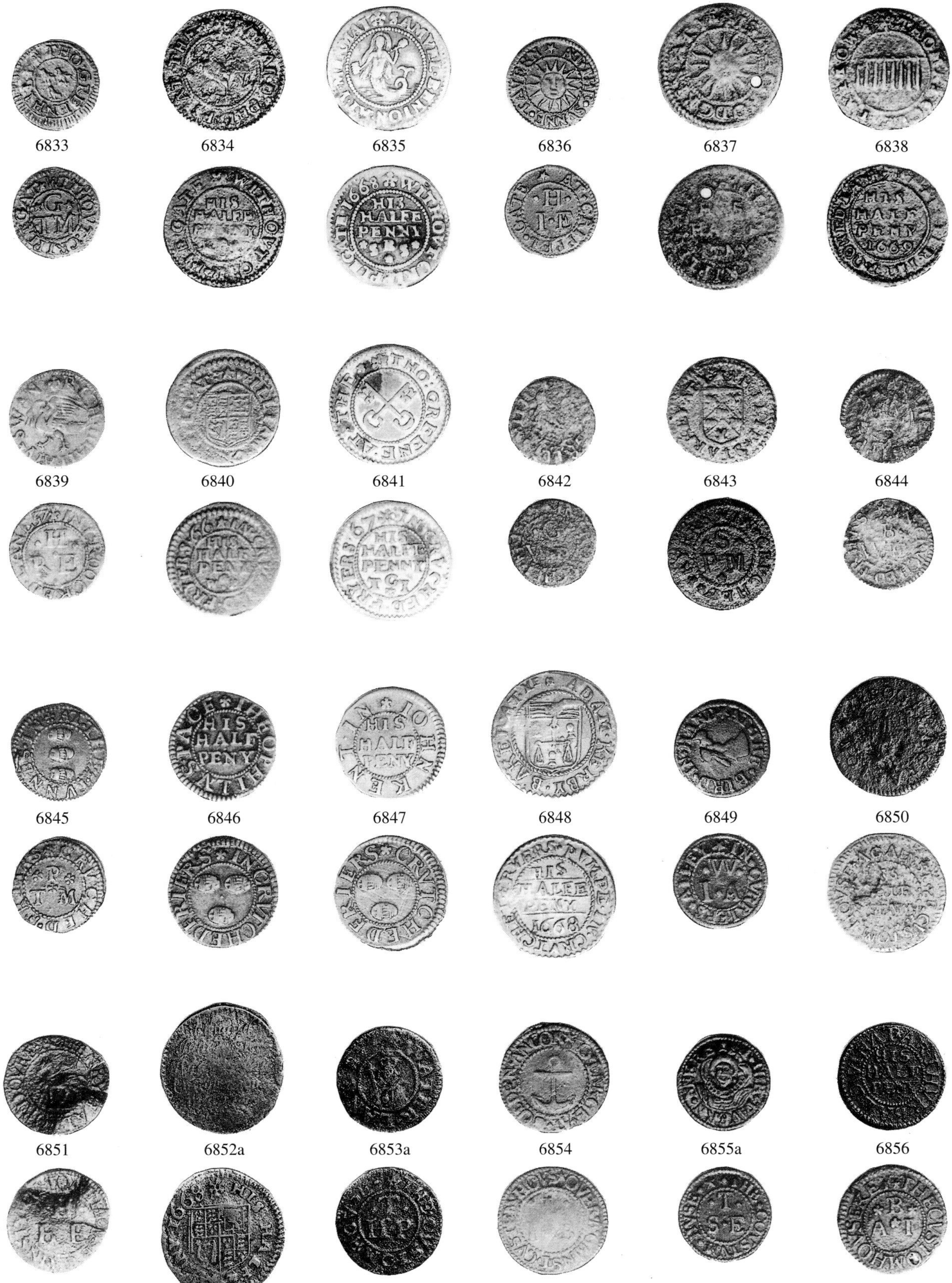

6833 6834 6835 6836 6837 6838

6839 6840 6841 6842 6843 6844

6845 6846 6847 6848 6849 6850

6851 6852a 6853a 6854 6855a 6856

CRUTCHED FRIARS. Aldgate Pump neighbourhood [29-G18: not identified]

The reading is AT Y^{E} PVMPE IN CRVTCHET FRYERS

	Weight g	Weight gr		Die axis	
6848	1.68	26.0	Br	180°	*Kerby,* Adam, baker. 1668 ½d. 5.14 Bakers (•ADAM•KERBY•BAKER•AT•Y^{E} around); 5.77 (HIS|[rule]|HALFE|[rule]|PENY[rule]|I668; •PVMPE•IN•CRVTCHET•FRYERS around). BW —; Greenall 1991, p. 98, n. 2 but I668. Baldwin. Adam Kirby of St Olave Hart Street, Baker, d. 1680 (Boyd 39101). The cubit arm appears to descend from outside the shield

CURRIERS' ALLEY *subsequently* ST BRIDE STREET (Farringdon ward Without, Shoe Lane) [23-H5, i11]

The reading is CVRRIERS ALLEY

Named signs

6849	1.11	17.1	M	180°	*Bird in Hand* (AT THE): ?W—, I/J—. nd. 3.6.22; W|IA. BW 817. Nott

CURSITOR'S ALLEY (Farringdon ward Without *and* Middlesex: Holborn *and* Westminster) *see* Middlesex I: Holborn

CUSTOM HOUSE neighbourhood *subsequently* CUSTOM HOUSE WOOL QUAYS (Tower ward) [39-K17]

The reading is AGAINST Y^{E} CVSTOM HOVSE on 6850; NEERE THE COVSTVM HVSE on 6855; *Ouer Against the Custome house in Thames Street* on 6852; OVER AGAINST CVSTEM HOVS on 6854; OVRE A\|GAINST Y^{E}CVSTOME HOVSE on 6851; WATER LANE BY THE CVSTOM HOVSE on 6853; cf. 6856

6850	2.16 (corroded)	33.3	Cu	270°	*Grafton* (GRAFṬON), Roger (ROGEṚ). nd ½d. (Ḥ̣IS –ALF). 3.10.0 (•ROGEṚ•GRAFṬON• around); 5.77 (Ḥ̣IS.|–ALF.|PENY; •AGAINST•Y^{E}•CVSTOM•HOVSE around). BW —. Baldwin. Legend starts between 10 and 11 o'clock each side
6851	0.63	9.8	Br	225°	*Halford,* Henry. nd. 3.60.4; H|HE. BW 825 but obv. OVRE•A, rev. GAINST. Nott [ex Taffs]. Reading confirmed from BM specimen. The F is perhaps flawed: it looks more like E
6852a	2.59	40.0	M	0°	*Jones,* Edward. 1668 ½d. 5.77.1; 5.14.5. BW 3105 but *Ouer Against, house,* apparently no stops at all on obv. Nott. Reading completed from MoL specimen
6852b	2.24	34.5	M	0°	Same dies. Nott [ex Taffs]
6853a	2.30	35.5	Br	180°	*?T—,* H—. nd. 3.5.87; T|HP. BW 3368. Nott
6853b	1.91	29.5	Br	180°	Same dies. Nott [ex Taffs]

Named signs

6854	1.48	22.8	M	180°	*Golden Anchor* (AT GOLDEN ANCOR): Large, Jo—. nd. 5.38.1 (•IO•LARGE•AT• GOLDEN•ANCOR around); L|IB (•L•|I•B; •OVER•AGAINST• CVSTEM•HOVS around). BW —; Dickinson 825A. Baldwin. C of ANCOR double-entered?
6855a	1.11	17.2	Br	180°	[*?Queen's Head*] *tavern* (AT THE): ?T—, S—. nd. 3.5.90; T|SE. BW 826 but TAVERN•NEERE. Nott [ex Taffs]
6855b	0.85	13.2	Br	180°	Same dies. [Baldwin]

CUSTOM HOUSE QUAY *subsequently* CUSTOM HOUSE WOOL QUAYS (Tower ward) [39-K17]

The reading is AT THECVSTOMHOVSE KEY

6856	2.30	35.5	M	180°	*Baldwin,* Arthur. nd ½d. 5.77; B|AI. BW 823 but THECVSTOMHOVSE. Baldwin -1969

DICE QUAY *otherwise* LITTLE DICE QUAY *subsequently* (new) CUSTOM HOUSE (Tower ward) [38-K16, n36]

The reading is AT DICE KEY on both, with NEAR BILLINSGATE on 6857

	Weight *g*	*gr*		*Die axis*	
6857	1.21	18.7	Cu	90°	*Dew,* William. 1668 ½d. 3.58.1; 5.77 (D|WM). BW 829 but BILLINSGATE. Seaby, [*SCMB* April 1967]. Reading confirmed from BM specimen
6858	0.83 (chipped)	12.8	Br	0°	*Turrall,* Francis. nd. 5.66.13; T|FA. BW 830. Nott [ex Taffs]. Description confirmed from BM specimen. Surname a form of Thorold (Reaney 1995, pp. 444-5)

DISTAFF LANE *subsequently* CANNON STREET (Bread Street ward) [35-I9]

The reading is DISTAFFE LANE on 6861-2; ḌESṬVF LANE on 6859; DISSTAFE LANE on 6860; DISTAF LANE on 6863; DISTAFE LANE on 6864

6859	1.17	18.0	M	0°	*Mason,* Rich—, tallow (ṬALLOWE) chandler. nd. 3.3.13; M|RI. *BW 833. Nott. Reading largely confirmed from MoL specimen
6860	1.00 (chipped)	15.5	Cu	270°	*Watersfeild,* Thomas, baker. nd ½d. 4.10.6 (W|TM); 5.77. BW 837. Spink 1971. Reading confirmed from BM specimen. Thomas Waterfield of St Margaret Moses, White Baker, d. 1670; wife Rebecca d. 1662; their children bap. 1650-62 (Boyd 31102); 'Mr Thomas Watersfield a White-Baker' 1664 (BW 837 n.). Foundation set out for Thomas Water(s)feild in (Little) Distaff Lane 1667[-8] (Mills 1962-7, i. 29, ii. 56). Surname presumably from Watersfield, Sussex

Named signs

6861	0.69	10.7	Br	180°	*Bell tavern* (THE BELL TAVERNE): T[aylor], R[ichard]. 1657. 5.70.1; T|RA. BW 835. Nott. Richard Taylor of St Margaret Moses, Vintner, Master 1677; wife Anne (Rogers 1928a, p. 73; Boyd 31118); appr. 1638 to Jonathan Barford (see BW 3031), whom he succeeded (Rogers 1928c, p. 147; Woodhead 1966, p. 160 (B)). See also Webb 1996-, xliii. 289, 386. Same rev. die as 6862, q.v.
6862	0.96	14.8	Br	180°	*Bell tavern* (THE): T[aylor], R[ichard]. 1657. 5.70.1 (•THE•BELL•TAVERN•IN around); T|RA (•T•|R•A; •DISTAFFE•LANE•I657 around). BW —, cf. 6861 (TAVERNE). Baldwin. Same rev. die as 6861, q.v. Succeeded Jonathan Barford at Temple Bar 1667/8, see BW 3070; d. 1698 (Rogers 1928c, pp. 147-8, Woodhead 1966, p. 160 (B))
6863	1.06	16.4	Cu	0°	*Death's Head* (AT THE DEATHES HEAD): ?M—, R—. 1652. 3.5.1; M|RD. BW 832. Nott [ex Taffs]. ?Robert Mellor, or Richard Meynell (but see Woodhead 1966, p. 115), or Robert Moore, apothecaries (Whittet 1983, p. 138)
6864	1.02	15.7	M	180°	*Sugarloaf* (AT THE SVGERLOFE): ?U/V—, I/J—. nd. 5.64.1; V|IE. BW 836 but SVGERLOFE. Coins & Antiquities 1976

DOCTORS' COMMONS neighbourhood (Castle Baynard ward) [34-I8, C10]

The reading is NEARE DOCTORS COMONS

Named signs

6865a	0.94	14.5	Br	180°	*Paul's Head* (AT THE PAVLE HEAD): ?H—, G—. nd. 3.5.71; G H. BW 839 (AT confirmed). Nott. ?Gregory Hardwick, Vintner, searcher for the Company 1656, 1663, Warden 1663 (Rogers 1928a, p. 73). Gregory Hardwicke appr. 1635 (Webb 1996-, xliii. 134, see also 359)
6865b	1.11	17.1	Br	—	Same obv. die. Nott [or Baldwin]. Obverse brockage

DOVE COURT (Langbourn & Walbrook wards, Lombard Street) (*lost*) [27-H13, i67]

The reading is DOVE COVRT AT Y^{E}LOWER END LVMBARD STREET

Named signs

6866a	3.77	58.2	Br	90°	*Six Bells* (AT Y^{E}6 BELLS): [anonymous]. nd. 5.70.20; 3.108.10. BW 1758. [Nott ex Taffs]. The diameters of the three specimens vary between 24 and 25 mm, suggesting a penny denomination
6866b	3.12	48.2	Br	90°	Same dies. [Nott]
6866c	2.69	41.5	Br	90°	Same dies. Nott [ex Spink]

DOWGATE neighbourhood (Dowgate ward) [36-K12]

The reading is AT DOWGATE on 6867, 6871-2, IN THAMES STREET BY DOWGATE on 6808, NEARE DOWGATE on 6870; DOWGAT on 6813; AT DOW GATE on 6869

6867	1.00	15.4	Br	270°	*Browne,* William. 1659. 4.3.13; B|WM. BW 842 but a star and crooked billet. Baldwin [or Nott ex Carthew]. Obv. legend starts between 10 and 11 o'clock
6868	1.70	26.3	Br	0°	*Hardie,* John. 1668 ½d. 1.41.2; 5.77. BW 3099 but BY•DOWGATE, BW 848 but as BW 3099 here amended. Nott [ex Carthew]. Reading confirmed from MoL specimen

[*continued overleaf*]

6857 6858 6859 6860 6861 6862

6863 6864 6865a 6866c 6867 6868

6869 6870 6871 6872 6873 6874

6875 6876 6877a 6878 6879a 6880

Plate 19 (*cont.*)

Weight *g* *gr* — *Die axis*

6869 1.14 17.6 M 180° *Paggan,* Sarah. 1652. 5.76.146 (S P); S P. BW 853. Nott [ex Taffs]

6870 1.06 16.4 Cu 0° *Sellers,* Michael (*Michaell*). 1664. 5.77.1; 3.2.9. BW 855 but *1664*. Nott [ex Taffs]

Named signs

6871 1.28 19.8 Br 0° *Red Lion* (AT THE RED LYON): Drue, John. 1667½d. 3.39.1; 5.77 (D|IH). BW 846. Nott [ex Spink]. Foundations set out for Mr John Drew(e) near Dowgate (Hill) 1667-8 (Mills 1962-7, i. 30, 74, ii. 50v; Fire Court 1966-, ii. 122-3)

6872 1.28 19.8 Br 0° *Sugarloaf* (AT THE SVĢER LOFE): Batt, Tho—, grocer. nd. 5.64.1; B|TH. *BW 840. Nott. Lower bar of E of LOFE weak

DOWGATE HILL (Dowgate ward) [36-J12]

See also DYERS' HALL neighbourhood. The reading is ONE DOWGATE HILL

6873 1.94 29.9 Cu 150° *Smith,* John. 1668 ½d. 5.60.20; 5.77. BW 856. Nott [ex Carthew]

DUKE'S PLACE *subsequently* DUKE'S PLACE *and* MITRE SQUARE *and* CREECHURCH PLACE (Aldgate & Portsoken wards) [29-G17]

The reading is DVKES PLACE on both

6874 1.46 (pierced) 22.5 Cu 0° *Empson,* John. 1667 ½d. 5.2.2 (NISI DOMINVS); 5.77 (E|IA). BW 894. Spink 1972. Reading of motto confirmed from *NCirc* 99 (1991), no. 5930. *Nisi Dominus*, 'Except the Lord…', occurs in Psalms 127:1

Named signs

6875 3.28 50.6 Br 0° *Last* (AT THE): Chevall, Edward. 1668 1d. 3.7.40; 5.77. BW 893 but I^{D}. Nott [ex Carthew]. Description confirmed from BM specimen. Edward Cheavall, Vintner; appr. 1611; will, PCC, 1668, St Katherine Cree (Boyd 25637; Webb 1996-, xliii. 59, see also 346)

DUNNING'S ALLEY (Bishopsgate ward Without) (*lost beneath Broad Street* and *Liverpool Street Station*) [18-C16, c13]

The reading is IN DVNINGS ALY WITHOVT BISHOPSGATE

6876 2.58 39.8 Br 0° *Sillet,* Will—. nd ½d. 3.53.30; 5.77 (S|WE). BW 328 but WILL:. Nott [ex Carthew]

DYERS' HALL neighbourhood *subsequently* DYERS' HILL WHARF (Dowgate ward, Dowgate Hill) [37-K13]

The reading is AT DIERS HAL: IN THAMES STREET

6877a 2.31 35.6 Cu 0° *Jones,* John. 1666 ½d. 3.52.6; 5.77. BW 3106 but HAL:. Nott [ex Taffs]
6877b 1.56 24.1 Cu 0° Same dies. [Nott]
6877c 1.17 18.0 M 0° Same dies. [Nott]

EAST INDIA HOUSE neighbourhood (Lime Street ward, Leadenhall Street) [28-H16, B88]

The reading is NEAR THE EAST INDIA HOVS IN LEADEN HALL STREET on 6878; AGIN Y^{E}ESTINDIA HOVS IN LEDEN HALL STREET on 6879

Named signs

6878 2.08 (chipped) 32.1 Br 0° [*John's coffee-house*]: ?John, [–]. nd John's ½d. 3.5.40; 5.77. BW 1670 but LEADEN•HALL. Nott [ex Baldwin]. Y of PENY double-entered. Sign name as Lillywhite 1972, no. 638

6879a 3.43 53.0 Br 180° [*North's coffee-house*]: North, Tho—. 1669 1d. 3.5.40; 5.77. BW 1674 but THO:, ESTINDIA. Nott [ex Taffs]. Sign name as Lillywhite 1972, no. 913
6879b 2.87 44.3 Br 180° Same dies. Nott

The EXCHANGE *see* The ROYAL EXCHANGE

EXCHANGE ALLEY *subsequently* CHANGE ALLEY (Cornhill & Langbourn wards) [27-H13, i66]

The reading is *Exchange Ally* on 6882-3; *Exch|laing Allie* on 6884; EXCHAINGE ALLEY on 6880; *Exchang Alley* on 6881

6880 2.25 34.7 Cu 180° *Stanley,* Arthur (AVRTHOR). 1666 ½d. 5.77; 5.8.5. BW 962 but PENNY; Thompson 1993, p. 78; Thompson 1997b, pp. 239-40. Nott [ex Taffs]. Arthur Stanley of St Mary Woolnoth, Vintner, d. 1674 (Boyd 5372); bound apprentices (Webb 1996-, xliii. 384)

EXCHANGE ALLEY (*cont.*)

Named signs

	Weight g	Weight gr		Die axis	
6881	2.91	44.9	Cu	0°	*Morat coffee-house (The):* [Elford, Walter]. nd. 3.5.42 (*Morat*); 5.77.1. BW 968 but *Mo*[Turk's head]*rat, The, house, Exchang.* Nott [ex Taffs or Carthew]. Reading *house* completed from Berry 1978, p. 121. New coffee-house, distinguishing sign 'The Great Turk', 1662 (BW 968 n.); almost certainly kept by Walter Elford (Pepys 1970-83, x. 71). Walter Elford of St Mary Woolnoth, b. 1611, merchant; fl. 1669 (Boyd 1897). Morat was Murād IV, sultan 1623-1640 (Matar 1998, p. 115)
6882	4.87	75.2	Cu	180°	[*Morat coffee-house*]: [Elford, Walter]. nd. 3.5.46; 5.77.1. BW 965 but Y^{e}GREAT, DID•|CALL MEE [i.e. MEE CALL?], rev. CONQVER•D•, *Tobacco•Sher=|bet•tea•&•Choco|lat• Retal'd•in•*. Nott [ex Spink]. Issuer as 6881, whence sign name. Obv. legend starts at 8 o'clock; reading Y^{e} confirmed from MoL specimen NN17572 = Cowan 2005, p. 179, on which some of the rev. lettering has been subsequently re-engraved. Slight traces of tinning both sides (cf. Greenall 1997, pl. 3.101 and MoL specimen NN17571). Same rev. die as 6883; rev. i.m. a crescent. The placing of the obv. legend requires the reading MORAT Y^{e} GREAT MEN DID CALL MEE, which metre could support; but 6883-4 suggest that MEE CALL was intended. The 26 mm diameter suggests a penny
6883a	4.25	65.6	Br	315°	[*Morat coffee-house*]: [Elford, Walter]. nd. 3.5.43; 5.77.1. BW 966 but obv. MEE[no stop]CALL, rev. corrected as 6882. Nott [or Baldwin]. Issuer as 6881, whence sign name. Obv. legend starts between 7 and 8 o'clock. Same obv. die as 6884; same rev. die as 6882, i.m. a crescent. Diameter 24-24.5 mm, suggesting a penny
6883b	4.10	63.3	Br	315°	Same dies. Nott. Diameter 24 mm, suggesting a penny
6884a	7.08	109.3	Br	180°	[*Morat coffee-house*]: [Elford, Walter]. nd. 3.5.43; 5.77.1. BW 967 but obv. MEE[no stop]CALL, rev. WHERE•EARE•I•*Came*•I•CONQVERD•*All* = •*Coffee*•|*Chocolat*•*tea*•|*Sherbett & tobac*|*Sould*•*in*•*Exch*|*aing*•*Allie*. Nott. Issuer as, and sign name from, 6881. Reading largely confirmed from MoL specimens. Obv. legend starts between 7 and 8 o'clock. Same obv. die as 6883. Diameter 25-25.5 mm, suggesting a penny
6884b	3.88	60.0	M	180°	Same dies. Nott [ex Taffs]. Diameter 24-24.5 mm, suggesting a penny

FENCHURCH STREET (Aldgate & Langbourn wards & Bridge ward Within) [38-I15]

See also ST GABRIEL FENCHURCH neighbourhood. The reading is FANCHVRCH STREET on 6885-6, 6888-9, 6891, 6893-4, 6898-9, 6902, STREETE on 6887, 6892, 6901, 6904-6, 6909; FAN\|CHVRCH STREET on 6896-7; FAN CHVRCH STREET on 6908; FENCHVRCH STREET on 6890, 6895, 6903, STREETE on 6907; FANCH STREETE on 6900

6885	2.17	33.5	Br	180°	*Baker,* John, oilman (OYLEMAN). nd ½d. 5.43.8; 5.77 (I B). BW 977 but three pruning-knives. Nott [ex Taffs]
6886	1.85	28.5	Br	270°	*Beebee,* Henry. nd ½d. 5.68.33; 5.77. BW 978. Nott [ex Taffs]
6887	0.89	13.7	Br	180°	*Brannd,* Ben—, grocer. nd. 5.64.1; B B. BW 979. Nott [ex Taffs]
6888	1.04	16.0	M	180°	*Conyers,* Emanuel (EMANVELL). nd. 4.12.2; E C. BW 981 but a rose and crown. Nott
6889	2.15	33.2	Cu	180°	*Davis,* Edward, grocer. 1669 ½d. 5.55.1; 5.77. BW 982 but PENY. Nott [ex Carthew]. Edward Davis of St Katherine Coleman, Grocer, free 1668, fl. 1677 (Boyd 54199)
6890	1.72	26.6	Cu	0°	*Davis,* Tobias. 1666 ½d. 3.6.39; 5.77. BW 983 but a hand holding a halbert. Nott [ex Taffs]
6891	1.44	22.1	M	180°	*Garner,* Ralph (RALPHE). nd. 4.10.13; G|RE. BW 985. Nott [ex Taffs]. See also 6909 (G|IA)
6892	0.69	10.7	M	0°	*Mathew,* Jerome (IEROM). nd. 5.64.30; M|IT. BW 990. Nott [ex Taffs]. Reading confirmed from MoL specimen. ?Jerome Mathew of St Olave Jewry, Grocer; md. Thomasin Stevens 1654 (Boyd 40421)
6893	1.16	17.9	M	180°	*Rudge,* James. nd. 3.57.3; R|IC. BW 995. Baldwin -1970. James Rudge of St Benet Gracechurch, Innholder; md. Christian Sharp 1636; will, PCC, 1658 (Boyd 27760)
6894	1.09	16.7	Cu	0°	*Smith,* Ambrose. nd. 5.3.20; S|AA. BW 997. Nott. See also 6904-5
6895	1.46	22.5	M	180°	*Tyler,* Franc[is], oilman (OYL MAN). nd. 5.64.50; T|FE. BW 999. Nott [ex Taffs]. Extension of forename from 6896. Francis Tiler of All Hallows Staining, Draper, free 1653; oilman; fl. 1685 (Boyd 23350); md. (1) Anne Spendlove 1656, (2) Elizabeth — (Woodhead 1966, p. 166). A different obv. die paired with the same rev. was in the Bird collection lot 290 ex Norweb ex Nott
6896	3.24	50.0	Br	180°	*Tyler,* Francis, oilman (OYLMAN). nd ½d. 5.77; 5.64.55 (F T). BW 998. Nott [ex Spink]. See also 6895. Same obv. die as 6897
6897a	3.81	58.8	Br	180°	*Tyler,* Francis, oilman (OYLMAN). nd ½d. 5.77; 5.64.55 (F T). BW 998. Nott [ex Taffs]. Same obv. die as 6896
6897b	2.69	41.5	Br	180°	Same dies. Nott
6898	1.97	30.4	Cu	270°	*Waggoner,* James. 1666 ½d. 3.3.13; 5.77. BW 1000. Nott [ex Taffs]. James Waggoner christened at the Dutch Church 1611 (Harl. Reg. 3 (1878), p. 94); will of James Waggyner, St Dionis Backchurch, Tallow Chandler, PCC 1667; cf. Boyd 12242

[*continued overleaf*]

PLATE 20

6881 6882 6883a 6884b 6885 6886

6887 6888 6889 6890 6891 6892

6893 6894 6895 6896 6897a 6898

6899 6900 6901 6902 6903 6904

Plate 20 (*cont.*)

	Weight *g*	*gr*		*Die axis*	
6899	3.09	47.7	Cu	0°	*Young,* John, stationer. nd ½d. 3.53.25; 5.77 (I Y). BW 1001. Nott. Foundation to be set out for John Younge 1669 (Mills 1962-7, i. 37)
Named signs					
6900	0.93	14.4	Br	180°	*Angel tavern* (THE ANGELL TAVERN): ?B—, W—. nd. 3.10.6; W B. BW 976. Nott [ex Carthew]
6901	3.05	47.1	Cu	0°	*Angel* (AT THE ANGELL): Miller, Mary. nd ½d. 5.77 (M M) (HER|HALFE|PENNY|M•M; •MARY•MILLER•AT•THE•ANGELL around); 3.10.1 (•IN•FANCHVRCH•STREETE• around). BW —; Dickinson 990A but ANGELL. Baldwin -1969. Dies engraved, i.e. not made up from punches
6902	1.82	28.1	Br	180°	*Exchange* (AT EXCHENG): Morris, John. nd ½d. 5.8.4; 5.77. BW 991; Thompson 1993, pp. 78-9; Thompson 1997b, p. 241. Nott [ex Spink]. ?John Morris of St Gabriel Fenchurch, Cooper, md. 1677, fl. 1696 (Boyd 42053)
6903	0.85	13.1	Br	0°	*Flower-de-luce* (AT THE FLOWERDELVCE): Heath, Ann. nd. 4.13.1; 5.77. BW 988 but FLOWERDELVCE, obv. and rev. transposed. Nott [ex Taffs]
6904	0.57	8.7	Br	180°	*Fountain tavern* (THE FOVNTANE TAVERN): K[ing], W[illiam]. nd. 5.3.21; K|WA. BW 989. Nott [ex Carthew]. Issuer William King (1607-1657), Vintner, md. Anne King [*sic*] 1636; at ye Fountaine 1641; bd. St Dionis Backchurch 1657 (Rogers 1928a, p. 76, 1928c, p. 192; Boyd 11828). Cf. Webb 1996-, xliii. 174, 366. Same rev. die as 6905

Named signs (*cont.*)

	Weight			Die	
	g	*gr*		*axis*	
6905	1.27	19.6	Br	180°	*Fountain tavern* (THE FOVNTIN TAVERN): K[ing], W[illiam]. nd. 5.3.20 (•THE•FOVNTIN•TAVERN around); K|WA (•K•|W•A; •IN•FANCHVRCH•STREETE around). BW —; Gilbert 1927, 128. Nott [ex Carthew]. Same rev. die as 6904, q.v. See also 6894
6906	1.06	16.3	M	180°	*Hatchet* (AT THE HATCHYT): ?A—, G—. nd. 5.45.1; A|GA. BW 974. Nott [ex Taffs]
6907a	1.54	23.8	Cu	180°	*Mitre* (AT THE MITETR): R[awlinson], D[aniel]. nd. 5.59.20; R|DM. BW 994. Baldwin. Rev. die slightly rusted to left of initial R: later than 6907b. Daniel Rawlinson of St Dionis Backchurch (1614-1679), Vintner, Steward 1644, Warden 1662, Master 1678; tavern keeper; wife Margaret (Pever) d. 1666, children born from 1641 (Rogers 1928c, pp. 126-9, 192; Boyd 11526; Woodhead 1966, p. 135; ODNB s.v. Rawlinson, Sir Thomas, bap. 1647, d. 1708). For apprentices see Webb 1996-, xliii. 378
6907b	1.08	16.6	M	180°	Same dies. Nott [ex Taffs, by whom exhibited to the British Numismatic Society, 22 March 1933 (Taffs 1933, p. 216)]
6908	0.99	15.3	M	180°	*Star tavern* (AT THE): C[lifton], J[ohn]. nd. 2.4.3; C|IM. BW 980. Nott [ex Taffs]. John Clifton was paid for 27 quarts of wine 1649; fl. 1670 (Rogers 1928a, p. 76). A John Clifton appr. a Vintner 1634, another 1639 (Webb 1996-, xliii. 65, see also 347)
6909	0.80	12.3	M	180°	*Wheatsheaf* (AT THE WHEAT SHEFE): ?G—, I/J—. nd. 4.10.1; G|IA. BW 984. Nott. Initial A confirmed from BM specimen. See also 6891 (Ralph Garner), though no trace here of a bird to right of the garb

FETTER LANE (Farringdon ward Without) [22-G3]

See also MAGPIE YARD. The reading is FETTER LANE on 6911-12, 6916-29, 6931, *Fetter Lane* on 6910, *Fetter lane* on 6930; FETER LANE on 6913-15; FETTERLANE on 7314

6910	2.19	33.8	Br	0°	*?B—,* T—. nd. 3.92.2; 5.77.1 (*•T B•|In Fetter|Lane•*). BW —; Dickinson 1001A but *T.B.* Nott [ex Taffs, by whom exhibited to the British Numismatic Society 1933 (Taffs 1933, p. 216)]
6911	1.59	24.6	M	180°	*Burman,* William. nd. 1.33.10; B|WI. BW 1003. Nott [ex Taffs]
6912	1.31	20.3	Cu	0°	*?D—,* W—. nd. 1.41.1; 5.77 (D|WE). BW 1006 but •IN•|FETTER|•LANE•|•D•|W.E, obv. and rev. transposed. Nott [ex Spink]. Restruck after turning over. See also 6916
6913	0.97	14.9	M	180°	*Dutch,* Thomas. nd. 3.67.31; D|TI. BW 1007 but talbot sejant. Nott. Same rev. die as 6914-15
6914	0.96	14.8	M	180°	*Dutch,* Thomas. nd. 3.67.31; D|TI. BW 1007 but talbot sejant. Nott. Same rev. die as 6913, 6915
6915	0.57	8.8	Br	0°	*Dutch,* Thomas. nd. 3.67.31; D|TI. BW 1007 but talbot sejant. Nott. Same rev. die as 6913-14
6916a	0.87 (chipped)	13.4	Cu	180°	*Gould,* James. 1664. 1.41.1; G|IS. BW 1011. Nott. See also 6912
6916b	0.60	9.2	Br	180°	Same dies. Nott [ex Taffs]
6917	0.96	14.9	Br	180°	*Harper,* George. nd. 3.49.5 (•GEORGE•HARPER• around); H|GM (.H.|•|G M; •IN•FETTER LANE around). BW —; Dickinson 1011B. Nott [ex Taffs]. Legend starts between 10 and 11 o'clock both sides. Description confirmed from Wetton 1989, pl. 8.177. Overstruck on a token of Will[iam] Middlemore of Holborn Bridge, from the same dies and with the same 90° axis as the BM specimen, the obv. legend starting between 10 and 11 o'clock (as BW London 1436, stops but no letters before HOLBORNE)
6918	0.85	13.1	Br	270°	*Higgs,* John. nd. H|IM; 3.3.13. BW 1012. Nott [ex Taffs]. Obv. legend starts between 5 and 6 o'clock, rev. at 10 o'clock
					?L—, G— *see* 7314 (Magpie Yard)
6919	0.89	13.7	M	0°	*Langborne,* Robert. nd. 3.92.6; L|RI. BW 1016. Nott. Reading LANE confirmed from BM specimen. Surname presumably from Langbourn ward
6920	1.45	22.4	Br	150°	*Poslet,* Thomas. 1667 ½d. 5.77; P|TA. BW 1018. Nott. Reading completed from BM specimen. Surname from Postlethwaite in Millom (Cumb), colloquially pronounced *Poslett* (Bardsley 1901, p. 617; Reaney 1995, p. 359)
6921a	2.99	46.1	Br	330°	*Simcoe,* John. 1666 ½d. 5.64.1; 5.77. BW 1021 but HALFE. Nott. John Simcoe of St Andrew Holborn, Haberdasher, b. 1625 (Boyd 17071). Two Foundations to be set out for John Simcoe 1670 (Mills 1962-7, i. 34)
6921b	2.32	35.8	Br	330°	Same dies. Nott
6922	1.17	18.1	M	180°	*Smith,* John. 1654. 3.10.17; S|IK. BW 1022. Nott. Same obv. die as 6923
6923	1.03	15.9	Cu	180°	*Smith,* John. 1654. 3.10.17; S|IK. BW 1022. Nott [ex Taffs]. Same obv. die as 6922
6924	0.54	8.4	Br	0°	*Tothaker,* Robert, mealman. 1657. T|RE; 5.77.1. BW 1024 but MEALMA^{N}. Nott. Reading confirmed from BM specimen. Obv. legend starts at 10 o'clock. Surname presumably as Toothaker etc., but closer to German *Todtenacker,* 'Churchyard' (Bardsley 1901, p. 758)

[*continued overleaf*]

6905 6906 6907a 6908 6909 6910

6911 6912 6913 6914 6915 6916b

6917 6918 6919 6920 6921b 6922

6923 6924 6925a 6926b 6927 6928

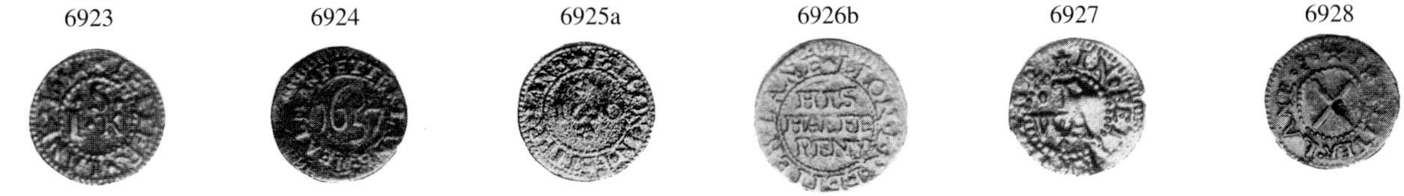

Plate 21 (*cont.*)

Named signs

	Weight			*Die*	
	g	*gr*		*axis*	
6925a	1.08	16.6	Br	180°	*Falcon* (AT THE): Gibbon, Henry. 1650. 3.92.5; date. BW 1010. Nott
6925b	0.82 (worn)	12.7	Br	180°	Same dies. [Nott]
6926a	1.72	26.6	Br	90°	*Lion* (AT Y^{E}): Redway, Robert. nd ½d. 3.11; 5.77. BW 1019; Kent 2005, p. 62. Nott. Diameter 20 mm. Robert Reddway or Rodway (Woodhead 1966, p. 136). Foundations set out for Robert Redway/Radaway 1667 (Mills 1962-7, i. 34, ii. 8v, 13). Bedloe 1679, p. 20, in an account of some other fires since that Grand Conflagration in [16]66, prints the substance of the examination of Robert Redway 'Victualler' at the 'Red-Lyon' in Fetter-Lane taken 6 Aug. 1670 by Sir Thomas Bludworth [1620-1682, MP]
6926b	1.55	24.0	Br	90°	Same dies. Nott [ex Taffs]. Diameter 18 mm
6927	0.44	6.9	Br	90°	*Sugarloaf* (AT THE SVGAR LOAFE): ?T—, W—. nd. 5.64.1; T|WA. BW 1023. Nott [ex Spink]. Reading confirmed from MoL specimen
					Three Golden Cocks: ?I/J—, R— *see* 6946 (Fleet Lane)
6928	0.98	15.1	Br	90°	*White Cross tavern* (WHITE CROSSE TAVERN): ?H—, W—. 1657. I6|W H|57 (I•6|W H|5•7; •WHITE•CROSSE•TAVERN around); 1.69.1 (•IN•FETTER•LANE•:• around). BW —; Dickinson 1011A. Nott. Punch-marked both sides

FETTER LANE (*cont.*)

Named signs (*cont.*)

	Weight			*Die*	
	g	*gr*		*axis*	
6929	1.30	20.0	Br	180°	*White Cross* (AT THE): Willcocks, Clement. 1666 ½d. 1.70.12 (W|CE); 5.77. BW 1025. Nott [ex Carthew]. Reading confirmed from BM specimen

FETTER LANE neighbourhood

The reading is *At Fetter lane End in Holborn* on 6930; AT FETTER LANE END NEXT FLEET STREETE on 6931

6930a	2.54	39.2	Br	0°	*Chandler,* Percival (PERCIFVLL). 1667 ½d. 4.13.12 (•PERCIFVLL•CHANDLER•AT•Y^E^ around); 5.77.1 (*At Fetter|lane End in|Holborn his|half•peny|1667*). BW —; Dickinson 1003C. Nott [ex Carthew]. Percival Chandler, Haberdasher; will, PCC, 1674, St Andrew Holborn (Boyd 24853)
6930b	1.55	23.9	Br	270°	Same dies. Baldwin
6931a	2.80	43.2	Br	180°	*Ivye,* John. 1670 ½d. 4.2.5; 3.3.13. BW 1014 but *1670*. Nott [ex Carthew]. The tallow-chandler appears to wear a flat hat as on 6674, and not the more usual conical cap
6931b	1.80	27.8	Br	180°	Same dies. Nott [ex Taffs]

FIELD LANE (Farringdon ward Without *and* Middlesex: Holborn) *see* Middlesex I: Holborn

FIELD LANE corner *see* Middlesex I: Holborn

FINCH LANE (Cornhill & Broad Street wards) [27-G14]

The reading is FINCH LANE on both

6932	1.64	25.4	Br	180°	*Stubs,* Thomas. 1669 ½d. 5.68.14; 5.77. BW 1035. Nott [ex Taffs]. Reading confirmed from MoL specimen A16528. Thomas Stubbs of St Peter Cornhill (1641-1674), Weaver (Boyd 16966)

Named signs

6933	1.01	15.6	Br	180°	*Horseshoe* (AT THE HORSE SHOOE): ?H—, R—. 1652. 5.68.1; R H. BW 1033. Nott

FIVE FOOT LANE (Queenhithe ward, Thames Street) [35-J10, m35] *see* Uncertain I

FLEET BRIDGE *subsequently* LUDGATE CIRCUS (Farringdon ward Without) [23-H6]

The reading is ONE FLET BRIGE; see also FLEET BRIDGE neighbourhood

Named signs

6934	0.66 (chipped)	10.1	Cu	0°	*Ball* (AT Y^E^): Ball, S—. nd. 1.40.3; B|SS. BW 1046. Nott [ex Taffs]. Reading completed from *NCirc* 112 (2004), TT3074

FLEET BRIDGE neighbourhood

See also GREEN'S RENTS. The reading is FLEET BRIDG on 7041; AT FLEET BRIDG on 6935, BRIDGE on 6937; NEERE FLEET BRIDGE on 6939; AT FLEETE BRIDG on 6940, BRIDGE on 6936, 6941; NEARE FLEETE BRIDGE on 6938

6935	0.89	13.7	Br	180°	*Brigstock,* Maurice (MORRIS). nd. 5.14 Tylers & Bricklayers 2 (•MORRIS•BRIGSTOCK around); B|MM (•B•|M•M; •AT•FLEET•BRIDG around). BW —; Dickinson 1046A but arms revised. Nott. Description confirmed from Greenall 1997, pl. 3.103
6936	1.13 (corroded)	17.5	Br	180°	*Tomkins,* Will—. 1657. T|WW; 3.95.1. BW 1052 but WILL:. Nott. Description confirmed from Greenall 1997, lot 105
6937	1.18	18.2	M	270°	*Wall,* Will, cap (CAPP) maker. nd. 5.14 Merchant Taylors; W|WM. BW 1053. Nott
6938	0.67 (chipped)	10.3	Br	180°	*Woodley,* Henry. 1657. Date; H W. BW 1054. Nott. Reading completed from MoL specimen. Same obv. die as ii. 1330, rev. AT NEW PORT POND, Essex; the rev. dies may be contemporaneous
6939a	2.18	33.6	Br	0°	*Wratten,* Edmond. nd ½d. 5.14.192; 5.77. BW 1055 but arms: three escutcheons. Nott. Struck off-centre. Description confirmed from BM specimen. Arms for the Painter-Stainers' Company, three escutcheons etc. (Bromley 1960, p. 184). Edmund Wratton bound Painter-Stainer apprentices 1667, 1670 (Webb 1996-, xxxviii. 44, 56)
6939b	1.46	22.5	Br	0°	Same dies. Nott [ex Taffs]

[*continued overleaf*]

6929 6930a 6931b 6932 6933 6934

6935 6936 6937 6938 6939b 6940

6941 6942 6943 6944 6945 6946

6947 6948 6949 6950 6951 6952

Plate 22 (*cont.*)

Named signs

	Weight *g*	*gr*		Die axis	
6940	0.93	14.3	M	180°	*Rose tavern* (AT THE): B[ellamy], W[illiam]. 1649. 4.12.1; B|WD. BW 1045. Nott [ex Taffs]. Reading FLEETE confirmed from Berry 1990, p. 36. Vintner 'Wm Bellamy, Rose neere fleetbridge' 1641 (Rogers 1928a, p. 76, 1928c, pp. 157, 190). William Bellamye appr. 1619 (Webb 1996-, xliii. 25, see also 339)
6941	0.50	7.6	Br	0°	*Three* [*?Lasts*] (AT THE 3): Stroud, Tho[mas]. nd. 3.7.43; S|TI. BW 1051 but THO:. Nott. Description confirmed from BM specimen. Thomas Stroud of St Bride, Glazier; md. Jane Blick or Black 1663 (Boyd 20416)

FLEET DITCH *subsequently* FARRINGDON STREET *and* NEW BRIDGE STREET (Farringdon ward Without) [23-H5: New Canal]

The reading is AT FLEETE DITCH

6942	0.85	13.1	Cu	180°	*Seale,* Robert. nd. 3.108.20 (•ROBERT•SEALE•AT•THE• around); S|RA (•S•|R·A|•; •AT•FLEETE•DITCH• around). BW —; Greenall 1991, p. 98, n. 3. Baldwin

FLEET LANE (Farringdon ward Without) [23-G6]

The reading is FLEET LANE on 6943, 6947-8, LANE on 6944; FLEETE LANE on 6945; FḶẸ–ṬẸ LANE on 6946

6943	1.79	27.6	Cu	0°	*Waterfall,* Henry. nd ½d. 5.77; W|HE. BW 1062. Nott. Reading confirmed from BM specimen

Named signs

6944	1.32 (chipped)	20.4	Cu	270°	*Plough* (AT THE): Yeo, Henry. nd ½d. 5.79.9; 5.54. BW 1063 but LANE, three knots. Nott. Henry Yeo, Embroiderer; will, PCC, 1665, St Sepulchre (Boyd 25552)
6945	1.15	17.7	M	180°	*Ship* (AT THE): ?O—, S—. 1649. 5.13.18; O|SA. BW 1061. Nott [ex Taffs]. In the Bird collection (lot 290) the same rev. occurred, perhaps in a fresher state, with a different obv. die at 180°, ex Norweb ex Nott
6946	0.66	10.1	Br	0°	*Three Golden Cocks* (Y^E3 GOVLDEN ÇOCḲES): ?I/J—, R—. 1657. 3.101.3 (•Y^E3 GOVLDEN•ÇOCḲES around); I|RM (•I•|R·M|•; •IN•FḶẸ–ṬẸ•LANE I657 around). BW —; Dickinson 1013A, from a report of this specimen, read as FETTER LANE. Nott [ex Taffs]

FLEET LANE. 'The Bridge' neighbourhood [23-H5]

The reading is FLEET LANE NEAR Y^EBRIDG on 6948, Y^EBRIDGE on 6947. By 1673 there was a bridge over the Fleet at Fleet Lane, but the work commenced 1668 only (Harben 1918, p. 234)

6947	1.75	26.9	Cu	180°	*Dugdale,* Wil—, mealman (MEALE MAN). 1663 ½d. 5.77; W D|date. BW 1057 but WIL:. Nott [ex Taffs]. Reading FLEET confirmed from BM specimen. Same obv. die as 6948
6948	2.17	33.4	Cu	0°	*Dugdale,* Wil—, mealman (MEALE MAN). 1664 ½d. 5.77; W D|date. BW 1058 but WIL:, BRIDG. Nott [ex Taffs]. Same obv. die as 6947, showing evidence that it had clashed with the rev. die of 6947 at an axis of 180°

FLEET STREET (Farringdon ward Without) [31-I2]

See also CHANCERY LANE neighbourhood; FETTER LANE neighbourhood; HERCULES' PILLARS ALLEY; INNER TEMPLE GATE neighbourhood; NEW FLEET STREET; RAM ALLEY; ST DUNSTAN IN THE WEST neighbourhood; WHITE LION COURT. The reading is FLEET STREET on 6751, 6950, 6952-5, 6957, 6959-61, 6969-70, 6973, 7073, 7156, 7571 (FḶẸET on 6961, STREEṬ on 6959), FLEET ST|REET on 7572; *fleet street* on 7070, *Street* on 7071; FLEET STREETE on 6931, 6949, 6964-6, 6972, 7072, 7570, STRET on 6968; FLEETE STREETE on 6750, 6967; FLEETSTREET on 6951, 6963, 6971, FLẸETSTR–ẸT on 6956; FLEETSTR: on 6962; FLET STREETE on 6958, FLET STRET on 7528

6949	0.88	13.6	Cu	90°	*Ashton,* John. 1664. 3.4.21; A|IL. BW 1064. Nott
6950	1.07	16.5	M	180°	*Bryan,* John. 1656. 3.52.25; B|IM. BW 1069. Nott. See also 7571
6951	2.66	41.0	Cu	90°	*Farr,* James. 1666 ½d. 2.12.1; 5.77. BW 1074 but FLEETSTREET. Nott. James Farr, 'barber' 1654, Barber Surgeon 1660, Master 1670, bd. St Dunstan in the West 1681 (BW 1074 n.; Boyd 48950; Whittet 1983, p. 137). The Rainbow coffee-house set up by Mr Farr c.1656 (Aubrey 1982, pp. 42-3). See also 7158
6952	1.00	15.4	M	180°	*FitzJefery,* N[icholas], mil[l]iner. 1656. F|NA; date. BW 1075. Nott [ex Taffs]. Nicholas FitzJeffries, Leatherseller; md. Abigail Webster 1655 (Boyd 24988). See also Middlesex I: Westminster: The Strand: *FitzJeoffery,* Nicholas

	Weight g	*gr*		*Die axis*	
6953	1.69	26.0	Cu	180°	*Halsted,* William. nd ½d. 5.14 Grocers; 5.76.147. BW 1078. Nott. Reading confirmed from MoL specimen. William Halsted of St Bride, b. 1633, Grocer; md. Elizabeth Bickerton 1662 (Boyd 28808)
6954	2.27	35.0	Br	0°	*Healey,* William. 1668 ½d. 3.65.10; 5.77 (H|WM). BW 1081 but THE. Nott. William Hayley, licensed victualler 1664, 1665 and 1669-80 (BW 1081 n.). Foundation to be set out for William Haley 1668 (Mills 1962-7, i. 35)
6955	0.72	11.1	Br	180°	*Hopley,* Thomas. nd. 3.1.37; 5.77 (H|TA). BW 1082. Nott [ex Taffs]
6956	0.46 (chipped)	7.2	Br	90°	*Mart,* William. nd. 3.5.81; W M. BW 1087 but FLẸETSTR–ẸT. Nott [ex Seaby ex ? ex Baldwin]. William Mart, Vintner, free 1658; by 1666 he had moved from the Queen's Head to the King's Head (Rogers 1928a, p. 78, 1928c, p. 152; Woodhead 1966, p. 112). See also 6751. For apprentices see Webb 1996-, xliii. 370
6957	0.86	13.2	Br	30°	*Sharpe,* John. nd. 3.5.87 (•IOHN•SHARPE•• around); I S (•••|I•S|•••; •IN•FLEET [?stop] STREET around). BW —; Dickinson 1097A, from a report of this specimen. Nott. John Sharp, haberdasher 1641, Leatherseller, Master 1676 (Boyd 58888)
6958	1.33	20.5	Br	180°	*Tisbery,* Thomas, oilman (OLE MAN). 1653. 5.76.148 (T T); date. BW 1099 but FLET. Nott. Reading completed from BM specimen. Thomas Tisberry, oilman, presented at the wardmote court 1664 'for selling his goods by light weight' (Burn 1855, 489 n.). For the monogram see 6959. Surname from Tisbury, Wilts.
6959	0.93 (chipped)	14.3	Br	180°	*Tisbery,* Thomas, oilman (OYL MAN). nd. 3.39.1; 5.76.148 (T T). *BW 1100. Nott [ex Taffs]. The wide Ns are believed to be later than the narrow Ns on 6958. Thomas Tisbery fl. 1649, bd. 1682. On the capital T in the monogram is a T in the Secretary Hand (Thompson 2005a)
Named signs					
6960	2.71	41.8	Cu	180°	[*Bear*] *tavern* (TAVERNE): B[rett], F[rancis]. 1665. 3.49.6 (B|FE); date. BW 1066. Brand. Reading completed from BM specimen. The Bear leased to Francis Brett, who was in possession at the time of the Fire (Rogers 1928a, p. 76). Francis Brett appr. Vintner 1647 (Webb 1996-, xliii. 39, see also 342)
6961	0.73	11.2	Br	180°	*Cock* (AT THE COK): ?T—, H—, ?m— (M. . .). 1649 (Ị6–9). 3.101.1 (•AT•THE•COK• IN•F̣ḶẸET around); T|HS (•T•|H•S; •STREET•M. . .Ị6–9 around). BW —; Dickinson 1097D, from Heal 1928, p. 10. Baldwin. Date determined from style of lettering
6962	1.20	18.5	Br	270°	*Feathers* (AT Y^E^ FETHERS): Tickner, Tho[mas]. nd. 3.107.1; T|TD. BW 1098 but THO:, FLEETSTR:. Nott. Rev. legend starts at 9 o'clock. Thomas Tickner md. Deborah Watts at St Bride, Fleet Street, 1657 (Biddle 2005, p. 308, wine-bottle seals no. 9). Tickner a Kent form of Titchener (Cottle 1978, p. 381)
6963	2.28	35.2	Cu	270°	*Golden* [*?Angel*] (AT THE): Hancox, John, grocer. nd ½d. 3.10.1; 5.77 (I H). BW 1079 but FLEETSTREET. Nott [ex Taffs]. Reading completed from BM specimen
6964	2.07	32.0	Br	90°	*Green* [*?Dragon*] *tavern* (AT Y^E^): Hammond (ḤAMMOND), Thomas. 1668 ½d. 3.114.1 (•THOMAS•ḤAMMOND•AT•Y^E^GREE^N^ around); 5.77 (HIS|[rule]|HALFE|[rule]|PENY|[rule]|I668; •TAVERN•IN•FLEET•STREETE• around). BW —; Dickinson 1078A (this specimen). Baldwin [ex Macfadyen, lot 151]. Thomas Ham(m)ond, Vintner, bound apprentices (Webb 1996-, xliii. 359)
6965	0.92	14.2	M	180°	*Horn tavern* (AT THE HORNE TAVERN): P[owell], P[hilemon]. nd. 5.62.1; P|PS. BW 1091. Nott [ex Taffs]. Reading confirmed from MoL specimen. Philemon Powell of St Dunstan in the West, Vintner, 'horne in fleetstreet' 1641, fl. 1651; wife Sarah, widow Powell 1652 (Rogers 1928a, p. 77, 1928c, pp. 155-6, 191; Boyd 56018). Philemon Powell appr. 1627 (Webb 1996-, xliii. 237, see also 377)
6966	0.88	13.5	Br	180°	*Jerusalem* (AT THE): ?P—, I/J—. nd. 5.12.10; P|IK. BW 1090. Nott [ex Taffs]
6967	1.05	16.3	Br	270°	*Jerusalem* (AT Y^E^): Grace (GRAC|E), Andrew (AND|REW). 1657. 5.77; 5.12.10. BW 1077 but IN[no stop]FLEETE[no stop]STREETE. Nott [ex Taffs]. Description confirmed from BM specimen
					King's Head: W[illson], L[ewis] [and] M[orris], H[enry] *see* 6750 (Chancery Lane neighbourhood)
6968	1.32	20.4	Br	0°	*Mitre* (AT THE MITER): Pagget, Will[iam]. nd. 5.59.20; P|WE. BW 1092. Nott [ex Carthew]. William Paget md. Elizabeth Watkins 1637; at the Mitre, Mitre Court, off Fleet Street, 1658-60; at the Mitre, Fleet Street, 1660-2 (Rogers 1928c, pp. 137-40)
6969	2.46	38.0	Br	180°	[*?Sun*] *tavern* (AT Y^E^ TAVERNE): Willson, Lewis. nd ½d. 2.1; 5.77. BW 1104. Nott. Lewis Wilson, vintner 1661-5 (Burn 1855, 492 n.). See also 6750 and Middlesex I: Westminster: The Strand: [*?King's Head*] tavern. Lewis Wilson appr. 1651 (Webb 1996-, xliii. 324, see also 392)
6970	1.39	21.5	Br	0°	*Temple* (AT Y^E^SINE OF Y^E^): Leigh, John. nd ½d. 5.3.28; 5.77 (L|IM). BW 1084 but HALF|PENY. Nott [ex Taffs]. John Leigh of St Dunstan in the West, Grocer; md. Mary Chelsham 1662 (Boyd 20194)

[*continued overleaf*]

6953 6954 6955 6956 6957 6958

6959 6960 6961 6962 6963 6964

6965 6966 6967 6968 6969 6970

6971 6972 6973 6974 6975 6976

Plate 23 (*cont.*)

	Weight *g*	*gr*		*Die axis*	
6971	0.84	12.9	Br	0°	*Three Legs* (AT THE 3 LEGS): Mayhew, Thomas. nd. 3.7.18 (•THOMAS:MAYHEW AT:THE: around); M|TP (M|T P; •3 LEGS:IN:FLEETSTREET: around). BW —; Dickinson 1087B. Baldwin -1970. Reading confirmed from MoL specimen
6972	1.13	17.4	M	180°	*Three Nuns* (AT 3 NVNS): Harward, Jo—. nd. 3.4.22; I H. BW 1080. Nott [ex Taffs]
6973	1.40	21.6	Cu	90°	*White Hart* (AT THE WHITE HART): Cordin, Tho—. nd ½d. 5.14 Grocers; 5.77. BW 1073 but THO:, WHITE . Nott [ex Taffs]. Reading confirmed from BM specimen. Thomas Cordin, son of Richard of Derby, vintner, bound 1653 for 8 years to John Beale of the Grocers' Company, cf. 7255 (Whittet 1983, p. 137); Mr Cordwin, seller of 'Mr Barnebies' Antipestilential Powder' 1665 (BW 1073 n.). For Richard Cordin cf. i. 588

'FLEET YARD' *i.e.* ?FLEET PRISON yard (Farringdon ward Without) [23-H6: Fleet]

The reading is FLEETE YARD

Named signs

6974	2.08	32.2	Cu	0°	*Barley-broth* (AT THE BARLY BROTH): Greene (GREENE), Thomas (–HOMAS). 1664 ½d. 5.77 (BARLY|BROTH|date); 5.77 (G|TM). *BW 1105 (THOMAS) but •G•|T M|•½•. Nott [ex Taffs]. Obv. struck off-centre. Reading partly completed from BM specimen. Barley-broth was strong ale (OED)

FORE STREET (Coleman Street ward & Cripplegate ward Without) [16-E11]

The reading is FORE STREET on 6976, 6978, STREETE on 6977; FORE S– –EET on 6975; FOARE STREET on 6981; FOR STRE^{T} on 6980; FORSTREAT on 6983; F–R STRET on 6979; – –WSTRET CRIPLEGAT on 6982

6975	1.88	29.0	Br	270°	*Minn* (MINN), Clemence (CLEMENTS). 1666 ½d. 3.92.7; 5.77. *BW 1111 (STREET) but CLEMENTS•MINN, bird of prey, HER|HALFE. Nott
6976	1.25 (edge cut)	19.3	Cu	90°	*Padgett,* Ralph. 1666 ½d. 5.77 ([rule]|•RALPH•|[rule]| •PADGETT•|[rule]| •IN• FORE•|[rule]| STREET|•••); 5.77 (B|RE) [*sic*] (•HIS•|[rule]|HALFEPENY| [rule]|•I666•|[rule]| •B•|R.E). BW —; Dickinson 1109B. Baldwin [ex Macfadyen, lot 152]. Reading completed from Sedgwick 1986, pl. 1.22. Letters E and F similar

FORE STREET (*cont.*)

	Weight *g*	*gr*		*Die axis*	
6977	1.32	20.3	Br	0°	*Papworth,* Thomas. nd. 3.11; P|TE. BW 1110. Nott [ex Taffs]. Reading STREETE confirmed from BM specimen
6978	1.54	23.7	Cu	0°	*White,* Thomas. 1661. 4.2.5; T W. BW 1112 but *16*[tree]*61*. Nott. ?Thomas Quait or White of Cripplegate, Cordwainer, md. Joan Whitlock 1659 (Boyd 40312)
6979	1.34	20.6	Br	0°	*Willcockes,* Sarah, milliner (MILENER). 1668 ½d. 2.4.7; S W|date. *BW 1113 (FAR) but STRET. Nott [ex Taffs]. K double-entered
Named signs					
6980	0.90	13.9	Br	90°	*Golden Lion* (AT Y^{E}GOV|DEN LYON): Hobs (ḤOBS), Israel. nd ½d. (HAḶF̣ PENỴ). 3.11 (•ISRAEL ḤOBS AT•Y^{E}GOV around); 5.77 (H|IM) (HIS|HAḶF̣|PENỴ|•H•|I•M; DEN LYON•IN•FOR STRE^{T} around). BW —; *Dickinson 1109A. Baldwin -1970. Israel Hobbs of St Giles Cripplegate, Grocer; md. Martha Jeffries 1665 (Boyd 29008)
6981	2.41	37.1	Cu	180°	*King's Head* (AT Y^{E}): Cheshire (CHESHỊRE), Thomas. 1669 ½d. 4.15.12 (KINGS|HEAD) (•THOMAS•CHESHỊRE•AT•Y^{E} around); 4.15.5 (HIS|HALF|PENY) (•IN•FOARE• STREET•I669 around). BW —; *Dickinson 1108A. Nott [ex Carthew]. Reading of date completed from Wetton 1989, lot 183
6982	0.96	14.8	Br	150°	*Tobacco Roll* (AT THE T– –ACCO ROLL): B[abington], ?J[ohn]. nd. B|– – (:B:|– –; •AT•THE•T– –ACCO ROLL around); 5.14.186 (– –WṢTRẸṬ•CRIP̣LEGAT around). BW —; Dickinson 788A, from a report of this specimen as B|NI, WITHIN CRIPLEGAT, and 2064A (New Street…), from Heal 1928, p. 12. Nott [ex Carthew]. Reading probably FAWSTRET, cf. BW 1108, I.B. at the Tobacco Roll in Fore Street (without Cripplegate). The arms are those of Babington *Argent ten torteaux four three two and one in chief a label of three points* (Papworth 1874, p. 1055). The issuer was perhaps John Babington b. c.1625 (Vis. Lond. 1633-5, p. 36)

FORE STREET. Ship neighbourhood

The reading is FORSTREAT NEXT Y^{E}SHIP

6983	0.78	12.0	Br	0°	*Reading,* Joh—, mealman. nd. 4.10.1 (•IOH•READING•MEALMAN around); I R (•|I•R|•; IN•FORSTREAT•NEXT•Y^{E}SHIP around). BW —; Dickinson 1110A. Nott [ex Carthew]

FOSTER LANE (Farringdon ward Within & Aldersgate ward) [25-G9]

The reading is FOSTER LANE on 6984-93 (LANẸ on 6990), ḶẠṆ– on 6994

6984	1.12	17.2	Br	180°	*Chambers,* John. nd. 5.64.50; C|IA. BW 1116. Nott. John Chambers, Merchant Taylor, fl. 1618-1681; Ordinary keeper 1666 (Woodhead 1966, p. 44). Foundations set out for John Chambers 1668-70 (Mills 1962-7, i. 33, iv. 34v, v. 26v)
6985	2.38	36.8	Cu	0°	*Dawson,* Samuel (SAMVELL). 1666 ½d. 3.60.30; 5.77. BW 1118. Nott [ex Taffs]
6986	0.48	7.4	Br	0°	*Ferne,* James. nd. 5.56.5; F̣|IS. *BW 1120. Nott [ex Taffs]. Legend starts between 10 and 11 o'clock both sides. ?James Fearne, Goldsmith, fl. 1647-?54 (Woodhead 1966, p. 68, s.v. Ferne, John)
6987	1.83	28.2	Cu	0°	*Hoult,* Matthew (MATHEW). 1665 ½d. 3.4.22; 5.77. BW 1123. Nott [ex Taffs]
6988	1.62	25.0	Cu	90°	*Jarves,* Edward. 1668 ½d. 2.1; 5.77 (I|EI). BW 1124. Nott [ex Taffs]. ?Same issuer as 6763
6989	1.68	25.8	Cu	0°	*Poole,* Anthony, ironmong[e]r. 1668 ½d. 3.60.30; 5.77. BW 1125 but IRONMONGR, PENY. Nott [ex Taffs]. Anthony Pool, b. 1643, Ironmonger; bd. St Leonard Foster Lane 1679 (Boyd 33392). Behind the nag's head the bridle appears to be held in a gloved hand
6990	2.27	35.1	Pb	135°	*?Rowthe* (R–W– –E), John. nd. 4.12.1 (•IOHN••R–W– –E around); I R (I R; •IN•FOSTER•LANẸ around). BW —; *Caldecott 1907, 4, *Dickinson 1125A (ROWTHE). Baldwin, by whom previously also read as RONTHE. *Rowthe* (for Roth?) not confirmed, though the fourth letter does seem to be an upright and not (e.g.) S
6991	0.56	8.6	Br	0°	*Wallis,* John. nd. 5.14.187; I W. BW 1128. Nott [ex Taffs]. John Wallis (d. 1695), Merchant Taylor, Master 1687, fl. Foster Lane 1655, 1664; ?Goldsmith and banker, ?Weigher and Teller in the Mint 1661 (Woodhead 1966, p. 170 but see note, Challis 1989, p. 176). Foundation set out for Major John Wallis 1668 (Mills 1962-7, i. 33, ii. 160v-161). The arms are of Wallis, unlocated (Berry 1828-40, ii. sig. 5X3v.)
Named signs					
6992	1.14	17.7	M	90°	*Dagger & Pie* (AT THE DAGAR AND PYE): D[annatt], M[oses]. nd. 5.42.4; 4.15.7 (D|MH). BW 1117 but AT[no stop]THE. Nott [ex Carthew]. Obv. legend starts at 1 o'clock. First A of DAGAR over [?]. 'Moses Dannet, at ye Dagger in Foster Lane, buried' 1657 (Smyth 1849, p. 46). Moses Dannett of St Leonard Foster Lane, Goldsmith; wife Hester (Boyd 27763). The crest of Dannett (etc.) was *A greyhound's head erased Argent collared Or rimmed and the ring Gules charged with three torteaux* (Fairbairn 1905, i. 151)

[*continued overleaf*]

6977 6978 6979 6980 6981 6982

6983 6984 6985 6986 6987 6988

6989 6990 6991 6992 6993 6994

6995 6996a 6997 6998 6999 7000

Plate 24 (*cont.*)

	Weight *g*	*gr*		*Die axis*	
6993	0.57 (chipped)	8.8	Cu	150°	[*Red Lion*]: Gerard, Robert. nd. 3.39.1; G|RE. BW 1122. Nott [ex Baldwin]. Foundation to be staked out for Robert Gerrard 1667 (Mills 1962-7, i. 33). Sign name assumed to be the same as for 6994 despite the different attitude of the lion
6994	1.47 (chipped)	22.7	Cu	90°	*Red Lion* (AT Y^{E} RED LYON): Gerard (GEARRARD), Robert. nd ½d. 3.11; 5.77 (G̣|RE). *BW 1121 (LANE) but PENY[–?]|[rule]|G̣|R E. Nott [ex Taffs]. Spelling of surname from 6993, q.v.

'FREEMAN'S LANE'

Stock, John *see* v. 4913

FRENCH CHURCH neighbourhood (Broad Street ward, Threadneedle Street) (*lost*) [27-G14, B62]

The reading is AG^{T}:Y^{E}:FRENCH CHVRCH IN THRED:|NEDLE STREET throughout

6995	2.71	41.9	Cu	0°	*Stonyer,* William (W^{M}:). nd ½d. 3.5.40; 5.77. BW 3138 but W^{M}:, ½•PENEY, AG^{T}:Y^{E}:, THRED:•:. Nott [ex Spink]. Stonyers Coffee-house (Lillywhite 1972, no. 1273). William Stonier, Saddler, of St Benet Fink, parish clerk, md. 1666 (Boyd 39728). The churchwardens of St Benet Fink recorded many payments at William Stonyer's (Rogers 1935, pp. 73-4, Murdoch 1985, p. 58, no. 53). Entire fraction ½ on obv. die, though fraction line doubtful; same rev. die as 6996-7
6996a	2.94	45.3	Cu	180°	*Stonyer,* William (W^{M}:). nd ½d. 3.5.40; 5.77. BW 3138 but W^{M}:, ½•PENEY, AG^{T}:Y^{E}:, THRED:•:. [Baldwin]. Same obv. die as 6997, in earlier state with 2 and fraction line of ½ absent from the die but 2 entered onto coin with incuse punch, i.e. sunk in relief; same rev. die as 6995 (q.v.), 6997
6996b	2.10	32.4	Cu	180°	Same dies, with 2 punched in as last. [Nott ex Taffs]
6996c	1.77	27.2	Cu	180°	Same dies, with 2 punched in as last. [Nott]
6997	3.34	51.6	Cu	180°	*Stonyer,* William (W^{M}:). nd ½d. 3.5.40; 5.77. BW 3138 but W^{M}:, ½•PENEY, AG^{T}:Y^{E}:, THRED:•:. Brand. Same obv. die as 6996, in later state with the fraction line and 2 of ½ added, clearer on MoL specimen illustrated Murdoch 1985, p. 59, no. 53. Same rev. die as 6995 (q.v.), 6996

FRESH WHARF neighbourhood (Billingsgate ward) [38-K15, n27]

The reading is AT FRESH WHARFE

Named signs

6998	1.16	17.9	Br	180°	*Three Mariners* (AT THE 3 MARRINERS): ?D—, T—. nd. 3.4.24; D|TS. BW 1130. Baldwin -1970

FRIDAY STREET (Bread Street ward & Farringdon ward Within) [25-H10]

The reading is FRYDAY STREET on 7002, STREETE on 6999, 7003, STREETẸ on 7004; FRYDAYSTREET on 7000; FRIDAY STREETE on 7001

6999	2.39	36.8	Cu	180°	*Watson,* Sam—. nd ½d. 3.6.51; 5.77. BW 1135. Spink [1977]

Named signs

7000	1.49	23.0	Br	240°	*Black Boy* (AT Y^{E}BLAK BOY): Jordan, Philip (PHILLIP). 1669 ½d. 3.1.34; 5.77 (I|PE). BW 1131 but FRYDAYSTREET. Nott [ex Taffs]. E of Y^{E} resembles F, probably from broken punch

FRIDAY STREET (*cont.*)

Named signs (*cont.*)

	Weight			Die	
	g	gr		axis	
7001	1.16	17.9	M	180°	*A Chand[ler's] shop:* Sanders, Edward. nd. S|EM (•S•|E•M; •EDWARD•SANDERS around); 5.77 (•A•|CHAND|SHOP|•; IN•FRIDAY•STREETE around). BW —; Dickinson 1133B. Baldwin. ?Edward Sanders of St Margaret Moses, box-maker, Joiner, fl. 1661; eldest child bap. 1642; wife Mary d. 1655 (Boyd 31088)
7002	2.12	32.6	Br	0°	*[Vincents] coffee-house* (Y^{E} COFFEE HOVSE): Vincent, Andrew. [16]71 1d. 3.6.51; 5.77. BW 1134 but I^{D}. Nott [ex Taffs]. Sign name from Lillywhite 1972, no. 1463
7003	0.72	11.1	Br	180°	*White Horse* (AT Y^{E}): M[iller], E[dward]. [16]57. 3.60.20; M|EM. BW 1133 but STREETE57. Nott. Reading completed from BM specimen. An Edward Miller appr. 1648 (Webb 1996-, xliii. 202, see also 371); of St Margaret Moses, Vintner, md. Mary, daughter of William Longe, 1657 (Rogers 1928a, pp. 78-9; Boyd 40893). For her father see Middlesex I: Westminster: Russell Street: *Rose tavern*
7004	0.50	7.7	Br	270°	*White Horse tavern* (AT Y^{E}WHIT ḤORS TAVRAN): P[etty] (P̣), H[enry]. nd. P̣|HE; 3.60.4. *BW 1132 but Y^{E}, •P̣•|HE|•. [Nott ex Baldwin]. Reading partly confirmed from BM specimen. Henry Petty or Pettitt of St Margaret Moses, Vintner; wife Elizabeth, their children bap. 1662-3, bd. 1665 (Rogers 1928a, pp. 78-9; Boyd 31129). Henry Petty appr. 1658 (Webb 1996-, xliii. 230, see also 376)

FULLER'S RENTS (Cripplegate ward Without *and* Middlesex: Finsbury: Golden Lane) [cf. 5-A9: not identified]/FULLER'S RENTS (Farringdon ward Within, Inner Temple) *subsequently* MITRE COURT BUILDINGS [cf. 32-I4: not identified] see Uncertain I

FYE FOOT LANE *see* Uncertain I: FIVE FOOT LANE

GARLICK HILL (Vintry ward) [36-I11]

The reading is GAR:\|LICK HILL on 6657; VPON GARLICKE HILL on 7005; cf. GARLICK HILL neighbourhood

Named signs

7005a	1.03	15.9	Br	180°	*Cooks' Arms* (AT THE COOKES ARMES): ?W—, R—. nd. 5.14 Cooks; W|RS. BW 1143. Baldwin. ?Robert Warter, Cook, fl. 1660; wife Susan (Boyd 25496, unlocated). He bound two apprentices 1659; the second was turned over 1662 (Webb 1996-, xxvi. 5, 57)
7005b	0.92	14.3	Br	180°	Same dies. Nott [ex Carthew]

GARLICK HILL neighbourhood (Vintry ward, Thames Street)

See also BLACK SWAN ALLEY. The reading is NERE GARLICK HILL on 7007; AT GARLICKE HILL on 7006

Named signs

7006	1.24	19.1	M	120°	*Greyhound tavern* (THE GRAHOVND TAVERN): B[randon], A[ndrew]. nd. 3.67.7; A B. BW 1142. Nott. Obv. legend starts between 1 and 2 o'clock. The Grayhound or Dog tavern demised to Andrew Brandon 1655 (Rogers 1928a, pp. 79, 338). Foundation set out May 1668 (Mills 1962-7, i. 39, iv. 54v); Andrew Brandon, haberdasher, to proceed with rebuilding Oct. 1668 (Fire Court 1966-, ii. 268)
7007	1.05	16.3	Br	0°	*Horseshoe* (AT THE HORSHOE): ?R—, I/J— (Ị). 1655. 5.68.1; Ị R. BW 1144 but HORSHOE, HILL•I655 = Ị• R. Nott [ex Seaby]. The axis could be 180°, with obv. legend starting at 6 o'clock

GEORGE YARD (Farringdon ward Without, Holborn Bridge neighbourhood) *subsequently* HOLBORN VIADUCT *etc.* [23-F5, f22: George Yard, Snow Hill]

The reading is GEORG YARD NEARE HOLBORNE BRIDG, perhaps the same as HOLBORN (*street*), 'George Yard' neighbourhood (q.v.)

7008a	1.30	20.1	Br	0°	*Scott,* Edmund. 1669 ½d. 3.5.23 (D Y); 5.77. BW 1459. Nott
7008b	1.03	15.9	Br	0°	Same dies. [Nott ex Taffs]

GILTSPUR STREET (Farringdon ward Within) [24-F7]

The reading is GILT SPVR STREET WITH\|OVT NEW\|GAT on 7011-12 (G̣–LT, W̩ỊṬḤ\|ỌVT on 7012); GILTSPVR STREET on 7010; GVILTSPVR STREET on 7009

7009	1.21	18.6	M	180°	*Botley,* Samuel (SAṂVEL). nd. 3.4.22; B|SH. *BW 1150 but rev. IN•GVILTSPVR. Nott [ex Taffs]. Rev. reading completed from BM specimen with obv. from a different die. ?Samuel Botley of St Sepulchre, shoemaker; md. Hannah White 1662 (Boyd 19813). See also 7011-12
7010	1.01	15.6	Br	180°	*Harris,* Thomas. nd. 5.14 Grocers; H|TA. BW 1151. Nott [ex Carthew]. Reading confirmed from BM specimen

[*continued overleaf*]

7001 7002 7003 7004 7005a 7006

7007 7008a 7009 7010 7011 7012

7013 7014 7015 7016b 7017 7018

7019 7020 7021 7022 7023b 7024

Plate 25 (*cont.*)

	Weight *g*	Weight *gr*		Die axis	
7011	1.53	23.6	Cu	0°	*Stephens,* James. nd. 3.4.22; 5.77. BW 1154. Nott. Obv. legend starts at 5 o'clock. H of WITH apparently double-entered. See also 7009
7012	1.38	21.3	Cu	0°	*Stephens,* James. nd. 3.4.22; 5.77. *BW 1154 (GILT). Nott [ex Taffs]. Restruck after turning over. Obv. reading completed from MoL specimen NN17500, struck from rev. die not represented in the Norweb collection. See also 7009

GLASSHOUSE HALL (Portsoken ward *and* Middlesex: Stepney) *see* Middlesex I: Stepney

GLOVERS' HALL neighbourhood (Cripplegate ward Without, Beech Lane) [15-C10, A20]

The reading is NEXT DORE TO GLOVERS HALL IN BEECH LANE

7013 1.32 20.4 Br 180° *Green,* Henry. 1669 ½d. 5.77; 5.77 (G|HA). BW 165. Nott [or Baldwin]. Reading confirmed from BM specimen

GOLDEN LANE (Cripplegate ward Without *and* Middlesex: Finsbury) *see* Middlesex I: Finsbury

GOODMAN'S YARD (Portsoken ward *and* Middlesex: Stepney) *see* Middlesex I: Stepney

GRACECHURCH STREET (Bishopsgate ward & Bridge ward Within) [28-H15: Gratious Street]

See also JERUSALEM ALLEY. The reading is GRA CHVRCH STREET on 7017; GRACE C STRET on 7019; GRACE CHVRCH STREET on 7022, STREETE on 7023; GRACE|CHVRCH STREET on 7015; GRASE CHVRCH STRET on 7021; GRASE|CHVRCH STREETE on 7020; GRACECHVRCH STREET on 7024, STREETE on 7025; GRACIOVS STREET on 7016, STREETE on 7014; GRATIOVS STREET on 7018, 7165, GRAṬIỌ–S STREEṬ on 7166.

The following were recorded but are now missing: BW 1200, two specimens, both axis 180°, ex Nott, one of larger diameter, on thick flan [another specimen illus. *S&B* no. 78, July-Sep. 2004, p. 19, T186]

7014	1.23	19.0	Br	180°	*King,* Samuel (SAMVELL). nd. 3.3.13; 3.2.8. BW 1204. Nott [ex Spink]
7015	1.38	21.3	Br	90°	*Potts,* John. 1669 ½d. 3.1.119 (•IOHN•POTTS•IN•GRACE around); 5.77 (HIS|HAḶF|PENY; •CHVRCH•STREET•I669 around). BW —; Dickinson 1205A but description revised. Baldwin. ?John Potts of St Peter Cornhill, Grocer, oilman; appr. 1658, d. 1705 (Boyd 23014). The standing figure holds an arrow or dart l., rt. a ?tobacco-pipe, so probably a North American Indian
7016a	2.19	33.7	Br	270°	*Urry,* David. nd ½d. 5.54; 5.77. BW 1207 but GRACIOVS. Nott. David Urry, Ironmonger, fl. 1659 (Webb 1996-, xxiv. 31), d. 1673, bd. St Leonard Eastcheap (Boyd 25462). Foundation to be set out 1668 (Mills 1962-7, i. 40). See also 7017
7016b	2.10	32.4	Br	270°	Same dies. Nott [ex Taffs]
7017	0.88	13.6	Br	270°	*Vernon,* Martin. [16]57. 5.54 (•MARTIN•VERNON•IN around); 5.77 (5 V 7|M A; •GRA•CHVRCH•STREET around). BW —; Dickinson 1207A. Nott. See also 7016
7018	0.87	13.4	Br	180°	*Warren,* Michael (MICHAELL). nd. 5.68.10; W|MA. BW 1209. Nott [ex Taffs]. 'Michael Warren at the Horse-shoe in Gracious Street' 1665, though a 1664 advertisement (if from the same house) expands the sign-name to the Gilded Horse-shoe (BW 1209 n.)

Named signs

7019	1.13	17.5	M	180°	*Boar's Head* (AT THE BORS HEAD): Cash (CASHE), L[aurence]. nd. 3.65.10; C|LA. BW 1197. Nott. After the Great Fire a foundation was staked out in Gracechurch Street for 'Lawrance Cash, Jerusalem Alley' (Mills 1962-7, i. 40). Surname and forename (normalized) from this, and a 1667 ½d. issued at [The Boar's Head]: LAVRANCE CASH IN IERVSALEM ALLY IN GRACECHVRCH STREET (Gilbert 1927, 150 = Dickinson 1563A)
7020	1.18	18.2	M	120°	*Red Lion* (THE RED LYON): ?F—, I/J—. 1650. 3.11; F|IS. BW 1201. Nott [ex Taffs]. Obv. legend starts between 1 and 2 o'clock. See also 7021
7021	0.97	15.0	Br	180°	*Red Lion* (AT THE RED LYON): ?P—, A—. nd. 3.11; P|AM. BW 1205 but STRET. Nott [ex Carthew]. See also 7020
7022	2.26	34.8	Cu	0°	*Ship tavern* (AT THE SHIP TAVERNE): [anonymous]. nd ½d. 5.13.18; 5.76.150. BW 1211. Nott [ex Carthew]. 'The monogram forms the word "Tavern"' (Thompson 1891, p. 302)
7023a	1.14	17.6	M	180°	*Three Tuns tavern* (THE 3 TVNN TAVERNE): K[ent], J[ohn]. nd. 5.64.33; K|IE. BW 1203. [Nott]. John Kent, Vintner, appr. 1631, Master 1681; Three Tonnes in Gracechurch Street 1651-66; md. (2) Elizabeth Barrett 1659; see also 6847; d. 1689 (Boyd 30268; Rogers 1928a, pp. 72-3, 1937, pp. 123-4; Woodhead 1966, p. 102 (B)). Apprentices bound to him (Webb 1996-, xliii. 365)
7023b	1.11	17.1	M	180°	Same dies. Nott [ex Taffs]
7024	0.89	13.7	Cu	180°	[*White Lion*]: Williams, William. nd. 3.11; W|WF. BW 1210. Nott [ex Taffs]. William Williams, Cordwainer at the White Lion, Master 1665, md. (1) Faith 1630, (3) Frances, d. 1666 (Rogers 1937, pp. 112-13; Woodhead 1966, p. 177(B))

GRACECHURCH STREET (*cont.*)

Named signs (*cont.*)

	Weight g	Weight gr		Die axis	
7025	3.12	48.2	Br	0°	*White* [*Lion*] (AT Y^{E}WHITE): Carter, Robert. 1668 1d. 3.11; 5.77. BW 1198 but GRACECHVRCH. Nott. White Lyon had been leased to Robert Carter 1666 (Fire Court 1966-, i. 116); foundation to be set out 1668 (Mills 1962-7, i. 40)

GRAVEL LANE (Portsoken ward, Houndsditch) [29-F18, d55]

The reading is GRAVY LANE NER HOVNDSDITCH

7026	0.92	14.1	Br	30°	*Stones,* Ben—. 1666. Date; S|BI. BW 1213 but BEN:. Baldwin. Reading confirmed from BM specimen

GRAY FRIARS *see* GREY FRIARS

GREAT CONDUIT neighbourhood (Cheap ward, Cheapside) [26-H11: removed after the Great Fire]

The reading is AGAINST THE GREAT COVNDVIT IN CHEAPSIDE on both (CHEAP̣SIDE on 7027)

7027	1.23	18.9	M	180°	*D*[*enny*], F[ulke]. nd. 3.2.8; D|FM. *BW 577. Nott [ex Taffs]. The initials correspond with those of Foulke Denny, 1654 (Rogers 1928c, p. 93)
7028a	1.17	18.1	Br	90°	*H*[*eath*], J[ohn]. nd. 5.64.33; H|IS. BW 583. [Baldwin]. The initials correspond with those of John Heath, 1654 (Rogers 1928c, p. 93)
7028b	0.99	15.2	Br	180°	Same dies. Nott

GREAT EASTCHEAP *subsequently* KING WILLIAM STREET *etc.* (Candlewick ward) [37-J14]

The reading is GREAT EAST CHEAP on 7031; GREAT EASTCHEAP on 7032; GREAT EASTCHIP on 7029-30

7029	1.85 (chipped)	28.5	Cu	0°	*Curtis,* Will—. nd ½d. 5.13.18; 5.77. BW 1257 but WILL:. Nott [ex Carthew]. Reading completed from Wetton 1989, pl. 8.188
7030	1.68	26.0	Br	180°	*Tew,* William, mealman. nd ½d. 3.61.2; 5.77 (T|WB). BW 1260 but .T.|line|2|W B|•; Thompson 2005c. Spink 1971. Reading confirmed from BM specimen. The upright of the T stands also for the numerator of ½. William Tew of St Dionis Backchurch, mealman; md. Bridget Gibbs 1665 (Boyd 20699). Foundation to be staked out for William Tewe 1677 (Mills 1962-7, i. 31)

Named signs

7031	0.97	15.0	M	180°	*Boar's Head tavern* (THE BORES HEAD TAVRNE): B[oyce], J[ohn]. nd. 3.65.10; B|II. BW 1256. Nott. John Boyce, Vintner, fl. 1642, d. 1658; wife Jane (Rogers 1928b, pp. 35-6, 41). John Boys appr. 1625 (Webb 1996-, xliii. 37, see also 341-2)
7032	4.23	65.3	Cu	0°	*Boar's Head tavern* (AT Y^{E}BORESHED TAVERNE): Sapcott, John. nd 1d. 3.65.10; 5.77 (S|IE). BW 1259 but I^{D}. Baldwin -1970. John Sapcott, Vintner, fl. 1667-78; wife Elizabeth (Rogers 1928b, pp. 29, 37-8, 41-2); appr. 1660 (Webb 1996-, xliii. 258, see also 381). Surname from Sapcote, Leics.

GREAT ST HELEN'S (Bishopsgate ward Within & Lime Street ward) [28-G16]

The reading is GREAT SAINT HELLEN

7033a	1.97	30.4	M	180°	*Adderley,* Hugh. 1666 ½d. 5.77.1; 3.109.1. BW 2515 but *His, 1666.* Nott [ex Carthew]. ?Hugh Adderley of St Helen Bishopsgate, Vintner; 1662 of St Bartholomew by the Exchange, where d. ?1674 (Boyd 4003); appr. 1649 (Webb 1996-, xliii. 2, see also 335)
7033b	1.62	25.0	M	180°	Same dies. [Nott]

GREAT TRINITY LANE (Vintry & Cordwainer & Bread Street & Queenhithe wards) [35-I10]

See also TRINITY LANE. The reading is GREAT TRENITY LAN^{E}

7034	1.06	16.3	Br	0°	*Cock,* John. nd. 3.107.3; C|IR. BW 1269 but TRENITY•LAN^{E}. Baldwin. Reading completed from BM specimen

GREAT WOOD STREET *see* WOOD STREET, southern part

[*continued overleaf*]

7025 7026 7027 7028b 7029 7030

7031 7032 7033a 7034 7035 7036

7037a 7038 7039a 7040 7041 7042

7043 7044 7045b 7046 7047 7048

GREEN DRAGON COURT *subsequently* HOLBORN VIADUCT *etc.* (Farringdon ward Without, Snow Hill) [23-G6, g63]

The reading is GREENE DRAGON COVRT on 7036, GREENEDRAGON COVR^{T} on 7035, with ON SNOW HILL on both

	Weight *g*	*gr*		*Die axis*	
7035	2.46	38.0	Br	0°	*Hide,* Joseph. 1669 ½d. 5.77 (•••IIOSEPHIHIDEI•••; •IN•GREENEDRAGON•COVRṬ around); 5.77 (HISIHALFEIPENNYI•••; •ON•SNOW•HILL•I669• around). BW —; Dickinson 2904A but GREENEDRAGON COVRṬ. Baldwin
7036	1.41	21.7	Br	180°	*?R—,* M—. 1659 (Ị659). M R (•••IMRI•••; •GREENE•DRAGON•COVRT around); 3.114.1 (•ON•SNOW•HILL•Ị659 around). BW —. Baldwin

The GREEN YARD (Lime Street ward & Bishopsgate ward Within, Leadenhall Market) [28-H15: see Harben 1918, p. 344]/The GREEN YARD (Cripplegate ward Without, London Wall) (*lost*) [16-E12]. Other possible attributions are disregarded, e.g. *Green Yard* off Goswell Street [4-A7, a5]

The reading is THE GREENE YARD throughout

7037a	1.74	26.9	Br	90°	*Eedes,* Humphrey. nd ½d. 3.60.30; 5.77. BW 1270. Nott. Diameter 19-19.5 mm
7037b	1.39	21.5	Br	270°	Same dies. [Baldwin ex Pridmore]. Diameter 18 mm
7038	1.46	22.5	Br	270°	*Nettelton,* Richard. nd ½d. 3.5.105; 5.77. BW 1274. Nott

Named signs

7039a	1.77	27.3	Br	0°	*Black* [*?Bull*] (AT THE): Payne, Will—. nd ½d. 3.52.6; 5.77. BW 1275 but WILL:. Nott [ex Taffs]. ?William Pain of St Andrew Undershaft, b. 1649, Distiller (Boyd 42610)
7039b	1.67	25.7	Br	0°	Same dies. [Nott ex Carthew]

GREEN'S RENTS *subsequently* BRIDE COURT (Farringdon ward Without, Bride Lane) [33-I6, k55]

The reading is FLEET BRIDG IN GREENES RENTS on 7041; GRE–NS ṚENTS on 7040

7040	0.67	10.3	M	180°	*W*[*arde*], W[illiam], a seacoal (SEACOLE) seller. nd. 3.44.7; WIWA. *BW 1278 (GREENS) but ṚENTS. Nott [ex Carthew]. Identification of issuer from 7041, q.v.
7041	1.41	21.8	Cu	0°	*Warde,* Will[iam] (WILL:). 1666 ½d. 5.14 Weavers; 5.77 (WIWA). BW 1279 but WILL:. Nott. Reading confirmed from BM specimen. William Ward, Weaver, fl. 1660; wife Anne (Boyd 25491, unlocated). Cf. 7375

GREY FRIARS (Farringdon ward Within) (*lost beneath Post Office Buildings*) [24-G7, g74]

The reading is GRAY FRIERS on 7042-4; GRAYE FRIERS on 7045

7042	0.76	11.7	Cu	315°	*Jones,* George. nd. 3.1.5 (•GEORGE•IONES around); 3.1.124 (••IN•GRAY•FRIERS• around). BW —, cf. 7043. Baldwin
7043	2.03	31.3	Br	0°	*Jones,* George. nd ½d. 3.1.124; IIGS. BW 1228. Nott [ex Carthew]. Reading completed from BM specimen
7044	1.78	27.5	Cu	300°	*Tart,* Richard. nd ½d. 3.1.67; R T. BW 1230. Nott. Reading completed from MoL specimen NN17548. ?Richard Tart of Christ Church, b. 1641, Haberdasher; md. Sarah Taylor 1665 (Boyd 17032)

GREY FRIARS. The Gate neighbourhood

The reading is AT GRAYE FRIERS GATE

7045a	0.90 (chipped)	13.9	Br	180°	*Waters,* James. nd. 3.1.5; WIIA. BW 1232. Baldwin. This specimen identified on ticket as 'White Friars Gate 3485A' and attributed to 'Whitefriars precinct: The Gate neighbourhood' (Greenall 1991, p. 106). James Waters of Christ Church, Cook; will, PCC, 1658 (Boyd 49034)
7045b	0.90	13.8	Br	180°	Same dies. Nott

GRUB STREET *subsequently* MILTON STREET (Cripplegate ward Without *and* Middlesex: Finsbury) [16-D11]

The reading is GRVB STREET on 7048, 7052-3, 7055, STREETE on 7049, 7051; GRVḄ STRET on 7054; GRVBB STREET on 7050; GRVBSTREET on 7046-7

7046	2.04 (chipped)	31.5	Br	270°	*Bell,* Marmaduke. 1670 ½d. 3.1.91 (M B) (•MARMADVKE•BELL•IN around); 5.77 (HISIHALFIPENY; •GRVBSTREET•I670: around). BW —; Dickinson 1281A, from Macfadyen, lot 152. Baldwin [ex Macfadyen, lot 152]
7047	1.42	21.9	Br	180°	*Branch,* James. 1664. Date (•••I1664I•••; •IAMES•BRANCH• around); BIIE (•B•II•E; •IN•GRVBSTREET around). BW —; Dickinson 1281B. Nott
7048	1.72	26.6	Br	45°	*Dawson,* John. 1666 ½d. 4.12.2; 5.77. BW 1282. Seaby 1969. Reading completed from MoL specimen

GRUB STREET *(cont.)*

	Weight g	Weight gr		Die axis	
7049	1.61	24.8	Br	90°	*Hatton,* William. 1666 ½d. 5.77; 4.10.6 (H|WM). BW 1285. Nott. Reading completed from BM specimen
7050	0.94	14.5	Br	180°	*Hide,* George, grocer. nd. 5.77.1; 5.82.28. BW 1287. Nott [ex Carthew]. Reading *Hide* completed from BM specimen
7051	2.20 (pierced)	33.9	Br	0°	*Winfeild,* Walter. 1666 ½d. 5.77 (HIS|HALF|PENY|••:••; •WALTER•WINFEILD•:• around); W|WF|date (•W•|W•F|1666; •IN•GRVB•STREETE•:• around). BW —; Dickinson 1294A. Nott

Named signs

7052a	1.89	29.2	Br	90°	[*Broad Arrow*] (AT THE): Pearce, Robert. 1666 ½d. 5.40.2 (R P); 5.77. BW 1290. Baldwin. Sign name from BW 1291. Rev. legend starts at 6 o'clock
7052b	1.57	24.3	Br	0°	Same dies. Nott [ex Taffs]
7053	1.50	23.2	Cu	180°	*Flying Horse* (AT Y^{E}): Robbinson, James. nd ½d. (HA–ḶFE). 3.62.5 (•IAMES•ROBBINSON•AT•Y^{E}: around); 5.77 (HIS|HA–ḶFE|PENY; •FLYING•HORSE •IN•GRVB•STREET around). BW —, cf. 1292. Baldwin. Evidence of die-clashing on rev. border. Description largely completed from BM and MoL specimens; these are from the same dies in later state, with one B cancelling the two in the surname and L cancelling the middle two characters in HA–ḶFE, as BW 1292
7054	1.27	19.6	Br	270°	*Naked Boy* (AT Y^{E} ṆẠḲED BOY): Tennant, William. nd ½d. (HALF̣Ẹ). 5.77; 3.1.2. *BW 1293. Nott. ?William Tennant of St Giles Cripplegate, b. 1614, Cordwainer, Sheriff's officer, fl. 1663 (Boyd 43069)
7055a	1.80	27.8	Br	180°	*White Lion* (AT Y^{E}): Threlkeld, Thomas, grocer. nd ½d. 5.77.1; 3.11. BW 1294 but no stops in rev. legend. Nott [or Baldwin]. Reading of surname completed from BM specimen
7055b	1.70	26.3	Br	180°	Same dies. [Nott ex Taffs]

GUILDHALL. Gate neighbourhood (Bassishaw & Cheap wards) [26-F11]

The reading is OVER AGAINS^{T} GVILD HALL GATE. See also 7057

7056	1.29	19.8	Br	270°	*Peete,* Robert. 1669 ½d. 3.11; 5.77. BW 1299 but AGAINS^{T}. Nott [ex Daniels]. Reading confirmed from BM specimen. ?Robert Peat of St Lawrence Jewry, Leatherseller and Clothworker; children bap. 1669-72 (Boyd 26461)

GUILDHALL. Gate neighbourhood. Three Tuns neighbourhood

For the Three Tuns at Guildhall Gate see BW 1296 and Lillywhite 1972, no. 15147. The reading is BEHIND THE 3 TVNS GVIL^{D}\|HAL

Named signs

7057	0.56	8.7	Br	150°	*Office* (AT Y^{E}OFIC^{E}): Tiler, Wil—. nd. T|WA; 5.77. BW 1301 but Y^{E}OFIC^{E}, GVILD|HAL. Baldwin. Reading largely completed from MoL specimen

GUN YARD (Bishopsgate ward Without, Bishopsgate)/GUN YARD *subsequently* GUN SQUARE (Portsoken ward, Houndsditch)

Blackle, William *see* Uncertain I

GUTTER LANE (Farringdon ward Without) [25-G10]

The reading is GVTTER LANE on 7059-60; GVTER LANE on 7058

Named signs

7058a	2.80	43.2	Br	330°	*Golden Anchor* (AT Y^{E}GOLDEN ANCKOR): FitzHugh, Thomas. nd 1d. 5.77; 5.38.20. BW 1304 but I^{D}. [Nott]
7058b	2.13	32.9	Br	240°	Same dies. No provenance
7058c	1.47 (chipped)	22.7	Br	330°	Same dies. Nott [ex Taffs]
7059	2.49	38.4	Cu	90°	*Horns & Horseshoe* (AT Y^{E}HORNES & HORSHOOE): Grainge, Will—. 1669 ½d. 3.53.33; 5.77 (G|WE). BW 1305 but WILL:, &HORSHOOE. Nott [or Baldwin ex Gilbert ex Baldwin 1937]
7060	0.59	9.0	Br	180°	*Wheatsheaf* [&] *Three Pigeons* (WHEATSHEIF 3 PIDGONS): ?W—, I/J—. 1657. 4.10.2 (•WHEATSHEIF•3•PIDGONS around); W|I (•W•|I•I; •IN•GVTTER•LANE 1657 around). BW —; Dickinson 1308A. Baldwin. Stop after IN confirmed from MoL specimen

[*continued overleaf*]

7049 7050 7051 7052a 7053 7054

7055b 7056 7057 7058c 7059 7060

7061b 7062 7063 7064 7065a 7066

7067b 7068 7069 7070 7071 7072

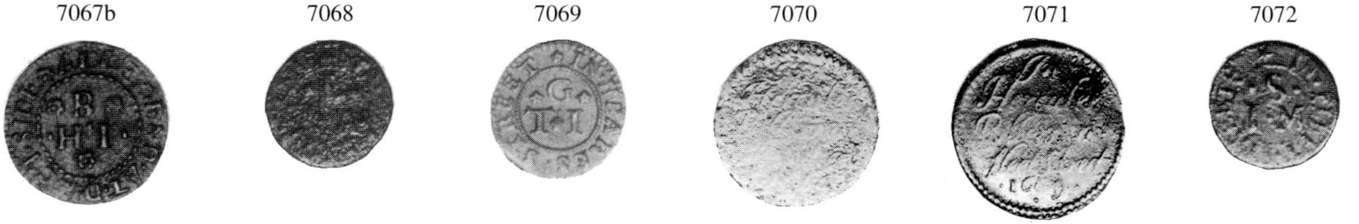

HALF MOON ALLEY (Bishopsgate ward Without) (*lost beneath Liverpool Street Station*) [18-D16, d36]

The reading is WITHOVT B GATE throughout

Named signs

	Weight g	*Weight gr*		*Die axis*	
7061a	0.96 (pierced)	14.8	Br	180°	*Half Moon brew-house* (THE HALFE MOONE BREW HOVSE): ?O—, G—. nd. 2.2; O|GI. BW 312. Nott [ex Taffs]. ?Griffith Owen of St Botolph Bishopsgate, Grocer, md. Jane Spencer 1641; both died 1669 (Boyd 54858)
7061b	0.96	14.7	Br	180°	Same dies. Nott [ex Carthew]
7062	1.08	16.6	Br	180°	*Half Moon brew-house* (THE HALFE MOONE BREW HOVS): ?O—, G—. nd. 2.2; O|GI. BW 311. Nott. Stop after WITHOVT double-entered. Same rev. die as 7063. For issuer see 7061
7063	1.05	16.3	Br	180°	*Half Moon brew-house* (THE HALFE MOONE BREW HOVS): ?O—, G—. nd. 2.2; O|GI. BW 311. Nott. R and stop after WITHOVT double-entered. Same rev. die as 7062, flawed below W. For issuer see 7061

HAMMOND'S QUAY (Billingsgate ward) (*lost*) [38-K15, n30]

The reading is AT HAMONSKEY on 7065-6; AT HAMONS KEY on 7064

7064	1.37	21.1	Cu	180°	*Fellsted,* Elizabeth. 1667 ½d. 3.101.21; 5.77 (E F). BW 1309. Nott [ex Spink]

Named signs

7065a	0.99	15.2	M	180°	*Hen & Chickens* (AT THE HEN AND CHICKINS): Sell, John. nd. 3.101.21; 5.77 (S...R). BW 1311 but HAMONSKEY, S|IOHN|SELL|R. Nott [ex Taffs]. See also 7066 (1659) and BW 1310 of Dorothy Sell (1668). She was administratrix of 'John Sell dec[ease]d', 20 July 1664 (Nightingale MS, cf. Rogers 1937, p. 40)
7065b	0.64	9.8	Br	180°	Same dies. [Nott ex Carthew]
7066	1.65	25.4	M	180°	*Hen & Chickens* (AT THE HEN AND CHICKINS): Sell, John. 1659. 3.101.21 (•AT•THE•HEN•AND•CHICKINS around); 5.77 (S|IR) (S|I.R|IOHN|SELL; •AT•HAMONSKEY•I659 around). BW —; Dickinson 1311A. Baldwin -1970. See also 7065

HARP ALLEY neighbourhood (Farringdon ward Without, Ditch Side) [23-H5, i10]

The reading is AT HARP ALLEY END AT DITCH SIDE

7067a	1.82	28.1	Cu	180°	*Browne,* Henry. nd ½d. 5.77; B|HI. BW 1312 but PENNY. [Baldwin]. Legend starts between 10 and 11 o'clock both sides. Identified on Baldwin ticket as '[BW] 838A|L[ondon] unp[ublishe]d'
7067b	1.06	16.3	Cu	180°	Same dies. Nott [ex Taffs]

HARP LANE (Tower ward, Tower Street) [38-J16]

The reading is HARPE LANE

Named signs

7068	0.87	13.4	Br	180°	*Star* (AT THE STARE): Lomax, Richard. nd. 2.4.3; L|RA. BW 1313 but HARPE. Baldwin [or Nott ex Taffs]. Reading confirmed from MoL specimen

HART STREET (Tower & Aldgate wards, Mark Lane *and* Crutched Friars) [39-I17]

The reading is HEARES STREET, cf. *Herestrete in the parish of St Olave, near the church of Crutched Friars* 1539 (Harben 1918, p. 294, and source); though this form is omitted by Ekwall 1954, p. 78, and Mills 2001, p. 105

Named signs

7069	0.90	13.9	Br	0°	*Golden* [*?Angel*] (AT GOLD): Garrard, Thomas. nd. 3.10.1 (•THOMAS•GARRARD• AT•GOLD around); G|TI (.G.|T•I; •IN•HEARES•STREET around). BW —; Dickinson 1337A (this specimen). Baldwin [ex Macfadyen, lot 152]. L partially overlaps D

'HEARES STREET' *see* HART STREET

HERCULES' PILLARS ALLEY *subsequently* TEMPLE BAR HOUSE (Farringdon ward Without, Fleet Street) [32-I3, k36]

The reading is FLEET STREET on 7073, STREETE on 7072; *Hercules Pillers in fleet street* on 7070, *Street* on 7071

	Weight			*Die*	
	g	*gr*		*axis*	
7070	1.70	26.2	Br	180°	*Cole,* Robert. 1666 ½d. 3.1.23; 5.77.1. BW 1072 but *Robert|Cole at the|his|*[man firing cannon]½, rev. *Pillers in|fleet street|1666.* Nott [ex Carthew]. Reading confirmed from BM specimen
7071	1.95	30.1	Cu	180°	*King,* William. 1664 ½d. 5.60.6; 5.77.1. BW 1083 but *fleet.* Nott [ex Carthew]. Reading confirmed from Berry 1978, p. 67, and BM specimens. William King fl. 1638-70 had made a fortune from the *Crown* ordinary, 30 Jan. 1668 (Rogers 1928c, pp. 144-5; Pepys 1970-83, ix.42, x.420)
Named signs					
7072	0.97	14.9	Br	180°	*Hercules' Pillars* (THE HERCVLVS PILLERS): ?S—, I/J—. nd. 3.1.4; S|IM. BW 1095. Baldwin -1970 [or Nott]. ?John Symonds, licensed victualler (Rogers 1928c, p. 144)

HERCULES' PILLARS ALLEY (*cont.*)

Named signs (*cont.*)

	Weight			*Die*	
	g	*gr*		*axis*	
7073	1.28	19.8	Br	0°	*Hercules' Pillars* (AT Y^{E}HERCVLES PILLERS): Oldham, Ed[ward]. nd ½d. 3.1.4; 5.77 (O|EP). BW 1088 but ED:. Nott [ex Carthew]. Reading ED: confirmed from BM specimen. Edward Oldham, Haberdasher, md. Priscilla Pell at St Mary le Strand Jan. 1656 (Boyd 25901); an unlicensed victualler 1657, in the lists of Cooks 1661-6 (Rogers 1928c, p. 144); bound apprentices 1665-73 (Webb 1996-, xxvi. 6, 14, 41)

HIGH TIMBER STREET (Queenhithe ward) [35-J10]

The reading is AT Y^{E}END OF HIGH TIMBER STREET NEAR QVEEN HITH

7074	1.38	21.3	Br	0°	*?F—,* L—. nd ½d. 5.84.30; 5.77 (F|LF). BW 1350. Nott. Obv. struck off-centre. Rev. initial mark apparently countermarked with a circle and a crescent conjoined. Reading completed from BM specimen

HOG LANE (Portsoken ward *and* Middlesex: Stepney: Minories) [40-I20: Rosemary Lane]/HOG LANE (Portsoken ward *and* Middlesex: Stepney: Whitechapel) [19-D17: Petticoat Lane] *see* Middlesex III

HOLBORN (*street*) (Farringdon ward Without *and* Middlesex: Holborn) [22-F3]

See also CASTLE YARD; FETTER LANE neighbourhood; ST ANDREW HOLBORN neighbourhood; THAVIE'S INN neighbourhood; STAPLE INN neighbourhood (Middlesex I: Holborn). The reading is HOLBORNE on 7075-8, 7080-1, 7084-6, 7089-91, 7093-4, 7096-7, 7100, 7747, HOLBORNE on 7099; HOLBORN on 6739, 7083, 7087-8, HOLBOR^{N} on 6737, 6742, HOL\|BORN on 7566; HOLBVRNE on 7079, 7082, 7092, 7098; HOLBON on 7095.

The following were recorded but are now missing: BW 1480, 0°, ex Nott; *BW 1484 (HOLḄ– –NE, Ạ W) but FLEC^{E}, 0°, ex Nott; *BW 1486 (M E Ẉ) but MICHAELL, 180°, ex Baldwin; BW 1488 but CROWNE&TOBACKO, 180°, ex Nott [another specimen illus. Greenall 1997, pl. 3.112]

7075	1.68	25.9	Cu	180°	*Broxon,* William. nd. 2.1 (•WILLIAM:BROXON around); 1.40.3 (•IN•:•HOLBORNE around). BW —; Dickinson 1379A but rev. a Ball. Nott
7076	0.93	14.3	Br	180°	*Burford,* Char—, tallow-chandler. nd. 5.32.9; B|CI. *BW 1382 but CHAR•BVRFORD, HOLBORNE. Nott. Reading TALLOW completed from Shuttlewood 2001, lot 650
7077a	3.29	50.8	Br	0°	*Edwards,* Henry, corn (CORNE) chandler. 1668 ½d. 3.67.1; 5.77. BW 1403 but CORNE, HALFE. [?Nott]
7077b	1.84 (pierced)	28.4	Br	0°	Same dies. Nott [ex Carthew]
7078	0.66	10.2	Br	90°	*Frere,* Baptist, oilman (OYLEMAN). 1661. Date; F|BS. BW 1408. Nott [ex Taffs]. Reading confirmed from BM specimen
7079a	1.45	22.4	Br	180°	*Sheers,* William. 1656. 5.38.1; date. BW 1461 but WILLIAM[no stop]SHEERS. Nott [ex Taffs]. Obv. legend starts at 6 o'clock
7079b	0.67	10.4	Cu	0°	Same dies. [Baldwin]
7080	0.89	13.8	Br	210°	*Simes,* Humphry. 1658. 3.7.24; 3.108.16. BW 1464 but three birds unspecified. Nott [ex Carthew]
7081	0.89	13.8	Br	180°	*Simons,* Bartholomew. 1654. B S; date. BW 1465. Nott [ex Carthew]
7082a	3.12	48.1	Br	270°	*Thody,* Robert. 1667 ½d. 3.5.105; 5.77. BW 1471. Baldwin
7082b	2.18	33.6	Br	180°	Same dies. Nott
7082c	1.93	29.8	Br	180°	Same dies. [Nott ex Taffs]
7082d	1.79	27.6	Br	180°	Same dies. [Nott]
7083	0.54	8.3	M	180°	*Turner,* John. 1657. 2.2.1; T|IR. BW 1473. Nott [ex Carthew]. Description completed from Greenall 1997, lot 111
7084	1.11	17.1	Br	180°	*Whetston,* William. 1653. 3.1.59; W|WI. BW 1482. [Nott ex Seaby]. Description completed from MoL specimen. Same obv. die as 7085, q.v.
7085	0.66	10.2	Br	180°	*Whetston,* William. 1653. 3.1.59; W|WI. BW 1482. [Nott]. Same obv. die as 7084. William Whetstone had erected five brick houses in Lincoln's Inn Fields without proper permission 1636, whence Whetstone Park WC2 (LCC 1914, pp. 6-7); William Whetston 'at ye Black Prince' 1665 (Rogers 1928a, p. 80); see also Wheatley 1891, iii. 490-1

Named signs

7086	1.91	29.5	Br	0°	*Crown tavern* (AT Y): Stirke, John, vintner (VINTINER). nd ½d. 5.60.5 (I S) (•I•S•; •IOHN•STIRKE•VINTINER•AT•Y around); 5.77 (HIS|HALFE|PENNY|•:•:•; •CROWN•TAVERN•IN•HOLBORNE around). BW —. Baldwin
7087	1.23	18.9	Br	180°	*Feathers* (AT THE FETHARS): Holmes, Rob[ert]. nd. 3.107.5; R H. BW 1424. Nott [ex Spink]. Forename completed from 7088, q.v.

[*continued overleaf*]

7073 7074 7075 7076 7077b 7078

7079a 7080 7081 7082a 7083 7084

7085 7086 7087 7088a 7089a 7090d

7091 7092 7093 7094 7095 7096

Plate 28 (*cont.*)

	Weight *g*	*gr*		*Die axis*	
7088a	2.06	31.8	Br	180°	*Feathers* (AT THE FETHARS): Holmes, Robert. nd ½d. 3.107.5; 5.77. BW 1423. [Nott ex Taffs]. Cf. 7099. Diameter 20 mm (excluding flattened area)
7088b	1.62	25.0	Br	0°	Same dies. Nott. Diameter 18.5-19 mm
7089a	1.08	16.7	Br	180°	*Fleece & Rose* (AT THE): W[illon], J[o—]. nd. 3.58.1; W|IH. BW 1476 but obv. •AT•[rosette]•THE•FLEECE•AND. Nott. The position of the obv. rosette suggests that the original intention was to start the legend with THE and end with ROSE, but there being insufficient space AT was substituted for ROSE, which was then placed at the start of the rev. legend; hence the obv. legend starts at 10 o'clock. Jo: Willon at the Rose in Holborn [vintner] presented for a 'deceitfull mixture' in his cellar 1653 (Rogers 1928a, p. 80). John Willon appr. 1636, John Willand 1639 (Webb 1996-, xliii. 321, 323, see also 392)
7089b	1.05	16.2	Br	180°	Same dies. [Nott ex Taffs]
7090a	1.09	16.8	M	180°	*Fleece tavern* (AT THE): ?S—, T—. 1651. 3.58.1; S|TM. BW 1457. [Nott]
7090b	1.06	16.4	M	180°	Same dies. [Baldwin]
7090c	1.02	15.8	M	180°	Same dies. [Nott]
7090d	0.87	13.4	M	180°	Same dies. Nott [ex Taffs]
7090e	0.79	12.1	M	180°	Same dies. [Nott]
7090f	0.77	11.9	M	180°	Same dies. [Nott]
7091	1.08	16.6	M	180°	*Globe tavern* (AT THE): ?H—, E—. 1651. 5.49.1; H|ES. BW 1414. Baldwin
7092	1.45	22.3	Cu	0°	*Globe tavern* (AT THE): Buggin, Anthony. nd. B|AM; 5.49.5. BW 1381. Nott. Anthony Buggins, Vintner, md. Mary Langston 1664; will, PCC, 1674, St Andrew Holborn (Boyd 24824). Anthony Buggin appr. 1652 (Webb 1996-, xliii. 46, see also 343)
7093	2.13	32.8	Br	270°	*Golden Falcon* (AT THE): Clay, Edmond. [16]67 ½d. 3.92.7; 5.77. BW 1389. Nott [ex Spink]. ?Edmond Clay of St Andrew Holborn (1645-1675), Haberdasher (Boyd 23436)
7094	1.06	16.3	M	180°	*Golden Griffin* (THE): ?P—, T—. nd. 3.64.4; P|TS. BW 1444. Nott [ex Taffs]. Cf. Middlesex I: Holborn: High Holborn: *Golden* [*?Griffin*] *tavern*
7095	0.93	14.4	M	180°	*King's Head tavern* (AT THE): ?H—, H—. nd. 3.5.77; H|HM. BW 1415 but HOLBON. Nott. Reading confirmed from BM specimen
7096	2.14	33.0	Br	180°	*Salutation tavern* (SALLVTATION TAVERNE): Grey, Daniel (DANIELL). nd ½d. 3.4.17; 5.77. BW 1412. Nott. Reading completed from BM specimen. Daniel Grey appr. Vintner 1647 (Webb 1996-, xliii. 125, see also 357)

HOLBORN (*cont.*)

Named signs (*cont.*)

	Weight *g*	Weight *gr*		Die axis	
7097	1.13	17.5	M	180°	*Star* (AT THE STARR): Deakes, John. nd. 2.4.3; D|IE. BW 1396 but STARR. Clark 1978. ?John Deaks, Innholder, wife Eleanor (Boyd 24937, unlocated). 'Mr Dawks at the Starre-Inne in Holborn near Turnstile' 1661 (BW 1396 n.)
7098	1.06	16.4	Br	0°	*Three Cups* (AT THE): ?B—, M—. 1658. B|MD; 5.64.104. BW 1359. Nott [ex Carthew]
7099a	1.56	24.1	Br	0°	*Vine tavern* (VINE TAVERNE): Marshal, Simon. nd. 4.9.1; M|SM. BW 1435 but VINE, TAVERNE, HOLBORNE. Nott [ex Taffs]. Simon Marshall appr. Vintner 1634 (Webb 1996-, xliii. 195, see also 370)
7099b	1.22	18.8	Br	180°	Same dies. Nott

HOLBORN (*street*). 'George Yard' neighbourhood (Farringdon ward Without) [23-F5, f22: George Yard, Snow Hill?]

The reading is GEORG YARD GATE IN HOLBORNE, perhaps the same yard as GEORGE YARD, Holborn Bridge

					U/V—, R—, 1652 *see* Burford (Oxon.): *George*. Read as AT GEORGE YARD, rev. IN HOLBORN 1652. Probably specimen iv. 3606b
7100	1.68	26.0	Br	180°	*Underwood,* Roger. nd ½d. V|RI (•V•|R•I|•; •ROGER•VNDERWOOD•GEORG around); 5.77 (HIS|HALF|PENY|•••; •YARD•GATE•IN•HOLBORNE around). BW —; Dickinson 1474A, from Glendining, 25-26 Sep. 1907, lot 61. Baldwin

HOLBORN BARS neighbourhood (Farringdon ward Without) [21-F2]

The reading is AT HOLBORNE BAṚẸṢ on 7101; AT HOLBVRNE BARRS on 7103; ṆẸARE HOLBORNE BARRS on 7102

7101	1.00	15.5	Br	180°	*Andrew,* Daniel (DANIELL). 1659. 5.14 Fishmongers 2; I6|DA|59. *BW 1357. Nott. Description largely completed from Greenall 1997, lot 109. Daniel Andrew bound apprentices 1635-57 (Webb 1996-, xliv. 72, 98)
7102	1.31	20.2	Br	0°	*Talbot,* Richard (RIC̣HARD). 1667 ½d. 5.77; Ṭ|RA. *BW 1469. Nott. Obv. reading largely completed from MoL specimen with different rev. die

Named signs

7103	0.78 (corroded)	12.0	Br	180°	*Feathers* (THE FETHARES): ?F—, O—. nd. 3.107.5; O F. BW 1404. Nott [ex Carthew]. Reading completed from MoL specimen. Cf. 7087-8

HOLBORN BRIDGE (Farringdon ward Without) [23-F5]

The reading is HOLBORNBRIDG on 7105-6, ỌN HOLB^{O}RN BRIDG on 7104

7104	0.90	13.9	Br	180°	*Sutton,* Natha— (NATHA– –). nd. 5.61.40 (•NATHA– – SVTTON around); S|NI (•S•|N I|•; •ỌN•HOLB^{O}RN•BRIDG around). BW —; *Dickinson 1468A, from a report of this specimen. Nott [ex Carthew]

Named signs

7105	0.63	9.6	Cu	180°	*White Horse* (AT THE): Birch, W—. nd. 3.60.4; B|WA. BW 1368 but a horse (no rider), HOLBORNBRIDG. Nott. Description confirmed from BM specimen. ?William Birch of St Sepulchre, Farrier; will, PCC, 1670 (Boyd 47524). Same rev. die as 7106, q.v.
7106	0.82 (chipped)	12.7	Cu	180°	*White Horse* (AT Y^{E}): Birch (BIRC̣H), W—. nd. 3.60.4 (•W•BIRC̣H•AT•Y^{E}•WHITE around); B|WA (•B•|W•A; •HORSE•HOLBORNBRIDG around). BW —, cf. 7105. Nott. William Birch appr. Farrier 1629; bound eight apprentices 1638-62 (Webb 1996-, xxviii. 7, 73). Same rev. die as 7105, q.v.

HOLBORN BRIDGE neighbourhood

See also GEORGE YARD. The reading is AT HOLBORN BRIDG on 7112, 7115, BRIDGE on 7108-9; AT HOLBORNE BRIDG on 7107, 7116, BRIDGE on 7110-11, 7113-14, 7119-20; AT HOLBVRN BRIDG on 7117; AT HOVLBVRN BRIDGE on 7118; NEARE HOLBORNE BRIDG on 7008

7107a	1.84	28.4	Br	0°	*Booth,* Robert. nd. 3.4.5; R B. BW 1375. Nott. ?Robert Booth of St Sepulchre, Salter; Poll Tax 1641, Holborn Cross precinct; will, PCC, 1654 (Boyd 47384)
7107b	1.10	17.0	M	180°	Same dies. Spink (envelope), Nott [ex Taffs] (ticket and record)
7108	1.27	19.5	Cu	0°	*Pytman,* Matthias (MATHIAS). nd. 3.4.32; P|MM. BW 1450 but AT[no stop]HOLBORN[no stop]BRIDGE. Nott. Device confirmed from MoL specimen NN17671
7109a	1.64 (chipped)	25.2	Cu	0°	*Skarvill,* John, distiller (DESTILLER). 1667 ½d. 3.1.19; 5.77 (S|I|I). BW 1466. Nott [ex Taffs]. John Scarvill (Scarvile), Distiller, bound four apprentices 1663-73 (Webb1996-, xi. 39). The Sussex family of de Scardeville appears as *Skarvile* 16c., usual forms now Scarfield etc. (McKinley 1988, pp. 50, 71-2, 93, 118). Diameter 21-22 mm.
7109b	1.45	22.4	Cu	0°	Same dies. Nott. Diameter 20-20.5 mm

[*continued overleaf*]

PLATE 29

7097 7098 7099a 7100 7101 7102

7103 7104 7105 7106 7107a 7108

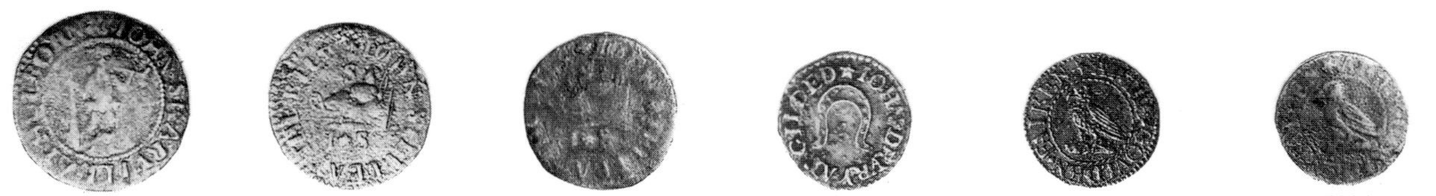

7109b 7110 7111 7112 7113 7114

7115 7116b 7117 7118 7119 7120

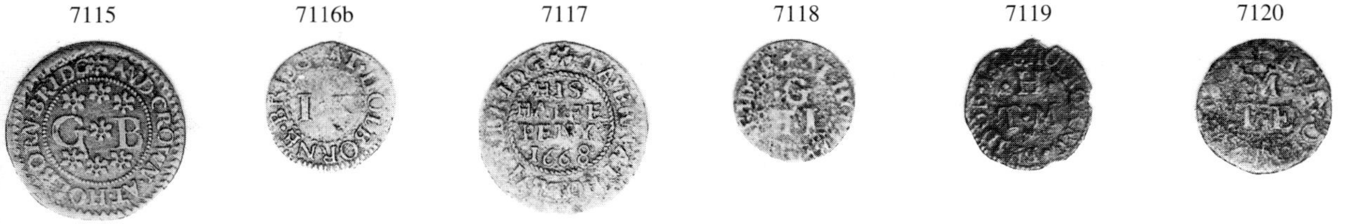

Plate 29 (*cont.*)

Named signs

	Weight *g*	*gr*		*Die axis*	
7110	1.21	18.7	Cu	0°	*Blue* [*?Boar*] (AT THE BLLW): Stelle, John. nd ½d. 3.65.12 (S|IS); 5.77. BW 1467 but BLLW. Nott [ex Taffs]. Reading confirmed from BM specimen. Same obv. die as 7111, q.v.
7111	1.20	18.4	Cu	270°	*Blue* [*?Boar*] (AT THE BLLW): Stelle, John. nd ½d. 3.65.12 (S|IS); 5.77. BW 1467 but BLLW. [Nott]. ?John Steele (1608-1670), Salter, Alderman 1668; will, PCC, 1670 St Andrew Holborn; Esq.; 1668 he md. (2)Lettice Brown, widow (Boyd 28220; Woodhead 1966, p. 156); but Cottle 1978, p. 360, and Hanks 1988, p. 512 s.v. Still, distinguish a surname Stell. Same obv. die as 7110
7112	0.68	10.4	Cu	270°	*Gilded* [*?Horseshoe*] (AT GILDED): Drury, John. nd. 5.68.10; D|IA. BW 1399. Nott. ?John Drury of St Andrew Holborn, Pewterer, bound ten apprentices 1637-75, Master 1673; will, PCC, 1678, 1682 St Andrew Holborn (Boyd 49069, Webb 1996-, xl. 109). Sign also described as *Golden* (AT Y^{E} GOLDEN, BW 1398, confirmed from MoL specimen)
7113	1.06	16.4	M	180°	*Golden Falcon* (AT THE GOVLDEN FAIKEN): P[argiter], T[homas]. nd. 3.92.1; P|TT. BW 1445. Nott [ex Taffs]. Same obv. die as 7114, q.v.
7114	0.59	9.1	M	180°	*Golden Falcon* (AT THE GOVLDEN FAIKEN): P[argiter], T[homas]. nd. 3.92.1; P|TT. BW 1445. No provenance. Same obv. die as 7113. The sign of the Falcon near Holborn Bridge had been leased 1661 to Thomas Pargiter; he declined to rebuild, Feb. 1668 (Fire Court 1966-, ii. 60-2)
					Golden [*?Horseshoe*] (AT Y^{E} GOLDEN): Drury, John see 7112 (*Gilded* [*?Horseshoe*])
7115	3.17	48.9	Cu	270°	*Hammer & Crown* (AT THE HAMER AND CROWN): Baggs, Giles. nd. 5.37.10; G B. BW 1361. Baldwin -1971. Giles Baggs of St Andrew Holborn, Ironmonger, b. 1640, appr. 1657; md. Deborah Nayler 1666; bound twelve apprentices 1666-1713 (Boyd 17322; Webb 1996-, xxiv. 3, 57)
7116a	1.00	15.4	Br	0°	*Raven* (AT THE): ?K—, I/J—. nd. 3.108.4; I K. BW 1428. [Nott]
7116b	0.75	11.5	Br	180°	Same dies. Nott [ex Taffs]
7117	1.18	18.2	Br	150°	*Sun tavern* (AT THE SVNN TAVERN): Clarveato, [Farnelius]. 1668 ½d. 2.1; 5.77. BW 1388 but CLARVEATO: [*sic*]. Nott. Fernelius Clarveate appr. Vintner 1662, son of William, London, doctor of medicine, deceased; apprentices bound to Farnelius Clarveato (Webb 1996-, xliii. 63, 346). Cf. Colonel Clarviato of St Sepulchre, Haberdasher, md. Blandina Thacker 1669 (Boyd 13955)
7118	0.47	7.2	Br	180°	*Sword & Ball* (AT THE): ?G—, H—. nd. 5.42.2; G|HI. BW 1409. Nott. Reading completed from MoL specimen
7119	0.73 (chipped)	11.3	M	180°	*Three Tuns* (AT THE 3 TVNS): ?H—, T—. 1648. 5.64.33; H|TM. BW 1418. Nott [ex Carthew]. For a purported identification of the issuer see Dickinson forthcoming. Same obv. die as 7120
7120	1.16	17.9	Br	180°	*Three Tuns* (AT THE 3 TVNS): ?M—, T—. nd. 5.64.33; M|TE. BW 1419. Nott. Reading completed from BM specimen. ?Thomas Mason (see Dickinson forthcoming). Same obv. die as 7119

HOLBORN CONDUIT neighbourhood (Farringdon ward Without) [23-F6]

The reading is AT HOBORN CONDED on 7122; AT HOLBORN CONDVIT on 7123; AT HOLBORNE COVNDID on 7126, CVNDIT on 7121, CVNDITC on 7128, CVNDVT on 7124-5; NEAR HOLBORN CVNDVIT on 7127

	Weight g	Weight gr		Die axis	
7121	0.80	12.4	M	180°	*Beale,* John, grocer (GROÇER). nd. 3.2.8 (•IOHN•BEALE•GROÇER around); B|IH (•B•|I•H; •AT•HOLBORNE•CVNDIT around). BW —; *Dickinson 1366A. Nott [ex Carthew]
7122a	0.98	15.1	M	180°	*Joyce,* Anthony (ANTHONEY). nd. 3.53.13; I|AK. BW 1427 but ANTHONEY. [Nott ex Taffs]. Anthony Joyce, tallow-chandler; Leatherseller 1654, but the stags are not the *three roebucks passant reguardant* of the Leathersellers; wife Katherine (Fenner) a cousin of Samuel Pepys; d. 1668 (Pepys 1970-83, x. 211-12, xi. 149). Token dates from 1658 o.s. (Dickinson forthcoming)
7122b	0.87	13.3	M	180°	Same dies. [Nott]
7122c	0.72	11.1	M	180°	Same dies. Baldwin

Named signs

7123a	1.17	18.0	M	180°	*Golden Still* (ATTHE GOVLDEN STILL): ?D—, R—. nd. 5.3.30; D|RE. BW 1393 but ATTHE. Nott [ex Carthew]
7123b	1.06	16.3	M	180°	Same dies. Nott [ex Taffs]
7124	1.17 (edge filed)	18.0	Br	180°	*Hen & Chickens* (THE HENN AND CHICHENS): ?B—, T—. nd. 3.101.21 (•THE•HENN•AND•CHICHENS around); T B (T•B; •AT•HOLBORNE•CVNDVT around). BW —, cf. 7125. Nott. Reading of obv. completed from Greenall 1997, lot 109. Same rev. die as 7125
7125	1.25	19.3	Br	180°	*Hen & Chickens* (THE HENN AND CHICKENS): ?B—, T—. nd. 3.101.21; T B. BW 1360. Nott [ex Spink]. Same rev. die as 7124
7126	0.90	13.9	M	180°	*Queen's Head tavern* (QVEENE HEAD TAVERNE): ?H—, E—. nd. 3.5.90; H|EE. BW 1413. Nott
7127	1.89	29.2	Br	0°	*Red Cow* (AT Y^{E}): Bayly, Matt—. nd ½d. 3.52.20; 5.77 (B|MT). BW 1366 but MATT:. Nott
7128	0.75	11.5	M	180°	*Three Sugarloaves* (THE 3 SVGAR LOVES): S[trudwick], T[homas]. nd. 5.64.16; S|TE. BW 1456 but CVNDITC [*sic*]. Nott [ex Taffs]. Issuer Thomas Strudwick fl. 1664-86, confectioner in Turnagain Lane 1666; wife Elizabeth (Pepys) a cousin of Samuel (Franks 1859-61; Pepys 1970-83, x. 405). A foundation set out for him at Snow Hill 1667 (Mills 1962-7, ii. 2v). ?Identical with Thomas Strudwick, grocer, fl. 1660, at the Star near Holborn Bridge 1692 (Woodhead 1966, p. 159). Surname from Strudgwick in Kirdford, Sussex (McKinley 1988, pp. 16, 120). See also 7699

HORN ALLEY *subsequently* EDMUND PLACE (Aldersgate ward, Aldersgate Street) [15-E9, e5]

The reading is HORN ẠḶḶY IN ALDERSGATE STREET

7129	1.04 (chipped)	16.0	Br	0°	*Maund,* Elizabeth (ELIZAḄETH). 1667 ½d. (PEṆNY). 3.11 (•ELIZAḄETH• MAVND•IN•HORN around); 5.77 (HER|HALFE|PEṆNY|1667; •ẠḶḶY•IN• ALDERSGATE•STREET around). BW —; Dickinson 1497A, from a report of this specimen. Baldwin. Placed in the collection at BW 44-45, where 'Three morris-dancers' must have been read from BW 43

HOSIER LANE (Farringdon ward Without) [23-F6]

The reading is HOSER LANE on 7132; HOSIER LANE on 7131; OSIER LANE on 7130

7130a	2.17	33.4	Br	0°	*Langhorne,* Richard, salter. nd ½d. 5.60.33; 5.77. BW 1499 but AT[no stop]Y^{E}. [Nott]
7130b	1.81	27.9	Br	0°	Same dies. [Nott ex Spink]
7130c	1.46	22.6	Br	180°	Same dies. Nott [ex Taffs]
7131a	2.10 (chipped)	32.4	Cu	180°	*Leake,* Andrew. nd ½d. 5.17.16; 5.77. BW 1500 but LANE•:•. Nott [ex Spink]
7131b	1.79	27.6	Cu	180°	Same dies. Nott

Named signs

7132	0.86	13.3	M	180°	*Sugarloaf* (AT THE SHVGER LOF̣E): ?P—, I/J—. 1651. 5.64.1; P|IR. *BW 1502. Nott [ex Spink]. Obv. reading largely completed from BM specimen, rev. reading from MoL specimen with different obv. die

[*continued overleaf*]

7121 7122c 7123a 7124 7125 7126

7127 7128 7129 7130c 7131b 7132

7133b 7134 7135b 7136 7137 7138a

7139 7140 7141a 7142b 7143 7144

HOUNDSDITCH (Portsoken ward & Bishopsgate ward Without) [29-F17]

See also GRAVEL LANE. The reading is HOVNDDICH on 7152; HOVNDICH on 7142; HOVNDS DICH on 7154, DITCH on 7148; HOVNDSDICH on 7139; HOVNDSDITCH on 7026, 7136; HOVNESDICH on 7153; HOVNSDICH on 7140-1, 7149, 7151; HOVNSDITCH on 7133-4, 7138, 7150; HOWNDS DITCH on 7147; HOWNSDITCH on 7135, 7137; HVENSDECH on 7143; HVNDICH on 7144-6

	Weight			*Die*	
	g	*gr*		*axis*	
7133a	1.83	28.2	Cu	90°	*Acton,* William. 1664. 5.50.1; 5.43.20. BW 1505. [Baldwin ex Pridmore]
7133b	1.23	19.0	Cu	90°	Same dies. Nott
7133c	0.87	13.4	Cu	90°	Same dies. [?Baldwin]
7133d	0.63 (chipped)	9.7	Cu	270°	Same dies. [Nott ex Taffs]
7134	1.88	29.1	Cu	0°	*Bly,* Giles. 1669 ½d. 5.70.17; 5.77 (B|GB). BW 1507 but five bells and a candlestick. Nott [ex Carthew]. Giles Bly, Loriner, wife Bridget (Boyd 24788, unlocated)
7135a	1.02	15.8	Br	0°	*Goodale,* Edmond. nd. 5.15.4; G|EA. BW 1511. Nott [ex Taffs]
7135b	0.76	11.7	Br	0°	Same dies. Nott
7136	1.43	22.1	Cu	180°	*Holbrough,* Richard. 1669 ½d. 3.6.21; 5.77. BW 1514. Nott. Reading confirmed from MoL specimen
7137	1.03	15.9	Br	270°	*Langrish,* John. nd. 3.3.13; I L. BW 1519. Nott. Reading confirmed from BM specimen. John Langrish appr. Tallow Chandler 1659, and bound an apprentice 1668 (Webb 1996-, xxxix. 10, 63)
7138a	0.78	12.0	Br	90°	*Merry,* John. 1663. 5.3.10; M|IS. BW 1520. Nott
7138b	0.66	10.2	Br	90°	Same dies. [Nott ex Spink]
7138c	0.61	9.4	Br	180°	Same dies. [Nott ex Taffs]
7139	1.34	20.6	Br	0°	*Nutell,* Thomas, baker (ḄAḲẸR). 1666. 5.14 Leathersellers (•THOMAS•NVTELL•ḄAḲẸR around); N|TS (•N•|T•S|•; •IN HOVNDSDICH•1666 around). BW —. Baldwin. Trade does appear to read BA… and not (e.g.) TANER
7140	1.05	16.1	Cu	0°	*Palmer,* John. 1667. 5.38.1; P|II. BW 1524. Nott
7141a	0.90	13.9	Cu	90°	*Rawlins,* William. nd. 5.68.33; 4.3.10. BW 1526. Nott. Rev. legend starts between 10 and 11 o'clock
7141b	0.67 (chipped)	10.4	Cu	0°	Same dies, rev. flawed. [Nott]
7141c	0.59	9.1	Cu	0°	Same dies, rev. flawed. [Nott]
7142a	1.02 (edge cuts)	15.7	Br	180°	*Shakmapell,* Samuel (SAMVELL). 1660. 3.108.19; S|SE. BW 1527. [Nott ex Taffs]. Samuel Shakemaple, Tallow Chandler, md. Elizabeth How 1643 (Boyd 25354); appr. 1636, bound five apprentices 1647-67 (Webb 1996-, xxxix. 91, 138)
7142b	0.93 (chipped)	14.4	Br	180°	Same dies. Nott
Named signs					
7143	1.00	15.4	Br	180°	*Bell* (AT THE): ?G—, I/J—. 1649. 5.70.1; G|IA. BW 1510. Nott
7144	1.05	16.3	Br	180°	*Golden Cock* (GOLDENCOCK): Jemmet, Philip (PHILLIP). nd. 3.101.1; I|PE. BW 1517-18 but GOLDENCOCK. Nott. Philip Jemmott (1618-78), Brewer, wife Elizabeth (Grimshaw); alderman 1667; daughter Anne md. (Sir) Jonathan Raymond MP who thereby 'gott a great estate' (Le Neve 1873, p. 333; Woodhead 1966, pp. 98, 136)

HOUNDSDITCH (*cont.*)

Named signs (*cont.*)

	Weight g	Weight gr		Die axis	
7145	1.03	15.9	Br	180°	*Golden Cock* (GOLDENCOCK): Jemmet, Philip (PHILLIP). nd. 3.101.1; I|PE. BW 1517-18 but GOLDENCOCK. Nott. Reading confirmed from MoL specimen
7146a	1.50	23.1	Br	0°	*Golden Cock:* Jemmet, Philip (PHILLIP). nd. 3.101.1; I|PE. BW 1517-18. [Nott]. Obv. flawed at first I of PHILLIP, more so than on 7146c and d
7146b	1.13	17.4	Br	270°	Same dies. Nott [ex Taffs]. First I of PHILLIP apparently unflawed
7146c	0.82	12.7	Br	90°	Same dies. [Baldwin]. Slight flaw above first I of PHILLIP
7146d	0.81	12.5	Br	90°	Same dies. [Nott]. Obv. flawed similarly to 7146c
7147	0.83	12.8	Br	0°	*Golden Lion* (AT THE GOVLDEN LIO^{N}): ?T—, G—. nd. 3.11; T|GA. BW 1528 but obv. and rev. transposed for consistency with other illustrations. Nott. Reading completed from BM specimen. Either side might be read as the obverse
7148	1.47	22.7	Br	180°	*Hand & Pen* (AT THE HAND AND PENN): ?T—, M—. 1653. 3.6.21; T|MA. BW 1529 but PENN, HOVNDS•DITCH. Nott. Double-struck. Reading completed from MoL specimen
7149a	1.07	16.5	Cu	180°	*Old Bunch [of Grapes]* (Y^{E}OLD BVNCH): Waples, Geo—. nd. 4.9.5; W|GA. BW 1531 but GEO:. Nott [ex Taffs]. ?George Waples, Haberdasher, fl. 1660; wife Abigail whose will, PCC, 1665 St Botolph Aldgate (Boyd 25485)
7149b	0.98	15.1	Cu	180°	Same dies. [?Baldwin]
7149c	0.59 (chipped)	9.1	Cu	180°	Same dies. [?Baldwin -1973]
7150	1.44	22.2	Cu	180°	*Seven Stars* (. . .SEVEN STARRS): Hollis, Robert. nd ½d. 2.4.9; 5.77. *BW 1515 (AT.Y^{E}) but HOVNSDITCH. Seaby, [*SCMB* May 1971]. Only six stars visible. Rev. reading completed from BM specimen with different obv. die
7151a	1.12 (chipped)	17.3	Cu	270°	*Shears* (AT THE SHEERS): ?T—, W—. 1664. 5.43.30; T|WM. BW 1530. Baldwin -1973. Diameter 17-17.5 mm
7151b	0.89	13.8	Cu	90°	Same dies. [Nott]. Diameter 16 mm
7151c	0.70	10.9	Cu	270°	Same dies. [Nott ex Spink]. Diameter 16 mm
7151d	0.69	10.6	Cu	90°	Same dies. [?Baldwin]. Diameter 16 mm
7152a	1.09	16.9	M	180°	*White Horse* (AT THE WHIT HORS): ?H—, L—. nd. 3.60.20; H|LE. BW 1512 but HOVNDDICH. [Nott]
7152b	1.07	16.6	M	180°	Same dies. Nott
7152c	0.93	14.3	M	180°	Same dies. [?Baldwin]
7153	0.76 (chipped)	11.7	Br	180°	*White Horse* (AT THE WHITE HORS): ?P—, I/J—. 1658. 3.60.21 (R); P|IA. BW 1523 but HOVNESDICH. Nott. Reading completed from MoL specimen. Initial R for Ramage, not Rawlins as in BW 1523 n.
7154	0.81	12.5	Cu	90°	*Woolsack* (AT WOLSAK): Hiet, Sarah (SARY). nd. 5.64.50; S H. BW 1513 but WOLSAK, HOVNDS•DICH. Seaby, [*SCMB* May 1971]. Reading confirmed from MoL specimen

HUGGIN LANE (Cripplegate ward Within, Wood Street) [25-G10]

The reading is HVGIN LANE NEAR WOOD STRET

7155	1.39 (chipped, corroded)	21.4	Br	180°	*Washburn,* Anthony. 1670 ½d. 3.6.14; 5.77. BW 1534 but I^{N}, WOOD[no stop]STRET. Nott. Description completed from BM specimen

INNER TEMPLE GATE neighbourhood (Farringdon ward Without, Fleet Street) [32-I3]

The reading is AT THE INNER TEMPLE GATE on 7157; AT THE INNERTEMPLE GATE IN FLEET STREET on 7156

7156	0.83	12.8	Br	180°	*?S—,* I/J—. nd. 5.64.80; S|II. BW 1094 but INNERTEMPLE. Nott. Reading completed from BM specimen
7157	1.31	20.1	Cu	0°	*Tomlinson,* Humphry (HVMFRY), milliner (MILIN|ER). nd. 5.4.1; 5.77. BW 1535 but an arched opening outlined in part with [stone] blocks, i.e. Inner Temple Gate. Nott. Reading completed from Harris 2002, lot 515

[*continued overleaf*]

7145 7146b 7147 7148 7149a 7150

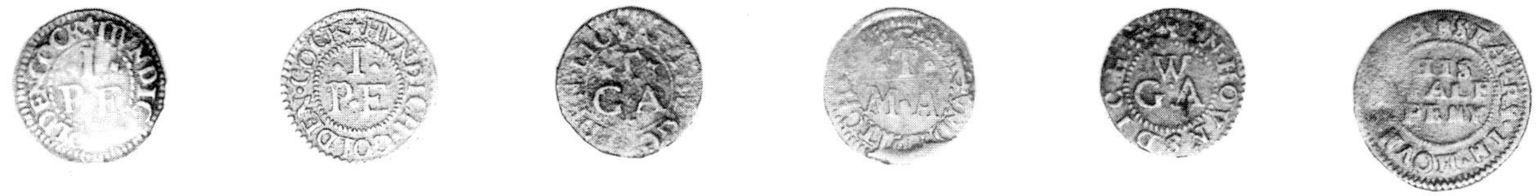

7151a 7152b 7153 7154 7155 7156

7157 7158 7159 7160 7161 7162

7163 7164b 7165a 7166 7167 7168

Plate 31 (*cont.*)

INNER TEMPLE GATE *and* MIDDLE TEMPLE GATE neighbourhood (Farringdon ward Without, Fleet Street) [32-I3]

The reading is BETWEENE Y^{E} TEMPLEGATES

Named signs

	Weight g	*gr*		*Die axis*	
7158	2.33	36.0	Br	240°	*?Farrs coffee-house* (AT Y^{E}F̣A. . . COF̣– –Ẹ HOVSẸ): Speed, Samuel. 1667 1d. 2.12.3 (•[?rainbow]•|COF̣– –Ẹ|HOVSẸ|•••; •SAMVEL•SPEED•AT•Y^{E}F̣A. . . around); 5.77 (HIS|PENNY|1667|•••; •BETWEENE•Y^{E}TEMPLEGATES around). BW —; *Dickinson 1097C (FARRS, COFFEE) but HOVSẸ BETWEENE, TEMPLEGATES. Nott. Tooling on and around last word of obv. legend makes reading difficult. FARRS would make good sense (Lillywhite 1972, no. 398), for Samuel Speed (bap. 1633, d. 1679?), printer and bookseller, was at James Farr's Rainbow 1663-9 (ODNB; cf. 6951)

IRELAND GATE neighbourhood (Farringdon ward Within, St Andrew's Hill) [34-I7, cf. k71]

The reading is AT IRELAND GATE, cf. *Ireland Yard* where Shakespeare in 1612 bt. a house erected over a great gate… (Harben 1918, p. 316)

7159	0.98	15.1	Br	270°	*Oyles,* William. [16]57. 5.43.35; O|WM. BW 1536 but OYLES, GATE•57. Nott [ex Taffs]

IRONMONGER LANE (Cheap ward) [26-H11]

The reading is IREMONGER LANE on 7160-1; IRONMVNGER LANE on 7162

7160	1.07	16.5	Br	270°	*Snow,* John, whit[e] baker. nd. 5.77; I S. BW 1554. Nott. Reading confirmed from MoL specimen. Same rev. die as 7161. Foundation set out for John Snow(e) 1671 (Mills 1962-7, i. 42, v. 78v.)
7161	1.00	15.5	M	90°	*Snow* (SNỌW), John (IOḤN), white baker (WHIT|ḄAKẸṚ). nd. 5.77; I S. *BW 1554. Nott [?ex Spink]. Same rev. die as 7160

IRONMONGER LANE neighbourhood

The reading is AT IRONMVNGER LANE

7162	1.03	15.8	Br	0°	*Davenport,* John. nd. 3.60.1; I D. BW 1551 but LANE. Nott [ex Spink]. Rev. legend starts at 10 o'clock. Foundation set out 1668 (Mills 1962-7, i. 42, iv. 39v.)

IVY LANE (Farringdon ward Within) [24-H8]

The reading is IVEY LANE on 7163; *Ivy Lane* on 7164

7163	0.91	14.0	M	180°	*Osman,* Wil—, corn chandler (CORNE CHANLER). nd. 1.33.10; W O. BW 1557. Nott [ex Daniels]. Reading completed from MoL specimen

Named signs

7164a	1.76	27.2	Cu	270°	[*Solyman*] *coffee-house (Att The Coffee Hou– –):* [anonymous]. 1663. 3.5.42; 5.77.1. *BW 1560 (*in*) but *Soly*[bust]*man*, rev. *Att|The Coffee|Hou– – – –|Ivy Lane|1663*. [Baldwin]. Sign name as in Lillywhite 1972, no. 13554
7164b	1.67	25.8	Cu	180°	Same dies. Nott [ex Taffs]

JERUSALEM ALLEY (Bridge ward Within, Gracechurch Street) *subsequently* ST BENET'S PLACE [38-I15, 147]

The reading is IERVSALEM ALLEY, with IN GRATIOVS STREET on 7165, I– ĢRAṬIỌ–S STREEṬ on 7166

7165a	0.87	13.4	Br	0°	*?H—,* F—. nd. 3.102.1; F H. BW 1566 but IN[no stop]GRATIOVS. Nott [ex Carthew]. Obv. legend starts between 5 and 6 o'clock
7165b	0.80 (chipped)	12.3	Br	0°	Same dies. Nott [ex Taffs]

Named signs

7166	1.26 (corroded)	19.4	Cu	180°	[*Boar's Head*]: B[lisse], J[ohn]. nd. 3.65.10; B|ID. *BW 1562 (IN.GRATIOVS). Nott [ex Taffs]. Sign name and identification of issuer from BW 1563. Cf. 7019

JEWIN STREET (Aldersgate ward & Cripplegate ward Without) [15-D9]

The reading is IEWEN STREET on 7170, 7172, 7176, STREEṬ on 7169, STREETE on 7167; IEWIN STREET on 7168, 7171, 7175, STREETE on 7173-4

7167	1.54	23.7	Br	0°	*Duncombe,* Henry. nd. 5.38.2; D|HS. BW 1571 but IEWEN. Seaby, [*SCMB* May 1971]. Reading completed from MoL specimen
7168	1.14	17.6	Br	0°	*Linford,* Thomas. 1667 ½d. 3.11 (•THOMAS•LINFORD:IN: around); 5.77 (L|TH) (HIS|HALFE|PENNY|L|T•H; •IEWIN•STREET•1667 around). BW —; Dickinson 1574A. Nott

JEWIN STREET (*cont.*)

	Weight g	Weight gr		Die axis	
7169	1.65	25.4	Br	270°	*Longman* (L–N. . .), George, silkman (. . .MAN). nd ½d. L|GA (L|G[flowerknot]A; •GEORGE L–N. . .•IN•:• around); 5.77 (HIS|HALFE|PENNY|•:•; •IEWEN•STREET. . .MAN around). BW —; *Gilbert 1927, 151, *Dickinson 1574B (LONGMAN, SILKMAN). Nott. Also read as BW 1573 (LANCASTER, CARMAN), which may have been a creative reading of the present specimen. ?George Longman of St Leonard Foster Lane, Mercer; md. Anne Becker 1665; will, PCC, 1668 (Boyd 20667)
7170a	2.61	40.2	Cu	0°	*Newton,* John, grocer. 1667 ½d. 3.5.35; 5.77 (N|IM). BW 1575. [Nott ex Taffs]
7170b	2.55	39.3	Cu	0°	Same dies. [Nott]
7170c	1.76	27.2	Cu	0°	Same dies. Nott
7171	2.12	32.7	Cu	0°	*Stanhopp,* Robert. 1667 ½d. 4.13.1; 5.77. BW 1576. Nott
7172	0.91	14.0	Br	90°	*White,* Tho—, grocer. nd. 5.14 Grocers; W|TE. BW 1578. Nott

Named signs

7173	0.72	11.2	M	0°	*Sun* (AT THE SVNN): ?D—, I/J—. 1659. 2.1.1 (I D); D|IM. BW 1569 but letters ID on face of sun. Nott [or Baldwin ex Pridmore]. Same obv. die as 7174; reading of rev. confirmed from BM specimen
7174	0.75 (corroded)	11.5	M	180°	*Sun* (AT THE SVNN): ?D—, I/J—. 1659. 2.1.1 (I D); D|IM. BW 1569 but letters ID on face of sun. Nott [ex Taffs]. Same obv. die as 7173
7175	1.84	28.4	Br	270°	*Sun & Red Cross* (AT Y^{E}SVNN & RED CROSS): Cross, John. nd. 1.55.37; C|IA. BW 1568 but Y^{E}SVNN. Nott. Reading completed from BM specimen
7176	1.85	28.5	Cu	210°	*White Lion* (AT Y): Lawson, Anthony. 1666 ½d. 3.11; 5.77. BW 1574 but apparently no ^{E} after Y. Nott. Reading completed from MoL specimen

KING STREET (Cheap ward, Cheapside) [26-G11] *see* Uncertain I

KNIGHTRIDER STREET (Castle Baynard & Bread Street & Queenhithe wards) [34-I8]

The reading is KNIGHTRIDER STREET on 7179; KNIGHTRIDER STREETE on 7177; – – RIDE. . .E– on 7178

7177	1.75 (corroded)	27.0	Br	90°	*Hobbs* (HOBB–), Richard (RICHARD), mealman (MEALMAN). 1671 ½d. H|RI; 5.77. *BW 1627 (HOBBS). Nott [ex Carthew]
7178	1.97	30.3	Pb	0°	*?L—,* T—. nd. 3.108.2 (T L)? (•IN•– –•RIDE. . .E– around); L|TM (L|T[flowerknot]M). BW —; cf. Sharman 1986, no. 2 (. . .RIDER STREET around a bird). Nott. Also attributed to Trim, Ireland, as 'W.718.A Unpub:', the source for Seaby 1970, p. 130, and Dickinson, Ireland 718A, which should be deleted

Named signs

7179	1.07	16.4	Br	180°	*Crown* (AT THE CROVN): ?S—, R—. nd. 5.60.1 (•AT•THE•CROVN•IN around); S|RI (•S•|R•I; •KNIGHTRIDER•STREET around). BW —; Dickinson 1628A, from Heal 1928, p. 11. Baldwin. G double-entered

LAD LANE *subsequently* GRESHAM STREET (part) (Cripplegate ward Within) [25-G10]

The reading is LAD LANE on both

7180	1.01	15.6	Br	90°	*Marsh,* John. 1669 ½d. 3.6.52; 5.77. BW 1629. Nott [ex Taffs]

Named signs

7181	1.11	17.1	M	180°	*St John the Baptist's Head* (AT THE S IOHN BAPTIS HEAD): ?A—, E—. nd. 3.5.75 (•AT•THE•S•IOHN•BAPTIS around); A|EI (•A•|E•I; •HEAD•IN•LAD LANE around). BW —; Dickinson 1628B. Brand

LAMBETH HILL (Castle Baynard & Queenhithe wards) [35-J9]

The reading is ON LAMBETH HILL throughout

7182	0.88	13.5	M	180°	*Stanes,* John. 1664. 5.64.1; I S. BW 1634. Nott [ex Carthew]. Reading confirmed from MoL specimen

Named signs

7183	1.35	20.8	M	180°	*Green Dragon* (AT THE): H[unt?], I/J—. 1651. 3.114.1; H|IE. BW 1633. Nott [ex Taffs]. Rogers 1928a, p. 81, documented a Mr Hunt at the Green Dragon. He suggested that the initials are for Edward Hunt (fl. 1646) in an unusual order, but more evidence for that is required
7184	0.66	10.1	Br	90°	*King's Head tavern* (Y^{E}): ?C—, W—. nd. 3.5.85; C|WE. BW 1632 but H[bust]VII. Baldwin, on whose ticket identified as 'Unp[ublishe]d. Surrey 161A'. ?William Croone, vintner, mentioned in the Churchwarden's Accounts of St Mary Magdalene, Old Fish Street, 1657-61. For an earlier issue from what was probably the same King's Head tavern see 7449 (Rogers 1928a, p. 81 and cf. p. 86)

[*continued overleaf*]

7169 7170c 7171 7172 7173 7174

7175 7176 7177 7178 7179 7180

7181 7182 7183 7184 7185 7186

7187 7188a 7189 7190 7191a 7192

Plate 32 (*cont.*)

LAWRENCE LANE (Cheap ward) [26-G11]

The reading is LAVRENCE LANE on 7185; Ṣ ḶẠẈṚẠṆÇ̣E on 7187; S^{T} LAVRANCE LAN^{E} on 7186; ST LAWRENCE LANE on 7188

	Weight g	Weight gr		Die axis	
7185	3.34	51.6	Br	180°	*Carllile,* [Thomas?]. 1671. 3.5.40; 5.76.151. BW 1637 but CARLLILE. No provenance 1979. Description confirmed from Dickinson, pl. 2. The monogram incorporates the letters of the surname and apparently THOMAS. Thomas Carlile appr. 1660 to Roger Carlile, Blacksmith; Thomas Carlile, Gunmaker, bound an apprentice 1683 (Webb 1996-, viii. 12, xli. 39). Child of Thomas Carlile of St Lawrence Jewry, Gunmaker, blacksmith, bap. 1671 (Boyd 25622). Carli(s)le Coffee-house 1671-1714 (Lillywhite 1972, nos. 220-2, 'Carllile' *recte* Carllile); 26-26.5 mm diameter suggests a penny
7186	1.58	24.4	Br	0°	*Peade,* Leonard. nd. 3.53.20; L P. BW 1639 but LAN^{E}. Baldwin [ex Pridmore]. Reading completed from MoL specimen. Leonard Pead of St Lawrence Jewry, Cook, d. 1663; churchwarden 1653, 1654 (Boyd 26364); Leonard Pead(e) bound apprentices 1655-62 (Webb 1996-, xxvi. 1, 6, 20, 27). The Dickinson reading PARDE was mis-copied from BW

Named signs

7187	0.99 (chipped)	15.2	Br	180°	*Cross Keys* (AT THE CROSSE KEYS): ?S—, T—. 1651. 5.66.20 (•AT•THE•CROSSE•KEYS around); S|TF̣ (•S•|T•F̣; •IN•Ṣ•ḶẠẈṚẠṆÇ̣E•I65I around). BW —; *Dickinson 1640A, from a report of this specimen. Nott. Obv. reading confirmed from Dickinson 2001, 9, on which the rev. initials are positioned F|TS
7188a	1.54	23.8	Cu	0°	*Cross Keys* (AT THE CROSE KEYES): ?S—, I/J—. nd. 5.66.30; I S. BW 1640 but ST•LAWRENCE. Nott [ex Spink]. Described on envelope as a halfpenny, 'denomination unlisted in Williams[on]'. Diameter 17.5-18 mm.; double struck. ?Mr John Sadler, for whom a foundation was set out in Lawrence Lane 24 Dec. 1667 (Mills 1962-7, ii. 53v)
7188b	1.30	20.1	M	180°	Same dies. [Nott ex Carthew]. Diameter 16-16.5 mm
7188c	1.29	19.8	M	0°	Same dies. Nott [ex Taffs]. Diameter 16 mm

LEADENHALL MARKET (Lime Street ward & Bishopsgate ward Within) [28-H15]

The reading is LEADEN HALL MARKET on 7192, STREET on 7191; LEADENHALL MARKET on 7190; . . .ḌEN HALL MARKẸ^{T} on 7189; cf. 7193-5

7189	0.69	10.6	Cu	0°	*Seale,* Tho[mas] (ṬHO:). nd. 4.12.2 (•ṬHO:SEALE•WITHIN around); S|TA (•S•|TA; . . .ḌEN•̣HALL•̣MARKẸ^{T} around). BW —. Baldwin. Thomas Seale of St Peter Cornhill, Butcher, d. 1681; wife Anne (Boyd 48962). Rev. reading LEADEN•HALL•MARKE^{T} observed on a specimen (from same dies?) seen Aug. 1988

Named signs

7190	0.92 (chipped)	14.2	Br	0°	*Bull's Head* (ẠṬ Y^{E} BVLL HEAD): O[nleey], A[lice]. 1657. 3.52.25; I6|A O|57. *BW 1658 but Y^{E} BVLL, LEADENHALL, I6|A O|57. Nott [ex Carthew]. Identification of issuer from 7191. Alice Only, widow 1657 of George Only of St Peter Cornhill, Vintner; she d. 1670 (Boyd 22937). 'White Bull head… in the occupation of… widow Onely' 1660 (Rogers 1928a, pp. 96-7). She bound apprentices (Webb 1996-, xliii. 373)
7191a	5.04	77.7	Br	0°	*Bull's Head* (AT THE): Onleey, Alice (ALLICE). 1668 1d. 3.52.25; 5.77. BW 1656 but ALLICE•ONLEEY, LEADEN•HALL, I^{D}. Baldwin. Location from 7190, q.v.
7191b	4.53	69.9	Br	0°	Same dies. [?Baldwin]
7191c	3.48	53.7	Br	0°	Same dies. [Nott]
7192	0.96	14.9	Cu	0°	*Golden Heart* (AT THE GOLDEN HART): [anonymous], a soap (SOPE) shop. nd. 3.9.1; 5.77. BW 1702 but LEADEN•HALL. Nott. Reading completed from BM specimen

LEADENHALL MARKET neighbourhood

The reading is BY ḶEAḌEN HALL on 7194; OVER AGAINST LEADENHAL on 7193

	Weight g	Weight gr		Die axis	
7193a	2.17 (chipped)	33.4	Br	90°	*Rugbey,* Edward. 1668 ½d. 3.10.4; 5.77. BW 1681. [Nott ex Seaby]. Edward Rugby (1631-1675), of St Peter Cornhill, Grocer and tobacconist (Boyd 22946)
7193b	1.87	28.9	Br	0°	Same dies. Baldwin, 'purchased in South St., Exeter, Aug. 1924'
7193c	0.93	14.4	Br	270°	Same dies. [Nott ex Taffs]
7194	0.44	6.8	Br	0°	*Trunket,* Ralph. nd. 5.38.5 (•RALPH•TRVNKET• around); T|RA (•T•|R A|•; •BY•̣ḶEAḌEN•HALL around). BW —; Dickinson 1691A, from Heal 1928, p. 11. Baldwin. Ralf Trunket of St Peter Cornhill, Cook, churchwarden 1664; md. Anne Wallis 1639; d. 1685 (Boyd 3414). Ralph Trunckett bound apprentices 1658-74 (Webb 1996-, xxvi. 56, 70)

LEADENHALL MARKET. 'The Gate' neighbourhood (Aldgate & Lime Street wards & Bishopsgate ward Within)

The reading is AT LEADEN HALL GATE. The principal gateway, on the northern side, was flanked by a number of small rooms (Masters 1974, p. 24, pl. vii)

Named signs

7195	1.05	16.2	Br	180°	*Dog & Duck* (AT THE DOGE AND DVCK): ?T—, G—. nd. 3.67.11; T|GA. BW 1690 but LEADEN•HALL. Nott [ex Carthew]

LEADENHALL STREET (Aldgate & Lime Street wards & Bishopsgate ward Within) [28-H15]

See also EAST INDIA HOUSE neighbourhood; ST KATHERINE CREE neighbourhood. The reading is LEADEN HALL STREET on 6878, 7191, 7199, 7201-5, 7207, 7213-14, 7227, 7229, 7231, STREETE on 7208, 7221-3, 7228, 7232-3; STRET on 7198, 7206, 7212, 7216, 7226, 7234-5, STREṬ on 7237, STRETE on 7230; LEA\|DEN HALL STREETE on 7210; LEADEN HAL STREET on 7218, 7584; LEDEN HAL STREEṬ on 7219; LEDEN HALL STREET on 6879; LEADENHALL STREET on 7196-7, 7200, 7209, 7215, 7225, 7236 (ḶEADENHAḶḶ ṢṬREET on 7196, ḶEADENHALL STREET on 7200), STREETE on 7211, 7217, 7224, STRET on 7220.

The following was recorded but is now missing: Gilbert 1927, 153 but ĢLOVFER = •••\|I67I\|•••, rev. = POVL\|TERER\|•••, =*Dickinson 1664A, axis 270°, ex Baldwin

7196	1.06	16.4	M	180°	*Amyes,* Jo[hn], oilman (OYLEMAN). nd. 5.40.4; A|IS. *BW 1643 but OYLEMAN. Nott. John Amis of St Peter Cornhill, Draper, free 1639; oilman, Bishopsgate Street, 1641; wife Mary to 1650; will, PCC, 1660 (Boyd 5603). Same obv. die as 7197
7197	1.21	18.6	M	180°	*Amyes,* Jo[hn], oilman (OYLEMAN). nd. 5.40.4; A|IS. BW 1643 but OYLEMAN. Nott [or Baldwin]. Same obv. die as 7196, q.v.
7198a	1.36	21.0	Cu	0°	*Bland,* John. 1666. 5.68.10; B|IE. BW 1649 but STRET. Baldwin
7198b	0.95	14.6	Cu	90°	Same dies. [Nott ex Taffs]
7199a	2.42	37.4	Br	0°	*Bonner,* Robert. nd ½d. (o|B). 5.3.21; 5.77 (o|B|RA). BW 1650 but LEADEN•HALL, o|•B•|R•A. [Nott ex Taffs]. Presumably the surname initial B serves also as the second letter of *ob[olus]* = ½d.; this is supported by the size of the flan, here 21 mm
7199b	2.29	35.3	Br	0°	Same dies. Baldwin ex B. G. J[ohnson]. Diameter 20 mm
7200	0.89	13.7	Br	180°	*Brimecome,* Joan (IONE). 1658 (I6•58). Date; I B. *BW 1651. Nott
7201a	1.50	23.1	M	0°	*Crowe,* John. nd. 5.38.20; C|IA. BW 1657. Nott
7201b	1.09	16.9	M	0°	Same dies. [Nott ex Taffs]
7202	2.50	38.6	Cu	90°	*Daniell,* George. nd ½d. (OB'). 3.45.7; 3.6.8. BW 1659 but LEADEN•HALL, HIS:OB (tittle above)|two hands or gloves. Nott [ex Spink]. R of STREET over ?; perhaps the token is overstruck on another
7203	1.73	26.7	M	0°	*Gardner,* Nathaniel (NATHANIELL). nd ½d. 3.101.6; 5.77. BW 1664 but NATHANIELL, a cock and unicorn, LEADEN[?no stop]HALL•STREET. Nott [ex Taffs]. 'Mr Gardners an Apothecary at the Unicorn' 1664 (BW 1664 n.)
7204	1.62 (chipped)	25.0	Br	180°	*Grigman,* George. nd ½d. 3.59.2; 5.77. BW 1665 but LEADEN•HALL. Nott. Reading confirmed from BM specimen. George Grigman of St Peter Cornhill, victualler; children bap. 1667-73 (Boyd 22987)
7205	1.78	27.4	Br	330°	*Hill,* Thomas, grocer. nd ½d. 5.64.15; 5.77. BW 1668 but sugarloaves not suspended, LEADEN•HALL. Nott [ex Taffs]

[*continued overleaf*]

7193b 7194 7195 7196 7197 7198a

7199b 7200 7201a 7202 7203 7204

7205 7206a 7207 7208b 7209 7210a

7211a 7212 7213 7214 7215 7216

Plate 33 (*cont.*)

	Weight *g*	*gr*		*Die axis*	
7206a	1.55	23.9	Cu	270°	*Kempster,* John. nd. 4.11.24; K|IE. BW 1671 but LEADEN•HALL. Nott [ex Taffs]. Same obv. die as another specimen, axis 180°, ex Nott, now lost, rev. •LEDEN•HALL•STREET = •K•|I•E (an earlier pairing). 'John Kempster potter . . . next to the Kings Arms Inne', 1662 (BW 1671 n.). Glass-sellers' Company: Master 1668, 1669; md. Elizabeth; d. 1687 (Woodhead 1966, p. 101). Bound apprentices 1674-84 (Webb 1996-, v. 33)
7206b	0.89 (chipped)	13.7	Cu	270°	Same dies. [Nott ex Seaby]
7206c	0.81 (chipped)	12.6	Cu	270°	Same dies. [Baldwin]. All struck from obv. die in flawed and rusted state
7207	1.97 (pierced)	30.4	Cu	0°	*Orpin* (OṚPIN), Robert. nd ½d. 3.4.2 (•ROBERT•OṚPIN•AT•TH̤E around); 5.77 (R O) (HIS|HALF|PENY|•R O•; –IN•LEADEN•HALL•STREET around). BW —; *Dickinson 1675A. Clark 1978. Robert Orpen of St Katharine Cree, b. 1644, (pastry)-cook; md. Mary New 1669 (Boyd 17588). Robert Orpin appr. 1662, bound apprentices 1667-75 (Webb 1996-, xxvi. 41, 68)
7208a	1.43 (chipped)	22.1	Br	330°	*Rowland,* John, mealman. 1669 ½d. 5.14.1 Tallow Chandlers (I R); 5.77. BW 1680 but LEADEN:HALL[?no stop]STREETE. [Nott ex Taffs]
7208b	0.69	10.6	Br	330°	Same dies. Nott [ex Carthew]
7209	1.25	19.3	Br	0°	*Sawyer,* Thomas. 1668 ½d. 3.1.25; 5.77. BW 1684. Nott [ex Spink]. ?Thomas Sawyer of St Peter Cornhill, b. 1640, Clothworker, fl. 1671 (Boyd 17326)
7210a	0.72	11.0	Br	90°	*Smith,* Henry. [16]57. 5.66.17; 5.76.42 (H S). BW 1688 but HENRY[no stop]SMITH. Nott [ex Taffs]
7210b	0.68	10.5	Br	90°	Same dies. [Nott]
7211a	1.58	24.4	Br	90°	*Tillard,* Christopher (CRISTOPHER). nd. 3.5.56; T|CA. BW 1692 but TILLARD[no stop]IN. Nott [ex Carthew]. Most letters E and R weakly punched into dies; obv. legend starts at 1 o'clock. Diameter 17-17.5 mm. Christopher Tillard of St Peter Cornhill, Vintner; wife Anne; children bap. 1663-65 (Boyd 22970); fl. 1669 (Harl. Reg. 4, 1879, p. 88). Christopher Tiller appr. 1649 (Webb 1996-, xliii. 295, see also 387)
7211b	0.71 (chipped)	10.9	Br	0°	Same dies. [Baldwin]. Diameter 16 mm
7212	1.78	27.5	Br	180°	*Vaston,* William. nd ½d. 5.77 (W V); 3.3.13. BW 1693. Nott [ex Carthew]. Description confirmed from BM specimen. William Vaston assessed in St Katherine Cree 1695 (Jones 1966, p. 300); Broderer, bound apprentices 1683-1712; Tallow Chandler apprentices turned over to William Vaston, broderer, 1706, 1712 (Webb 1996-, vi. 30, 40, xxxix. 29, 92). See also 7647, perhaps the same issuer since the surname is rare
7213	0.70	10.8	Cu	0°	*Vere,* Joseph. nd. 3.60.30; I V. BW 1694 but the head couped and bridled. Spink 1973. Struck off-centre. Reading completed from BM specimen
7214	4.04	62.3	Cu	0°	*Webb,* Joseph, flaxman (FLEXMAN). 1668 1d. 3.1.79?; 5.51.12. *BW 1700 but I^{D}. Nott. Copper surround with plug of brass. Denomination completed from BM specimen. The woman on the obv. is not clear
7215	0.81	12.5	Br	90°	*Wonde,* John. nd. 4.1.1; W|IE. BW 1701. Nott [ex Taffs]. Second T of STREET cancels ?initial mark. Rev. legend originally began IN, repeating the last word of obv. legend, but a mullet and ?pierced rosette respectively cancel these letters

Named signs

7216	0.97	15.0	M	180°	*Bird in Hand* (AT THE BVRD IN HAND): ?M—, N—. nd. M|NA (•M•|N:A; •AT•THE•BVRD•IN•HAND around); 3.6.24 (•IN•LEADEN•HALL•STRET around). BW —; Dickinson 1672B. Baldwin

LEADENHALL STREET (*cont.*)

Named signs (*cont.*)

	Weight g	*Weight* gr		*Die axis*	
7217a	0.96	14.8	M	180°	*Black Horse* (THE): [anonymous]. nd. 3.60.20; 5.76.152. BW 1703. Nott. Second T of STREETE double-entered
7217b	0.64 (chipped)	9.9	M	180°	Same dies. [Nott ex Taffs]
					Bull's Head: Onleey, Alice *see* 7191 (Leadenhall Market)
7218a	1.90	29.3	Br	270°	*East India House* (AT THE SIGNE OF Y^{E}): Wait, George. nd ½d. 5.77; 1.69.8. BW 1699 but PENY|three saltires. Nott. Diameter 21 mm
7218b	1.55	23.9	Br	0°	Same dies. Nott [ex Taffs]. Diameter 19 mm
7219a	0.87	13.5	Br	180°	*Gilt Frying Pan* (AT THE GILT FRIINPAN): ?B—, H—. nd. 5.50.33; B|HM. BW 1645 but FRIINPAN, HAL. Baldwin. Reading confirmed from BM specimen
7219b	0.71 (chipped)	11.0	Br	180°	Same dies. [Nott ex Taffs]
7220	0.80	12.3	Cu	180°	*Golden* [*?Ball*] (AT): Davice, Rob—. nd. 5.50.1; R D. BW 1660. Nott [ex Carthew]. D of surname double-entered
7221a	0.95 (chipped)	14.7	Br	180°	*Grave Maurice* (THE GRAVE MORYES): ?T—, G—. nd. 3.5.21; T|GE. BW 1691 but LEADEN•HALL, •T•|G•E. [Nott ex Taffs]. Maurice (1567-1625), Count (*Graaf*) of Nassau, Prince of Orange, Stadholder of the Netherlands, occurs in English as *Grave Maurice* 1597-1614 (British Library Catalogue)
7221b	0.91	14.0	Br	180°	Same dies. Nott
7221c	0.86	13.3	Br	180°	Same dies. [Nott]
7222	0.83	12.8	M	180°	*Grocers' Arms* (AT ṬHE GRỌÇẸṚS ẠRMES): ?M—, T—. nd. 5.14 Grocers; M|TB. *BW 1673 but LEADEN•HALL. Nott. Same rev. die as 7223
7223	1.07	16.5	M	180°	*Grocers' Arms* (AT THE GROCERS ARMES): ?M—, T—. nd. 5.14 Grocers; M|TB. BW 1673 but LEADEN•HALL. Nott [or Baldwin ex Pridmore]. Same obv. die as 7224; same rev. die as 7222
7224a	1.12 (chipped)	17.3	M	180°	*Grocers' Arms* (AT THE GROCERS ARMES): ?M—, T—. nd. 5.14 Grocers; M|TB. BW 1673. Nott. Same obv. die as 7223
7224b	1.06	16.4	M	180°	Same dies. Nott
7225	0.77	11.9	M	180°	*Hoop tavern* (THE HOOPE TAVEREN): ?P—, T—. nd. 1.41 (•THE•HOOPE•TAVEREN•IN around); P|TF (•P•|T•F; •LEADENHALL•STREET around). BW —; Gilbert 1927, 157 (this specimen), whence Dickinson 1675C, but obv. legend revised, •P•|T•F. Nott [ex Carthew ex Gilbert]
7226a	1.14	17.6	M	180°	[*Hoop*] *& Three* [*?Tuns*] (AT THE AND 3): S[tubbs], P[hilip]. nd. 1.41.5 (P S); 5.64.40. BW 1682 but LEADEN•HALL. Nott [ex Taffs]. Issuer and part of sign name identified from 7227. Philip Stubbs (1636-1705), of St Peter Cornhill, Vintner (Boyd 23098). Philip Stubbs appr. 1646 (Webb 1996-, xliii. 284, see also 385)
7226b	0.72	11.1	M	180°	Same dies. [Nott]
7227	1.43	22.0	M	0°	*Hoop & Three* [*?Tuns*] (AT Y^{E}HOOP AND 3): Stubbs, Philip (PHILLIP). nd ½d. (–ALF̣). 1.41.6; 5.64.42. *BW 1689 (HALF) but STVBBS, LEADEN•HALL•STREET = AND|3|three tuns. Nott [ex Taffs]. See 7226
7228	1.43	22.1	Cu	0°	*King's Head* [*tavern*] (AT Y^{E}): A[thy], J[ohn]. nd. A|II (.A.|I•I; •AT•Y^{E}•KINGS•HEAD•IN around); 3.5.56 (•LEADEN•HALL•STREETE around). BW —, cf. 7229, but bust with cap and feather, holding sceptre ?and orb; Rogers 1928d. [Nott, on whose ticket identified as BW 1642, ex Taffs]. John Athy of St Peter Cornhill; children bap. there 1651-7; Haberdasher, vintner; Alderman 1667; d. 1687 (Rogers 1928a, p. 82; Boyd 22905; Woodhead 1966, p. 20). Same obv. die as 7229 (q.v.)
7229a	1.22	18.9	Br	90°	*King's Head* [*tavern*] (AT Y^{E}): A[thy], J[ohn]. nd. A|II; 3.5.84. BW 1641 but LEADEN•HALL, crowned bust. Nott [ex Carthew]. Same obv. die as 7228, q.v. BW 1642 supplies 'tavern', but in the note read 1695 for '1681', and the King's Arms Inn was on the other side of the street, see Rogers 1928d
7229b	0.77	11.9	Br	90°	Same dies. [Nott ex Taffs]
7230	0.67	10.4	Br	180°	*Nag's Head tavern* (THE): ?P—, W—. nd. 3.60.30; P|WA. BW 1676 but TAVERN. Nott
7231a	3.16	48.7	Br	0°	*Peel* (AT Y^{E}PEALE): Alder, John. 1668 ½d. 5.34.11; 5.77 (A|IA). BW 1644. [Nott]. John Alder of St Katherine Cree, b. 1631, Baker; md. Anne Hendis 1655 (Boyd 39539)
7231b	2.91	44.9	Br	0°	Same dies. [Baldwin]
7231c	2.78	42.8	Br	0°	Same dies. Nott [ex Taffs]
7231d	2.37	36.5	Br	0°	Same dies. [Nott]
7231e	1.80 (chipped)	27.8	Br	0°	Same dies. [?Baldwin]
7231f	1.80	27.7	Br	0°	Same dies. [?Baldwin]

[*continued overleaf*]

7217a 7218b 7219a 7220 7221a 7222

7223 7224b 7225 7226a 7227 7228

7229a 7230 7231c 7232a 7233a 7234b

7235 7236a 7237 7238 7239 7240

Plate 34 (*cont.*)

	Weight			*Die*	
	g	*gr*		*axis*	
7232a	1.12	17.2	M	180°	*Plough* (AT THE): ?S—, R—. nd. 5.54; S|RI. BW 1683 but LEADEN•HALL. Nott [ex Carthew]
7232b	0.92	14.2	M	180°	Same dies. [Nott ex Taffs]
7233a	0.91	14.1	M	180°	*Prince's Arms* (THE PRINÇES ARMES): ?W—, I/J—. nd. 3.107.5; W|IS. *BW 1696. Nott. Reading largely completed from BM specimen
7233b	0.60	9.2	M	180°	Same dies. [Nott ex Taffs]
7234a	1.75	27.0	M	180°	*Red* [*?Lion*] (AT THE): Scott, John. nd ½d. 3.11; 5.77. BW 1685 but THE. Nott [ex Carthew]
7234b	1.50	23.2	M	180°	Same dies. [Nott]
7235	0.81	12.6	Cu	0°	*Two Sugarloaves* (AT TWO SVGER LOVES): Brond [*i.e.* Brand], John, grocer. nd. 5.15.39; 5.77. BW 1652 but STRET. Nott. Obv. legend starts between 10 and 11 o'clock; rev. legend starts at 11 o'clock. The arms are those of Brand, of Holborn or of Gray's Inn and Suffolk (Burke 1884, p. 116). John Brand was aged 11 in 1634 (Vis. Essex 1552-1634, i. 357)
7236a	1.15	17.8	Cu	0°	*White* [*?Bell*] (AT WHITE): Palmer, Rob[ert]. nd. 5.70.1; R P. BW 1677 but ROB:. Nott [ex Taffs]. Robert Palmer, Clothworker, appr. 1621; will, PCC, 1674, St James Dukes Place (Boyd 25254; Woodhead 1966, p. 125)
7236b	0.72	11.1	Cu	90°	Same dies. [Baldwin]
7236c	0.64	9.8	Cu	180°	Same dies. [Nott]
7237	0.94	14.6	Br	180°	*White Hart* (AT THE WHIT HART): ?E—, W—. nd. 3.53.20 (•AT•THE•WHIT•HART•IN around); E|WE (E|W E; •LEADEN•HALL•STREṬ around). BW —; Dickinson 1660A. Baldwin

LILYPOT LANE (Aldersgate ward) [25-F9]

The reading is LILLY POTT LANE

7238	0.96 (chipped)	14.8	Cu	270°	*Dowse,* John. nd. 5.14 Drapers; D|IM. BW 1705. Nott [ex Carthew]

LIME STREET (Aldgate & Lime Street & Langbourn wards) [28-H16]

The reading is LIME STREETE throughout (STREẸTE on 7239, ḶỊME on 7241)

Named signs

7239	0.76	11.7	Cu	0°	*Jack of Newbury* (AT Y^{E} IACK OF NEWBV:^{Y}): ?P—, U/V—. – –58. 3.1.40 (•AT•Y^{E}•IACK•OF•NEWBV:^{Y} around); P|VI (•P•|V•I|•; •IN•LIME•STREẸTE•– –58 around). BW —; Dickinson 1706A but – –58. [Baldwin ex Macfadyen, lot 154]. Same obv. die as 7240, q.v. For Jack of Newbury 'the most considerable Clothier… England ever beheld' see ODNB s.v. Winchcombe, John (d. 1520), and for his popular fame (e.g.) Spufford 1985, pp. 241-4
7240	1.37	21.1	Cu	270°	*Jack of Newbury* (AT Y^{E} IACK OF NEWBV:^{Y}): ?P—, U/V—. 1658. 3.1.40 (•AT•Y^{E}•IACK•OF•NEWBV:^{Y} around); P|VI (•P•|V I|•; •IN•LIME•STREETE•I658 around). BW —; Dickinson 1706A but I658. Nott. The E of Y^{E} from a broken punch, appearing as F; on rev. the 5 and Ts double-entered, the 8 from two *o* characters. Traces of original tinning on rev. Same obv. die as 7239 (q.v.)

Named signs (*cont.*)

	Weight *g*	*gr*		Die axis	
7241	2.02	31.1	Br	270°	*Rose tavern* (AT Y^{E}ROSE TAVERNE): Futter (FVTTER), Tho— (THO:). nd ½d. 5.77 (HIS|HALFE|PENY; •THO:FVTTER•AT•Y^{E}ROSE•– around); 4.12.1 (•TAVERNE•IN•LIME•STREETE around). BW —, cf. 'THO. HUNTER' (Webb 1915). Baldwin. Surname also read as FVLLER. ?Thomas Futter of St Mary at Hill, b. 1632, Salter; children bap. 1662, 1664 (Boyd 23515). Thomas Futter appr. Vintner 1648 (Webb 1996-, xliii. 112)

LION QUAY [*i.e.* LYON KEY] neighbourhood *subsequently* BOTOLPH WHARF *and* NICHOLSON'S WHARF *etc.* (Billingsgate ward) [38-K15, n31]

The reading is AT LYON KEY IN THEMSTRET on 7242; THEMES STREETE on 7243. On 7243 Lyon Key (spelling from Harben 1918, p. 374) is unnamed, but is implied by the obverse

7242	0.89	13.7	Br	180°	*Hawkins,* James. nd. 3.31.9; H|IV. BW 3100 but •H•I•v. Nott [ex Carthew]
7243a	1.10	16.9	Br	0°	*?R—,* F—. 1651. 3.31.9; R|FE. BW 3118. [Nott]
7243b	0.99	15.3	Br	180°	Same dies. Nott [ex Taffs]

LITTLE BRITAIN (Aldersgate ward & Farringdon ward Without) [24-F8]

The reading is LITTLE BRITTAIN on 7244, BRITTAINE on 7249-50, 7253, BRITTEN on 7248, BRITTIN on 7246, 7251; LITLE BRITTAINE on 7247, 7252; LITTL BRITTAIN on 7245

7244	0.52	7.9	Cu	180°	*Allen,* Zachary. nd. 5.64.79; A|ZA. BW 1709. Baldwin. Rev. legend starts at 1 o'clock. ?Zachariah Allen, Brewer; md. Anne Haiward 1662 (Boyd 24717, unlocated). Zachary Allen appr. Brewer 1651 (Webb 1996-, xxxvi. 2)
7245	0.98	15.0	Br	90°	*A[ttley],* S[amuel], pewterer. 1667. 5.14 Pewterers; 5.77 (A|SM). BW 1708 but LITTL, inscription in six lines, obv. and rev. transposed. Nott. Issuer identified by Cotterell 1929, p. 64; Liveryman 1667 (p. 150, no. 142). Samuel Atlee (Attley) appr. Pewterer 1653, free 1660, bound apprentices 1661-1701, struck from Livery at his request 1683 (Webb 1996-, xl. 4, 105; Ricketts 2001, p. 39). Samuel Atly of St Mildred Bread Street [no company noted] md. Mary Harford 1663 (Boyd 30920)
7246a	1.26	19.5	Br	270°	*Gasley,* Thomas, grocer. 1666 ½d. 4.9.5; 5.77. BW 1712 but IN[?no stop]LITTLE. Nott [ex Taffs]
7246b	0.93 (chipped)	14.4	Br	270°	Same dies. [Nott ex Carthew]
7247	0.67	10.4	Br	90°	*Holland,* Ralph. nd. 3.6.33; H|RD. BW 1716. Nott. Description confirmed from BM specimen
7248a	2.57	39.6	Cu	90°	*Midwinter,* Daniel (DANIELL), tallow-chandler. nd ½d. 5.14 Leathersellers (•DANIELL•MIDWINTER•TALLOW around); 5.77 (M|DA) (HIS|HALF|PENNY|M|D•A; •CHANDLER•IN•LITTLE•BRITTEN around). BW —; Dickinson 1718B. [Nott ex Taffs]
7248b	2.14	33.0	Cu	90°	Same dies. Nott
7248c	1.79	27.6	Cu	90°	Same dies. [?Baldwin]
7249	0.95	14.6	Cu	0°	*Papworth,* John. 1667 ½d. 3.60.4; 5.77. BW 1720 but BRITTAINE. Seaby, [*SCMB* April 1967]. Reading confirmed from MoL specimen
7250	2.33	36.0	Br	0°	*Torshell,* Samuel (SAMVELL), grocer (GROÇER). [16]67 ½d. 5.64.3 (T|SD); 5.77. *BW 1723. Nott [ex Carthew]. Surname presumably from Tattershall, Lincs., occurring as 'Tortoiseshell' 1861 (Bardsley 1901, p. 759)
7251a	0.95	14.7	Br	0°	*Whittingham,* Tho—. nd. 5.76.153 (TB); W. BW 1725 but THO:. [Nott]
7251b	0.81	12.5	Br	0°	Same dies. Nott [ex Spink]
7252	2.51	38.7	Cu	135°	*Willmer,* Robert, leather (LETHER) cutter. [16]63. W|RM; 3.7.33. BW 1726 but WILLMER, rev. •6•3•|LETHER|CVTTER|[shoe]. Nott [ex Spink]
7253a	1.09	16.8	Cu	0°	*Wray,* Daniel (DANIELL), soap boiler (*Soap boyler*). [16]61. 5.77.1; W|DI. BW 1727 but obv. = *Soap|boyler|61.* [Baldwin]
7253b	0.99	15.2	Cu	0°	Same dies. Nott [ex Spink]

LITTLE CHEAPSIDE (Vintry ward) (*lost*) [36-J11, m53]

The reading is LITELL CHEPSIDE. Harben 1918, p. 352, records the name first from Ogilby; Ekwall 1954, p. 185, gives 1667 in error. Though undated, 7254 must be earlier

Named signs

7254	1.02 (chipped)	15.7	Br	0°	*Dyers' Arms* (A– –HE DIERS ARMES): ?H—, I/J—. nd. 5.14 Dyers; H|ID. *BW 578 but A– –HE, •H•I D. Nott. Reading CHEPSIDE completed from BM and MoL specimens which are all from another obv. die

[*continued overleaf*]

PLATE 35

7241 7242 7243b 7244 7245 7246a

7247 7248b 7249 7250 7251b 7252

7253b 7254 7255 7256b 7257b 7258

7259 7260b 7261 7262 7263 7264

Plate 35 (*cont.*)

LITTLE DICE QUAY *see* DICE QUAY

LITTLE EASTCHEAP *subsequently* EASTCHEAP (part) (Billingsgate ward) [38-I15]

The reading is LITTLE EAST CHEAP on 7259, CHEAPE on 7257, CHEP on 7255; LITTLE EASTCHEAP on 7256, EASTSHIP on 7258

Weight (*g*, *gr*) — *Die axis*

7255 0.54 8.3 Br 270° *Beale,* John. 1664. 5.60.1; B|IA. BW 1728. Spink 1971. See also 6973
7256a 1.15 17.7 Br 90° *Rolston,* John. nd. 3.107.2; R|IA. BW 1732. Nott [ex Spink]
7256b 1.13 17.4 Br 90° Same dies. Baldwin

Named signs

7257a 1.02 15.7 Br 330° *Globe* (AT THE): ?R—, I/J—. nd. 5.49.1; R|IA. BW 1731. [?Baldwin]. Attribution to John Rose (Fleet 2000, p. 151) unsafe because style suggests a date no later than 1649 o.s. (Dickinson forthcoming)
7257b 0.96 14.8 Br 150° Same dies. Nott [ex Taffs]
7257c 0.95 14.7 Br 150° Same dies. [?Baldwin]
7258 1.16 18.0 Br 0° *King's Head* (AT Y^{E}): Green, Emanuel (EMANVELL). nd ½d. 5.77 (G|EP); 3.5.81. BW 1729. Spink 1972. Appears to read PE•NY but the 'stop' is a compass point. Emanuel Green of St Mary at Hill, Cordwainer; wife Priscilla, children bap. 1649, 1650; will, PCC, 1682 (Boyd 16747)
7259 0.52 8.0 (chipped) Br 180° *Red Lion* (AT THE): ?U/V—, I/J—. nd. 3.11; V|IS. BW 1734. Nott

LITTLE MOORFIELDS *subsequently* MOORFIELDS (Cripplegate ward Without) [16-D12]

The reading is LITLE MOOR FELDS

Named signs

7260a 1.12 17.3 Cu 0° *Green House* (AT THE): Bond, Simon. 1666. 5.77; B|SA|date. BW 1954 but LITLE. [Nott]. 'The Green-house… fam'd for good Liquors' (Ward 1715, ii. 6), i.e. a tavern
7260b 0.65 10.0 Cu 270° Same dies. [Nott]

LITTLE OLD BAILEY *subsequently* OLD BAILEY (part) (Farringdon ward Without) [23-G6]

The reading is LITTLE OVLD BALY on 7263, –ẠỴLEY on 7261; LITLE OVLD BAYLEY on 7265; THE LITLE OVLD BEALEY on 7266-7, OVLDE BAYLEY on 7264, OVLDE BAYLY on 7268-9; THE LITTLE OLD BAYLY on 7262

7261 0.90 14.0 Br 90° *Eaveson* [i.e. *Paulson*?], Thomas. nd. 3.95.1; P|TE. *BW 2101 (BAYLEY) but •P•|T•E [*sic*]. [Nott]. Cf. 7409 (same initials and device)
7262 1.66 25.6 Br 270° *Hose,* Thomas. nd ½d. 3.108.5; 5.77 (H|TR). BW 2106. [Nott ex Seaby]. Description confirmed from MoL specimen
7263 0.60 9.2 Br 0° *Townsond,* Robert. nd. 3.5.54; T|RA. BW 2119. [Nott ex Taffs]. Obv. legend starts between 10 and 11 o'clock; rev. legend starts at 11 o'clock
7264 0.73 11.3 M 180° *Wates,* Alice (ALCE). nd. 3.108.15; A W. BW 2123. [Nott ex Taffs]

LITTLE OLD BAILEY (*cont.*)

Named signs

	Weight g	gr		Die axis	
7265	0.92	14.2	Br	150°	*Rose* (AT THE): ?C—, I/J—. nd. I C; 4.12.1. BW 2098. [Nott ex Spink]. Rogers 1928a, p. 86, suggested that John Carr may have moved here after 1641 from the Three Cranes in Old Bailey; evidence is desirable
7266a	1.00	15.4	M	180°	*Seven Stars* (AT THE 7 STARS): ?F—, I/J—. nd. 2.4.11; F|II. BW 2103. [Nott]. Same rev. die as 7267
7266b	0.83 (chipped)	12.9	Br	180°	Same dies. [Nott]
7267	1.10	17.0	M	180°	*Seven Stars* (AT THE 7 STARS): ?F—, I/J—. nd. 2.4.11; F|II. BW 2103. [Nott ex Taffs]. Same rev. die as 7266

LITTLE OLD BAILEY neighbourhood

The reading is AT THE CORNER OF THE LITLE OVLDE BAYLY on both

7268	1.01	15.6	M	180°	*?B—,* I/J—. nd. 4.13.1; B|IE. BW 2095. [Nott]. Same rev. die as 7269
7269	0.97	15.0	M	180°	*?B—,* I/J—. nd. 4.13.1; B|IE. BW 2095. [Nott ex Taffs]. Reading confirmed from MoL specimen. Same rev. die as 7268

LITTLE ST BARTHOLOMEW (Farringdon ward Without, St Bartholomew's Hospital neighbourhood) [14-E7]

The reading is LITTLE S^{T}BARTHOLEMEWS on 7270; LITTLL S BARTHELMEWS on 7271. 'Probably near St Bartholomew's Hospital' (Harben 1918, p. 351), but it is named as *Little St Bartholmew* by Ogilby, running from [West] Smithfield past the Hospital and St Bartholomew the Less [24-F7]

7270	1.44	22.2	Br	270°	*Banckes,* Noah, chees[e]mong[e]r. 1667 ½d. 0.7 (NOAH•BANCKES•CHEESMONG^{R} around); 5.77 (HIS|HALFE|PENY•|I667; •IN•LITTLE S^{T}BARTHOLEMEWS around). BW —; Dickinson 1735A, from a description of this specimen. Nott [ex Taffs]

Named signs

7271	1.10 (pierced)	17.0	Br	180°	*Cock* (THE COCKE): ?I/J—, S—. 1652. 3.101.1; S I. BW 1738 but LITTLL. Nott [ex Carthew]. Reading confirmed from BM specimen

LITTLE SOMER'S KEY *subsequently* BILLINGSGATE MARKET (Billingsgate ward) [38-K15, n33]

See also 6670. The reading is AT LITLE SOMERS KEY on 6670, SOM\|ERS KEY NEAR BILLINGS\|GATE (the Ns retrograde) on 7272; AT LITTLE SAMERS KEY on 7274; ON LITTLE SVMMER KAY on 7273

7272a	3.43	52.9	Br	0°	*Michell,* John, 'living at Little (LITLE) Somers Quay (KEY) near Billingsgate.' nd 1d. 3.4.31; 5.77. BW 2917 but A•PENNY•|a tilt-boat, etc., LIVING[no stop]AT|LITLE[no stop]SOME•|RS[no stop]KEY, obv. and rev. transposed, all Ns on rev. retrograde. Baldwin [ex Gilbert]
7272b	3.42	52.8	Br	0°	Same dies. Nott
7272c	3.30	50.9	Br	0°	Same dies. [Nott ex Carthew]
7273a	3.56	54.9	Br	90°	*Simmons,* John. 1666 ½d. 5.64.76; 5.77 (S|IH). BW 2919 but PENNY. Nott (envelope), Baldwin (record and ticket). John Symonds of St Mary at Hill, strong-water man, md. Hannah Seymour 1663 (Boyd 20540); John Simonds/Symonds, Distiller, bound apprentices 1669-78 (Webb 1996-, xi. 39)
7273b	2.88	44.5	Br	90°	Same dies. [Nott ex Daniels]
7273c	2.20	33.9	Br	90°	Same dies. [?Baldwin]
7273d	1.93	29.8	Br	180°	Same dies. [Nott]
7273e	1.67	25.8	Br	180°	Same dies. [Nott ex Taffs]

Named signs

7274a	5.14	79.3	Br	240°	*Queen's Head* (AT Y^{E}): Pascall, Alice (AILLIS). nd 1d. 5.77; 3.5.94. BW 2918 but AILLIS, I^{D}. [Nott ex Carthew]
7274b	2.77	42.8	Br	240°	Same dies. Nott

LITTLE TOWER STREET *subsequently* EASTCHEAP (part) (Billingsgate & Tower wards) [38-I16: from Tower Street to St Mary at Hill]

The reading is LITTLE TOWER STREET

7275a	2.62	40.5	Cu	0°	*Tayler* (. . .LER), Thomas. nd ½d. 2.4.12; 5.40.2 (T T). BW 3224 but . . .LER. Nott [ex Taffs]. In MoL there is a token of this issuer reading as Burn 1855, 1215 and Boyne 1858, London 2583 (viz. BW 3224 but LITTLE, HALF)
7275b	2.43	37.5	Cu	0°	Same dies. Nott [ex Carthew]. Struck off-centre

[*continued overleaf*]

7265 7266a 7267 7268 7269 7270

7271 7272b 7273a 7274b 7275a 7276b

7277 7278b 7279 7280 7281 7282

7283 7284 7285 7286b 7287b 7288

LITTLE TRINITY LANE (Queenhithe ward) [35-J10]

See also TRINITY LANE. The reading is LITTLE TRINITY LANE

	Weight			*Die*	
	g	*gr*		*axis*	
7276a	2.73	42.2	Br	0°	*Langdell,* Joan (IOANNE). 1666 ½d. 5.38.1; 5.77 (I L). BW 3232. [Nott ex Taffs]
7276b	1.93	29.8	Br	0°	Same dies. Nott

LITTLE WOOD STREET *otherwise* WOOD STREET, northern part (Farringdon & Cripplegate wards Within) [15-E10: north of Addle Street, 25-F10]

See also WOOD STREET, southern part. The reading is LITTLE WOODSTREET throughout

7277	0.60 (pierced four times)	9.3	Cu	0°	*Clarke,* Philip (PHILLIP). nd. 5.64.1; C|PA. BW 3510 but WOODSTREET. Nott
7278a	2.03	31.4	Br	0°	*Halford,* Thomas. 1669 ½d. 5.77; 4.10.1. BW 3523. [Nott ex Carthew]. Thomas Halford of St Alban Wood Street, b. 1647, Brewer; md. 1670 (Boyd 17702)
7278b	1.76	27.2	Br	0°	Same dies. Nott [ex Taffs]
7279	1.53	23.7	Cu	0°	*Plomer,* Francis. 1666 ½d. 5.64.173; 5.77. BW 3530 but WOODSTREET. Nott [ex Spink]. Reading completed from MoL specimen

LOMBARD STREET (Langbourn ward & Bridge ward Within & Walbrook ward) [27-H13]

See also DOVE COURT. The reading is LOMBARD STREET on 7284; LVMBARD STREET on 6866; LVMBER STREET on 7280, STREETE on 7282, STRETE on 7283; LVMBERT STREETE on 7281

7280	1.76	27.1	Br	270°	*Goodall,* Rich[ard]. nd ½d. 3.102.19; G|RA. BW 1752 but RICH:. Nott. Richard Goodall of St Michael Cornhill, Merchant Taylor; md. Abigail Strong 1665; both fl. 1672 (Boyd 43026)
7281	0.97	15.0	Br	180°	*Rolfe,* John. nd. 3.6.62; I R. BW 1755. Nott. Struck off-centre. Reading confirmed from MoL specimen
7282	1.12 (chipped)	17.2	Cu	0°	*Smith,* William. 1666 ½d. 4.1.4; 5.77. BW 1757. Nott [ex Taffs]. Description completed from MoL specimen, illustrated by Hulbert 1972. William Smith, vintner, kept this Royal Oak tavern: 9 hearths 1666 (Pepys 1970-83, iv. 100, vi. 38, x. 426). See also Webb 1996-, xliii. 273-4, 383

Named signs

7283	0.93	14.4	Br	180°	*Plough* (AT THE PLOW): Jones, Robert. nd. 5.54; 5.54. *BW 1754 but PLOW•IN•LVMBER•STRETE. Nott [ex Carthew]. Reading partly confirmed from a specimen available to the authors. Robert Jones of St Mary Woolnoth, Grocer, confectioner, comfit maker, d. 1663; children bap. from 1644 (Boyd 2164)
7284	2.32	35.7	Br	180°	*Salutation* (AT Y^{E}): ?H—, T—. nd ½d. 3.4.2; H|TM. BW 1753. Nott [ex Taffs]. Contrary to BW 1753 n., the Salutation was at No. 66, and existed in 1658 (Rogers 1935, pp. 107-8)

LONDON BRIDGE (Bridge ward Within) [37-K14]

The reading is ON LONDON BRIDG on 7286-7, BRIDGE on 7288, BRIDGẸ on 7285

7285	0.60 (chipped)	9.2	Br	90°	*Wallker,* George (ĢEORGE). 1667 ½d. 4.12.1; 5.77 (W|GA). *BW 1762. Baldwin

Named signs

7286a	1.65	25.5	Cu	180°	*Black [?Bull]* (AT BLAK): Harrison, Nicholas. 1666 ½d. 3.52.6 (•NICHOLAS•HARRISON•AT•BLAK around); 5.77 (HIS|HALF|PENY|•:•; •ON• LONDON•BRIDG•I666: around). BW —; Dickinson 1759A. [Nott ex Carthew]. Reading BLAK confirmed from Gilbert 1927, pl. vii.10
7286b	1.41	21.8	Cu	180°	Same dies. Baldwin
7287a	2.50	38.5	Cu	0°	*Sugarloaf* (AT THE SVGER LOAF): Muns, Edward. 1668 ½d. 5.64.1; 5.77. BW 1760. [Baldwin]. Edward Munns, Draper, Warden 1678 and later; girdler 'on the Bridge' 1641; will 1689 PCC (Boyd 38180). Diameter 21.5-22 mm
7287b	2.37	36.5	Cu	0°	Same dies. Nott [ex Seaby]. Diameter 21-21.5 mm
7287c	1.67	25.8	Cu	0°	Same dies. [Nott ex Taffs]. Diameter 22.5-23 mm
7288	1.05 (edge filed)	16.2	Cu	180°	*Three Bibles* (AT THE 3 BIBLES): T[yus], C[harles]. nd. T|CS; 5.85.5. BW 1761 but T[YUS]. [Longman] 1958, lot 452. Named in BW as 'Tyns' through a misreading of T. Calvert, *The Wise Merchant*, 1660 (Wing 1972-88, C327). Charles Tyus, Stationer, fl. 1656-64; widow Sarah (Plomer 1907, p. 185). On his stock of chapbooks and ballads see Spufford 1985, pp. 92-110. Surname there spelled Tias; from Old French *tieis*, 'German' (Reaney 1995, p. 460)

LONDON STONE neighbourhood (Walbrook ward, Cannon Street) [37-I13]

On the south side of Cannon Street, opposite the SW corner of St Swithin's Church (Harben 1918, p. 367); subsequently moved to the north side. The reading is AT LONDON STONE

	Weight g	Weight gr		Die axis	
7289	1.28	19.8	Cu	90°	*Burges,* William. 1667 ½d. 5.14 Coopers; 5.77. BW 461. Nott. ?William Burgess of St Lawrence Jewry, Cooper, fl. 1682 (Boyd 32441)

LONDON WALL neighbourhood (Broad Street & Bassishaw & Coleman Street wards & Cripplegate ward Within) [17-E13 etc.]

See also BALL ALLEY; BROAD STREET neighbourhood; CARPENTERS' HALL neighbourhood; WHITE HORSE YARD. The reading is LONDON WALL on 6504, 7816; AT LONDON WALE on 7292, LONDON WALL on 6721, LONDO^{N} WALL on 6719; BY LONDON WAL on 6735, LONDON WALL on 7290; NEAR LONDON WALE on 7291

7290 0.92 (chipped) 14.2 Cu 90° *Trotter,* Hester. [16]67. 3.60.1; H T. BW 1772. Baldwin. Reading LONDON confirmed from BM specimen. ?White Horse Inn 1676 (Ogilby 1676, 17-E13, A68). The horse is shown as a Trotter

Named signs

7291 1.85 28.5 Br 270° *Ball* (AT Y^{E}): Buckly, Randolph. 1669 ½d. 5.50.1 (•RANDOLPH•BVCKLY•AT•Y^{E} around); 5.77 (HIS|HALF|PENY|1669; •BALL•NEAR•LONDON•WALE around). BW —; Dickinson 1764A. Nott. Reading completed from MoL specimen. ?Randolf Buckl(e)y of St Sepulchre, b. 1638 (Boyd 20586). Withycombe 1977, p. 249, considered *Randolph* an 18th-c. antiquarian coining from Latin *Randulfus*

7292 2.07 31.9 Br 315° *Sledge* (AT Y^{E}SLEDG): Alin, Oliver. nd. 5.53.24 (•OLIVER•ALIN•AT•Y^{E}SLEDG around); A|OI (•A•|O·I|•; ••AT•LONDON•WALE• around). BW —; Dickinson 1763A. Baldwin. The device is apparently the Sledge used for conveying condemned persons to execution (OED Sledge sb.^{2} 2b)

LONG LANE (Aldersgate ward & Farringdon ward Without) [14-D7]

See also THREE FOX COURT. The reading is LONG LANE throughout (LANE on 7294), including 7752

7293a 1.51 23.3 Br 90° *Morton,* Thomas. 1666 ½d. 3.116.1; M|TM|date. BW 1825. [Nott]. Reading confirmed from MoL specimen

7293b 1.07 (chipped) 16.5 Br 0° Same dies. Nott

7294 0.98 15.2 Cu 0° *Seymor,* Roger. nd. 5.70.1; S|RE. *BW 1827. Nott [ex Taffs]. Obv. legend starts between 10 and 11 o'clock, rev. legend between 5 and 6 o'clock

Named signs

7295a 1.29 19.9 Br 0° *Acorn* (AT THE ACORNE): ?S—, I/J—. 1656. 4.8.10; S|IS. BW 1826. Baldwin

7295b 0.85 13.1 Br 0° Same dies. [Nott]

7295c 0.79 12.1 Br 180° Same dies. [Nott ex Taffs]

7296 0.84 12.9 Br 0° *Golden Ball:* [anonymous], meal shop (MEALE SHOPP). nd. 5.50.1; 5.50.1. BW 1831. Nott, on whose ticket identified as 'Southwark. . .W.297.B. unpub:'

7297 0.84 (chipped) 12.9 Cu 0° *Green* [*?Dragon*] (AT GREENE): Burr, Tho—. nd. 3.114.1; T B. BW 1817 but THO:. Nott [ex Spink]. Obv. legend starts between 10 and 11 o'clock

LOTHBURY (Broad Street & Coleman Street wards) [27-G13]

The reading is LOATHBVRY on 7300-1; LOTHBVRY on 7298-9, LOTHBVRY on 7303, LOTHBVRY on 7302; LOTHEBVRY on 7304

7298 4.67 72.0 Br 180° *Brisco,* Edward. 1670. 5.77; 3.67.28. BW 1832. Nott. *Argent three greyhounds courant in pale Sable* were the arms of Briscoe, which John Brisco(e) of London brought to the Visitation, 1634; his eldest son and heir apparent was Edward Brisco (Vis. Lond. 1633-35, i. 103). Edward Brisco, Grocer; will of his widow Frances, PCC, 1673, St Margaret Lothbury (Boyd 47628). The 24.5-25 mm diameter suggests a penny

7299 1.21 18.6 Cu 240° *Varney,* John. [16]63. 4.9.5 (•IOHN•VARNEY 63 around); V|IM (•V•|I·M|•; ••IN•LOTHBVRY• around). BW —; Dickinson 1839A. Seaby, [*SCMB* April 1967]. Rev. legend starts between 4 and 5 o'clock. John Varn(e)y free of the Drapers' Company 1651; chandler, Lothbury; by 1683 of Fulham, gent.; will proved PCC 1691 (Boyd 38857; PROB/11/403)

7300 0.73 (chipped) 11.2 Br 180° *Wolrich,* Michael. 1656. 3.107.5; M W. BW 1840. Nott [ex Taffs]. Reading completed from MoL specimen N2081. Michael Woolrich bound apprentices 1659-64 (Webb 1996-, xxvi. 71). Decree 1668 that M. Woolrich, Cook, should rebuild the messuage leased to John Woolrich 1656 (Fire Court 1966-, i. 275); foundation set out for M. Wooldredge/ Woolridge 1669 (Mills 1962-7, i. 44, iv. 125v). See also 6680-2 (J. Wolrich). Same rev. die as 7301

[*continued overleaf*]

7289 7290 7291 7292 7293b 7294

7295a 7296 7297 7298 7299 7300

7301 7302 7303 7304 7305 7306a

7307 7308 7309b 7310 7311 7312

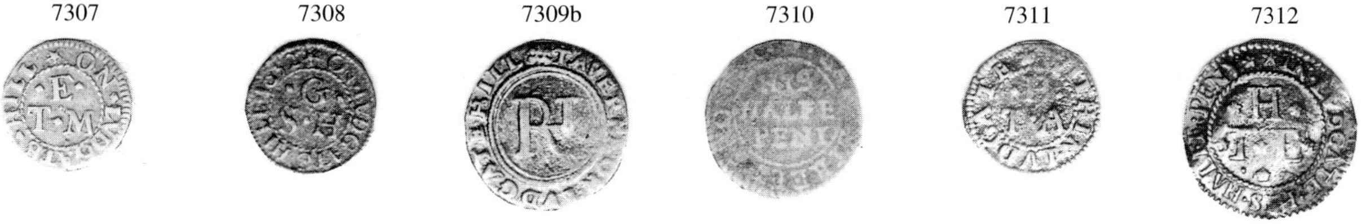

	Weight *g*	*gr*		*Die axis*	
7301	1.15	17.8	Br	180°	*Wolrich,* Michael. 1656. 3.107.5; M W. BW 1840. Nott. Same rev. die as 7300 (q.v.), in later state with upper counter of B filled
Named signs					
7302	1.94	30.0	Br	0°	*Golden Falcon* (AT Y^{E} GOLDEN FAVLCON): Terrill, Avery, cook (COOKE). [16]69 ½d. 3.92.4; 5.77 (T|AM). BW 1838 but LOTHBVRY. Nott [ex Taffs]
7303	1.15	17.7	Br	0°	*Martinico* (AT THE MARTI|NEECO): Carter, Will—, cook (COOKE). 1669 ½d. 5.77 (THE|MARTI|NEECO|•••; •WILL:CARTER•COOKE•AT around); 5.77 (C|WM) (HIS|HALF|PENY|C|W.M; •IN•LOTHBVṚY•I669• around). BW —; Dickinson 1833A. Nott [ex Taffs]. Martinique was called 'Martinico' in John Davies of Kidwelly's *History of the Caribby-Islands* (London, 1666), and later
7304	2.42	37.4	M	180°	*West Country coffee-house* (AT THE WEST CVNTRY COFFE HOVSE): ?S—, I/J—. nd. I S; 3.6.51; BW 1837 but COFFE. Nott. Reading confirmed from MoL specimen. Several prick marks above initials

LOVE LANE *subsequently* LOVAT LANE (Billingsgate ward) [38-J15]

The name is generally held to refer to houses of ill fame (Ekwall 1954, p. 166), and this tradition is promoted on 7305 by the tooling(?) of the Pillars into an exotic portal, and of Hercules into a long-haired female standing with thighs apart. The reading is LOVE LANE on both

7305	1.89	29.2	Br	180°	*Whitting,* John. nd ½d. 3.5.83 (•IOHN•WHITTING•AT•Y^{E}•IN around); 3.1.4 (•LOVE•LANE•HIS•HALF•PENY around). BW —; Dickinson 1842A, from a report of this specimen. Nott [ex Taffs]. Attribution to this Love Lane supported by the 1679 administration for John Whiteing, All Hallows Staining (Fitch 1992-8, iii. 731). The rev. device not being the Apothecaries' Arms, identification of the issuer as an apothecary (Whittet 1983, p. 136) is unsafe. Rev. ?tooled, see above. Cf. 7306

LOVE LANE. The Post-house

'It seems quite possible… that the King's Head, Love Lane, was solely a post house for letters, not only because its nearness to the Thames suggests traffic by water, rather than [a place where horses and vehicles could be hired for] travelling by road, but also it appears to have been the predecessor of the post office mentioned in the "Mercurius Publicus" news-sheet of 1661… [see BW 1841 n.]. This advertisement was probably to inform the public that the post office had been moved from one building to another in the same lane' (Bagust 1937, pp. 5-6). It was a separate receiving office for the Kent road, otherwise the Dover Post House, destroyed in the Fire; its removal in 1667 to the Grand office in Bishopsgate Street seems to have been the end of a separate post house (Willcocks 1975, p. 21). The reading is POST-\|HOVSE LOVE LANE

Named signs					
7306a	1.03	15.9	Br	90°	*King's Head Post-house:* L[ong], W[illiam]. [16]57. 3.5.89; L|WI. BW 1841 but POST- (hyphen), LANE57. Nott. A of LANE an inverted V. Identification of issuer from Baldwin's Auction 38, lot 751 (illus.), a halfpenny dated 1667. Cf. 7305
7306b	0.84	12.9	Br	90°	Same dies. [Nott]

LUDGATE neighbourhood (Farringdon wards Within & Without) [24-H7]

The following was recorded but is now missing: BW 1854 but THOMAS, [probably I^{D}], possibly LVDGAT^{E}, axis 180°, ex Baldwin

LUDGATE HILL [Ludgate to Fleet Bridge] (Castle Baynard ward & Farringdon ward Without) [23-H6]

The reading is ON LVDGATE HILL throughout.

The following was recorded but is now missing: BW 1856, axis 0°, ex Nott

Named signs					
7307	1.12	17.3	M	180°	*Hand & Mouth* (THE): ?E—, T—. nd. 3.5.123 (•THE•HAND•AND•MOVTH around); E|TM (•E•|T•M; •ON•LVDGATE•HILL around). BW —; Dickinson 1843A, from Heal 1928, p. 11. Nott [or Baldwin]
7308	1.30	20.0	Br	180°	*Mermaid tavern* (THE MERMAIDE TAVERN): ?G—, S—. 1652. 3.10.17; G|SH. BW 1844. [Nott ex Taffs]
7309a	2.54	39.2	Cu	0°	[*?Three Tuns*] *tavern* (AT THE TAVERNE): Hawkins, Richard. nd. 5.64.33; 5.76.154 (RH). BW 1846. [Nott ex Taffs]. A Richard Hawkins appr. Vintner 1639, and another 1657, son of Thomas of Marcham, Berks. (Webb 1996-, xliii. 140, see also 360). Cf. Woodhead 1966, p. 86, but not the same
7309b	2.26	34.9	Cu	0°	Same dies. [Nott]
7309c	2.12	32.6	Cu	0°	Same dies. [Nott]

LUDGATE HILL. Belle Savage gate neighbourhood [23-H6, g28 cancelling i28: *Bell Savage Yard*]

The following was recorded but is now missing: BW 1853 but BELL|•SAVIG•GAT•LVD•GATE•HILL• = Portcullis(?), axis 180°, ex Nott

LUDGATE STREET *otherwise* LUDGATE within *subsequently* LUDGATE HILL [Old Bailey to St Paul's] (Castle Baynard ward & Farringdon ward Within) [24-H7]

The reading is LVD|GATE STREET on 7310; WITHIN LVDGATE on 7311, 7313; WTH|IN LVDGATE on 7312.

The following were recorded but are now missing: BW 1849 but A swan close and beneath its head a suspended ball (?), LVDGATE, axis 180°; BW 1851, 180°; *BW 1855 (SYLVẸ. . .Ṛ, LVDGA. . .ṬREET), two specimens, both 90°. All ex Nott

	Weight			*Die*	
	g	*gr*		*axis*	
7310	1.37	21.1	Cu	180°	*Benett,* John, grocer. nd ½d. I B; 5.77. BW 1843. Nott [ex Taffs]. Reading completed from MoL specimen. John Bennet of St Martin Ludgate, b. 1635, Grocer; md. 1665 (Boyd 16946)
7311	0.70	10.8	Cu	0°	*Holmden,* Thomas. nd. 3.53.1; H|TA. BW 1848. [Nott]. Reading HOLMDEN confirmed from BM specimen. Initial A cancels ?N or ?H. Another specimen from the same dies, also ex Nott, now lost, had axis of 180°. Foundation set out for Thomas Hol(m)(e)den, and ground taken away at Blackfriars Gate in Ludgate Street, 1669 (Mills 1962-7, i. 48, iii. 87, 113v)
Named signs					
7312	1.90	29.3	Cu	270°	*Globe* (AT THE): Heath, Tho[mas]. nd ½d. 5.49.5; H|TE. BW 1847 but THO:. [Nott ex Carthew]. Tho. Heath, Stationer within Ludgate, 1664 (BW 1847 n.); fl. Russell Street near the Piazza of the Covent Garden 1651-54 (Plomer 1907, p. 95). Foundations set out for Thomas Heath in Holiday Yard [Ludgate Square] 1669-70 (Mills 1962-7, i. 48, iii. 105, 147)

LUDGATE STREET *(cont.)*

Named signs *(cont.)*

Weight g gr — *Die axis*

7313 1.62 24.9 Br 180° *St John the Baptist's Head tavern* (AT THE S IOHNS HEAD TAVERN): ?H—, I/J—. nd. 3.5.75; H|IE. BW 1845. [Seaby, *SCMB* July 1968]

LYON KEY *see* LION QUAY neighbourhood

MAGPIE YARD (Farringdon ward Without, Fetter Lane) [22-G3]

On or near the site of Norwich Street. The reading is FETTERLANE MAGPY YARD

7314 0.81 12.5 Br 180° *?L—,* G—, heel-maker. nd. L|GP; 3.108.44. BW 1015 but FETTERLANE, HEEL=MAKER around, obv. and rev. transposed. Nott [ex Taffs]. Bird perhaps a magpie

MAIDEN LANE (Cripplegate ward Within & Aldersgate ward) [25-G10]/MAIDEN LANE (Vintry ward) [36-J11] *see* Uncertain I

MARK LANE (Tower & Aldgate & Langbourn wards) [39-J17]

See also Middlesex I: Westminster: Westminster *and* 'Mar Lane'. The reading is MARK LANE on 7317; MARKE LANE on the remainder (LAṆẸ on 7322)

7315 1.05 16.3 Cu 0° *Adams* (–DAMS), Joseph (IOSEP–). nd. 2.4.3; A|IE. *BW 1866 (IOSEPH.ADAMS). [Nott]

7316 1.62 25.0 Cu 0° *Hills* (HILḶṢ), Daniel (ḌANIELL). 1666̣ ½d. 5.77 (HIS|HALF|PENY|••:••; •ḌANIELL•HILḶṢ ỊN around); 3.6.50 (•MARKE•LANE•I666̣ around). BW —; *Dickinson 1869A but HILḶṢ. [Baldwin], on whose ticket originally read as SAMVELL•HILL. 'Mark Lane Coffee House' (Lillywhite 1972, 10308; also in error 10484 Miles's…)

7317a 1.86 28.8 Br 0° *Parkar,* William, oilman (OYLEMAN). 1669 ½d. 5.64.40; 5.77 (P|WK). BW 1871 but OYLEMAN. [Baldwin ex Pridmore]

7317b 1.42 22.0 Br 0° Same dies. [Nott ex Carthew]

7318a 1.02 15.7 Br 180° *Payne,* W[illiam], tal[low]-chandler. 1651. 3.3.13; P|WM. BW 1872. [Nott ex Taffs]. William Pain of St Olave Hart Street, Tallow Chandler; wife Martha d. June 1651 (Boyd 42595). See also 7319

7318b 0.83 12.8 Br 180° Same dies. [Nott ex Seaby]

7319 1.37 21.2 Br 0° *Payne,* William. 1667 ½d. 3.3.13; 5.77 (P|WC̣). BW 1873 but P|W.C̣. Nott. Issuer's second wife Christian d. 1676; he d. 1680, 'Citizen and embroiderer' in will (Boyd 42595). See also 7318

7320 0.90 14.0 Cu 180° *Stringer,* Alexander. 1666. 5.14 Clothworkers; S|AM. BW 1874. Nott [ex Carthew]

MARK LANE neighbourhood

The reading is AT MARKE LANE END on both (LAṆẸ on 7322)

Named signs

7321 0.95 14.7 M 180° *Fox & Goose* (AT THE): ?B—, T—. nd. 3.66.3; B|TP. BW 1867 but MARKE. [Nott ex Carthew]. Same obv. die as 7322

7322 0.81 12.5 M 180° *Fox & Goose* (AT THE): ?B—, T—. nd. 3.66.3; B|TP. *BW 1867 but MARKE. [Nott ex Taffs]. Same obv. die as 7321

'MARY MAUDLIN'S' *i.e.* ?ST MARY MAGDALENE CHURCHYARD (Castle Baynard ward, Lambeth Hill) [35-J9]

Dobson, Edward *see* 'MARYMAYDLENS' (Uncertain I)
Midleton, Roger *see* 'MARYMAYDLENS' (Uncertain I)
Richardson, Henry *see* 'ST MARY MAUDLING COURTYARD' (Uncertain I)
Wood, Francis *see* 'MARYMAYDLENS' (Uncertain I)

MAUDLIN'S CHURCH *see* ST MARY MAGDALENE MILK STREET neighbourhood/ST MARY MAGDALENE OLD FISH STREET neighbourhood

MICHAEL'S LANE *see* ST MICHAEL'S LANE

MICHAEL'S QUEENHITHE *see* ST MICHAEL QUEENHITHE

MIDDLE TEMPLE GATE *see* INNER TEMPLE GATE *and* MIDDLE TEMPLE GATE neighbourhood

[*continued overleaf*]

7313 7314 7315 7316 7317a 7318a

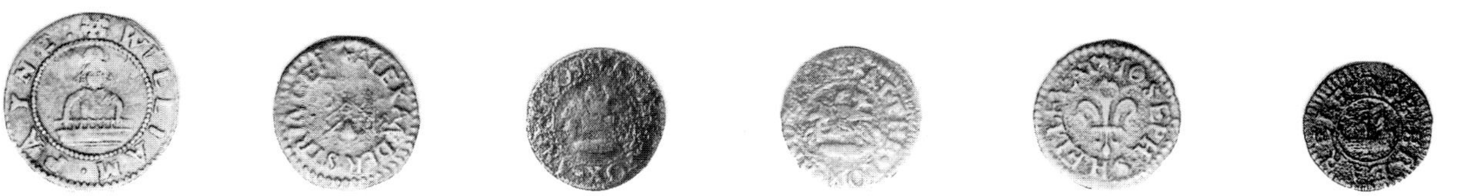

7319 7320 7321 7322 7323 7324b

7325 7326 7327 7328 7329 7330

7331a 7332 7333 7334 7335 7336b

Plate 38 (*cont.*)

'MILES CROOKED LANE' *i.e.* ?ST MICHAEL'S LANE *subsequently* MILES LANE (Candlewick ward & Bridge ward Within) [37-J14]

See also CROOKED LANE. The reading is MILES CROOKED LANE, i.e. ?ST MICHAEL'S LANE, named from St Michael Crooked Lane church (Harben 1918, p. 415)

	Weight g	*gr*		*Die axis*	
7323	0.92	14.2	Cu	30°	*Shelley,* Joseph. nd. 4.13.1; S|IE. BW 804. Seaby, [*SCMB* April 1967] ex R. C[arlyon-]B[ritton]. In St Michael's Lane, west side, in 1638 James Sleigh was at the *Flore de Luces* [Fleur-de-lis] (Dale 1931, p. 147, cf. Rogers 1928b, pp. 46-47). See also 7616

MILK STREET (Cripplegate ward Within) [25-G10]

The reading is MILK STREET on 7325; AT LOWER END MILK –[–?] on 7326; MILKSTREETE on 7324; MILKE STREET on 7327-9

7324a	0.64	9.8	Br	270°	*Breareley,* Rob—. nd. 5.13.18 (•ROB:BREARELE^{Y} around); B|RA (•B•|R•A|•; •IN MILKSTREETE around). BW —; Dickinson 1900A. [Nott]. Reading BREARELE^{Y} confirmed from MoL specimen A17659. Diameter 16-16.5 mm
7324b	0.60	9.2	Br	90°	Same dies. Baldwin [ex Macfadyen, lot 154]. Diameter 14.5-15 mm
7325	1.12	17.3	Cu	90°	*Gardiner,* Robert. nd. 2.3.8; G|RA. BW 1901. Nott [ex Carthew]. Robert Gardner of All Hallows Honey Lane, Vintner, d. 1673; wife Anne (Boyd 25007). Robert Gardiner appr. 1649, Robert Gardner 1654 (Webb 1996-, xliii. 113, see also 355)
7326	0.75	11.5	Br	180°	*Lukey,* Rich[ard]. nd. 5.2.20; 5.14 Broderers. *BW 1903 (MILK.S) but RICH•LVKEY•AT, rev. Broderers' Arms. Nott [ex Carthew]. Reading of obverse confirmed from Greenall 1997, pl. 4.117. Richard Luky of St Lawrence Jewry, embroiderer, d. 1693; wife Mary; children bap. 1654, 1656 (Boyd 26407). Cf. RICHARD LVKEY AT THE PVMP IN CHICK LANE, nd ½d. (L|RM) (Burn 1855, 325; BW 614). The pump presumably locates the issuer near 'the meeting of the corners of the old Iurie [Jewry (*district*)], Milkestreet, Ladlane, and Aldermanburie' where 'there was of old time a fayre Well... of late yeares conuerted to a Pumpe' (Stow 1603, i. 294)
Named signs					
7327	1.04	16.0	M	180°	*Boar's Head* (AT THE BOARES HEAD): I/J—, W—. nd. 3.65.10; I|WS. BW 1902. Nott [ex Baldwin]
7328	1.05	16.2	M	180°	*Boar's Head* (AT THE BOARES HEAD): I/J—, W—. nd. 3.65.10; I|WS. BW 1902. Nott
7329	2.31	35.6	Br	0°	*Red Cow* (AT THE): Rixon, William. nd ½d. token. 3.52.21; 5.77. BW 1904. Nott [ex Spink]. ?William Rixon of St Mary Colechurch, b. 1631, surgeon (Boyd 19784)

MINORIES (Portsoken ward *and* Middlesex: Stepney) [30-H19]

See also Middlesex I: Stepney: Heydon House, Little Minories. The reading is THE MINEORYS on 7334, MINEREESE on 7349, MINERES on 7356-7, MINIRIS on 7358, MINEREYES on 7331, MINERIS on 7335, MINERYES on 7330, 7344, MINNERIS on 7332-3, 7352; Y^{E} MINERYS on 7341, MINIOREIS on 7350; Y^{E}MINERYES on 7354; Y^{E}MINOREIS on 7345-6; Y^{E}MINORIES on 7342, 7355; THE MINORIES on the remainder

7330	1.66	25.6	Cu	0°	*Chubb,* Richard. 1666 ½d. 5.13.18; 5.77 (C|RS). BW 1915. Baldwin. Reading confirmed from MoL specimen
7331a	1.72	26.5	Br	180°	*Clarke,* Richard. 1668 ½d. 3.102.1; 5.77 (C|RF). BW 1916 but HALF. Nott [ex Seaby]. ?Richard Clark, Merchant Taylor; ?md. Frances Street at Holy Trinity Minories 1660; will, PCC, 1673, All Hallows Barking (Boyd 24868)
7331b	1.31	20.1	Br	180°	Same dies. [Nott]
7332	1.21	18.7	M	180°	*Cox,* Thomas. nd. 3.2.9 (•THOMAS•COX•IN around); 3.101.1 (•THE•MINNERIS around). BW —, cf. 7333. Nott [ex Taffs]
7333	0.95	14.7	Cu	180°	*Cox,* Thomas. nd. 3.2.16; C|TI. BW 1918. Nott [ex Seaby]. Cf. 7332. In chief of St George and the Dragon a cock penetrates the outer circle
7334	2.36	36.3	Br	180°	*Garbert,* Timothy. 1666 ½d. 5.3.23; 5.77. BW 1922. Nott [ex Taffs]. B double-entered, E of surname cancels B. Reading confirmed from BM specimen, which shows in chief of both cisterns what appear to be ornamental balls. Timothy Garbut, Vintner; will, PCC, 1667, St Botolph Aldgate (Boyd 25004). Timothy Garbert appr. 1648, bound an apprentice 1661 (Webb 1996-, xliii. 112, 182). See also 7348
7335	1.05	16.2	Br	180°	*Gillam,* Ralph (RAFE), baker. 1656. 5.14 Bakers (•RAFE•GILLAM•BAKER around); G|RA (•G•|R•A; •IN•THE•MINERIS•I656 around). BW —; Dickinson 1922A. Baldwin [ex Macfadyen, lot 154]
7336a	1.20	18.5	Br	180°	*Hancock,* Arthur. nd. 5.70.7; H|AA. BW 1923. [Nott]
7336b	1.02	15.8	Br	180°	Same dies. Nott [ex Taffs]

	Weight g	gr		Die axis	
7337	1.83	28.3	Br	270°	*Keaine,* Christopher. 1669. 4.13.2; 5.76.155. BW 1928. Nott. The monogram comprises the letters of the issuer's entire name (confirmed from BM specimen)
7338	1.61	24.8	Br	180°	*Minching,* Mary. 1671 1d. 3.1.79 (•MARY•MINCHING•• around); 5.77 (M M) (•I^{D}•|M M|I67I|•••; •IN•THE•MINORIES••• around). BW —; Dickinson 1932A. Baldwin. Description completed from Gilbert 1927, pl. vii.14
7339	0.98	15.1	M	180°	*Peirson,* Thomas. 1655. 3.3.13; P|TL. BW 1935. Nott [ex Taffs]. Same rev. die as 7340. A Thomas Peirson, Tallow Chandler, bound apprentices 1679-85 (Webb 1996-, xxxix. 11, 59)
7340	0.97	15.0	M	180°	*Peirson,* Thomas. 1655. 3.3.13; P|TL. BW 1935. [Nott]. Same rev. die as 7339 (q.v.)
7341	1.67	25.8	Br	0°	*Plumstead,* Francis, ironmonger (IRON|MONG|ER). 1669 ½d. 5.42.30 (•FRANCIS• PLVMSTEAD•IN•Y^{E} around); 5.77 (IRON|MONG|ER|I669; •MINERYS•HIS• HALF•PENY around). BW —. Baldwin. Cf. Clement Plumsted, ironmonger (BW 1936)
7342	2.27	35.0	Cu	0°	*Sadd,* Henry. [16]66 ½d. (A COFFE HALFE PENNY). 4.12.3 (H S); 3.5.44 (H S). BW 1940. [Nott ex Taffs]. Description confirmed from BM specimen ex Symonds; the E of Y^{E} from a broken punch resembling F. 'Sadd's Coffee House' (Lillywhite 1972, no. 1144 etc.)
7343	1.31	20.2	Br	90°	*Sae,* Edward. nd. 3.31.6; S|EM. BW 1941 but a lion rampant and sugarloaf. [Nott ex Carthew]. Reading confirmed from R. H. Thompson specimen
7344a	0.75 (chipped)	11.6	Cu	180°	*Smith,* Henry. nd. 5.14 Merchant Taylors (•HENRY•SMITH around); S|HM (•S•|H M; •IN•THE•MINERYES around). BW —; Dickinson 1942A. [Nott ex Carthew]. Henry Smith of St Botolph Aldgate, Merchant Taylor; md. Mary Gilman 1662 (Boyd 20180)
7344b	0.61	9.3	Cu	180°	Same dies. [Baldwin]
7345	0.84	12.9	Br	180°	*Smith* (ṢMITH), John, mealman (–ẸẠLE MAN). nd. 4.10.2 (•IOHN•ṢMITH•–ẸẠLE around); S|IM (•S•|I•M|•; •MAN•IN•Y^{E}MINOREIS around). BW —, cf. 1943 (MINEREYS). [Nott ex Taffs]. Same rev. die as 7346
7346	1.37	21.2	Br	180°	*Smith,* John (IOH–[flaw]), mealman (MEALE MAN). nd. 4.10.2 (•IOH–̣ SMITH•MEALE around); S|IM (•S•|I•M|•; •MAN•IN•Y^{E}MINOREIS around). BW —, cf. 1943 (IOHN, MINEREYS). [Nott ex Seaby]. Same rev. die as 7345
7347	1.09	16.8	M	180°	*Stone,* Henry. 1656. 3.82.1; S|HS. BW 1946. [Nott]
7348	1.35	20.8	Br	0°	*Walker,* Thomas. 1668 ½d. 5.3.53 (•THOMAS•WALKER•• around); 5.77 (HIS|HALF|PENY; •IN•THE•MINORIES•I668 around). BW —; Greenall 1997, lot 119, which confirms description (obv. illus. on front cover). [Baldwin]. Obv. device a well with raised bucket between two persons, left with container for water and apparently female, right apparently male with halo. Jacob's Well (John 4: 6-26), between a woman of Samaria and Jesus Christ. See also 7334
Named signs					
7349	0.89	13.8	Br	180°	*Golden Anchor* (AT THE GOVLDEN ANKER): F[irebrace], J[ohn]. nd. 5.38.1; F|IS. BW 1921. Baldwin [or Nott ex Taffs]. 'John Firebrace [Vintner] at ye Anchor in ye Minories' 1641 (Rogers 1928a, p. 83, 1928c, p. 192). John Firebrasse appr. 1639 (Webb 1996-, xliii. 104, see also 354)
7350	1.33	20.5	Cu	180°	*Golden Lion* (AT Y^{E}GOVLḌEN LYON): Hill, John. 1669 ½d. (HAḶF̣E). 3.11; 5.77. *BW 1927 but GOVLḌEN, LYON, MINIOREIS•I669. Nott [ex Taffs]. ?Mr Hill of the Minories, free 1668, listed in the Society of Apothecaries' minutes of 21 Aug. 1718 (Whittet 1983, pp. 135-6). ?John Hill of Whitechapel, gold wire drawer, md. 1656 (Boyd 40877); John Hill(s), Goldsmith, bound apprentice Gold and Silver Wyre Drawers 1707-28 (Webb 1996-, xv. 10, 27)
7351	0.88	13.5	M	180°	*Hand & Pen* (AT THE): ?M—, I/J—. nd. 3.6.21; M|IE. BW 1931. Nott [ex Taffs]
7352	0.92	14.2	Br	180°	*Pie* (AT THE PIY): ?S—, I/J—. 1659. 3.108.7; 5.55.26 (S|IA). BW 1938. [Nott ex Carthew]. Description confirmed from BM specimen
7353	0.98	15.1	Br	180°	*Porter & Car* (THE PORTER AND CARR): ?B—, M—. nd. 5.64.33 (•THE•PORTER•AND•CARR around); M B (M•B; •IN•THE•MINORIES around). BW —; Dickinson 1910B. Baldwin
7354	1.04	16.0	Cu	0°	*Red* [*?Lion*] (AT Y^{E}): Knight, Will[iam]. 1666. 3.11; K|WS. BW 1929 but WILL:. Nott. Foundation to be set out for William Knight 1673 (Mills 1962-7, i. 4)
7355	0.79 (chipped)	12.2	Br	0°	[*?Still*] *& Swan* (AT THE): Hanson, Tho—. nd. 5.64.69; 3.102.1. BW 1924 but THO;. Nott [ex Carthew]. Reading AT confirmed from MoL specimen. ?Thomas Hanson, Innholder, fl. 1641, Master 1659 (Boyd 48829, unlocated)
7356a	1.29	19.8	Br	180°	*Three Sugarloaves* (AT THE 3 SVGAR LOFES): ?T—, H—. nd. 5.64.16; T|HI. BW 1947. Nott. Same obv. die as 7357
7356b	0.61 (chipped)	9.4	Br	180°	Same dies. [Nott ex Taffs]
7357	1.11	17.1	Br	180°	*Three Sugarloaves* (AT THE 3 SVGAR LOFES): ?T—, H—. nd. 5.64.16; T|HI. BW 1947. [Baldwin]. Same obv. die as 7356

[*continued overleaf*]

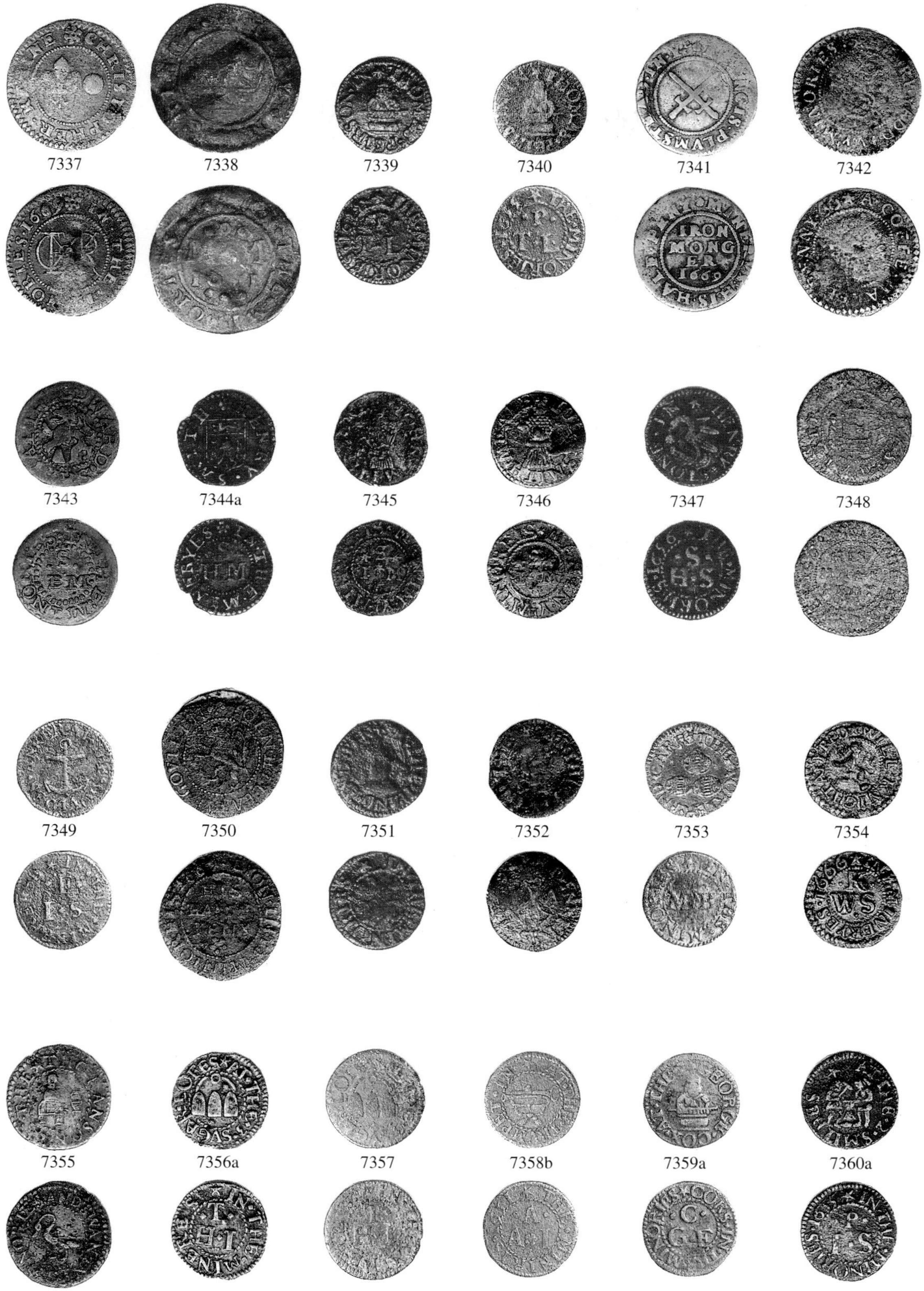

7337 7338 7339 7340 7341 7342

7343 7344a 7345 7346 7347 7348

7349 7350 7351 7352 7353 7354

7355 7356a 7357 7358b 7359a 7360a

Plate 39 (*cont.*)

	Weight			*Die*	
	g	*gr*		*axis*	
7358a	1.11	17.2	Br	180°	*Trumpet* (AT THE): ?A—, A—. 1651. 5.62.10; A|AI. BW 1910. [Nott ex Carthew]
7358b	0.92	14.1	Br	180°	Same dies. Brand
7359a	1.10	16.9	M	180°	*Two Cocks* (AT THE 2 COKS): Cox, George. nd. 3.3.13; C|GE. BW 1917. Nott. George Cox fl. here 1665-75 (Woodhead 1966, p. 53)
7359b	0.75	11.5	M	180°	Same dies. [Nott ex Taffs]
7360a	0.93	14.4	Br	180°	*Two Smiths* (AT THE 2 SMITHES): ?P—, I/J—. 1655. 3.4.9; P|IS. BW 1933 but I655. Baldwin
7360b	0.93	14.3	Br	180°	Same dies. [Nott ex Carthew]

MONKWELL STREET *otherwise* MUGWELL STREET (Cripplegate & Farringdon wards Within) [15-E10]

The reading is MVGGWELL STREETE

	Weight g	Weight gr		Die axis	
7361	2.00	30.8	Br	120°	*Michell,* Montague (MOVNTAGVE). nd ½d. 5.77; M|MA. BW 1952. [Baldwin]

MOOR LANE (Cripplegate ward Without *and* Middlesex: Finsbury) [16-D11]

The reading is MORE LANE on 7363; MORELANE on 7364; *Upper Ẹnd Moore Lane* on 7362

7362	1.30	20.0	Br	0°	*Hartley (Hartlẹy),* Lowe (*Loe*), tobacconist (*Tobacco|nist*). nd ½d. (*pẹny*). 5.77.1 (*Loe|Hartlẹy|Tobacco|nist*); 5.77.1 (*Upper•Ẹnd|Moore•Lane|his.halfe|pẹny*). BW —. [Baldwin]. Cf. 6433

Named signs

7363	0.94	14.5	Br	150°	*King & Harp* (A^{T} Y^{E}): Bell, John. 1661. 3.1.120 (16 61); 5.77 (HARP|MORE|LANE; •IOHN•BELL•A^{T}•Y^{E}•KING•& around). BW —. [Baldwin]. The figure 1 is arabic but not in script. For the sign cf. Dickinson 1973A and 7406 below; earlier apparently named as a meeting-place for Ranters: 'the house of one Middleton, at the sign of *David and the Harp*, in Moore-lane' (Routing 1650, p. 4)
7364	1.18	18.2	Br	180°	*Three Flower-de-luces* (AT THE 3 FLOWERDELVC): ?C—, P—. 1653. 4.13.11; C|PM. BW 1971 but FLOWERDELVC, MORELANE. [Nott ex Carthew]

MOORGATE neighbourhood (Coleman Street ward) [16-E12]

The reading is AT MORE GATE (the last three letters in monogram) on 7367; AT MOORE\|GATE on 7366; NEER MORGAT on 7816; NEERE MOORGATE on 7365; cf. 7368

7365	1.82	28.1	Cu	90°	*Clarke,* John, grocer. nd ½d. 5.77 (C|IB); 3.65.2. BW 1966. Seaby, [*SCMB* April 1967]. Struck off-centre
7366a	3.34	51.6	Br	0°	*Randall,* John. 1666 ½d. 5.4.4 (R|IM); 5.4.4 (R|IM). BW 1970. [Nott ex Taffs]
7366b	1.85 (pierced)	28.5	Br	0°	Same dies. [Baldwin] ex Faulkner
7366c	1.52	23.4	Br	0°	Same dies. [Nott]

Named signs

7367a	1.46	22.5	Br	45°	*Sun & Moor's Head* (AT Y^{E}SONN & MORES HEAD): More, Pelham. nd ½d. 2.1.4; 5.77. BW 1968 but MORE•GATE, last three letters in monogram. [Nott]. Obv. legend starts between 6 and 7 o'clock. Pelham More, Vintner 'at ye Sun at Moregate' 1641 (Rogers 1928a, p. 83, 1928c, p. 192). Petham [*sic*?] More appr. 1621 (Webb 1996-, xliii. 206, see also 371)
7367b	1.30	20.0	Br	45°	Same dies. [Baldwin]

MOORGATE within (Coleman Street ward) [16-E12]

The reading is WITHIN MOOREGATE; cf. 7867

7368a	0.79	12.1	Br	0°	*Holmes,* Oliver. nd. 3.65.1; H|OA. BW 1967. [Nott]. Struck twice, second time off-centre
7368b	0.63	9.7	Br	270°	Same dies. [Nott]

MOORGATE without (Coleman Street ward) [16-E12]

White Swan: Baker, John *see* 7867 (Addendum)

MOSLEY'S COURT (Langbourn ward, Philpot Lane) (*lost*) [38-I15, 145]

The reading is MOSELIES COVRT IN FILPOT LANE; perhaps named after Sir Nicholas Mosley or his family; he was ald. Langbourn ward 1594-1602, Lord Mayor 1599-1600 (Harben 1918, p. 424)

7369a	2.78	42.8	Br	0°	*Mosely,* Will[iam]. 1667 ½d. 3.5.12 (S^{T}|HVGH); 5.77 (M|WR). BW 2231 but S^{T}|HV[half-length figure]GH. [Nott ex Taffs]. Reading MOSELIES confirmed from BM specimen. William Moseley of St Dionis Backchurch, shoemaker, d. 1673; wife Rebecca d. 1670 (Boyd 11977). The legend of St Hugh may be found in Larwood 1866, pp. 282-3; 'Saint Hugh's Bones' were the tools of a shoemaker. Drawn in Boyne 1858, pl. 21.2, with a tall hat, but the figure may be seen to have a long bearded face with high forehead and hair around
7369b	1.94	29.9	Br	0°	Same dies. [Nott]

[*continued overleaf*]

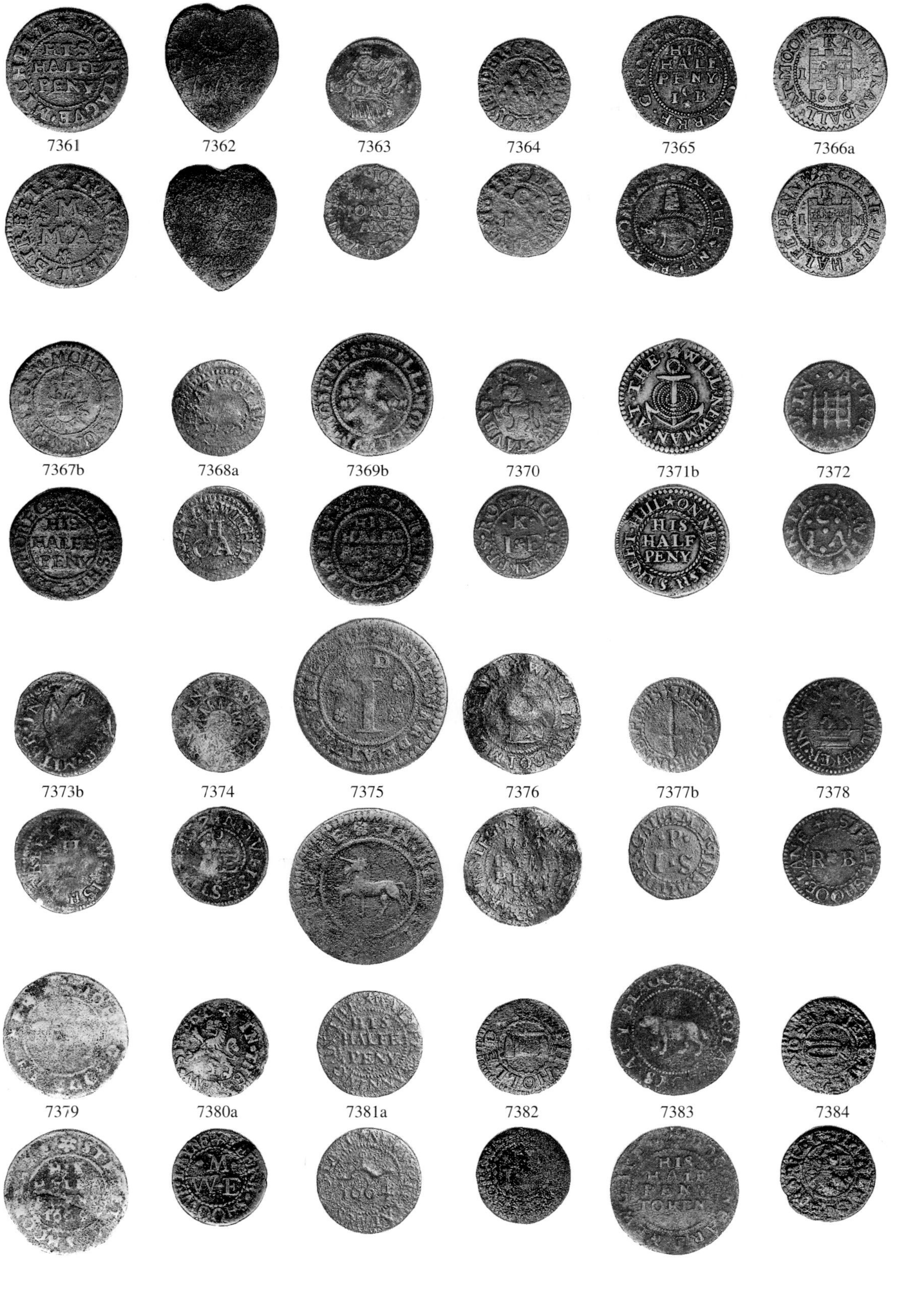

7361 7362 7363 7364 7365 7366a

7367b 7368a 7369b 7370 7371b 7372

7373b 7374 7375 7376 7377b 7378

7379 7380a 7381a 7382 7383 7384

Plate 40 (*cont.*)

MOULDMAKER'S ROW (Aldersgate ward, St Martin le Grand) (*lost beneath old GPO Building*) [25-G9, g93]

The reading is MOOLEMAKERS ROE, cf. *Mold-Maker Row* (Ogilby 1677, p. 8), first mention ap. Harben 1918, p. 424, but the token must be earlier

Named signs

	Weight g	Weight gr		Die axis	
7370	1.08	16.7	M	150°	*Talbot* (AT THE TAVBVT): ?K—, I/J—. nd. 3.67.4 (•AT•THE•TAVBVT•IN around); K|IE (•K•|I•E; •MOOLEMAKERS•ROE around). BW —; Dickinson 1976A (this specimen). [Baldwin ex Macfadyen, lot 154]. The surname initial is clearly K, not R as described in Greenall 1991, p. 121, 9

NEW FISH STREET *subsequently* FISH STREET HILL (Bridge ward Within) [37-J14]

The reading is NEW FISH STREET on 7373-4; NEW FISHSTREETE on 7372; ON NEW FISH STREET HILL on 7371

7371a	2.47	38.1	Cu	0°	*Newman,* Will—. nd ½d. 5.38.20; 5.77. BW 2014 but WILL:. [Nott ex Taffs]
7371b	1.99	30.8	Cu	180°	Same dies. [Nott]. Slightly double-struck
7371c	1.62	25.0	Cu	180°	Same dies. Brand
7371d	1.46	22.5	M	180°	Same dies. [Nott]

Named signs

7372	1.07	16.5	Br	0°	*Harrow* (AT Y^{E}): ?C—, I/J—. nd. 5.17.10; C|IA. BW 2010 but obv. AT•Y^{E}HARROW•IN, rev. NEW[?no stop]FISHSTREETE. [Nott ex Spink]. Description virtually confirmed from MoL specimen
7373a	1.03	16.0	Cu	90°	*Mitre* (AT THE MITER): H[arman], W[illiam]. nd. 5.59.20; H|WA. BW 2012. [Nott ex Taffs]. 'Mr Groby, a victualling house, at the Mytor' 1638 suggests that the Mitre was then an eating house (Rogers 1928c, p. 159). 'Mr William Harman at the Miter in new Fish-street' 1661 (BW 2012 n.)
7373b	0.96	14.8	Cu	90°	Same dies. [Nott]
7374	0.88	13.5	Br	270°	*Sun tavern* (Y^{E}SVN TAVERNE): P[adnoll], T[homas]. [16]57. 2.1; P|TE. BW 2015 but FISH. Nott [ex Baldwin]. Reading confirmed from Baldwin's Auction 38, lot 796. Thomas Padnoll, Vintner at the Sun, which he rebuilt after the 1666 Fire; md. Elizabeth Jackson 1637; 'Lieut.-Colonel' after 1660; will, PCC, 1668 (Rogers 1937, pp. 84-8; Boyd 26832; Woodhead 1966, p. 124; Mills 1962-7, i. 54). Thomas Padnall appr. 1626 (Webb 1996-, xliii. 220, see also 374). For his wine-bottle seal (.T.P.|sun) see Hume 1956, fig. 25

'NEW FLEET STREET' (Farringdon ward Without, Fleet Street) [32-I4]

The reading is NEW FLEETE STREETE, probably the new buildings east of Fetter Lane, re-erected after the Fire of 1666 (Harben 1918, p. 236, from the token)

Named signs

7375	4.47	69.0	Br	180°	*Unicorn* (AT THE VNICORNE): Warde, Will—. nd 1d. 5.77; 3.61.1. BW 1103 but WILL:, I^{D}. Nott [ex Taffs]. Reading confirmed from BM specimen. Cf. 7040-1

NEW RENTS (Aldersgate ward, St Martin le Grand) (*lost beneath old GPO Buildings*) [25-G9, g89]

The reading is NEVRENTS MARTINS ALLDERSGATE on 7377; THE NEW RENTS IN S^{T}MARTINS LEGRN^{D} on 7376

7376	2.12	32.7	Cu	0°	*Solmon,* William. nd ½d. 3.56.2; 5.77. BW 2657 but LEGRN^{D}. Nott [ex Taffs]. Reading completed from MoL specimen

Named signs

7377a	1.08	16.6	M	180°	*Dagger* (THE): ?P—, I/J—. nd. 5.42.1; P|IS. BW 48, and 2652 but NEVRENTS = a dagger, rev. MARTINS•ALLDERSGATE = •P•|I•S. Nott [ex Carthew]
7377b	1.01	15.6	M	180°	Same dies. Nott

NEW STREET *subsequently* LITTLE NEW STREET *and* NEW STREET SQUARE (Farringdon ward Without, Shoe Lane) [22-G4]

See also Uncertain I. The reading is NEW STREET SHOOE LANE on 7378, IN SHOOE LANE on 7379; THE NEW STREET NEAR SHOO LANE on 7381, NEERE SHOOWE LAYNE on 7380

7378	1.18	18.3	M	180°	*Baker,* Randal. nd. 3.3.13 (•RANDAL•BAKER•IN•NEW around); R B (R•B; •STREET•SHOOE•LANE around). BW —; Dickinson 2064B. [Nott ex Spink]
7379	1.06	16.3	Br	270°	*Goode,* John. 1669 ½d. 3.51.1 (•IOHN•GOODE•IN•NEW• around); 5.77 (HIS|HALFE|PENNY|1669; •STREET•IN•SHOOE•LANE around). BW —; Dickinson 2064C. [Baldwin]. Reading completed from Harris 2002, lot 519 (illus.)

	Weight g	gr		Die axis	
7380a	1.11	17.2	M	180°	*?M—,* W—. nd. 3.11; MIWE. BW 2065 but LAYNE. [Nott ex Taffs]
7380b	1.00	15.5	M	180°	Same dies. [Nott]
7381a	2.33	36.0	Br	90°	*Manning,* Walter. 1664 ½d. 5.77; 4.3.12. BW 2066. [Baldwin]
7381b	1.27	19.5	Br	90°	Same dies. [Nott]

NEWGATE neighbourhood (Farringdon ward Within & Without) [24-G7]

The reading is AT NEWGAT on 7382; NEARE NEWGATE on 7383; cf. 7397-7401

7382	0.71	11.0	Br	270°	*Holled,* Joseph, grocer. nd. 5.64.14; HIIA. BW 2036 but obv. description revised. [Nott ex Carthew]. Reading completed from MoL specimen and Wetton 1989, lot 217. ?Joseph Holled of St Mary Aldermary, Grocer; wife Anne; children bap. 1657, 1659 (Boyd 50535)

Named signs

7383	1.19	18.3	Br	0°	*Black Dog* (AT Y^{E}BLACK DOGG): Roys, Nicholas. nd ½d. token. 3.67.10; 5.77. BW 2040. [Nott ex Spink]. Reading confirmed from MoL specimen

NEWGATE MARKET (Castle Baynard ward & Farringdon ward Within) [24-G7]

Before the Fire the Market was in the centre of Newgate Street (e.g. Prockter 1979, p. 8). The reading is NEW GATE MARKET on 7389, 7391, 7393 (MARḲET on 7391); NEWGAT MARKET on 7384, 7392 (NEWGẠṬ on 7384), MAR^{T} on 7395; NEWGATE MARKET on 7385, 7387-8, 7390, 7394 (MARKEṬ on 7394), MARIKETT on 7396, MARKIT on 7386

7384	1.22	18.8	Br	330°	*Arnold,* Jeremiah. nd. 5.62.10; 3.51.2 (AIIE). BW 2017 but a trumpet, NEWGẠṬ, AIIE above elephant & castle. [Nott] Overstruck or double-struck(?)

NEWGATE MARKET (*cont.*)

	Weight g	Weight gr		Die axis	
7385	2.00	30.8	Br	330°	*Bonner,* Will—, chees[e]monger. 1670 ½d. 3.1.25; 5.77 (B|WE). BW 2018 but WILL:. [Baldwin]. Reading completed from BM specimen
7386	1.03	15.9	Br	180°	*Robinson,* Ri—, clerk (CLARKE) of Newgate Market (MARKIT). 1658. 5.14 London City 1 (•RI•ROBINSON•CLARKE around); R R|date (R•R|I658; •OF•NEWGATE•MARKIT around). BW —. [Baldwin]. The cross of St George appears to be hatched for *Gules*. Richard Robinson, Clothworker, a tenant of the City; two foundations set out for him, 1669; he surrendered two leases for the building of Newgate Market, which replaced the pre-Fire street market (Mills 1962-7, i. 53, iii. 90v., 111v.; Masters 1974, pp. 39, 43). Robinson perhaps was clerk of that
7387a	0.73	11.3	Br	180°	*Snesby,* Robert (ROBERṬ). nd. 5.70.1; R S. *BW 2029. [Baldwin]. Origin of York & district surname Sneesby not identified (Rogers 1991, p. 87)
7387b	0.57 (chipped, corroded)	8.8	Br	180°	Same dies. [Nott]
7388a	2.36	36.3	Br	90°	*Warner,* Edmund, pou[l]terer. 1666 ½d. 5.77; 5.77. BW 2031. [Nott ex Spink]
7388b	2.26	34.8	Br	90°	Same dies. [Nott]

Named signs

7389	0.65	10.0	Cu	180°	*Fox* (AT THE): Fox, Thomas. nd. 3.66.1; F|TA. BW 2020 but NEW•GATE. [Nott ex Spink]. Description completed from MoL specimens. Thomas Fox(e) of Christ Church, b. 1601, Merchant Taylor; md. Alice Watson 1629; will, PCC, 1666 (Boyd 30669)
7390	0.90	13.9	M	180°	*Fox & Goose* (THE): ?W—, D—. nd. 3.66.3; W|DE. BW 2030. [Nott ex Spink]. Obv. legend starts at 1 o'clock
7391	0.79	12.2	M	180°	*George* (AT THE): ?D—, I/J—. nd. 5.14 Grocers (•AT•THE•GEORGE•IN around); D|IS (•D•|I•S; •NEW•GATE•MARḲET around). BW —. [Baldwin]
7392a	1.18	18.2	Br	90°	*Golden Plough* (AT Y^{E}GOLDEN PLOWE): ?H—, I/J—. nd. 5.54.5; H|II. BW 2023 but no stops in legends either side. [Baldwin], on whose ticket identified as 'Unp[ublishe]d 646A Newmarket', *i.e.* Clare Market (Westminster). Obv. legend starts at 10 o'clock
7392b	0.94	14.5	Br	90°	Same dies. [Nott ex Taffs]
7392c	0.69	10.6	Br	90°	Same dies. [Nott ex Seaby]
7393	0.84	13.0	M	180°	*King's Head* (AT THE): ?T—, C—. nd. 3.5.56 (•AT•THE•KINGS•HEAD around); T|CI (•T•|C•I; •IN•NEW•GATE•MARKET around). BW —; Dickinson 2029A. Baldwin ex Macfadyen, lot 154 (initials read as G.I.T.)]. Reading confirmed from Sedgwick 1986, pl. 1.35
7394	0.92	14.2	Br	180°	*Three Tobacco Pipes* (AT THE 3 TOBAKO PIPS): ?F—, W—. nd. 5.84.36; W F. *BW 2021. [Nott ex Carthew]. Reading largely completed from MoL specimen
7395	1.04	16.0	Br	180°	*Wheatsheaf & Three Pigeons* (WHEAT SHEAF AND 3 PIDGONS): ?F—, M—. nd. 4.10.2; 5.76.156 (MF). BW 2019 but PIDGONS, merchant's mark and MF in monogram, ?no stops in legends either side. Nott [ex Taffs]. Reading AND 3 confirmed from Wetton 1989, lot 217

NEWGATE MARKET. Rose tavern neighbourhood

For the Rose tavern cf. Lillywhite 1972, no. 12539, and BW 2027. The reading is NEXT DORE TO Y^{E} ROSE TAVERN IN NEWGATE MAR\|KETT

7396	2.03	31.3	Br	0°	*Hyde,* John. 1669 ½d. 5.77 (HIS|HALF|PENY|I669; •IOHN•HYDE•NEXT•DORE•TO•Y^{E} around); 5.77 (H|IM) (MAR|KETT|•H•|I•M; •ROSE•TAVERN•IN•NEWGATE• around). BW Addenda; Dickinson 2025A. [Baldwin ex Macfadyen, lot 154]

NEWGATE without (Farringdon ward Without) [24-G7]

See also GILTSPUR STREET. The reading is WITH\|OVT NEW\|GAT on 7011-12 (WỊṬḤ\|ỌVT on 7012); WITHOVT NEV GATE on 7401, NEW GATE on 7397-8, NEWGAT on 7399; WI–ḤOVT NEWGAT on 7400

7397a	1.11	17.1	Br	180°	*Andrews,* Thomas. nd. 5.68.13; T A. BW 2033 but NEW•GATE. [Nott]. Same rev. die as 7398
7397b	1.04	16.0	Br	180°	Same dies. [Nott ex Taffs]
7398	1.22 (chipped)	18.9	Br	0°	*Andrews,* Thomas. nd. 5.68.13; T A. BW 2033 but NEW•GATE. [Baldwin]. Obv. legend starts at 6 o'clock. Same rev. die as 7397
7399a	0.95	14.7	Cu	90°	*Packman,* Ralph. nd. 5.14 Merchant Taylors; 5.61.45 (P|RI). BW 2038. [Nott ex Taffs]
7399b	0.69	10.6	Cu	90°	Same dies. [Nott ex Carthew]
7400	1.52	23.5	Cu	180°	*Packman* (–ACKMAṆ), Ralph (ṚALP̣–). nd. 5.14 Merchant Taylors; 5.61.45 (P̣|ṚỊ). *BW 2038 (RALPH.PACKMAN, WITHOVT). [Baldwin]. Rev. legend starts between 10 and 11 o'clock

Named signs

7401a	1.28	19.7	M	180°	*Fountain tavern* (THE FOVNTANE TAVERN): ?R—, W—. nd. 5.3.20; R|WM. BW 2039. [Nott ex Baldwin]
7401b	0.95	14.6	M	180°	Same dies. [Nott ex Taffs]

[*continued overleaf*]

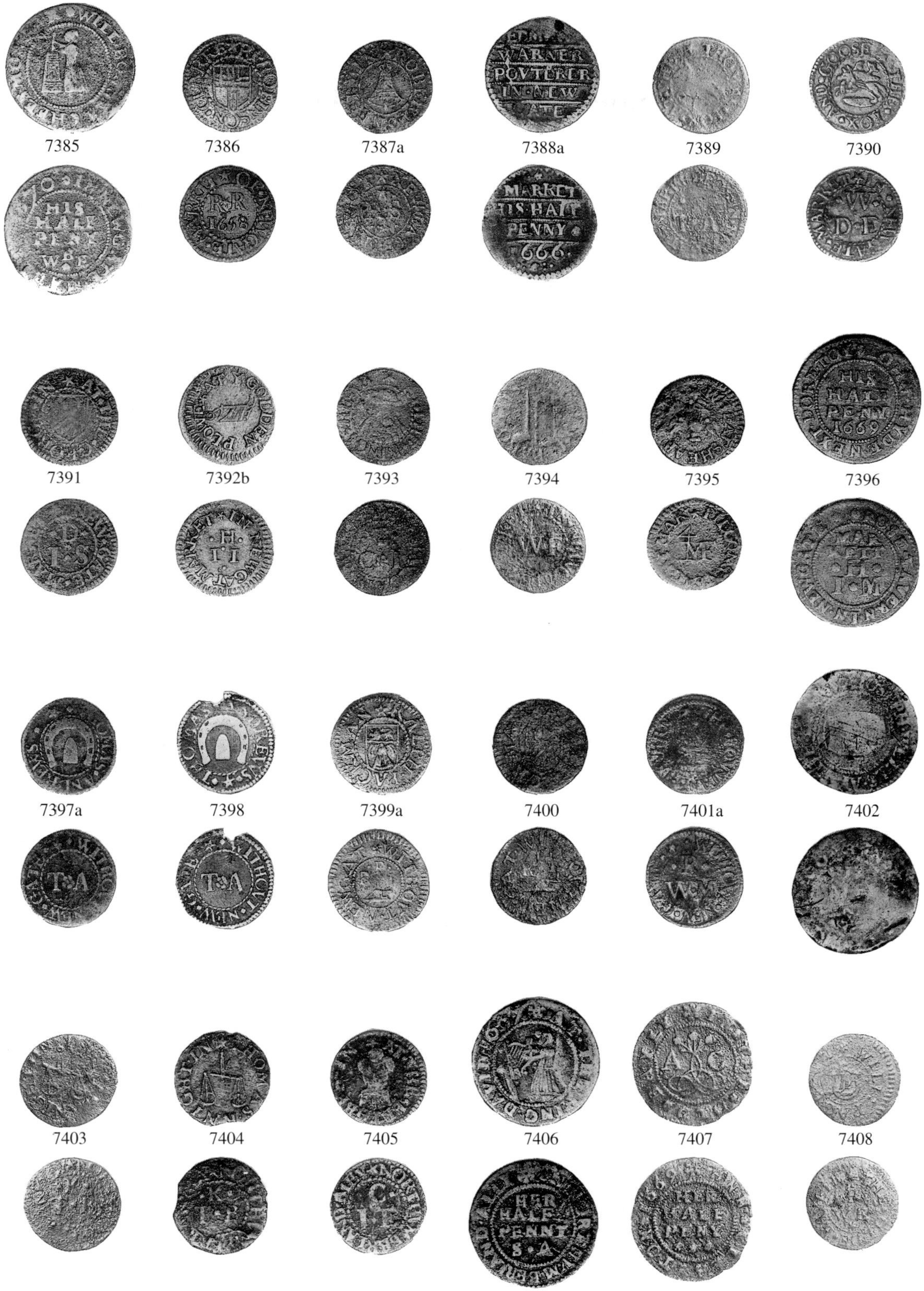

7385 7386 7387a 7388a 7389 7390

7391 7392b 7393 7394 7395 7396

7397a 7398 7399a 7400 7401a 7402

7403 7404 7405 7406 7407 7408

Plate 41 *(cont.)*

NOBLE STREET (Aldersgate ward & Farringdon ward Within) [25-F9]

The reading is NOBELL STREET

Named signs

	Weight g	Weight gr		Die axis	
7402	2.47	38.1	Br	0°	*Tun* (AT THE TVNN): Wells, Joseph. 1665 ½d. 5.64.30; 5.77. BW 2078. [Nott]. Reading completed from BM specimen

NORTHUMBERLAND ALLEY (Aldgate ward) [29-H18, i89]

The reading is NORTHVMBERLAN ALY on 7403-4; NORTHVMBERLAND ALEY on 7405, ALLY on 7406

7403	0.73	11.2	Cu	0°	*Knight,* Thomas. nd. 5.65.30; K|TB. BW 2082. [Nott ex Taffs]. Struck from flawed obv. die. Reading completed from BM specimen. Another, obv. ?unflawed, not now in the collection, axis 180°, ex Baldwin. Same rev. die as 7404
7404	0.88	13.6	Cu	270°	*Knight,* Thomas. nd. 5.65.30; K|TB. BW 2082. Brand. Reading confirmed from MoL specimen. Same rev. die as 7403

Named signs

7405	1.25	19.2	Br	180°	*Feathers* (AT THE FETHERS): ?C—, I/J—. nd. 3.107.5; C|IE. BW 2081. [Nott ex Taffs]
7406	2.06	31.9	Cu	0°	*King David* (AT THE): ?A—, S— (f.). 1667 ½d. 3.1.54; 5.77 (S A). BW 2079 but ALLY. Nott [ex Taffs]. *Pace* Lillywhite 1972, p. 149, the *King David* is apparently not distinct from the *David & Harp*, cf. 7363

OLD BAILEY (Farringdon ward Without) [24-H7]

See also LITTLE OLD BAILEY. The reading is OLD BAILY on 7417; OVLD BALY on 7421; THE OLD BAILYE on 7411, BALEY on 7412-13, BAYLEY on 7415-16, BAYLY on 7407, 7418, BAYLYE on 7414; THE OLDE BAYLIE on 7408; THE OVLD BALY on 7420, BAYLEY on 7410; Y^{E} OLD BAYLEY on 7419; Y^{E}OVLD BAYLEY on 7409

7407	0.79 (chipped)	12.2	Br	180°	*Cleayton,* Ann. 1669 ½d. 5.77; A C. BW 2099 but HER. Nott [ex Taffs]
7408	1.40	21.6	Cu	270°	*Page,* Will—. nd. 2.2.8 (•WILL:PAGE•ỊN around); P̣|WE (•P̣•|W E|•; •THE•OLDE•BAYLIE around). BW —. [Baldwin]. See also 7417

OLD BAILEY (*cont.*)

	Weight			*Die*	
	g	*gr*		*axis*	
7409a	1.10	17.0	Br	90°	*Paulson,* Thomas. nd. 3.95.1; P|TE. BW 2112. [Nott]. 'Thos. Paulson 4 [hearths]' 1663 (Dale 1934, p. 53, f. 85). The same initials and device appear on 7261 (LITTLE OLD BAILEY: *Eaveson* [i.e. *Paulson*?], Thomas), which suggests that OVLD BAYLEY here means Little Old Bailey. Diameter 17-17.5 mm
7409b	1.04	16.0	Br	270°	Same dies. [Nott ex Taffs]. Diameter 16 mm
7409c	1.00	15.5	Br	180°	Same dies. [Nott]
7410	2.31	35.7	Br	180°	*Sandys,* Henry (HENREY). 1668 ½d. 3.10.9; 5.77 (S|HF). BW 2115. [Nott ex Taffs]

Named signs

7411a	0.80	12.4	M	180°	*Black Spread Eagle* (THE): ?E—, P—. 1650. 3.95.1; E|PS. BW 2100. Nott
7411b	0.71	10.9	M	180°	Same dies. Nott
	(chipped)				
7412	1.05	16.1	M	180°	*Blue Bell* (AT THE BLEW BELL): ?F—, T—. 1650. 5.70.1; F|TK. BW 2104. [Nott ex Carthew]. Reading confirmed from MoL specimens. Another specimen, not now in the collection, axis 180°, ex Baldwin, had the same obv. die; the bar of the initial T on rev. pointed to I, whereas on the present specimen it points to Y
7413	1.24	19.1	M	0°	*George* (AT THE): Kenn, Philippa (PHILLIPA). nd. 3.2.8; P K. BW 2110. Nott [ex Taffs]. First P in forename double-entered
7414	1.16	17.8	Br	180°	*Golden Falcon* (THE GOVLDEN FAVLCON): ?N—, M—. nd. 3.92.1; M N. BW 2111. [Nott ex Taffs]
7415a	1.06	16.4	M	180°	*Lion & Ball* (AT THE LYON AND BALL): ?S—, N—. nd. 3.39.2; S|NE. BW 2113. [Nott ex Taffs]. Same rev. die as 7416
7415b	0.91	14.1	M	180°	Same dies. [Nott] ex 'C.B.'
7416a	1.08	16.7	M	180°	*Lion & Ball* (AT THE LYON AND BALL): ?S—, N—. nd. 3.39.2; S|NE. BW 2113. [Nott ex Taffs]. Same rev. die as 7415
7416b	1.05	16.2	M	180°	Same dies. [Nott] ex 'C.B.' Struck off-centre
7416c	1.00	15.4	M	0°	Same dies. [Baldwin]
7416d	0.98	15.1	M	180°	Same dies. [Nott]
7417	1.25	19.3	M	180°	*Man in the Moon* (THE): ?W—, T—, tal[low]-chandler. nd. 2.2.9; 5.32.10 (T W). BW 2122 but BAILY, T•W|candles. [Nott]. Reading confirmed from MoL specimen. See also 7408
7418a	1.18	18.2	Br	180°	*Plough* (AT THE PLOW): Vere, John. nd. 5.54; V|IB. BW 2120. [Baldwin]. See also 7419
7418b	1.02	15.8	Br	180°	Same dies. [Nott]
7419	1.60	24.6	Br	90°	[*Plough*]: Vere, John, mealman. 1664 ½d. 5.54.2; V|IM. BW 2121 but •IOHN•VERE MEALMAN•• = HIS•|HALFE|[plough]|PENNY; rev. •IN•Y^{E} OLD•BAYLEY•I664 = •V•|I M|• . [Nott ex Carthew]. Sign name from 7418. Reading completed from MoL specimen
7420a	1.29	19.8	M	270°	*Three Candlesticks* (AT THE 3 CANDLESTICKS): ?K—, A—. 1649. 5.32.6; K|AI. BW 2109. [Nott]. Obv. legend starts at 9 o'clock
7420b	1.23	19.0	M	90°	Same dies. [Nott ex Taffs]

OLD BAILEY. Three Cranes tavern neighbourhood

The Three Cranes is recorded from 1634 (Lillywhite 1972, 14648). The reading is NEXT TO THE 3 CRANES TAVERN

7421	0.84	13.0	M	180°	*B*[*arnes*], W[illiam], salter. 1651. Date|W B; date|W B. BW 2096. Baldwin, on whose ticket identified as '3139A, Three Cranes Wharf'. Reading completed from BM specimen. William Barnes 'next ye 3 Craine tavern' assessed on eight hearths 1678 (Rogers 1928a, p. 86)

OLD BARGE HOUSE *subsequently* BARGE YARD (Cheap ward, Bucklersbury) [26-H12, i61]

Liske, Thomas *see* Uncertain I

OLD BARGE HOUSE neighbourhood

Named signs

Meal shop: Gun, Jane *see* Uncertain I

OLD BETHLEHEM HOSPITAL. Gate into Bishopsgate neighbourhood (Bishopsgate ward Without) [18-E15, e59: White Hart Court]

The reading is AT THE WHITE HART AT BEDLAM GATE; cf. 7423-5

Named signs

7422	1.10	17.0	M	180°	*White Hart* (AT THE): ?K—, E—. 1657. 3.53.20; K|EE. BW 188. Nott [ex Carthew]. Reading confirmed from MoL specimen NN16485

[*continued overleaf*]

7409b 7410 7411a 7412 7413 7414

7415a 7416a 7417 7418b 7419 7420a

7421 7422 7423 7424a 7425a 7426

7427 7428 7429 7430 7431 7432

Plate 42 (*cont.*)

OLD BETHLEHEM HOSPITAL. Gate into Moorfields neighbourhood (Bishopsgate ward Without) [17-E14]

The reading is AT THE MOREFEILDS NEARE BEDLAM GAT^{E} on 7423, BADLAM GAT on 7424; NEARE BEDLAM GATE IN MORE FEILDES on 7425; cf. 7422. A gateway from Bedlam into Moorfields is visible on the Copperplate-map of c.1553-9 (e.g. Prockter 1979, p. 30), the 'Agas' map of 1561-70 (ibid. 11), and Newcourt 1658. [*New Bethlehem* in Moorfields was not built until 1675-6 (Weinreb 1993, p. 62)]

	Weight			*Die*	
	g	*gr*		*axis*	
7423	0.58	8.9	Cu	0°	*?C—*, H— (Ḥ). nd. 3.10.1; C|ḤS. *BW 1958. [Nott ex Baldwin]. Same obv. die as 7424
7424a	1.14	17.5	Cu	90°	*?C—*, H—. nd. 3.10.1; C|HS. BW 1957. [Nott]. Same obv. die as 7423, flawed
7424b	0.66	10.1	Cu	0°	Same dies (obv. unflawed). [Nott ex Taffs]
7425a	5.01	77.3	Br	180°	*Young,* Henry. nd 1d. 5.77; 5.3.30. BW 1964 but I^{D}. [Nott ex Carthew]
7425b	4.40	68.0	Br	180°	Same dies. Brand [or Nott]

OLD BETHLEM *subsequently* LIVERPOOL STREET (Bishopsgate ward Without) [18-E15: Bethelem]

The reading is BEDDLAM on 7429; BEDLAM on 7427, 7435; BEDLAME on 7434; BETHALEM on 7430; BETHELAM on 7426, 7431; BETHELEM on 7433; BETHLEHEM on 7428; BETHLEM on 7432

7426	1.42 (chipped)	22.0	Cu	0°	*Badgett,* Ralph. 1668 ½d. 3.7.45; 5.77 (B|RE). BW 180. Nott [ex Carthew]. Description completed from BM specimen
7427	1.29	19.9	Br	90°	*Bonny,* Thomas. 1667 ½d. 5.14 Clothworkers; 5.77 (B|TṂ). *BW 181. Brand
7428	0.72	11.1	Br	0°	*Ground,* Elizabeth. nd. 3.7.48; 3.7.34. BW 184 but rev. a last. Nott [ex Carthew]. Description confirmed from BM specimen (toe of last to right)
7429	0.63	9.8	M	0°	*Leare,* Thomas. 1662. 2.2; T L. BW 189. Nott. The O, apparently from a broken punch, resembles C. Reading LEARE confirmed from BM specimen
7430	1.89	29.1	Br	90°	*Mallin,* Richard. 1668 ½d. 5.50.43 (RICHARD•MALLIN•AT Y^{E}• around); 5.77 (M|RR) (HIS|HALFE|PENY|M|R.R; •IN•BETHALEM•I668 around). BW —; Dickinson 190A. Baldwin [or Nott]. Description completed from Sedgwick 1986, pl. 1.5. If the device is a frying-pan the arms suggest it was made of pewter (?)
7431	1.22	18.8	Br	90°	*Panke,* Ralph. 1667 ½d. (HAḶFE). 5.14 Blacksmiths; 5.77 (P|RS). *BW 191. Nott [ex Carthew]. Reading largely completed from BM specimen. Surname a short form of Pancras (Hanks 1988, s.v. Pank)

Named signs

7432	1.88	28.9	Cu	90°	*Black* [*?Bull & ?Dog*] (AT): Hilton, Will—. 1666 ½d. 3.52.2; 5.77. BW 186 but WILL:. Nott [ex Taffs]. Description confirmed from BM specimen

OLD BETHLEM (*cont.*)

Named signs (*cont.*)

	Weight g	Weight gr		Die axis	
7433	2.55	39.3	Br	270°	[*Claptons*] *coffee-house* (AT THE): Clapton, John. 1669 1d. 3.6.51; 5.77. BW 182 but hand pouring coffee from pot into bowl. Nott [ex Baldwin]. Reading confirmed from MoL specimen. Sign name from Lillywhite 1972, no. 249
7434	1.36	21.0	M	180°	*Half Moon* (THE SINE OF THE HALF MOVN): ?B—, T—. nd. 2.2; T B. BW 179. Nott
7435	1.18	18.2	M	180°	*Plough* (AT THE PLOW): Reddall, James. nd. 5.54; R|IS. BW 193. Nott [ex Taffs]

OLD CHANGE (Farringdon ward Within & Bread Street & Castle Baynard wards) [25-H9]

The reading is THE OLD CHAINGE on 7439, 7442; THE OVLD CHANGE on 7438, 7444; Y^{E} OLD CHANGE on 7440, 7443; Y^{E} OLDE $CHANG^{E}$ on 7437; Y^{E}OLD CHANGE on 7436; Y^{E}OLD CHANG NEARE CHEAPE SIDE on 7441

7436	1.18	18.2	Br	180°	*Andrewes,* Edward. nd. 4.12.2 (•EDWARD•ANDREWES around); L|IE [*sic*] (.L.|•|I E|•; •IN•Y^{E}OLD•CHANGE around). BW —, cf. 7437. [Baldwin]. Same obv. die as 7437
7437a	1.02	15.8	Cu	0°	*Andrewes,* Edward. nd. 4.12.2; A|EI. BW 2125 but $CHANG^{E}$. [Nott ex Carthew]. Same obv. die as 7436
7437b	0.66	10.2	Cu	0°	Same dies. [Nott ex Taffs]
7438	2.07	32.0	Cu	0°	*Dobson,* Edmond. nd ½d. 3.1.58; 5.77. BW 2129. [Nott ex Spink]
7439	0.58	8.9	Br	0°	*Fisher,* Ann. 1664. 5.14 Merchant Taylors; A F. BW 2131. [Nott ex Taffs]. Charles Fisher of St Mary Magdalene, Old Fish Street, Merchant Taylor, b. 1574; administration of PCC will 1653 to relict Ann (Boyd 43192)
7440	0.42	6.4	Br	210°	*Grifeith,* John. nd. 5.64.205; G|IM. BW 2132. [Nott ex Taffs]. Reading confirmed from MoL specimen. Device a Case of Knives, see Thompson 2002a, p. 168. John Griffith of St Vedast, fl. 1663; md. Margaret Cockram 1655 (Boyd 51802), but had md. Margaret Gislingham 1650 (Harl. Reg. 30, 1903, p. 16)
7441	0.56	8.6	Br	270°	*Imings,* George, oilman (OYLE MAN). nd. 5.77 (GEORGE|IMINGS;|OYLE[?no stop]MAN|IN.Y^{E}OLD|CHANG); I|GM (•I•|G M|•; •NEARE•CHEAPE•SIDE: around). BW —; Dickinson 2132A. [Nott]. George Imminge of St Michael le Querne, Leatherseller; md. Mary Smith 1662; will, PCC, 1676, St Sepulchre (Boyd 20110)
7442a	1.14	17.5	Br	180°	*Lidgould,* Richard, baker. 1669 ½d. 5.65.5 (•RICHARD•LIDGOVLD•IN around); 5.77 (HIS|HALFE|PENNY|I669; •THE•OVLD•CHAINGE•BAKER around). BW —; Dickinson 2132B. [Baldwin]. Obv. struck off-centre
7442b	1.09	16.9	Br	180°	Same dies. [Nott ex Carthew]. Obv. struck off-centre
7442c	1.02	15.7	Br	0°	Same dies. [Nott]

Named signs

7443a	1.11	17.1	Cu	180°	*Three* [*?Morris-dancers*] (AT Y^{E}3): Lisle, John. nd. 3.4.27; L|IA. BW 2134. [Nott ex Taffs]. Legends start between 10 and 11 o'clock both sides. Lease from the Town of Sheffield assigned to John Lisle, who was to rebuild (Fire Court 1966-, i. 240); three foundations set out for John Lyle 1667 (Mills 1962-7, i. 56, ii. 40). For the Three Morris-Dancers, Old Change, see Lillywhite 1972, 14936, also BW 2133; see also BW 43, John Lisle in Aldersgate Street
7443b	0.91	14.1	Cu	0°	Same dies. [Nott ex Carthew]
7444a	1.19	18.4	M	180°	*Willow Tree* (AT THE): ?B—, N—. nd. 4.1.1; B|NI. BW 2127. [Nott]. Initial N upside down. Same obv. die as 6784, the original die-pairing (Cloak Lane, whence the issuer evidently moved); on 7444 letters occurring on both sides are from different punches
7444b	1.03	15.9	M	180°	Same dies. [Nott ex Taffs]
7444c	1.01	15.5	M	180°	Same dies. [Baldwin]
7444d	0.94	14.5	M	180°	Same dies. [Nott]

OLD FISH STREET *subsequently* KNIGHTRIDER STREET (Bread Street & Queenhithe wards) [35-I9]

The reading is OLD FISH STREET on 7446, FISHE STREET on 7449; OVLD FISH STREET on 7450-3, FISH STREETE on 7448, FISHSTREETE on 7445, FISHTREET on 7447

7445	1.77	27.3	Br	270°	*Betteris,* Edward. nd ½d. 3.61?; 5.77. *BW 2137 but FISHSTREETE, HALF. [Nott ex Baldwin]. Reading completed from MoL specimen, but not device. Edward Bettrice of St Mildred, Bread Street, b. 1628, Grocer; will, PCC, 1666 (Boyd 17039)
7446a	2.27	35.0	Cu	0°	*Hearon,* George. 1662 ½d. 3.66.1; 5.77. BW 2139. [Nott ex Taffs]. See also 7448
7446b	1.63	25.2	Cu	0°	Same dies. [Nott ex Spink]
7447	2.07 (chipped)	32.0	Br	0°	*Robinson,* William. 1668 ½d. 5.7.20 (•WILLIAM•ROBINSON•AT•Y^{E} around); 5.77 (HIS|HALFE|PENY•|•••; •IN•OVLD•FISHTREET•I668 around). BW —; Dickinson 2145A. [Baldwin]. Reading FISHTREET confirmed from MoL specimen

[*continued overleaf*]

7433 7434 7435 7436 7437b 7438

7439 7440 7441 7442c 7443a 7444a

7445 7446b 7447 7448 7449 7450

7451a 7452 7453 7454a 7455 7456a

Plate 43 (*cont.*)

Named signs

	Weight g	gr		Die axis	
7448	0.42	6.4	Br	0°	*Fox* (AT Y^E): Gay, Will[iam]. nd. 3.66.1; G|WM. BW 2138 but WILL:, the upper stop like an apostrophe. [Nott ex Spink]. William Gay of St Matthew Friday Street, d. 1665; md. Mary Jennings 1655 (Boyd 32149). See also 7446
7449	1.11	17.1	Br	180°	*King's Head tavern* (THE): A[ndrewes], W[illiam]. nd. 3.5.78; A|WR. BW 2135 but his note incomprehensible. [Nott ex Carthew]. Reading completed from BM specimen and Greenall 1997, pl. 4.123. Payments to William Andrewes for wines and dinners, and payments at the King's Head, noted in the St Mary Magdalen, Lambeth Hill, churchwardens' accounts 1648-52; Andrewes gone by c.1657 (Rogers 1928a, p. 86). William Andrewes appr. Vintner 1627, William Andrews 1632 (Webb 1996-, xliii. 6, cf. 336). See also 7184
7450	1.13	17.5	M	315°	*Swan tavern* (AT THE SWAN TAVERNE): M[arshall], J[ohn]. nd. 3.102.1; M|IA. BW 2142-3. [Nott ex Carthew]. Obv. legend starts at 1 o'clock. Mr John Marshall at the Swan in Old Fish Street, vintner, in churchwardens' accounts of St Nicholas Cole Abbey 1632-50 (Rogers 1928a, p. 87, 1928c, p. 187). John Marshall appr. 1614 (Webb 1996-, xliii. 195, see also 370)
7451a	1.11	17.2	M	150°	*Swan tavern* (AT THE): M[arshall], J[ohn]. nd. 3.102.1; M|IA. BW 2141. [Nott ex Taffs]. Obv. legend starts at 1 o'clock. For identification of issuer see 7450. Same rev. die as 7452
7451b	1.07	16.6	M	150°	Same dies. [Nott ex Taffs]
7452	1.29	19.9	M	180°	*Swan tavern* (AT THE): M[arshall], J[ohn]. nd. 3.102.1; M|IA. BW 2141. [Nott] ex 'C.B.' For identification of issuer see 7450. Same rev. die as 7451

OLD FISH STREET neighbourhood

The reading is BACKSIDE|OVLD FISH STREET, cf. the sign of the Will Somers, on the backside of Old Fish Street, leased 1658 (Mills 1962-7, i. xxvii)

Named signs

7453	1.55	24.0	Br	0°	*Will Somers* (AT Y^E): ?W—, I/J—. 1666 ½d. (OB). 3.1.121; W|IM. BW 2147 but WILL:, figure holding a horn. [Nott ex Taffs]. William Somer [Sommers] (d. 1559), court fool (ODNB)

OLD FISH STREET HILL *subsequently* QUEEN VICTORIA STREET *and* LAMBETH HILL (Queenhithe ward) [35-J9: Fishstreet Hill]

The reading is ON OVLD FISH STREET HIL

7454a	0.97	15.0	M	180°	*Baggot,* Wil—, brewer. nd. 3.4.20; W B. BW 2136. [Nott ex Taffs]. Mr Bagott, brewer, died insolvent 1656 (Smyth 1849, p. 43). His sign gave its name to *Oldfish str. (or Labour in vain) hill* (Hatton 1708, ii. 405; Harben 1918, p. 449)
7454b	0.94	14.5	M	180°	Same dies. [Nott]

OLD JEWRY (Cheap & Coleman Street wards) [26-H12]

See also ST LAWRENCE JEWRY. The reading is AT THE LOWER END OVLD IVRY on 7456; Y^E OLD IVRY on 7455

7455	1.61	24.9	Br	0°	*Auberry,* Henry. 1668 ½d. 1.33.12 (H A) (H A|AT[chequers]Y^E|1668|•); 5.77 (••|[rule]|HENRY•|[rule] AVBERRY•|[rule]|IN•Y^E•OLD•|[rule]|IVRY•HIS•|[rule]|HALFE•|[rule]|PENY•|[rule]|•. BW —. [Baldwin]
7456a	1.76	27.1	Cu	180°	*Pelling,* Henry. 1668 ½d. 5.59.20; 5.77. BW 2151. [Nott ex Taffs]
7456b	1.62	25.0	Cu	180°	Same dies. [Nott ex Carthew]

PANYER ALLEY (Farringdon ward Within) [25-G9, g82]

The reading is PANIER ALLEY on 7458; *Pannyer Ally* on 6516; PANYER ALLEY on 7457

Named signs

	Weight g	Weight gr		Die axis	
7457	0.74	11.4	Br	0°	*Acorn* (AKORNE): Lacke, Hen[ry]. nd. 4.8.10; H L. BW 2182. [Nott ex Taffs]. An acorn *pendent* would appear to be without parallel, so obv. placed with legend starting at 6 o'clock. A messuage on east side of Panyer Alley demised 1647 to Henry Lacke, Haberdasher (British Library Add MS. 5080 no. 1, cit. Nightingale MS)
7458	2.05	31.6	Cu	180°	[*Hayes*] *coffee-house* (AT Y^E COFFE HOVSE): Hayes, Robert. nd ½d. 3.5.40; 5.77. BW 2181. [Nott ex Carthew]. See also 6516. Sign name from Lillywhite 1972, no. 555

PATERNOSTER ROW (Farringdon ward Within & Castle Baynard ward) [24-H7]

The reading is PATER NOSTER ROW on 7460-1; PATERNOSTER ROE on 7459

Named signs

7459a	1.11	17.2	M	180°	*Castle tavern* (THE CASTELL TAVERN): B[roughton], J[ohn]. nd. 5.5.1; B|ID. BW 2188 but PATERNOSTER. [Nott]. John Broughton, vintner, mentioned in the accounts of St Michael le Querne (Rogers 1928a, p. 88); 6 hearths b[urnt 1666] (Dale 1934, p. 8, f. 13). John Broughton appr. 1638 (Webb 1996-, xliii. 43, see also 343)
7459b	1.04	16.0	M	180°	Same dies. [Baldwin]
7460	0.98	15.0	M	0°	*Mermaid tavern* (THE MER MAYDE TAVERN): ?F—, R—. nd. 3.10.17; F|RI. BW 2190; Rogers 1928c, p. 81. [Nott]. Reading confirmed from MoL specimen
7461	1.05	16.2	Br	0°	*Mermaid tavern* (Y^E MEARMAYD TAVERN): B[all], S[ilvester]. nd. 3.10.17; B|SE. BW 2189 but ROW. [Nott]. Rev. legend starts between 10 and 11 o'clock. Silvester Ball appr. Vintner 1649 (Webb 1996-, xliii. 14, see also 337); md. Elizabeth Dolleveris, St Dionis Backchurch, 1658 (Harl. Reg. 3, 1878, p. 34); sons bap. St Faith under St Paul's 1664-6 (IGI); assessed on 10 hearths in Castle Baynard ward 1662 (Rogers 1928c, p. 81)

PAUL'S ALLEY *subsequently* ST PAUL'S ALLEY (Castle Baynard ward & Farringdon ward Within) [24-H8, i35]/PAUL'S ALLEY (Cripplegate ward Without, Redcross Street) [15-D9, c83]

The reading is PAVLS ALLEY

7462a	1.06	16.3	Br	0°	*Broome,* John. 1657. 5.17.13; B|IE. BW 2192. [Nott ex Taffs]
7462b	0.87	13.4	Br	0°	Same dies. [Nott ex Carthew]

PAUL'S CHAIN *subsequently* GODLIMAN STREET (Castle Baynard ward) [34-I8: St Paul's Chaine]

The reading is PALLES CHAINE on 7463; S^T PAVLES CHAINE on 7464

7463a	0.98	15.2	Cu	0°	*Adkinson,* William. nd. 5.14 Apothecaries; A|WC. BW 2193. [Nott ex Taffs]. William Atkinson, free 1658 (Whittet 1983, p.134)
7463b	0.85	13.1	Cu	0°	Same dies. [Nott ex Carthew]
7464	1.61 (chipped)	24.8	Br	0°	*Swettingham,* Thomas. nd ½d. 5.7.20; 5.77. BW 2194. Deane 1976. Reading confirmed from MoL specimen. Surname presumably from Swettenham, Cheshire

PAUL'S WHARF neighbourhood (Castle Baynard ward) [34-J8]

See also BELL YARD (Castle Baynard ward). The reading is BY PAVLS WHARFE on 7467, POWLS WHARF on 6544; NEAR PAVLES WHARFE on 7466; NEERE PAVLES WHARFE on 7465

Named signs

7465	2.21	34.2	Cu	0°	*Ball* (THE): ?H—, I/J—. nd 2d. 5.77 (2^D; •THE•BALL•NEERE around); I H (I H; •PAVLES•WHARFE• around). BW —, cf. 2198-9 and Dickinson 2199A. [Baldwin ex Macfadyen, lot 155]
7466a	2.22	34.2	Cu	0°	*Bell brew-house* (AT Y^E BELL BREW|HOVS): Chitty, Abraham. 1669 ½d. 5.77; 5.70.3. BW 2197 but BREW|HOVS. [Baldwin]. Irregular, nearly round flan; unclear whether originally thus or trimmed from an octagonal shape. Abraham Chitty of All Hallows Barking (1619-85), Cooper; churchwarden, St Benet Paul's Wharf 1679 (Boyd 39841)
7466b	2.06	31.8	Cu	0°	Same dies. [Nott ex Carthew]

[*continued overleaf*]

7457 7458 7459a 7460 7461 7462b

7463a 7464 7465 7466a 7467a 7468a

7469 7470b 7471 7472 7473a 7474

7475a 7476b 7477 7478 7479 7480b

PAUL'S WHARF *and* ST PETER'S HILL neighbourhood (Castle Baynard ward) [34-J8]

The reading is BY PAVLS WHARFE AT PETERS HILL FOOT. The tokens appear to be the only evidence for an establishment here called The Next Boat (Lillywhite 1972, 10804)

	Weight g	*gr*		*Die axis*	
7467a	2.21	34.0	M	0°	*Next Boat* (AT Y^{E}): ?B—, M—. nd. 3.4.29 (NEXT|BOAT); B|MM. BW 2196. [Nott ex Taffs]. The Greenall specimen (1997, pl. 4.124) is from an earlier obv. die, probably the original pairing, with NEXT|BOAT adjacent to a building behind the boat
7467b	1.99	30.7	Br	0°	Same dies. [Nott]
7467c	1.94	29.9	Br	180°	Same dies. [Nott]

PETTICOAT LANE *subsequently* MIDDLESEX STREET (Portsoken ward *and* Middlesex: Stepney: Whitechapel) [19-D17]

The reading is PETTECOATE LANE on 7469; PETTICOAT LANE on 7470; PETTICOATE LANE on 7468; PETTICOTE LANE on 7472; PITE COT LANE on 7471

7468a	2.24	34.5	Br	0°	*Bickcem,* John. [16]68 ½d. 3.5.105; 5.77. BW 2210. [Baldwin]
7468b	1.15 (corroded)	17.7	Br	270°	Same dies. [Nott]
7469	0.94	14.5	Cu	0°	*Hiller,* Edmond. nd. 3.11 (•EDMOND•HILLER•IN around); H|ES (•H•|E S|•; •PETTECOATE• LANE: around). BW —; Dickinson 2215B. [Nott]. Cf. 7472 (WHIT LYON)
Named signs					
7470a	2.38	36.7	Br	270°	*Red Cross* (AT Y^{E}): Markland, Ralph. 1667 ½d. 1.44; 5.77. BW 2217. [Nott ex Taffs]
7470b	2.27	35.1	Br	270°	Same dies. [Nott ex Carthew]
7471	0.97	14.9	Br	180°	*Rose & Crown* (THE ROSE AND CROVNE): ?M—, W—. nd. 4.12.2 (THE•ROSE•AND• CROVNE around); M|WB (•M•|W•B; ••IN•PITE COT•LANE• around). BW —; Dickinson 2216A, from Heal 1928, p. 13. [Baldwin ex Macfadyen, lot 155]
7472	0.87	13.4	Br	180°	*White Lion* (AT THE WHIT LYON): ?D—, R—. nd. 3.11; D|RE. BW 2212. [Nott]. Cf. 7469

PETTY FRANCE *subsequently* NEW BROAD STREET (Bishopsgate ward Without) [18-E15]

Barnes, John *see* Uncertain I
Rack, William *see* Uncertain I

Named signs

Ball: Hunt, Sam— *see* Uncertain I

PHILPOT LANE (Billingsgate & Langbourn wards) [38-I15]

See also MOSLEY'S COURT. The reading is FILPOT LANE on 7369; PHILLPOT LANE on 7473; PHILPOT LANE on 7474-5

7473a	2.09	32.2	Br	90°	*Hewson,* Samuel (SAMVELL). 1668 ½d. 4.10.12; 5.77 (H|SA). BW 2229 but on a garb three birds. [Nott ex Taffs]
7473b	1.72	26.5	Br	90°	Same dies. [Baldwin]
7473c	1.57	24.2	Br	90°	Same dies. [Nott ex Carthew]
7474	0.39 (chipped)	6.0	Br	0°	*Nevell,* Robert. nd. 5.14.188; N|RA. BW 2232 but not the *reguardant* roebucks of the Leathersellers. [Baldwin]. Robert Nevell of St Dionis Backchurch, mealman; md. Anne Pease 1654; children bap. 1657, 1661 (Boyd 11991)
Named signs					
7475a	1.48	22.8	Br	180°	*Sugarloaf* (AT THE SVGAR LOAFE): ?B—, R—. nd. 5.64.1; B|RS. BW 2233 but rev. = •B•|R•S. [Nott ex Spink]. Diameter 16.5-17 mm
7475b	0.78	12.0	Br	180°	Same dies. [Nott]. Diameter 15.5-16 mm

PIE CORNER *see* PYE CORNER

POPE'S HEAD ALLEY (Cornhill & Langbourn wards) [27-H13, i65, confirmed by Ogilby 1677 p. 10 but in Ogilby 1676 indexed as i60]

The reading is POPESHEAD ALLEY

	Weight *g*	*gr*		Die axis	
7476a	1.07 (chipped)	16.5	Br	0°	*Sawyer,* John. nd. 3.5.50 (?); S|IF̣. BW 2256 but •S•|I•F̣. [Baldwin]. Description largely confirmed from BM specimen. John Sawyer or Sayer, bd. 1687, wife Frances (Rogers 1928a, p. 83, 1935, p. 15). Kept the Pope's Head at least 1660-74 (Pepys 1970-83, x. 425). See also Fire Court 1966-, i. 167-8, ii. 30; Mills 1962-7, i. 28, 60
7476b	1.03 (chipped)	15.8	Br	0°	Same dies. Nott [ex Carthew]

POPPINGE ALLEY *subsequently* POPPIN'S COURT (Farringdon ward Without, Fleet Street) [23-H5, i16]

The reading is POPENG ALLEY

Named signs

7477	0.69	10.6	Br	0°	*Green* [*?Dragon*]: Penycot:, Simon. nd. 3.114.0; P|SD. BW 2257 but G^{REEN}. Nott [ex Taffs]. Reading confirmed from MoL specimen. Rev. struck off-centre

The POSTERN *subsequently* FORE STREET (Coleman Street ward & Cripplegate ward Without) [16-E12]

Called *The Posterne Street* in 1720 (Harben 1918, p. 240). The reading is AT Y^{E} P̣OS\|TERN BY MORE FEILDES on 7478; IN Y^{E}POSTERN BY CRIPLEGAΤE on 7479; IN POSTERNE STREET on 7480 (dated 1666)

7478	0.75	11.5	M	225°	*Mills,* Rob—. nd. 5.2.30; M|RE. *BW 2267 but ROB:, TERN[?no stop]BY[?no stop]MORE[?stop]FEILDES. [Baldwin], on whose ticket identified as 'Unp[ublishe]d|1963A'
7479	1.94	29.9	Br	0°	*Rawlinson,* Tho[mas], distiller. nd ½d. 5.77; 5.3.30. BW 2268 but THO:RAWLINSON, CRIPLEGAΤE . Seaby, [*SCMB* April 1967]. Reading confirmed from BM specimen. Thomas Rawlinson (A), free of the Distillers 1662, bound apprentices 1666-74, d. 1691 (Woodhead 1966, p. 135, Webb 1996-, xi. 6, 20, 27)

Named signs

7480a	2.10	32.4	Cu	0°	*White* [*?Hart*] (AT Y^{E}): Looe, Hugh. 1666 ½d. 3.53.21 (L|HE); 5.77. BW 2271. [Nott ex Taffs]
7480b	1.85	28.5	Cu	90°	Same dies. [Nott]
7480c	1.62	24.9	Cu	180°	Same dies. [Nott]

POSTERN GATE *see* Middlesex I: Stepney: Tower Postern neighbourhood

POULTRY (Cheap ward) [26-H12]

The reading is THE POVLTREY throughout

	Weight *g*	Weight *gr*		Die axis	
7481a	2.79	43.0	Cu	0°	*Twine,* George. 1665 ½d. 3.99.4; 5.77. BW 2278. [Nott]. George Twine of St Mary Woolnoth, Vintner, at the Three Cranes tavern until 1666; 'Captain' 1697 (Boyd 2439; Rogers 1931, pp. 111-12, 122). Apprentices bound to him (Webb 1996-, xliii. 388)
7481b	2.18	33.6	Cu	0°	Same dies. Nott [ex Taffs]
Named signs					
7482	1.21	18.7	M	180°	*Exchange tavern* (THE): K[ing], W[illiam]. 1651. 5.8.1; W K. BW 2277; Thompson 1993, p. 78. [Nott ex Carthew]. 'Mr King himself was up and standing at the Bar, telling of Brass farthings' 1663 (Kirkman 1673, p. 28; Burn 1855, 915). See also 7483; for the 'counterfeit lady' see ODNB s.v. Carleton, Mary (1634x42-1673). A William King appr. a Vintner 1624, another 1625, and a third 1631 (Webb 1996-, xliii. 174, see also 366)
7483a	3.19	49.3	Br	90°	*Exchange tavern* (THE): [King, William]. 1668 ½d. 5.8.2; 5.77. BW 2276; Thompson 1993, p. 78. [Baldwin]. John Oliver 'sett out one Foundac' on Feb: 28th 1667 for Mr Will: Kinge which was the Exchange in the Poultrey' (Mills 1962-7, iv. 16v.). See also 7482
7483b	1.46	22.5	Br	180°	Same dies. [Nott]
7484	1.22	18.9	Br	180°	*Rose tavern* (AT THE): D[yott], T[homas]. nd. 4.12.1; D|TE. BW 2273. [Nott ex Carthew]. Issuer named as on BW 2275, though also called *Dius, Diouse, Dyas* (Mills 1962-7, i. 62, ii. 4v., 63). Sons bap. St Mildred Poultry 1651-60; Thomas bd. 1679; Elizabeth Dyose bd. 1681 (Rogers 1931, p. 128). A Thomas Dios appr. Vintner 1635, another 1639 (Webb 1996-, xliii. 87, see also 352)

PRINCES STREET (Broad Street & Cheap & Coleman Street wards) [26-H12]

Morton, Walter *see* Uncertain I
Snelling, Thomas *see* Uncertain I

Named signs

Sun: Rixon, John *see* Uncertain I

PUDDING LANE (Billingsgate ward & Bridge ward Within) [38-J15]

The reading is PVDDING LANE on 7486; PVDIN LANE on 7487-90 (P̣VDIN on 7490); PVDING LANE on 7485; REDRIF(FE) LANE on 5034-5, cf. 'PUDDING LANE ALIAS REDERIFFE LANE' 1667-73 (Mills 1962-7, i. 60), *Retherhethe Lane* 1551-2, *Raderiff Lane* 1571, due to association with the place-name Rotherhithe (Ekwall 1954, p. 154 s.v. Rother Lane *now* Pudding Lane)

					Farener, Thomas, baker *see* v. 5034 and Thompson 2005b
7485a	0.92	14.2	M	180°	*Hands,* John. 1664. H|IM; 5.64.16. BW 2284. [Nott ex Taffs]. John Hands of St George Botolph Lane, Haberdasher; md. Mary Lawrence 1662 (Boyd 20078)
7485b	0.84	12.9	M	180°	Same dies. [Baldwin]
Named signs					
7486a	0.89	13.7	Br	270°	*Black Bull* (AT THE BLACKE BVLL): ?P—, W—. nd. 3.52.1; P|WI. BW 2285. [Nott ex Taffs]. Struck from rusted dies
7486b	0.84	13.0	Br	180°	Same dies. [Nott]
					Dark House: ?F—, M— *see* v. 5035 and Thompson 2005b
7487a	0.83	12.8	Br	0°	*Maidenhead* (AT Y^{E}MAYDENHEADE): A[ppleby], B[rian]. 1657. 3.5.96; A|BW. BW 2283 but MAYDENHEADE. [Nott ex Taffs]. Brian Appleby of St George Botolph Lane, Vintner, fl. 1656-76 (Rogers 1928a, p. 89, 1937, p. 41; Boyd 26995). Brian Applebye appr. 1636 (Webb 1996-, xliii. 7, see also 336). Same obv. die as 7488
7487b	0.76	11.7	Br	0°	Same dies. [Baldwin]. Another, not now in the collection, axis 180°, ex Nott
7488	0.79	12.2	Br	0°	*Maidenhead* (AT Y^{E}MAYDENHEADE): A[ppleby], B[rian]. 1657. 3.5.96; A|BW. BW 2283 but MAYDENHEADE. [Nott ex Taffs]. Same obv. die as 7487, q.v.
7489a	1.69	26.1	Br	240°	*Maidenhead* (AT THE MAYDENHEADE): A[ppleby], B[rian]. 1668 ½d. 3.5.96; 5.77 (A|BW). BW 2282 but MAYDENHEADE. [Nott]. For identification of issuer see 7487
7489b	1.01	15.5	Br	240°	Same dies. [Nott ex Taffs]
7489c	0.85	13.1	Br	240°	Same dies. [Baldwin]
7489d	0.57 (chipped, pierced)	8.8	Br	0°	Same dies. [Baldwin], on whose ticket identified as 'Unp[ublishe]d . . . 2286B'
7490	1.15 (chipped)	17.8	Br	270°	*Spaniel Dog & Three* [*?Hats*] (AT Y^{E} SPANILDOG & 3): Sell (–ELL), Tho—. nd ½d. 3.67.34 (•THO:–ELL•AT•Y^{E}•SPANILDOG•&•3 around); 5.61.24 (S|TE) ([Hat]|[Hat]S[Hat]|T E; •I–P̣VDIN•LANE•HIS•HALFE•PENY around). BW —; *Dickinson 2285A (SELL). [Baldwin ex Macfadyen, lot 155]. Double-struck. Reading partly confirmed from Sharman 1983, p. 123, illus. 17

[*continued overleaf*]

7481b 7482 7483a 7484 7485a 7486a

7487a 7488 7489a 7490 7491a 7492

7493a 7494 7495 7496 7497 7498

7499 7500 7501 7502a 7503 7504

Plate 45 (*cont.*)

PUDDLE DOCK neighbourhood (Castle Baynard ward) [cf. 34-J7]

First mention 1666 (Harben 1918, p. 489), though some tokens are earlier. The reading is AT PVDDELLDOCKE on 7492, PVDDLE DOCK on 7497-8 (P̣VDDLE on 7498), PVDELL DOCKE on 7500, PVDLE DOCK on 7493, 7495; NEAR PVDLE DOC WHARF on 7496, NEẠ. . .VDLE WHARF on 7499, NERE PVDLE DOCK on 7491; IN THAMẸṢ STREET AT P̣ỴDDLE WHARF on 7494

	Weight g	Weight gr		Die axis	
7491a	2.86	44.2	M	270°	*Baker,* Tho[mas]. 1659 (59|I6). 3.107.2; B|TA. BW 2287 but THE59; Woodhead 1966, p. 22, Thomas (A). [Nott]. Diameter 20 mm
7491b	1.78	27.5	M	180°	Same dies. [Nott]. Diameter 18.5-19 mm
7492	0.56 (chipped)	8.7	Br	0°	*Colsill,* Francis. nd. 5.14 Bakers (•FRANCIS[?stop]CỌḶSILL••• around); C|FE (.C.|F·E; •AT•PVDDELLDOCKE• around). BW —. [Baldwin], on whose ticket surname read as COESILL. I.m. both sides a fleur-de-lis. Surname presumably local, from *Coleshill,* with Coleshill, Warks. occurring as *Colsell* 1540, 1626 (Watts 2004, p. 150)
7493a	1.77	27.3	Cu	0°	*Hale,* Robert, chandler. 1662 ½d. 5.77; H|RM. BW 2291 but ROBER^{T}. [Nott ex Taffs]. Obv. legend starts at 3 o'clock
7493b	1.72	26.6	Cu	0°	Same dies. [Nott]
7493c	1.52	23.4	Cu	180°	Same dies. [Nott]
7494	0.64	9.9	Br	180°	*Howe,* Benjamin (–ẸNIAMIN). nd ½d. 3.2.9; 5.77 (H|BE). *BW 2293 but –ẸNIAMIN. [Nott ex Carthew]. Reading largely confirmed from MoL specimen
7495	1.40	21.5	Br	90°	*Osman,* John. 1664 ½d. O|IM; 5.77. BW 2295. [Nott ex Carthew]. Foundation set out on Puddle Wharf Hill 1668 for John Osmond/Osman (Mills 1962-7, i. 59, ii. 141)
7496	0.84	13.0	Cu	0°	*Veare* (VEẠRE), William (W^{M}), woodmonger (WOODMVNGR). nd. 5.60.9 (•W^{M} VEẠRE•WOODMVNGR•AT around); V|WA (.V.|WA|•; NEAR•PVDLE•DOC•WHARF around). BW —; Dickinson 2001, 3. Baldwin. Corrosion on the obverse has left raised lines that give the impression of being part of a design. Cf. John Vere, Woodmonger, Castle Baynard ward 1675-81 (Woodhead 1966, p. 167)
Named signs					
7497	1.05	16.2	Br	0°	*Brew-house* (AT THE BREW HOVSE): ?S—, R—. nd 1d. 5.14 London City 1 (•AT•THE•BREW•HOVSE around); 5.77 (R S) (I^{D}|R̤• S; •AT•PVDDLE•DOCK• around). BW —, cf. 2297 (PVDLE). [Baldwin]. Reading largely confirmed from specimen in BM, which has another example from the same obv. die but with a rev. reading PVDLE (a later die pairing), as BW 2297. See also 7498
7498	1.65 (chipped)	25.4	Br	0°	*Brew-house* (AT THE ḄREW ḤOṾṢE): ?S—, R—. nd 2d. 5.14 London City 1 (•AT•THE•ḄREW•ḤOṾṢE• around); 5.77 (R S) (II^{D}|R S; (•AT•P̣VDDLE•DOCK around). BW —. [Baldwin]. See also 7497. Lillywhite 1972, 3897, with reference to the Old Brew-house (10898)
7499	1.29 (chipped)	20.0	Br	180°	*Green Dragon* (AT Y^{E} GREEN[E?] DRAGON): West, Will. nd ½d. 5.77 (HIS|HALFE|PENY; WILL•WEST•AT•Y^{E}•GREEN[E?] around); 3.114.1 (•DRAGON•NEẠ. . .VDLE•WHARF around). BW —; Dickinson 2297B. [Nott ex Spink]
7500	1.66	25.6	Cu	270°	*White Swan* (AT Y^{E}WHTE SWAN): Rogers, John. nd ½d. 3.102.4; 5.77. BW 2296 but WHTE [*sic*], PVDELL. [Nott ex Taffs]. Reading confirmed from Wetton 1989, pl. 9.225

PUDDLE DOCK HILL neighbourhood *subsequently* ST ANDREW'S HILL (Castle Baynard ward & Farringdon ward Within) [34-J7]

The reading is AT Y^{E} CORN\|ER OF PVDLEDOCK HILL

7501	1.71	26.4	Br	0°	*Harris,* Samuel. 1669 ½d. 5.14 Tallow Chandlers; 5.77. BW 2292. [Nott]. Samuel Harris bound one Tallow Chandler apprentice 1678, and his widow Elizabeth another two 1700 (Webb 1996-, xxxix. 96; 50, 68)

PYE CORNER (Farringdon ward Without, Giltspur Street) (*lost*) [24-F7: Pie Corner]

The reading is AT SPY CORNER WEST SMITHFLD on 7505, SPYCORNER on 7506; IN PYE CORNER on 7503, P̣ỴE – –ṚNE– on 7504; PY CORNER on 7502.

The following were recorded but are now missing: BW 2249, two specimens, both 90°, ex Nott

7502a	0.93	14.4	Br	180°	*Marston,* John, tallow-chandler. [16]59. 2.3.9; M|ID. BW 2251 but PY, TALLOW[no stop]CHANDLER. Nott [ex Taffs]
7502b	0.90 (chipped)	13.9	Br	180°	Same dies. [Nott ex Carthew]
7503	1.45	22.4	Br	30°	*Marston,* John, tallow-chandler. nd ½d. 2.3.9; 5.77. BW 2250. [Nott ex Taffs]
7504	1.38	21.3	Br	90°	*Marston* (MAṚ. . .), John (ỊOHN), tallow-chandler (ṬALḶ. . .ÇḤẠND. . .). nd ½d. 2.3.9; 5.77. *BW 2250 (MARSTON.TALLOW, CHANDLER, CORNER). [Nott]

PYE CORNER (*cont.*)

	Weight g	Weight gr		Die axis	
7505	1.73	26.7	Br	90°	*Parkins,* Sam— (SAM•), mealman. nd ½d. 4.10.12; 5.77 (P|SM). BW 2252 but On a garb three birds, SPY, SMITHFLD. [Nott ex Taffs]. SMITHFLDSPY is apparently one unbroken word; SMITHFLDS as in BW has not been found elsewhere, so legend probably intended to begin SPY (cf. 7506) and end SMITHFLD

Named signs

7506	1.75	27.0	Br	0°	*Spy Corner brew-house:* Wilcocks, Stephen. nd. 3.53.30; S W. BW 2253 but WILCOCKS, SPYCORNER. [Nott ex Taffs]. Description confirmed from BM specimen. Sign name as in Lillywhite 1972, 11411, cf. 16572

QUEEN STREET (Vintry & Cordwainer & Cheap wards) [36-I11: New Queen Street]

Made after the Fire of 1666; the northern portion occupies the site of Soper['s] Lane (Harben 1918, p. 495). The reading is QVEENE STREET on 7508; QVEENS STREET on 7507; QVEENSTR on 7509; SOPER LANE on 7510-11

7507a	1.30	20.1	Cu	210°	*Cannon,* John. nd. 3.5.8; C|IS. BW 2315. [Nott ex Taffs]
7507b	1.03	15.9	Cu	210°	Same dies. [Nott]
7508	1.31	20.3	M	180°	*Eddenburro,* Thomas. nd. 4.2.1; E|TA. BW 2317. [Nott ex Taffs]
7509	1.13	17.5	Br	180°	*Moss,* Robert, mealman. nd. 5.14 Tallow Chandlers 2; M|RF. BW 2319 but QVEENSTR. [Nott ex Taffs]. Description confirmed from BM specimen. Robert Moss(e) appr. Tallow Chandler 1638, bound an apprentice 1656 (Webb 1996-, xxxix. 73, 104)

Named signs

7510	1.03	15.9	M	180°	*Plough* (AT THE PLOW): Holms, William (WILLAM). nd. 5.54 (•WILLAM•HOLMS•AT THE around); H|WA (•H•|W•A; •PLOW•IN•SOPER•LANE around). BW —, cf. 7511. [Nott]
7511	0.80	12.4	M	0°	*Plough* (AT THE PLOW): Holms, William. nd. 5.54; H|WA. BW 2318. [Nott ex Taffs]. William Holmes of St Pancras Soper Lane; md. Anne Harrison 1626; she d. 1651 (Boyd 14829)

QUEENHITHE [*i.e.* THAMES STREET]/QUEENHITHE DOCK neighbourhood (Queenhithe ward) [35-J10]

See also QUEENHITHE 'GATE' neighbourhood; ST MICHAEL QUEENHITHE parish. The highway called *Quenehith* (*Queenhith*) 1546-7, 1585 must be Thames Street in Queenhithe ward (Ekwall 1954, p. 29). The reading is AT QVEEN HITH on 7515, QVEEN HITHE on 7514, QVEENE HITH on 7513, 7518, QVEENE HITHE on 7522, 7525, QVEENE HIVE on 7517, 7520 (QVẸENE on 7517), QVEENE HIFE on 7523, QVEENEHITHE on 7524, with LONDON on 7515; IN QVEENE HITH on 7512, 7521, with LONDON on 7521; NEAR QVEEN HITH on 7074; NEARE QVEENE HIVE on 7519; IN THAMES STREET NEERE QVEEN HITH LON on 7516

7512	2.30	35.6	Br	0°	*Baker,* Thomas. 1668 ½d. 5.64.1; 5.77 (B|TI). BW 2298 but HITH. [Nott ex Carthew]. ?Thomas Baker of St Mary Somerset, Fishmonger, appr. 1626, free 1633, md. Susan Jones 1633; salter, Queenhithe, 1641; bound apprentices 1655-68 (Boyd 44724; Webb 1996-, xliv. 6, 150). Woodhead 1966, p. 22, identifies token-issuer with Thomas Baker (B), though wife's initial does not agree. Foundations to be set out for Thomas Baker 27 Apr. and 24 Sep. 1668 (Mills 1962-7, i. 63)
7513	2.26	34.8	Br	0°	*Briggs,* Richard. 1660 ½d. 5.14 Fishmongers; 5.77 (B|RA). BW 2299. [Nott]. Figure I in the fraction ½ omitted. Reading QVEENE confirmed from MoL specimen. Richard Briggs, Fishmonger, appr. 1651, md. Anne Moriot 1657, bound apprentices 1658-72; will, PCC, 1674, St Michael Queenhithe (Boyd 24810; Webb 1996-, xliv. 16, 152). He paid for a foundation 1667, and 1670 after petitioning (Mills 1962-7, i. 63, ii. 34v., Fire Court 1966-, ii. 70)
7514	1.86 (pierced)	28.6	Br	0°	*Canham,* Robert. 1669 ½d. 4.12.2; 5.14 Coopers (C|RI). BW 2300. [Nott]. Initial I confirmed from MoL specimen
7515	1.74	26.9	Cu	180°	*Cooper,* Josiah (IOSIAS). 1658. 5.13.18 (•IOSIAS•COOPER•AT•I658 around); 5.38.23 (AD SVPEROS:) (•QVEEN•HITH•LONDON• around). BW —; Dickinson 2300A but SVPEROS. [Nott ex Carthew]. The P of the motto (which resembles a wide I) is punched into the die on the cross-piece of the anchor; reading confirmed from MoL specimen; 'To those above'
7516a	2.27	35.1	Cu	210°	*Field,* Will—. nd. 3.111.4; F|WS. BW 3095 but WILL;. Nott. Description virtually confirmed from BM and Greenall 1997, lot 132, specimens
7516b	1.97	30.5	Cu	210°	Same dies. [Nott ex Spink]
7517	1.06	16.3	Br	210°	*Hester,* Bartholomew. nd. 5.14 Fletchers; H|BA. *BW 2306. [Nott]. Reading partly confirmed from BM specimen
7518a	0.97	15.0	Br	90°	*Longe,* Samuel. 1657. 3.1.32; L|SM. BW 2308 but boy holding pineapple. [Nott ex Taffs]. I.m. fleur-de-lis both sides. See also 7522
7518b	0.40 (chipped)	6.2	Br	270°	Same dies. [Nott]

[*continued overleaf*]

7505 7506 7507b 7508 7509 7510

7511 7512 7513 7514 7515 7516a

7517 7518a 7519 7520a 7521 7522

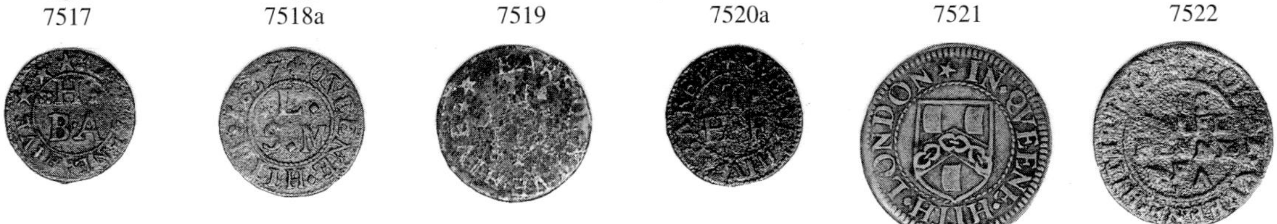

7523b 7524a 7525 7526 7527 7528

Plate 46 (*cont.*)

	Weight g	Weight gr		Die axis	
7519	1.84	28.4	Br	0°	*Neale,* John. nd ½d. 5.45.11; 5.77 (N|IA). BW 2309 but •N•|I A|½. [Nott ex Carthew]. Reading confirmed from MoL specimens. Legends start between 10 and 11 o'clock both sides; the head of the axe is to left (not clear on photo). ?John Neal who md. Anne Gatwood of St Mary Somerset 1655 (Boyd 56508)
7520a	1.15	17.7	M	180°	*Tatum,* Henry (HENREY), baker. nd. 3.9.1; T|HF. BW 2312. [Nott ex Taffs]. Henry Tatham, Baker; Master 1672, 1674 (Boyd 43907, unlocated). Three foundations set out for him 1667, but ground cut off 1669 (Mills 1962-7, i. 63, ii. 3, iii. 71)
7520b	1.07	16.5	M	180°	Same dies. [Nott ex Carthew]. Double-struck

Named signs

7521	4.03	62.1	M	180°	*Bull* (AT THE): Skrine, Robert. nd. 3.52.1; 5.14 Ironmongers. BW 2310. [Nott ex Carthew]. Robert Skrine of St Michael Cornhill, Ironmonger; will, PCC, 1666, St Michael Queenhithe (Boyd 16602). Bound apprentices 1660 (Webb 1996-, xxiv. 9, 18)
7522	0.77	11.8	Br	90°	*Naked Boy* (AT Y^{E}): Feild, Robert. 1667 ½d. 3.1.32; 5.77 (F|RA). BW 2302 but boy holding ?pineapple (cf. 7518). [Nott ex Taffs]. Reading confirmed from MoL specimen. Foundation to be set out 1668 (Mills 1962-7, i. 63)
7523a	0.99	15.2	M	180°	*Noble Garter* (AT THE): F[ish], B[artholomew]. nd. 3.109.12; F|BM. BW 2301 but three fishes naiant. [Nott]. Issuer identified from 7524. Bartholomew Fish of St Michael Queenhithe, Fletcher, will, PCC, 1676; widow Martha (Boyd 17831)
7523b	0.80	12.3	Cu	180°	Same dies. [Nott ex Taffs]
7524a	2.02	31.2	Cu	180°	[*Noble Garter*]: Fish, Bartholomew (BARTHOLLOMEW). 1667 ½d. 3.109.12; 5.77. BW 2303. [Nott ex Taffs]. Sign name from 7523, q.v. A foundation to be set out, 1671 (Mills 1962-7, i. 63). Diameter 20-20.5 mm
7524b	1.72	26.6	Cu	180°	Same dies. [Nott]. Diameter 21 mm
7524c	1.70	26.2	Cu	90°	Same dies. [Baldwin]. Diameter 21-21.5 mm
7525	0.92	14.3	M	0°	*Queen's Head tavern:* [anonymous]. 1662. Date; 3.5.65. BW 2314 but QVEENE•HITHE. [Nott ex Taffs]. Rev. legend starts between 10 and 11 o'clock

QUEENHITHE 'GATE' neighbourhood (Queenhithe ward) [35-J10]

The reading is IN THAMESSTREE^{T} and NEAR QVEENE HITHGAT^{E}, which may simply mean Queenhithe Dock, for Stow 1603, ii. 359, refers to it as 'this gate and Hith'

7526	1.79	27.6	Br	90°	*Hinde,* John, baker. 1668 ½d. 4.10.1; 5.77. BW 3102 but THAMESSTREE^{T}, HITHGAT^{E}. Nott [ex Taffs]. The superscript E, perhaps from a broken punch, resembles F

RALPH'S QUAY *subsequently* (new) CUSTOM HOUSE (Tower ward) [38-K16, n38]

The reading is AṬ ṚAPHS KEY THAM STR

Named signs

7527	0.82	12.7	Br	180°	*Half Moon* (AT THE HALFE MOON): ?H—, T—. nd. 2.2; H|TI. *BW 3097. Baldwin, on whose ticket identified as [BW] 961 (THE ROYAL EXCHANGE neighbourhood). Reading partly confirmed from BM specimen

RAM ALLEY *subsequently* HARE PLACE (Farringdon ward Without, Fleet Street) [32-I4, k40]

The reading is RAM ALEY IN FLET STRET on 7528, RAM ALLEY on 7529

Named signs

7528	1.06	16.3	M	180°	*Sugarloaf* (AT THE SHVGER LOFE): ?C—, M—. nd. 5.64.1; C|MA. BW 1070 but SHVGER, ALEY. Nott. Reading confirmed from Kent 2005, illus. 148

RAM ALLEY neighbourhood

The reading is AGAINST RAM ALLEY

Named signs

	Weight g	gr		Die axis	
7529	0.94	14.6	Br	180°	*Blue Boar* (AT THE BLEW BOARE): ?W—, W—. nd. 3.65.1 (•AT•THE•BLEW•BOARE around); W|WM (•W•|W•M; •AGAINST•RAM•ALLEY around). BW —; Dickinson 1102A, from Heal 1928, p. 9. [Baldwin], on whose ticket identified as 'Unp[ublishe]d . . . 2321A'

RED LION COURT (Bishopsgate ward Without, Bishopsgate Without) (*lost*) [18-C16, c12: Red Lyon Alley]

The reading is REDLION COVRT WITHOVT BISHOPGA^T

7530	2.16	33.3	M	180°	*Lamle,* John. nd ½d. (ḤIṢ). 5.77; 3.11. *BW 306 but LAMLE, REDLION, HALF, BISHOPGA^T. Nott [ex Baldwin]. Reading largely completed from MoL specimen

RED LION COURT (Cripplegate ward Without, Whitecross Street *and* Middlesex: Finsbury) *see* Middlesex I: Finsbury

REDCROSS STREET (Cripplegate ward Without) [15-C10]

The reading is RED CROS STREET on 7532-3; RED CROSS STREET on 7534, 7536, STREETE on 7535; REDCROS STREET on 7531

7531	0.57	8.9	Br	90°	*Ballett,* Thomas. nd. 3.10.21; B|TA. BW 2374. [Nott]. Description completed from MoL specimen. Thomas Ballett of St Giles Cripplegate, oilman; md. Anne Gardner 1663 (Boyd 20523)
7532	1.37	21.1	Br	90°	*Brandred,* Margaret (MARGRET). 1668 ½d. 5.85.1; 5.77 (M B). BW 2376. [Longman] 1958, lot 452
7533	2.20	33.9	Cu	0°	*Holloway,* Thomas. 1666 ½d. 3.5.88; 5.77. BW 2385 but bust of ?Elizabeth I. [Nott ex Taffs]. Thomas Holloway of St Giles Cripplegate, b. 1639, Salter (Boyd 17044)
7534a	1.23	19.0	Cu	90°	*Wallis,* Oliver. 1667. 3.67.14; W|OI|date. BW 2388. Seaby 1961. Oliver Wallis, Mercer, free 1643; silkman; d. by 1699; wife Judith (Woodhead 1966, p. 170). Diameter 16-16.5 mm
7534b	0.89	13.7	Cu	0°	Same dies. [Nott]. Diameter 16.5-17 mm
7534c	0.78 (chipped)	12.1	Cu	0°	Same dies. [Baldwin]. Diameter 15-15.5 mm

Named signs

7535a	1.11	17.1	M	180°	*Red Cross tavern* (THE): ?W—, F—. nd. 1.60 (•THE•RED•CROSS•TAVERN around); F W (F•W; •IN•RED•CROSS•STREETE around). BW —; Dickinson 2387C. [Baldwin]
7535b	0.76 (corroded)	11.8	M	180°	Same dies. [Nott]
7536a	1.98	30.5	Br	210°	*Sun* (AT THE SVNN): Dickenson, T—. 1666 ½d. 2.1; 5.76.158 (T D). BW 2379 but TD[monogram]ICKENSON. [Baldwin]
7536b	1.69	26.1	Br	210°	Same dies. [Nott ex Taffs]

ROOD LANE (Billingsgate & Langbourn wards) [38-I16]

The reading is ROOD LANE on 7538; ROODE LANE on 7537

7537	0.74	11.5	M	0°	*Coulson,* William. nd. 5.68.10; C|WM. BW 2391. [Nott]. Reading confirmed from MoL specimens
7538a	0.70	10.8	Br	240°	*Lyndall,* Daniel (DANIELL). nd. 5.14.189; L|DI. BW 2392. [Nott]
7538b	0.47 (chipped)	7.2	Br	240°	Same dies. [Nott]

ROSEMARY LANE (Farringdon ward Without) (*lost*) [24-F7, f33]/ROSEMARY LANE *subsequently* ROYAL MINT STREET (Portsoken ward *and* Middlesex: Stepney: Minories) [40-I20]

The reading is ROASE MARY LANE on 7543; ROSEMARYE LANE on 7555-6; ROSMARY LANE on 7542, 7560; ROSEMARY LANE on the remainder (ṚOSEMARỴ ḶANE on 7553)

7539	1.32	20.3	Br	180°	*Carpenter,* Robert. 1668 ½d. 5.15 Blacksmiths; 5.77 (C|RK). BW 2395. Nott. Same obv. die as 7540
7540a	1.74	26.8	Cu	270°	*Carpenter,* Robert. 1668 ½d. 5.15 Blacksmiths; 5.77 (C|RK). BW 2395. [Nott ex Carthew]. Same obv. die as 7539
7540b	1.72	26.6	Br	270°	Same dies. [Baldwin]
7541	0.99	15.3	Br	0°	*Cooles,* Richard. 1669 ½d. (HAḶF). 5.77; 3.11. *BW 2396 but I669. [Nott ex Carthew]

[*continued overleaf*]

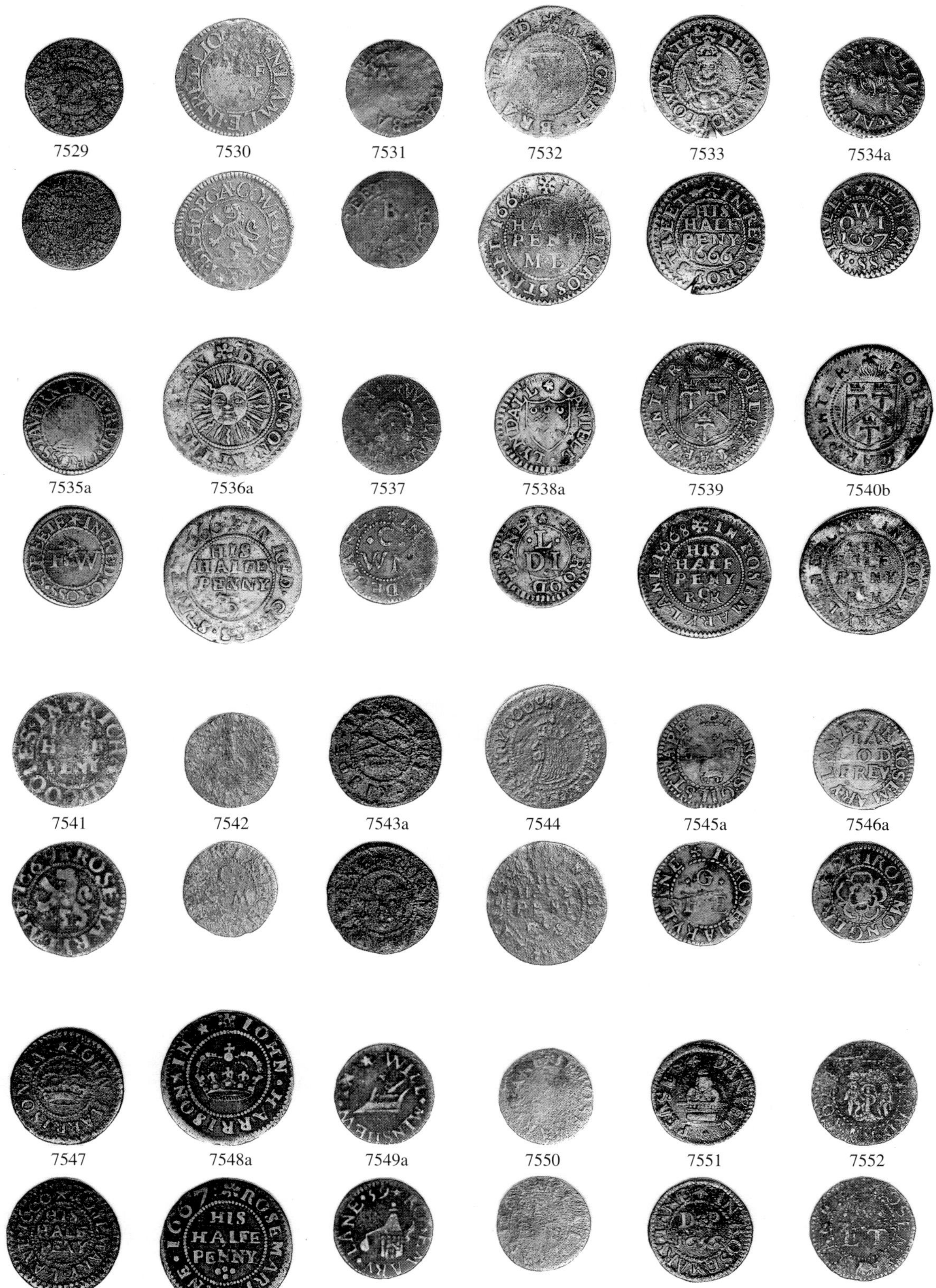

7529 7530 7531 7532 7533 7534a

7535a 7536a 7537 7538a 7539 7540b

7541 7542 7543a 7544 7545a 7546a

7547 7548a 7549a 7550 7551 7552

Plate 47 (*cont.*)

	Weight *g*	*gr*		*Die axis*	
7542	0.89	13.8	M	180°	*Crisp,* Sam—, cheesemonger. nd. 5.3.30; C|SM. BW 2398. [Nott]. Description completed from BM specimen
(edge filed and chipped)					
7543a	0.87	13.4	Cu	180°	*Crispe,* Henry. nd. 5.84.14; C|ḤM. *BW 2397. [Baldwin]. Reading MARY confirmed from MoL specimen
7543b	0.74 (chipped)	11.4	Cu	180°	Same dies. [Nott]
7544	1.55	23.8	Br	0°	*Cryer,* Robert, pastry-cook. 1668 ½d. 3.5.105; 5.77 (C|RS). BW 2399. [Nott ex Carthew]. Reading confirmed from MoL specimen
7545a	1.18	18.2	Br	180°	*Gilstrape,* Francis. nd. 3.53.13; G|FE. BW 2404 but GILSTRAPE, three stags, probably ROSEMARY (flaw between E and M). [Nott ex Carthew]. The surname presumably derives from Gelsthorpe in Yorks. WR (Redmonds 1973, p. 121)
7545b	1.05	16.3	Cu	0°	Same dies. [Baldwin]
7545c	0.85	13.1	Cu	180°	Same dies. Nott [ex Taffs]
7546a	1.10	16.9	Br	180°	*Godfrey,* Ja[mes], ironmonger (IRON MONGER). 1662. 5.77; 4.12.1. BW 2405. [Nott ex Taffs]. See also Middlesex I: Stepney: Tower Hill, for another 1662 token of this issuer, but with different rev. die. James Godfrey bound apprentices 1670-77 (Webb 1996-, xxiv. 59)
7546b	0.87	13.5	Br	180°	Same dies. [Nott ex Carthew]
7547	2.09	32.2	Cu	0°	*Harrison,* John. 1666 ½d. 5.60.1 (•IOHN•HARRISON•IN: around); 5.77 (HIS|HALF|PENY; •ROSEMARY•LANE•I666 around). BW —, cf. 7548; Dickinson 2407A. [Baldwin]
7548a	1.75	27.1	Br	0°	*Harrison,* John. 1667 ½d. 5.60.1; 5.77. BW 2407. [Nott]
7548b	1.60	24.7	Br	0°	Same dies. [Nott]
7549a	0.96	14.9	M	0°	*Minshew,* Will. [16]59. 5.54; 5.3.30. BW 2411. [Nott]
7549b	0.88 (chipped)	13.6	M	0°	Same dies. [Nott ex Taffs]
7550	1.02	15.8	Br	0°	*?P—* (P̣), E— (Ẹ), mealman (MEALEMAN). 166!̣ (I66Ị). 5.7.1? (•IN•ROSEMARY•LANE around); P̣|ẸẸ (P̣|Ẹ Ẹ; •MEALEMAN•I66Ị around). BW —. [Nott]. Initials have also been read as F.F.P. (Nott ticket). Device possibly a church
7551	1.11	17.1	Br	180°	*Pease,* Daniel. 1656. 3.3.13; D P|date. BW 2412. Nott [ex Taffs]
7552	0.88	13.5	Cu	180°	*Reade,* Edward (EDWAṚD). nd. 4.2.1; R|ET. *BW 2413. [Nott ex Carthew]. Reading largely confirmed from MoL specimen

ROSEMARY LANE *(cont.)*

No.	Weight g	Weight gr	Metal	Die axis	Description
7553	1.87	28.8	Br	0°	*Taylor,* William (ẈỊḶLIAM), brewer. 1668 ½d. (HẠḶF PẸṆY). 2.1; 5.77 (T|WM). *BW 2416. Nott [ex Carthew]. There were Brewers' Company apprentices named William Taylor in 1620, 1638, 1641, and 1655, also Masters so named (Webb 1996-, xxxvi. 93, 120)
7554	1.17	18.0	Br	0°	*Whitbourne,* Robert. 1668 ½d. 5.64.7; 5.77 (W|RE). BW 2419. [Nott ex Carthew]. Description completed from BM specimen
Named signs					
7555	1.02	15.7	Br	180°	*Falcon* (AT THE): ?D—, N—. nd. 3.92.1 (••AT•THE•FALCON•IN• around); D|NI (•D•|N•I; ••ROSEMARYE•LANE• around). BW —; Dickinson 2399A. [Nott ex Spink]. Same obv. die as 7556
7556	0.58	9.0	Br	180°	*Falcon* (AT THE): ?H—, R—. nd. 3.92.1; R H. BW 2406 but ROSEMARYE. [Nott]. Reading confirmed from MoL specimen. Same obv. die as 7555
7557	0.86 (pierced)	13.3	M	180°	*Plough* (AT THE PLOW): ?W—, C—. nd. 5.54; W|CE. BW 2417 but •W•|C•E. Nott [ex Carthew]
7558	1.06	16.4	Br	0°	*Three [?Tuns]* (AT THE 3): Lane, Richard. 1670 ½d. (HIṢ). 5.64.33; 5.77 (L|RH). *BW 2408. [Nott ex Taffs]. Reading largely confirmed from BM specimen

ROSEMARY LANE 'end'

The reading is ROSEMARY LANE EN

No.	Weight g	Weight gr	Metal	Die axis	Description
7559	1.28	19.7	Br	150°	*Flowers,* Ed—. nd. 4.9.5; F|EM. BW 2403 but ED:, TH^{E}. [Nott ex Spink]. Reading confirmed from MoL specimen

ROSEMARY LANE (Portsoken ward *and* Middlesex: Stepney: Minories) *and* HERMITAGE BRIDGE neighbourhood (Middlesex: Stepney: Wapping)

The reading is IN ROSMARY LANE ỌR ARMETAGE BRIGE

No.	Weight g	Weight gr	Metal	Die axis	Description
7560	0.99	15.3	M	0°	*Doe,* Ph—. nd. 4.10.1; 5.54. BW 2400 but PH:, OṚ•ARMETAGE•BRIGE. [Nott ex Seaby ex ? ex Baldwin]. Reading largely confirmed from BM specimen; the present specimen was perhaps the source of the main BW reading

ROUND COURT (Cripplegate ward Without, Barbican) [15-C9, west of b64]/ROUND COURT (Bishopsgate ward Without, Bishopsgate Street) [18-C16, c9: Angel Alley]/ROUND COURT (Aldersgate ward, St Martin le Grand) [25-G9, g90] *see* Uncertain I

'ROUND COURT' neighbourhood *see* Uncertain I

The ROYAL EXCHANGE neighbourhood (Broad Street & Cornhill wards) [27-H13]

The reading is BEHIND THE EXCHANG on 7563, THE EXCHANGE on 7561, THE EXCHENG on 7564-5, THE ROY EXCHA on 7562

No.	Weight g	Weight gr	Metal	Die axis	Description
7561	1.13	17.5	M	180°	*Browning,* Tho[mas] (TḤO). nd. 3.5.79; B|TS. *BW 958. Nott. Reading largely confirmed from Berry 1978, p. 60. 'Mr Browning, at the King's head, behind the Old Exchange' 1664 (BW 958 n.). Thomas Browning, Cook (Rogers 1935, p. 74); bound apprentices 1659-79 (Webb 1996-, xxvi. 64), including 1664 Henry son of James Boone, Tottenham, moneyer, deceased (cf. Challis 1989, p. 179)
7562	0.87	13.5	—	—	*Towers,* Sam—. nd 2d. 5.77; 0.1. BW Appendix A.14 (p. 803, this specimen). Nott (record), [Baldwin] ex Hodgkin [1914], [pl. iv], lot 199 (envelope). Uniface, *leather*, all incuse. Reading BEHIND confirmed from MoL specimen (Burn 1855, 1161 but SAM•, ROY)
Named signs					
7563	0.58	8.9	Br	180°	*Antwerp tavern* (THE): T[aylor], P[eter]. nd. 2.9.1; T|PA. BW 963. Nott. Reading confirmed from BM specimens. The Antwerp was in Threadneedle Street. Peter Taylor appr. Vintner 1642 (Webb 1996-, xliii. 289, see also 386); bd. 1662, wife Abigail (Rogers 1935, pp. 77-9)
7564	0.80	12.4	M	180°	*Globe tavern* (AT THE): W[illson?], S—. nd. 5.49.1 (•AT•THE•GLOBE•TAVERN around); W|SM (•W•|S•M; •BEHIND•THE•EXCHENG around). BW —; Dickinson 963A, from Heal 1928, p. 9. Baldwin. Rent for the Globe Tavern paid by Mr Willson 1649 (Rogers 1928a, p. 75, 1935, p. 51). Samuel Wilson appr. Vintner 1634, Simon Wilson 1638 (Webb 1996-, xliii. 324, see also 392). Same obv. die as 7565
7565	1.13	17.5	M	180°	*Globe tavern* (AT THE): ?E—, W—. nd. 5.49.1 (•AT•THE•GLOBE•TAVERN around); W E (W•E; •BEHIND•THE•EXCHENG around). BW —; Dickinson 960A. Nott [ex Carthew]. Same obv. die as 7564, apparently slightly corroded

[*continued overleaf*]

7553 7554 7555 7556 7557 7558

7559 7560 7561 7562 7563 7564

7565 7566 7567c 7568 7569 7570

7571 7572 7573 7574 7575 7576

ST ANDREW HOLBORN neighbourhood (Farringdon ward Without *and* Middlesex: Holborn) [22-F4]

The reading is AGAINST S^{T} ANDREWS CHVRCH HOL|BORN

Named signs

	Weight g	Weight gr		Die axis	
7566	1.60	24.7	Br	210°	*Pied* [*?Bull*] (AT Y^{E}PID): Catterall (CATTERALL), Tho—, oilman (OYLMAN). nd ½d. 3.52.4 (T C); 5.77. *BW 1386 but THO:, S^{T}. Nott [ex Taffs]. Reading largely confirmed from BM specimen

ST ANN'S LANE *subsequently* GRESHAM STREET (Aldersgate ward) [25-F9]

Perrot, John *see* Uncertain I

Named signs

[*Strainges*] *Coffee-house:* Strainge, Nich— *see* Uncertain I

ST BENET'S HILL *subsequently* BENNET'S HILL (Castle Baynard ward) [34-I8]

The reading is ONE S^{T} BENNETS HIL

Named signs

7567a	3.02	46.6	Br	300°	*Harrow* (AT THE): Tunstale, Matthew (MATHEW). nd 1d. 5.17.16; 5.77. BW 2450 but S^{T}:, I^{D}. [Nott]
7567b	2.96	45.7	Br	300°	Same dies. [Nott ex Taffs]
7567c	2.70	41.7	Br	120°	Same dies. Baldwin

ST BRIDE'S CHURCHYARD (Farringdon ward Without) [33-I5]

The reading is S^{T} BRIDES CHVRCHYARD

Named signs

7568	1.72	26.5	Cu	180°	[*Noke's*] *coffee-house* (COFFEE HO–SE): Noke, William. nd. 3.5.40; 5.77. *BW 2451 (HOVSE) but NOKE, CHVRCH[no stop]YARD. Nott [ex Carthew]. Reading largely confirmed from Shuttlewood 2001, lot 643; CHVRCHYARD can be taken as one word. The present specimen may have been the source of BW reading NORSE. Sign name from Lillywhite 1972, no. 912 corrected

ST CLEMENT EASTCHEAP neighbourhood (Candlewick ward) [37-I14] *see* Uncertain I

ST CLEMENT EASTCHEAP CHURCHYARD (Candlewick ward) *see* Uncertain I

ST CLEMENT'S LANE *subsequently* CLEMENT'S LANE (Langbourn & Candlewick wards) [37-I14] *see* Uncertain I

ST DUNSTAN IN THE EAST neighbourhood (Tower ward) [38-J16]

The reading is AT S DVNSTONS EAST

Named signs

7569	1.07	16.5	Br	180°	*Lock & Shears* (THE LOCK AND SHEERS): ?C—, T—. 1649. 5.67.7; C|TC. BW 2478. Nott [ex Taffs]

ST DUNSTAN IN THE WEST neighbourhood (Farringdon ward Without, Fleet Street) [32-I3]

The reading is AGAINS S^{T}DVNSTANS CHVRCH IN FLEET ST|REET on 7572; AT DVNSTONS CHVRCH IN FLEET STREET on 7571; AT S DVNSTANS CHVRCH FLEET STREETE on 7570

7570	1.31	20.2	M	180°	*Secol,* John. nd. S|IP; S|IP. BW 1096. Baldwin -1970. John Seacole, licensed victualler, 1649-50; 'the widow Seacole' 1652 (Burn 1855, 486 n.)

Named signs

7571	0.94	14.5	Br	180°	*Bull's Head* (THE BVLL HEAD): ?Y—, H—. nd. 3.52.25 (•THE•BVLL•HEAD•AT•DVNSTONS around); Y|HM (•Y•|H•M; •CHVRCH•IN•FLEET•STREET around). BW —; Dickinson 1104A. Baldwin [ex Macfadyen, lot 151 (surname initial read as V)]. See also 6950
7572	3.50	53.9	Br	180°	*Seven Stars* (AT THE): Markham (MARKHAM), Robert (ROBERT). 1672 1d., 'in lieu of this to the (Y^{E}) bearer a penny (PENY) is due'. 5.77; 5.77 (M|RE). *BW 1085 but THE, S^{T}:. Baldwin. Robert Markham, apothecary, of 'the Seven Stars . . . and at his shop in Westminster Hall' (Whittet 1983, p. 136); *pace* Whittet, Mrs Markham, toyman, was widow of George (Jowett 2005, p. 113). 'This is the last *Trader*, they being this year cryed down' (Heal 1928, p. 2)

ST DUNSTAN'S HILL neighbourhood (Tower ward) [38-J16]

The reading is AT DVNSTONES HILL. Although the issuer evidently belonged in the parish of St Dunstan in the West, no (St) Dunstan's Hill is apparent there

	Weight			*Die*	
	g	*gr*		*axis*	
7573	1.16	17.9	Br	180°	*Parslou,* Anthony. nd. 5.68.1; P|AE. BW 2479. Nott [ex Carthew or Taffs]. Anthony Parslow, Fletcher; at Holborn Bridge 1641; will, PCC, 1665, St Dunstan in the West; wife Elizabeth (Boyd 25257). If there be no mistake, he appears to have lived and worked at opposite ends of town

ST GABRIEL FENCHURCH neighbourhood (Langbourn ward) [38-I16]

The church stood in the middle of Fenchurch Street, between Rood Lane and Mincing Lane, but was burnt in the Great Fire and not replaced (Harben 1918, pp. 248-9). The reading is AT FENCHVRCH on 7575-6; BY FANCHVRCH on 7574

7574	1.41	21.8	Cu	0°	*Homfrey,* Pharaoh (PHARO). 1664 ½d. 5.64.1; 5.77. BW 993 but PHARO•HOMFREY. Nott [ex Carthew]. Reading confirmed from MoL specimen. ?Pharoah Humphry of St Mary Woolchurch, confectioner, d. 1671 (Boyd 1378)

Named signs

7575	1.10	17.0	Br	180°	*Blue Boar's Head* (AT THE BLEW BORES HEAD): ?N—, I/J—. nd. 3.65.10; N|IS. BW 992. Nott
7576	1.03	15.9	Br	180°	*Blue Boar's Head* (AT THE BLEW BORES HEAD): ?N—, I/J—. nd. 3.65.10; N|IS. BW 992. Nott [ex Taffs]

S T GEORGE'S LANE *subsequently* FLEET LANE (Farringdon ward Without) [23-G6: Fleet Lane from Old Bailey to Seacoal Lane]

The reading is S^{T}GEORGES LANE

	Weight g	Weight gr		Die axis	
7577	0.88	13.6	Br	90°	*Bovery,* Samuel (SAMVELL). nd. 3.1.73; B|SA. BW 2480 but SAMVELL. Nott [ex Taffs]. Reading confirmed from BM specimen

S T GILES WITHOUT CRIPPLEGATE parish (Cripplegate ward Without) [15-D10] *see* S T GILES. . . (Uncertain I)

S T GILES WITHOUT CRIPPLEGATE neighbourhood (Cripplegate ward Without) [15-D10]

The reading is AGAINST CRIPEL GATE CHVRCH on 7579, CRIPPLEGATE CHVRCH on 7581; AGAYNS^{T} CRIPPLGATE CHVRCH on 7578; AT CRIPLEGATE CHVRCH on 7580

7578	0.72 (chipped)	11.1	Br	180°	*Amy,* Robert. nd. 3.116.1; A|RP. BW 787 but AGAYNS^{T}, CHVRCH. Nott. Reading confirmed from BM and MoL specimens. Robert Amy, apothecary, free 1654, fl. 1666 (Whittet 1983, p. 135); 1672 bound an apprentice who was turned over 1675 (Webb 1996-, xlii. 15)
7579	0.85	13.1	Br	180°	*Cornel,* Tho—, milliner (MILNNR). 1657. C|TM; date. BW 790. Nott [ex Carthew]. Overstruck or corroded. ?Thomas Corny of St Giles without Cripplegate, Leatherseller; md. Margaret Johnson 1657 (Boyd 39947)
7580	0.53 (chipped)	8.1	Br	0°	*Spencer,* Tho—. 1658. Date; S|TP. BW 800 but THO:, CRIPPLEGATE[?stop]CHVRCH = .S.|T P. Nott [ex Carthew]. Description virtually confirmed from Greenall 1997, lot 100

Named signs

7581	0.70	10.8	Br	180°	*Oil shop* (OYLE SHOP): Barnes, Will[iam]. nd. B|WM; 5.77. BW 789 but WILL:, CRIPEL•GATE. Nott [ex Taffs]. Reading confirmed from MoL specimen. William Barnes of St Giles without Cripplegate, Salter; md. Margery Cash 1662 (Boyd 13330). Identified by Woodhead 1966, p. 24, with William Barnes (d. by 1697), appr. a Leatherseller 1653

S T JOHN STREET (Farringdon ward Without *and* Middlesex: Finsbury) *see* Middlesex I: Finsbury

S T KATHERINE CREE neighbourhood (Aldgate ward, Leadenhall Street) [29-G17, B68]

The reading is BY CRE CHVRCH on 7585, CREECHVRCH on 7586; IN LEADEN HAL STREET BY CREEDCHVRCH on 7584; NERE CREE CHVRCH on 7582-3

7582	1.23	19.0	Br	180°	*Clarke,* Will, chan[d]ler. nd. C|WA; C|WA. BW 782. Nott
7583	0.86	13.2	Br	330°	*Ludington,* Wil—. nd. L|WM (•L•|W M|•; .•.WIL•LVDINGTON around); 3.101.1 (•NERE•CREE•CHVRCH around). BW —; Dickinson 782A. Nott
7584	1.17	18.1	Br	0°	*Welch,* Michael. nd ½d. 3.53.20 (•MICHAEL•WELCH•IN•LEADEN around); 5.77 (M W) (HIS|HALF|PENY|M•W; •HAL•STREET•BY•CREEDCHVRCH around). BW —; Dickinson 1700B. Baldwin

Named signs

7585	1.10	17.0	Br	180°	*Bull's Head* (AT THE BVLL HEAD): C[leredge], J[onathan]. 1653. 3.52.25; C|II. BW 780 but CRE•CHVRCH. Nott [ex Taffs]. Identification of issuer from 7586
7586	2.46 (corroded)	38.0	Br	0°	[*Bull's Head*]: Cleredge, Jonathan. 1668 ½d. 3.52.25; 5.77 (C|II). BW 781 but CREECHVRCH. Nott [ex Spink]. Sign name from 7585. Description confirmed from MoL specimen

S T LAWRENCE JEWRY (Cheap ward, Cateaton Street) [26-G11]

The reading is IVRYE S L

7587	2.37 (pierced)	36.6	Cu	180°	[*St Lawrence Jewry* (parish)]. 1656. 5.17.37; 5.77 (S L). BW 2149 but *16*[gridiron]*56*, obv. and rev. transposed. Nott [ex Carthew]. The gridiron symbolised St Laurence, and probably this was a communion token

S T MARTIN LE GRAND liberty/street *otherwise* S T MARTIN'S LANE (Aldersgate ward) [25-G9]

See also NEW RENTS; ST MARTIN'S LANE (Uncertain I). The reading is MARTINES LEGRAND on 7601; MARTINS ALLDERSGATE on 7377, LEGRAND on 7596; S MARTINS ALDERSG on 7597, NERE ALLDERS GATE on 7600, WITH IN ALDERS GATE on 7599; S^{T}MARTINS on 7592; S^{T} MARTINS (or S^{T}MARTINS) ALDERSGATE on 7598, LE GRAN on 7588, LE GRAND on 7591, LEGRAND on 7590, 7593-5, LEGRN^{D} on 7376, NEERE ALDERSGATE on 7589

7588	0.94	14.5	Br	0°	*Fullerton,* John. nd. 5.68.33; I F. BW 2636 but LE[no stop]GRAN. Nott [ex Spink]. Stop after MARTINS confirmed from Wetton 1989, pl. 9.238. John Fullerton had four foundations set out in St Martin le Grand 1668-9 (Mills 1962-7, i. 50-1, ii. 115v, cf. Fire Court 1966-, ii. 308-9)

[*continued overleaf*]

7577 7578 7579 7580 7581 7582

7583 7584 7585 7586 7587 7588

7589 7590 7591a 7592 7593 7594

7595 7596 7597a 7598 7599 7600

Plate 49 (*cont.*)

	Weight *g*	*gr*		*Die axis*	
7589	2.90	44.7	Cu	0°	*Holden,* William. nd ½d. 3.1.75; 5.77. BW 2646. Nott [ex Taffs]. Reading S^{T} confirmed from MoL specimen
7590	1.20	18.6	Cu	0°	*Huggines,* Henry. nd ½d. 4.3.11 (H|HE); 5.77. BW 2647 but HVGGINES•IN, S^{T}•MARTINS•LEGRAND. Nott. Reading completed from Harris 2002, lot 522
7591a	1.30	20.1	Br	180°	*Mason,* Will—. nd. 3.6.22 (•WILL:MASON•IN•S^{T} around); M|WA (.M.|W A|•; •MARTINS LE GRAND around). BW —; Dickinson 2650A. Nott [ex Taffs]. Die-clashing evident on rev.
7591b	0.91	14.0	Br	0°	Same dies. [Baldwin]
					Porter, Will— *see* 'ST MARTIN'S' (Uncertain I)
7592	0.94	14.5	Br	0°	*Rickards,* Samuel (SAMVELL). 1666. 2.1.12; S R. BW 2654 but SAMVELL. Nott. Reading SAMVELL confirmed from BM specimen. ?Samuel Rickard, Draper, free 1663; will, PCC, 1707, Newington Butts [Newington, Surrey]; son of Philip Rickard of St Martin le Grand (Boyd 38709)
7593	2.20	33.9	Cu	180°	*Thompson,* Ralph. nd ½d. 3.4.35; 5.77. BW 2659 but S^{T}, HALF. Nott [ex Spink]
7594	0.57	8.7	Cu	180°	*Thorne,* George. nd. 5.13.23; G T. BW 2660 but LEGRAND. Nott. Obv. legend starts between 10 and 11 o'clock
7595	2.40	37.0	Cu	0°	*Waller,* John. [16]64 ½d. 3.10.1 (•IOHN•WALLER•HIS•HALF•PENY around); W|II (•W•|I•I|•; •IN•S^{T}MARTINS•LEGRAND•64 around). BW —; Dickinson 2660B. Baldwin
7596	1.41	21.7	Br	180°	*Wilson,* Jos—, chandler. 1669 ½d. 3.7.34 (W|IM); 5.77. BW 2663 but IOS:, LEGRAND. Nott [ex Taffs]
Named signs					
					Black [*?Eagle*]: Lee, Joseph *see* 'ST MARTIN'S' (Uncertain I)
7597a	1.22	18.8	Br	180°	*Blackamoor's Head* (THE BLACKMORES HEAD): ?F—, E—. nd. 3.5.37; F|EA. BW 2642 but BLACKMORES, S•MARTINS; Dickinson 31A, from a report of this specimen. Nott [ex Taffs]
7597b	0.93 (chipped)	14.3	Br	180°	Same dies. Baldwin
7598	0.71	11.0	Br	270°	*Cross Keys* (AT Y^{E}CROSSE KEYES): ?H—, T—. nd. 5.66.20; T H. BW 2644 but ST:. Nott [ex Taffs]
7599	0.95	14.7	Br	180°	*Harrow* (THE HAROW): ?T—, T—. nd. 5.17.13; T|TA. BW 2658 but WITH•IN•ALDERS•GATE. Nott [ex Taffs]
					King's Head: Marriott, Matt— *see* 'ST MARTIN'S' (Uncertain I)
7600	1.18	18.2	Br	180°	*Sun* (THE SONNE): ?M—, T—. nd. 2.1; M|TA. BW 2649 but ALLDERS•GATE. Nott [ex Taffs]

ST MARTIN LE GRAND liberty/street (*cont.*). 'The Boarded Entry'

The reading is THE BORDET ENTRY IN S MARTINES LEGRAND

	Weight *g*	*gr*		*Die axis*	
7601a	1.14	17.6	M	180°	*?S—,* W—. nd. 5.14 Drapers; S|WA. BW 2656 but BORDET. [Nott]
7601b	0.96	14.8	M	180°	Same dies. Nott [ex Spink]

ST MARY AT HILL (*street*) (Billingsgate ward) [38-J15]

The reading is ON ST MARY HILL on 7608, S^{T}MARY HILL on 7602-3, S^{T} MARYS HILL on 7604; S^{T}MARYS HILL on 7605-7 (Ṣ˙ on 7605); cf. 7609-10

7602	1.40	21.6	Br	180°	*Galatly,* James. 1668 ½d. 5.12.1; 5.77. BW 2685. Nott. James Gallantly [Golightly] of St Peter Cornhill, Haberdasher, perfumer; bd. St Mary at Hill 1674 (Boyd 22833)
7603a	1.89	29.2	Cu	0°	*Hive,* John. 1667 ½d. 5.3.10; 5.77 (H|ID). BW 2687 but ON•S^{T}MARY. [Nott ex Taffs]
7603b	1.66	25.6	Cu	0°	Same dies. Nott
7604	0.91	14.1	Cu	180°	*Lawrence,* Edmond. nd. 5.14 Fishmongers; L|EE. BW 2691. Nott [ex Taffs]. Edmund Lawrence bound apprentices 1655-74 (Webb 1996-, xliv. 38, 129, 136)
7605	1.04	16.0	M	180°	*Lawrence,* Edmond. nd. 5.14 Fishmongers; L|EE. *BW 2691 (S^{T}). Nott. See also 7604. Same obv. die as 7606
7606	0.91	14.1	M	180°	*Lawrence,* Edmond. nd. 5.14 Fishmongers; L|EE. BW 2691. [Nott ex Daniels]. Same obv. die as 7605, q.v.
7607a	1.96	30.2	Br	180°	*Lawrence,* Edmond. nd ½d. 5.77; 5.14 Fishmongers. BW 2690. [Nott ex Taffs]. See also 7604
7607b	1.59	24.5	Br	180°	Same dies. Nott
7608	2.86	44.1	Cu	0°	*North,* Margaret (MARGRET). 1668 ½d. 5.13.18; 5.77. BW 2692. Nott [ex Taffs]. Reading completed from BM specimen. Margaret, widow of John North (d. 1665), ?md. (2) William Devon, vintner (Hume 1974, pp. 116-19)

ST MARY AT HILL neighbourhood

The reading is AT S^{T}MARY HILL on 7609, S^{T} MARY HILL on 7610

7609	0.58	9.0	Br	60°	*Lafton,* Will, mealman (MEAL|MAN). nd. 4.10.1; L|WS. BW 2689 but S^{T}. Nott [ex Taffs]. Reading S^{T} confirmed from MoL specimen

Named signs

7610 (corroded, chipped)	0.87	13.4	Br	180°	*King's* [*?Arms*] (AT Y^{E}): Hall, William (WILLIAṂ). 1668 ½d. 5.14.5; 5.77 (H|WK). *BW 2686 but MARY•HILL. Nott [ex Taffs]. Reading largely confirmed from BM specimen

ST MARY AXE (*street*) (Lime Street & Aldgate wards) [28-G16]

See also AXE YARD. The reading is SENMARYACTS

7611	1.00	15.4	M	0°	*Dell,* Mary. 1657. 5.70.1; M D. BW 2694. Nott [ex Taffs]. Reading completed from MoL specimen

ST MARY LE BOW neighbourhood (Cordwainer & Cheap wards, Cheapside) [25-H10]

The reading is VNDER BOW CHVRCH IN CHEAPSIDE

Named signs

7612	1.14	17.5	M	180°	*King's Head:* ?E[aton], E[dward]. nd. E|EM; E|EM. BW 580. Seaby, [*SCMB* April 1967]. Edward Eaton had children bap. at St Mary le Bow 1653-9; Martha Eaton, widow, occurs 1674 (Rogers 1931, p. 46)

ST MARY MAGDALENE MILK STREET neighbourhood (Cripplegate ward Within) [25-G10: Honey Lane Market]/ST MARY MAGDALENE OLD FISH STREET neighbourhood (Castle Baynard ward) [35-I9]

See also 'MARY MAUDLIN'S'. The reading is NEARE MAVLINS $CV^{H}RCH$

7613a	0.99	15.2	Br	180°	*Green,* George (GEORG). nd. 5.38.1; G G. BW 2724 but THE, MAVLINS:$CV^{H}RCH$ [*sic*], colon stops throughout. [?Baldwin]. E of THE thin, perhaps engraved individually onto die; possibly a superscript D above VL. Reading largely confirmed from MoL specimen. ?George Green of St Lawrence Jewry (1628-?1675), Goldsmith (Boyd 20429); if so, the Milk Street location (near Cheapside) would be more likely. On the misreading of this token see Greenall 1991, p. 104, n. 9
7613b	0.88	13.6	Br	180°	Same dies. Nott

[*continued overleaf*]

7601b 7602 7603b 7604 7605 7606

7607b 7608 7609 7610 7611 7612

7613b 7614a 7615 7616 7617 7618

7619 7620 7621a 7622 7623a 7624

Plate 50 (*cont.*)

ST MICHAEL QUEENHITHE parish (Queenhithe ward) [35-J10]

The reading is MICHELLS QVEENE HITH

	Weight g	*gr*		*Die axis*	
7614a	1.45	22.3	Br	180°	*Stevenson,* Percival (PEARCIVALL). nd ½d. 4.12.2; 5.77 (S|PE). BW 2311. [Nott ex Taffs]
7614b	0.94 (chipped)	14.5	Br	180°	Same dies. [Baldwin]. Another, not now in the collection, die axis 0°, ex Nott

ST MICHAEL'S ALLEY (Cornhill ward) [27-H14, i70: Michael's Alley]

The reading is *St Michells Ally*

Named signs

7615 1.58 (chipped) 24.4 Cu 180° *[Backler's] coffee-house, formerly Bowman's (At the ould Coffee house, formerly Bomans):* Hayward, Steph[en] [and] Backler, Geo[rge]. nd ½d. 3.6.51; 5.77.1. BW 2695 but STEPH:, GEO:, *S^{t}*, no stops visible in rev. legend. Nott. Reading completed from BM and MoL specimens. The first coffee-house in London, set up c.1652 by Christopher Bowman, bd. 1662; George Backler and Stephen Hayward assessed together on 8 hearths 1668 (Aubrey 1898, i. 110; Rogers 1928a, pp. 90-1, 1935, pp. 30-1). Sign name from Lillywhite 1972, no. 62

ST MICHAEL'S LANE *subsequently* MILES LANE (Candlewick ward & Bridge ward Within) [37-J14]

Often called *Crooked Lane* (Rogers 1928b, p. 47); see also 'MILES CROOKED LANE'. The reading is MICALS LANE on 7619; S M C L on 7617-18; the place is unnamed on 7616

7616 2.06 31.8 Pb 0° *Flower,* Christopher (CRISTOPHER). nd. 4.13.1 ([fleur-de-lis]•; •CRISTOPHER•FLOWER around); 5.14 Innholders 2 (••|•[Arms]•). BW —; Gilbert 1927, 349 (this specimen); Dickinson, Uncertain 62D but early Innholders' arms. [Baldwin ex Gilbert ex Day -1926]. Attributed to Christopher Flower, Innholder, to be bd. St Michael Crooked Lane (Prob/11/233, proved 1654; Boyd 48142). The Flore de Luces existed in St Michael's Lane 1638 (Dale 1931, p. 147). Cf. Caldecott 1907, fig. 12 (different dies). See also 7323

7617 1.13 17.4 Br 180° *H[ardwin]*, G[race] (m.), wax-chandler (VAX CHANDLLER). nd. H|GE; 3.52.35. BW Uncertain 88 but VAX•CHANDLLER; BW Uncertain 13 but as 88 corrected. [Baldwin]. Attributed to Grace Hardwin (Hardman), Wax Chandler, who bound apprentices 1668-9 (Webb 1996-, xxxi. 15, 25); md. Hester [otherwise Esther] Daws 1621; Master 1650-52 (Boyd 25388; Dummelow 1973, p. 170). Grace Harden at Cowe's face, St Michael's Lane, 1638 (Dale 1931, i. 147); Grace Harding paid for a foundation in Crooked Lane 1668 (Mills 1962-7, i. 23); will of Grace Hardwin, St Michael Crooked Lane, house called the Cowes face, PCC, 1672/1679. The Cowface and the Cowhead were both names for a house in Cheapside (Rogers 1931, pp. 76-8), so the letters SMCLATCH may be expanded as St Michael Crooked Lane At The Cow's Head. Same rev. die as 7618

7618 1.02 15.7 Br 180° *H[ardwin]*, G[race] (m.), wax-chandler (VAX CHANDLLER). nd. H|GE; 3.52.35. BW Uncertain 88 but VAX•CHANDLLER; BW Uncertain 13 but as 88 corrected. [Nott ex Carthew]. Same rev. die as 7617, q.v.

ST MICHAEL'S LANE. Swan neighbourhood

The reading is IN MICALS LANE NEER THE OLD SWAN, which appears to be the same as the (old) Swan tavern in Crooked Lane, consumed 1666, dating from 1537 but distinct from the Old Swan in Thames Street (Lillywhite 1972, 14243, 11046). For the Swan see 6839 and BW 802; it is marked on the map in Rogers 1928b, pp. 44-9

7619 2.38 36.8 Br 270° *Nutt,* Thomas. nd ½d. 3.109.1; 5.77. BW 2696. Baldwin [ex Pridmore]

ST NICHOLAS LANE *subsequently* NICHOLAS LANE (Langbourn & Candlewick wards) [37-I14]

The reading is S NICOLAS LANE on 7621; S^{T} NICHOLAS LANE on 7620

7620 2.02 31.1 Cu 0° *Dodsworth,* Francis. nd ½d. 3.11; 5.77. BW 2698. Nott. Struck off-centre. Reading confirmed from BM specimen. 'Coffee-Berrie . . . is to be seen every day at the house of Mr Francis Dodsworth at the Signe of the Golden Lyon at the upper end of St Nicholas Lane' 1663 (BW 2698 n.)

Named signs

7621a 1.15 17.8 M 180° *Bell* (AT THE BEL): B[illingsly], J[ohn]. nd. 5.70.1; B|IK. BW 2697. Baldwin. John Billingsly (1616-1680), of St Martin Orgar, Vintner; 1648 md. Catherine who d. 1669 (Boyd 23986, 31251; Woodhead 1966, p. 31). The Bell in St Nicholas Lane conveyed to him 1655 (Rogers 1928a, p. 91, 1937, p. 55). He paid for a foundation 1667 (Mills 1962-7, i. 52). John Billingsley appr. a Vintner 1634; bound apprentices 1646-76 (Webb 1996-, xliii. 29, 339)

7621b 0.92 14.2 M 180° Same dies. [Nott ex Taffs]

ST NICHOLAS SHAMBLES *see* The SHAMBLES

ST PAUL'S CATHEDRAL (Castle Baynard ward). East End neighbourhood [25-H9]

The reading is AT Y^{E}EAST END OF S^{T} PAVLS; cf. 7623-9

Named signs

	Weight g	Weight gr		Die axis	
7622	2.51	38.7	Cu	0°	*Lamb & Ink-bottle* (THE): Rooks, Tho[mas] (THỌ), [ink-maker]: 'best ink for records'. nd ½d. (ob'). 5.77 (THE|LAMB &|INK BOTTLE|AT Y^{E}EAST|END OF S^{T}|PAVLS); 5.77 (ṬHER THỌ|ROOKS MA. . .|Y^{E}BEST INK|FOR RECORDS|ob'). BW —; cf. Sharman 1994. [Longman] 1958, lot 452, bt by Spink for the Norwebs not Nott, *pace* Preston-Morley 1994. Letters of irregular size both sides; tittle on b of ob. The rev. is probably to be understood as *Ther*[*e*] *Tho*[*mas*] *Rooks makes*..., cf. Larwood 1866, pp. 229-30 (Thomas Roch). Thomas Rook(e)s, stationer & bookseller, Lamb, at the East End of St Paul's 1658-66, made a speciality of writing inks (Plomer 1907, pp. 156-7). Holy Lamb near the school 1661; Lamb & Ink-bottle 1660-71, 'has changed his sign from the Holy Lamb' (Price 1906, pp. 137, 139), date of change unclear. See also Heal 1931, p. 147, and Hyde in Ogilby 1676, p. v (Thomas Rookes)

ST PAUL'S CATHEDRAL. West End neighbourhood [24-H8]

The reading is AT THE WEST END OF S^{T} PAVLS LONDON; cf. 7622, 7624-9

Named signs

7623a	5.59	86.3	Br	180°	[*Turk's Head*] *coffee-house* (THE COFFE HOVSE): [anonymous]. nd. 3.5.43; 5.76.159. BW 2730 but COFFE, no denomination. Baldwin. The Bishop of London in 1662 leased to John Hayes a coffee-house, the sign of the Turkes Head, then in the possession of Luke Petley, parish of St Gregory (Fire Court 1966-, ii. 138). Sign name as Lillywhite 1972, no. 1414, but also listed as The Coffee House (no. 1335, p. 551), Petley's (no. 1651), and Turkes Head (no. 1658). Possibly visited by Pepys 1663 (Pepys 1970-83, iv. 80). The diameters of the Norweb specimens vary between 24 and 25 mm, suggesting a penny
7623b	3.84	59.3	Cu	180°	Same dies. [?Baldwin]
7623c	3.47	53.5	Br	180°	Same dies. [Nott]
7623d	3.24	49.9	Br	180°	Same dies. [Nott ex Taffs]

ST PAUL'S CATHEDRAL neighbourhood [24-H8]

The reading is AT S^{T} PAVLES CHVR^{CH}; cf. 7622-3, 7625-9

Green, George *see* 7613 (St Mary Magdalene neighbourhood)

Named signs

7624	1.07	16.5	Cu	0°	*St Peter & St Paul* (AT S^{T} PETER AND S^{T} PAVLE): H[anson], F[rancis]. nd. 3.5.70; 3.5.71. BW 2725. Nott [ex Baldwin]. Reading completed from Greenall 1997, pl. 4.126. The Turk's Head (see 7623) 'abutting... east on the Peter and Paul in the possession of Francis Hanson' (Fire Court 1966-, ii. 138-9)

ST PAUL'S CHURCHYARD (Castle Baynard ward) [34-I8]

The reading is PALLES CHVRCH YARD on 7625; PAVLES CHVRCH YARD on 7626, YEARD on 7629, CHVRCHEYARD on 7627; S PAVLS CHVRCH YARD on 7628; cf. 7622-4

Weight (*g*, *gr*) — *Die axis*

7625 0.95 14.7 Cu 0° *Chester,* Tho— (ṬHO). nd. 5.64.15 (•ṬHO•CHESTER•AT•THE around); 5.14 Grocers (•PALLES•CHVRCH•YARD around). BW —; *Dickinson 2723A. Spink 1975 ex Mabbot[t]. ?Thomas Chester of St Bartholomew by the Exchange, Grocer; md. Elizabeth Lewis 1653 (Boyd 23233). John Pottinger bound to him 1654 (Woodhead 1966, p. 133)

7626 1.05 16.2 Cu 180° *Dickenson,* John. nd. 5.64.1; I D. BW 2720 but CHVRCH•YARD. Nott [ex Taffs]

Named signs

7627a 1.17 18.0 M 180° *Samson* (AT THE): ?C—, W—. nd. 3.1.11; C|WA. BW 2718. Nott [ex Taffs]

7627b 1.11 17.2 M 180° Same dies. [Nott]

7627c 0.79 12.1 (chipped) M 180° Same dies. [Nott]

7628a 0.95 14.7 M 180° *Three Tuns tavern* (AT THE 3 TVNN TAVERNE): C[lare], E[lizabeth]. nd. 5.64.33; E C. BW 2716. Nott. Rev. legend starts at 9 o'clock. John Clare of St Gregory, Vintner; at the Three Tuns 1641; will, PCC, 1653, relict Elizabeth (Boyd 45000). Apprentices bound to Elizabeth Clare 1650, to Elizabeth widow of John Clare 1655-74 (Webb 1996-, xliii. 188, 346). Her estate had come to another in trust, 1668 (Fire Court 1966-, i. 199, 200). See also Rogers 1928a, p. 91

7628b 0.92 14.1 (chipped) Br 180° Same dies. [Nott]

7629a 1.09 16.8 Br 180° *Tobacco Roll* (THE TOBACCO ROWLE): ?H—, S—. nd. 5.82.1; H|SM. BW 2727 but YEARD. [Baldwin]

7629b 0.97 14.9 Br 180° Same dies. Nott [ex Carthew]

7629c 0.74 11.5 Br 180° Same dies. [Nott ex Taffs]

'ST PAUL'S MARKET' *i.e.* ?ST PAUL'S CHURCHYARD (Castle Baynard ward) [34-I8] *see* Uncertain I

ST PETER'S HILL *and* PAUL'S WHARF neighbourhood *see* PAUL'S WHARF *and* ST PETER'S HILL neighbourhood

ST SWITHIN'S LANE (Walbrook & Langbourn wards) [37-I13]

The reading is S SWETHINS LANE on 7630; S^{T}SWITHENS LANE on 7631; S^{T}SWITHINS LANE on 7632; SWETHINS LANE on 7633

7630 1.19 18.4 Cu 210° *Clarke,* Samuel (SAMWELL). nd. S C; 3.1.105. BW 2732. Nott

7631 1.39 21.4 Cu 180° *Emet,* Wm. nd ½d. 3.49.12; 5.77. BW 2733 but obv. and rev. transposed. Nott [ex Taffs]

7632 0.64 9.9 Br 180° *Langhorne,* Rob—. nd. 3.5.79 (•ROB:LANGHORN$^{E:}$IN around); L|RE (•L•|R•E|•; •S^{T}SWITHINS•LANE around). BW —; Dickinson 2733B. Nott. Description confirmed from Sedgwick 1986, pl. 2.49. Robert Langhorn, Innholder, will, PCC, 1665, widow Emma (Boyd 17803). Prob/11/318 mentions son Robert and appoints as overseer Thomas Phipps of St Mary Woolnoth, so confirming location. Bound apprentices 1661-2; the 1681 apprenticeship must have been to his son (Webb 1996-, xvii. 34)

Named signs

7633 1.73 26.7 Cu 0° *Meal shop* (AT THE MEALE SHOPP): ?C—, I/J— (f.). 1666 ½d. 4.10.6 (I C); 5.77. BW 2731. Nott [ex Spink]

ST THOMAS APOSTLE parish (Vintry *and* Cordwainer wards) [36-I11]

The reading is LON[don]; the parish is unnamed

7634 1.49 23.0 Cu 0° *Olliffus* [i.e. *Oliffe*], Ralph (RADVLPHVS), 'made it in Lon[don]' (FECIT LON). 1629. 3.1.123 (IN HORAS AD ARMA SVM PARATVS around); 1.42.4. BW Uncertain 115 but SVM•PARATVS, RADVLPHVS•OLLIFFVS; Thompson 2002b. [Baldwin]. Struck off-centre. Attributed to Ralph Oliffe (d. 1636), Cooper, of St Thomas Apostle; 'Gent', son of John Oliffe of Shipton Oliffe, Glos. (Vis. Som. 1672, p. 39), where in 1608 [?the issuer's uncle] Ralph Oliffe, gent., aged 'about Forty', was a trained soldier, and of the tallest stature fit to make a pikeman (Smith 1980, pp. 1, 274)

[*continued overleaf*]

7625 7626 7627b 7628b 7629b 7630

7631 7632 7633 7634 7635 7636b

7637 7638 7639 7640a 7641 7642

7643a 7644 7645 7646 7647a 7648

ST THOMAS APOSTLES backside *subsequently* LITTLE ST THOMAS APOSTLES (Cordwainer & Vintry wards) [36-I11]

The reading is IN Y^{E} BACK SIDE OF S^{T} THO:APOSTLES, cf. *Backside of St Thomas Apostles* 1722, 1732 (Harben 1918, p. 355)

	Weight g	Weight gr		Die axis	
7635	1.06	16.4	Br	0°	*R[edman]*, H[enry]. nd. 3.5.54; R|HM. BW 2736 but Y^{E}•BACK. Nott. Rev. legend starts at 10 o'clock. Probably the issuer was Henry Redman, of St Thomas Apostle 1660, who supplied wine to the church (Rogers 1928a, p. 91). Henry Redman, Vintner; md. (1) Isabel d. 1654, (2) Mary; will, PCC, 1676, St Dunstan in the West (Boyd 25301). Appr. 1642; apprentices bound to him 1658-74, and to Mary his widow 1676-81 (Webb 1996-, xliii. 245, 378). See also Middlesex I: Holborn: Chancery Lane: Redman [at the Pope's Head], a sign name which Rogers also applies here; but this bust has none of the attributes of a pope, and might as well represent St Thomas

SALISBURY COURT (Farringdon ward Without, Fleet Street) [33-I5]

The reading is SALSBVRY COVRT on 7637, COVRTE on 7636

7636a	1.22	18.8	Br	0°	*Burmby,* Richard. nd. 5.14 Tallow Chandlers; B|RM. BW 2738. Baldwin [or Nott ex Carthew]. Richard Burmbie appr. 1648; Richard Burnby [*sic*] bound an apprentice 1657 (Webb 1996-, xxxix. 16, 104)
7636b	0.73	11.2	Br	0°	Same dies. [Nott ex Taffs]

Named signs

7637	1.28	19.8	Br	90°	*Cat* (AT Y^{E}CATT): Harvey, Will— (WILL;). nd. 3.63.1; H|WA. BW 2739 but WILL;. Nott

SCALDING ALLEY *subsequently* ST MILDRED'S COURT (Broad Street & Cheap wards) [26-H12, i60]

The reading is SCAVLDING ALLEY on 7638; the place is unnamed on 7639

7638	0.91	14.0	Br	0°	*Russell,* Francis. [16]57. 5.14 Clothworkers; R|FE. BW 2751. Nott

Named signs

7639	2.15	33.2	Cu	0°	*Post House coffee-house (at y^{e})*: Lansdell, John. nd ½d. 5.77.1 (*Iohn|Lansdell·at|y^{e}post house|Coffee•house|•••*); 3.5.45 (HIS HALF PENY). BW —; Dickinson 2750A but *Coffee*, inscription in italic. Baldwin. Reading confirmed from MoL specimen. John Lansdell, b. 1632, Vintner, coffee-man (Boyd 30283). Placed like BW 2750 in Scalding Alley, parish of St Mildred Poultry, where John, son of John Lansdel, was bap. 1657 (IGI), and Susan Lansdell was bd. 1664, St Christopher le Stocks but carried to St Mildred Poultry. After the Fire, however, 'Mr Lansdell's Child, the Coffeeman' was bd. 12 Oct 1666, and John, son of John Lansdall 'Coffeman', was bap. 1668, both at St Helen Bishopsgate (Harl. Reg. 31 (1904), pp. 43, 312). His coffee-house might refer either to the Post-house at the junction of Threadneedle Street and Cornhill, opposite the Stocks, or to the Post-house in Bishopsgate Street, cf. BW 261. Surname from Lonsdale

SEACOAL LANE (Farringdon ward Without) [23-G6]

The reading is SEACOALE LANE on 7644; SEACOL:LANE on 7643; SEACOLE LANE on 7640-2

7640a	2.28	35.2	Br	180°	*Barker,* George. [16]66. 5.64.34 (B|GA); 4.10.1. BW 2755. [Nott ex Taffs]. Reading confirmed from BM specimen
7640b	2.04	31.4	Br	180°	Same dies. Spink 1971
7641	0.95	14.6	Cu	0°	*Mereifeild,* John. nd. 5.14 Blacksmiths; M|IM. BW 2757. Nott. Same obv. die as 7642 (q.v.); rev. reading completed from BM specimen
7642	1.25	19.3	Cu	270°	*Mereifeild,* John. nd. 5.14 Blacksmiths; M|IM. BW 2757. [?Baldwin]. Same obv. die as 7641. John Merriefeild appr. 1654; bound apprentices 1667-89 (Webb 1996-, xli. 152, 288)

Named signs

7643a	1.47	22.7	Cu	180°	*Red [?Cross]* (AT): West, Rich—. 1662. 1.44; W|RS. BW 2758 but SEACOL:. Baldwin
7643b	1.37	21.2	Cu	180°	Same dies. [Nott ex Taffs]

SEACOAL LANE. 'The Pump' neighbourhood

The reading is AT THE PVMP IN SEACOALE LANE

	Weight			*Die*	
	g	*gr*		*axis*	
7644	1.47	22.7	Br	0°	*Hone,* Giles. [16]68 ½d. 5.14.190 (•GILES•HONE•AT•THE•PVMP around); 5.77 (H|GD) (HIS|HALF|PENY|H|G.D; •IN•SEACOALE•LANE•68 around). BW —; Searle 1902, 2756 bis but SEACOALE; Dickinson 2756A. Baldwin. Reading completed from BM specimen

SEETHING LANE (Tower ward) [39-I17]

The reading is SEATHING LANE on 7645, 7649; SEETHING LANE on 7646-8

7645	1.40	21.6	Br	180°	*Babington,* Ann. nd ½d. 5.77 (HER|HALF|PENY; •ANN•BABINGTON around); 5.60.1 (•IN•SEATHING•LANE around). BW —; Dickinson 2758A. Baldwin [ex Macfadyen, lot 157]
7646	0.93	14.4	Cu	90°	*Rivers,* Thomas. nd. 5.14 Grocers; R|TI. BW 2761. Nott [ex Spink]
7647a	1.01	15.6	M	180°	*Vaston,* William. nd. 3.3.13; W V. BW 2762. Nott [ex Taffs]. See also 7212, perhaps the same issuer since the surname is rare
7647b	0.76	11.7	M	180°	Same dies. [Baldwin]
7647c	0.55 (chipped)	8.5	M	180°	Same dies. [Nott]

Named signs

7648	2.03	31.3	Br	0°	*Black Dog* (AT Y^{E}): Bonnick, Ralph. [16]68 ½d. 3.67.1; 5.77 (B|RL). BW 2759 but B|R L. Nott [ex Carthew]. Reading confirmed from MoL specimen

SEETHING LANE (*cont.*)

Named signs (*cont.*)

	Weight g	Weight gr		Die axis	
7649	2.98	45.9	Br	0°	*Pied Dog* (AT THE PIDE DOG): Radcliffe, Edward. 1667 ½d. 3.67.32 (R|EM); 5.77. BW 2760. Nott. Reading completed from BM specimen

The SHAMBLES *subsequently* NEWGATE STREET (Farringdon ward Within) [24-G7]

S.N. shambles may be seen in Prockter 1979, p. 8. The reading is NICKLES SHAMBLES on 7656; S NICHALAS SHAMBLES on 7658; S NICHOLAS SHAMBLES on 7650, 7660; S NICKLES SHAMBLES on 7655, 7657; S^{T} NICOLAS SHAMBLES on 7653; S^{T}̣NICOLAṢ SHAMBLES on 7652; S^{T}NICOḶAS S. . . on 7651; SHAMBLS on 7659, THE SHAMBLES on 7661-3; VPPER END OF SHAMBLS on 7654

7650	1.77	27.3	Br	0°	*Aspinall,* Joh—. nd ½d. 3.102.1; 5.7.44. BW 2700 but IOH:. Nott [ex Taffs]. Reading confirmed from BM specimen. No sign of superscript T before NICHOLAS, but stop low to accommodate it. Subsequently gilt. John Aspinal of Christ Church (1630-1673), Innholder (Boyd 24732). Bound apprentices 1660-64 (Webb 1996-, xvii. 31)
7651	0.79	12.1	Br	90°	*Bullock,* John. nd. 5.64.1 (•IOHN•BVLLOCK•AT•THE around); B|IṂ (B|IṂ; IN S^{T}NICOḶAS•S. . . around). BW —; *Dickinson 2700A. Nott [ex Sotheby 25 July 1938, lot 88, attributed to St Nicholas Street]
7652	1.90	29.3	Cu	330°	*Harper,* John. nd ½d. (HAḶF̣– PENṆY). 5.64.30; 5.77. *BW 2708 but HAḶF̣–|PENṆY. Baldwin. Reading partly completed from BM specimen
7653	2.02	31.2	Br	120°	*Hurst,* Richard. nd ½d. 3.102.1; 5.77. BW 2707. Spink 1975. Richard Hurst, Cook; bd. St Vedast 1681 (Boyd 25819). Richard Hurst, son of John (see 7661-3, BEHIND the Shambles), appr. 1658; bound apprentices 1669-79 (Webb 1996-, xxvi. 29, 67)
7654a	1.31	20.2	Br	180°	*Lyfe,* William. nd. 5.64.15 (•WILLIAM•LYFE•AT around); W L (•|W•̣L|•; VPPER END.OF SHAMBLS around). BW —; Dickinson, Middlesex 186A (Shadwell), from a report of this specimen. Nott [ex Carthew], on whose tickets attributed to Shadwell. Diameter 16-16.5 mm
7654b	0.74	11.4	Br	0°	Same dies. Baldwin, on whose ticket surname read as 'Dyer'. Diameter 15 mm
7655a	1.09	16.9	M	180°	*?S—,* E—, the tallow-chandler (CAHANDLER). nd. 3.3.13; S|EA. BW 2713. Nott
7655b	1.04	16.1	M	180°	Same dies. [Nott ex Daniels]

Named signs

7656	0.79	12.2	M	180°	*Butchers' Arms* (AT THE BVCHERS ARMES): ?M—, I/J—. nd. 5.14 Butchers 2; M|IS. BW 2710. Nott [ex Carthew]. Reading completed from BM specimen
7657	1.34	20.6	Br	180°	*Flying Horse* (AT THE): ?B—, P—. nd. 3.62.1; B|PM. BW 2701. Nott [ex Taffs]
7658	1.00 (pierced)	15.4	M	210°	*Red Lion* (AT THE RED LYON): ?C—, A—. nd. 3.11; C|AE. BW 2703. Nott. Obv. legend starts at 3 o'clock

The SHAMBLES neighbourhood

The reading is BACKSIDE SHAMBLS on 7659; BEHIND S NICHOLAS SHAMBLES on 7660; BEHIND THE SHAMBLES on 7661-3

7659a	1.40	21.6	Br	0°	*Larke,* Joseph. nd. 5.14 Grocers; I L. BW 2709. [Nott ex Taffs]
7659b	1.22	18.8	Br	0°	Same dies. Nott [ex Carthew]

Named signs

7660	0.99	15.3	M	180°	*Red Cross* (THE READ CROSE): ?B—, T—. nd. 1.44; B|TE. BW 2702. Nott [ex Taffs]. Reading confirmed from BM specimen
7661	0.80 (pierced and plugged)	12.3	M	225°	*Swan* (AT THE SWANN): H[urst], J[ohn]. 1649. 3.102.1; H|IM. BW 2706. Nott. Same rev. die as 7662-3. 'Mr Hurst who keeps the Swan behinde St Nicholas Shambles' 1648 (BW 2707 n.). John Hurst, Cook, bound an apprentice 1656; son Richard (see 7653, IN St Nicholas Shambles) appr. to Mary, widow of John Hurst, 1658 (Webb 1996-, xxvi. 29, 42)
7662a	1.32	20.4	M	150°	*Swan* (AT THE SWANN): H[urst], J[ohn]. 1649. 3.102.1; H|IM. BW 2706. [Nott ex Taffs]. Obv. legend starts at 1 o'clock. Same rev. die as 7661 (q.v.), 7663
7662b	1.23	18.9	M	150°	Same dies. No provenance
7662c	0.91	14.0	M	150°	Same dies. [Nott] ex 'C.B.'
7663	1.20	18.5	M	135°	*Swan* (AT THE SWANN): H[urst], J[ohn]. 1649 [i.e. 1658 o.s.]. 3.102.1; H|IM. BW 2706. Nott. Obv. legend starts between 1 and 2 o'clock. Datable from N punch (see Dickinson forthcoming). Same rev. die as 7661 (q.v.), 7662

[*continued overleaf*]

7649 7650 7651 7652 7653 7654a

7655a 7656 7657 7658 7659b 7660

7661 7662c 7663 7664 7665 7666

7667 7668a 7669 7670 7671b 7672

Plate 52 (*cont.*)

SHARP'S ALLEY (Farringdon ward Without *and* Middlesex: Finsbury) *see* Middlesex I: Finsbury; *see also* Uncertain I

SHIRE LANE (Farringdon ward Without *and* Middlesex: Westminster) *see* Middlesex I: Westminster

SHOE LANE (Farringdon ward Without) [22-G4]

The reading is SHEW LANE on 7677; SHOE LANE on 7667, 7675; SHOO LANE on 7381, 7666; SHOOE LANE on 7378-9, 7665, 7668-72, 7676, 7678, ṢHOOE ḶẠṆE on 7664; SHOOELANE on 7673; SHOOWE LAYNE on 7380; SHOWE LANE on 7674; SHVE LANE on 7679

	Weight			*Die*	
	g	*gr*		*axis*	
7664	1.56 (chipped)	24.0	Br	180°	. . .*hart* ([?. . .]HARṬ), ?Abigail (. . .E–ALL. . .). 16̣6̣5̣ ½d. 5.70.18 (. . .E–ALL. . . HARṬ•AT•Ṭ– – around); 5.77 (HER|HALFE|PENNY|•••; •IN•ṢHOOE•ḶẠṆE•I6̣6̣5̣• around). BW —; Dickinson 2793B, from a report of this specimen. Nott. See also 7673
7665	2.86	44.2	Cu	0°	*Hiscock,* Robert. 1666 ½d. 3.7.34; 5.77. BW 2794. Nott. Reading of date completed from Greenall 1997, pl. 4.129. Robert Hiscocke (Hitchcock), Haberdasher (Woodhead 1966, p. 91). Foundation for Robert Hiscock(e), and one for Robert Hitchcocke, paid and set out 1668 (Mills 1962-7, i. 69, ii. 163-4)
7666	1.03	15.8	Br	90°	*?K—,* I/J—, pastry-cook (COOKE). 1657. 5.60.1; K|IH. BW 2802 but I657, •K•|I•H. Baldwin. Reading confirmed from Shuttlewood 2001, lot 648. *Pace* Rogers 1928a, p. 91, initials not those of John Renolds, yet by coincidence a foundation for him was set out 1669 'formerly the Sign of the Crowne in Shoe Lane' (Mills 1962-7, iii. 98v)
7667	0.96	14.8	Cu	0°	*Lawrence,* Ann. 1662. A L; date. BW 2797. Nott [ex Carthew]
7668a	2.83	43.7	Br	0°	*Mayne,* Elizabeth. 1668 ½d. 5.14 Merchant Taylors; 5.77 (E M). BW 2799. Nott [ex Taffs]. Diameter 21 mm
7668b	1.35 (pierced)	20.8	Br	180°	Same dies. Baldwin (record and ticket), Nott (envelope). Diameter 19 mm
7669	1.22	18.8	Br	0°	*Payne,* John, mealman (MEALEMAN). 1669 ½d. 5.77; P|ID. BW 2801. Nott [ex Taffs]. Reading confirmed from MoL specimen
7670	1.36	21.0	Cu	0°	*Winch,* Amos. nd ½d. 3.5.55; W|AM. BW 2807. Nott [ex Carthew]. Description completed from MoL specimen. Foundation set out for Mr Amos Winch 1670 (Mills 1962-7, i. 70, iii. 134)
Named signs					
7671a	4.09	63.1	Br	270°	*Ben Jonson's Head* (BENIOHNSONS HEAD): [?Johnson, William]. 1672. Date; 3.5.33. BW 2808. [Nott ex Taffs]. Suggested name of issuer from BW 2795, obv. read by Rogers 1928a, p. 97 as 'Imort…al Ben', i.e. Ben Jonson, who was poet laureate 1616-37; BW pl. xii.8 does not recognise the bust as laureate. A foundation set out for William Johnson 1667, 1671 (Mills 1962-7, i. 69-70, ii. 35v). The 24.5-25 mm diameter suggests a penny
7671b	3.62	55.8	Br	270°	Same dies. Nott [ex Carthew]. Diameter 24.5 mm
7672	3.15	48.7	Br	0°	*Cross Keys* (ATT THE CROSE KEYES): [anonymous]. nd 1d. 5.77; 5.66.30. BW 2809 but I^D^. Baldwin

SHOE LANE (*cont.*)

Named signs (*cont.*)

Weight g gr — *Die axis*

7673 1.43 22.1 Br 120° *Five Bells* (AT Y^E 5 BELLS): Catstree, Ann. nd. 5.70.15; A C. BW 2791 but SHOOELANE. Nott [ex Taffs]. See also 7664

7674 0.94 14.5 Br 180° *George* (AT Y^EGEORG): Fox, John. nd. 3.2.11 (•IOHN•FOX•AT•Y^EGEORG: around); F|IA (•F•|I•A|•; •IN•SHOWE•LANE•• around). BW —; Dickinson 2792A. Nott [ex Carthew]. Obv. legend starts between 10 and 11 o'clock, rev. at 11 o'clock. Fleur-de-lis counterstamp behind St George

7675a 3.52 54.3 Br 270° *Mansfield's coffee-house:* [Mansfield], [?]. nd, 'in Shoe Lane by providence'. 3.6.50; 5.32.4. BW 2798 but rev. description amended. [Nott ex Taffs]. Diameter 22.5-23 mm

7675b 2.67 41.2 Br 0° Same dies. Baldwin [or Nott]. Diameter 21.5-22 mm

7675c 2.41 37.2 Br 0° Same dies. [Nott ex Sotheby 25 July 1938, lot 88]. Diameter 22-22.5 mm

7676a 1.30 20.0 M 180° *Plough* (AT THE PLOW): Love, Richard. nd. 5.54 (•RICHARD•LOVE•AT•THE around); L|RD (•L•|R•D; •PLOW•IN•SHOOE•LANE around). BW —; Dickinson 2797A. Baldwin. See also 7677. Diameter 17 mm

7676b 1.01 15.5 M 180° Same dies. Spink 1975 ex ? ex Carthew. Diameter 15.5-16 mm

7677 1.33 20.6 Br 180° *Plough* (THE PLOWE): Hickin, Michael. nd. 5.54 (•MICHAEL•HICKIN•THE around); M H (M•H; •PLOWE•IN•SHEW•LANE around). BW —; Heal 1928, p. 15; Dickinson 2793A (this specimen). Baldwin [ex Macfadyen, lot 157]. I of forename double-entered. See also 7676

SHOE LANE. Windmill Inn neighbourhood [23-F5, A88 indexed as A81*bis*]

The symbol A88 appears to have been cancelled, but is *Wind Mill Inn* in Ogilby 1677, p. 16. The Windmill Inn is Lillywhite 1972, no. 16606. The reading is SHOOE LANE BEHIND THE WINDMILL

7678 2.38 36.8 Br 180° *Langworth,* Charles. nd ½d. 4.1.1; 5.77. BW 2796. Spink 1975. Reading confirmed from MoL specimen

SHOE LANE neighbourhood

The reading is AT SHVE LANE END

7679 1.44 22.2 Br 0° *Busher,* Jeremy, smoker. nd. B|IS (.B.|I S|•; •IEREMY:BVSHER•AT•SHVE around); 5.64.1 (•LANE•END:SMOKER•AT•Y^E around). BW —, cf. 2790. Seaby, [*SCMB* May 1971]. ?Jeremy or Jeremiah Busher, Girdler, b. 1632, md. Susan Larimore 1653 (Boyd 24835); or his father Jeremy, of St Mary Bothaw (Boyd 49837). Issuer presumably would have cured fish, bacon etc. by means of smoke, though cf. Roberts 1803, whose reference is Holme 1688, 3.6.61

SILVER STREET (Cripplegate & Farringdon wards Within) [15-E10]

The reading is SILVER STREET on both

7680a 0.88 (chipped) 13.6 M 180° *Laurence* (LAWRANCE), John. 1659. Date; L|IS. BW 2838. Nott [ex Taffs]. Form of surname from 7681

7680b 0.68 10.5 M 180° Same dies. [Nott]

7681 1.84 28.4 Cu 0° *Laurence,* John. 1665 ½d. 5.77; 5.77 (L|IS). BW 2837 but IN•SILVER. No provenance 1979. Reading confirmed from Dickinson, pl. 2

SMITHERS LANE (Billingsgate ward, Little Eastcheap) *subsequently* EASTCHEAP (part) [38-I15]

The portion of Little Eastcheap from St Mary (at) Hill west to Botolph Lane (Leake 1666; Harben 1918, p. 212). The reading is SMITHEY LANE

7682 0.57 (chipped) 8.8 Br 180° *Wilson,* Jarvis. nd. 2.4.7 (•IARVIS•WILSON• around); W|IS (•W•|I•S|•; •IN•SMITHEY•LANE• around). BW —. Baldwin. Jarvis Wilson of St Margaret Pattens, Grocer; md. Sarah Woodward 1662 (Boyd 19955)

SMITHFIELD, West *see* WEST SMITHFIELD

SMITHFIELD BARS neighbourhood (Farringdon ward Without *and* Middlesex: Finsbury) [13-D6]

See also Middlesex I: Finsbury: Smithfield Bars without. The reading is AT SMITHFEILD BARS on 7683, 7687-9, BARRS on 7684, 7686; SMITH FEILD BARRS on 7685; cf. 7690-2

7683 1.37 21.2 Br 180° *?B—,* T—, comfit (CVMFIT) maker. nd. 3.10.6; B|TH. BW 2886. Nott [ex Taffs]. See also 7686, 7688-9

7684a 1.68 25.9 Br 330° *Curtis,* Robert. 1669 ½d. 5.77; 4.13.7 (R C). BW 2891 but PENY. Nott [ex Carthew]

7684b 1.44 22.1 Br 330° Same dies. [Nott ex Taffs]

[*continued overleaf*]

7673 7674 7675b 7676b 7677 7678

7679 7680a 7681 7682 7683 7684a

7685a 7686 7687b 7688 7689 7690a

7691a 7692 7693a 7694 7695 7696b

Plate 53 (*cont.*)

	Weight g	Weight gr		Die axis	
7685a	1.10	17.0	Br	270°	*Streame,* Tho[mas], grocer. nd. 3.65.10; S|TM. BW 2898 but THO:STREAME, SMITH•FEILD. Nott [ex Taffs]. Thomas Stream, Grocer, wife Mary (d. 1674); both b. St Sepulchre (Boyd 58744). 'Mr Tho. Stream at the Bores-head in Smithfield' 1661 (BW 2898 n.). Thomas Stream(s) d. 1679 (Woodhead 1966, p. 157)
7685b	0.65	10.0	Br	90°	Same dies. Nott
Named signs					
7686	2.47	38.2	Cu	270°	*Angel* (AT Y^E^ANGELL): Fell, Thomas. [16]67 ½d. 3.10.2 (F|TI); 5.77. BW 2892 but SMITHFEILD. Nott [ex Taffs]. Reading SMITHFEILD confirmed from MoL specimen. See also 7683, 7688-9
7687a	2.40	37.1	M	0°	*Bull's Head* (AT THE): Bond, John. nd ½d. 3.52.26 (B|IM); 5.77. BW 2888. [?Baldwin]
7687b	2.39	36.9	M	0°	Same dies. Nott [ex Daniels]
7687c	1.59	24.6	M	0°	Same dies. [Spink 1973+]
7688	3.20	49.3	Br	0°	*Golden* [*?Angel*] (AT Y): Foljambe, Godfrey, confection[e]r. 1666 ½d. 3.10.1; 5.77. BW 2893 but Y•GOLDEN [*sic*], rev. AT•SMITHFEILD•BARS•CONFECTIONR =. Nott [ex Taffs]. Y of Y[e] double-entered. Same rev. die as 7689. See also 7683, 7686
7689	1.99	30.7	Br	0°	*Golden* [*?Angel*] (AT Y^E^): Foljambe, Godfrey, confection[e]r. 1666 ½d. 3.10.1; 5.77. BW 2893 but rev. AT•SMITHFEILD•BARS•CONFECTIONR =. Nott [ex Daniels]. Reading confirmed from MoL specimen. Same rev. die as 7688, q.v.

SMITHFIELD PENS neighbourhood (Farringdon ward Without) [13-E6]

The reading is OVER AGAINST Y^E^ SHIPPENS IN SMITH\|FEILD on both, i.e. The Sheep Pens; see also 'SMITHFIELD ROUNDS'

7690a	2.09	32.1	Br	0°	*Smith,* George, chees[e]monger. nd ½d. 5.77 (HIS|HALF|PENY|•••; •GEORGE•SMITH• CHEESMONGE^R^ around); 5.77 (•IN•|SMITH|FEILD|•••; •OVER•AGAINST•Y^E^• SHIPPENS: around). BW —; Dickinson 2878B. [Baldwin]. The superscript E weakly punched onto die: it resembles F
7690b	2.04	31.4	Br	0°	Same dies. [?Baldwin]
7690c	1.93	29.8	Br	0°	Same dies. Nott
7690d	1.22	18.9	Cu	180°	Same dies. [Nott ex Taffs]
7691a	2.22	34.3	Cu	180°	*Thomas,* Jeffrey (IEFFERY), grocer. nd ½d. 5.77; 5.77. BW 2880 but IEFFERY. Nott [ex Spink]. Diameter 21 mm
7691b	1.85	28.5	Cu	0°	Same dies. [Baldwin] ex Snell 1922. Diameter 19.5-20 mm
7691c	1.67	25.7	Cu	180°	Same dies. [Nott]. Diameter 21.5-22.5 mm
7691d	1.44	22.2	Cu	0°	Same dies. [Nott ex Taffs]. Diameter 19-19.5 mm

'SMITHFIELD ROUNDS' *i.e.* ?SMITHFIELD PENS (Farringdon ward Without)

The reading is *In Smithfeild Rounds*; possibly in error for *Pounds*, which would mean much the same as *Pens*

7692	1.79	27.6	Br	0°	*Inman,* Euodias, goldsmith (*Gouldsmith*). nd ½d. 5.77.1; 5.77.1. BW 2862. Nott. Reading confirmed from MoL specimen. The name *Euodias* occurs in Philippians 4: 2. Euodias Inman fl. 1641 in St Leonard Foster Lane (Heal 1972, p. 181)

SNOW HILL (Farringdon ward Without) [23-F6]

See also GREEN DRAGON COURT. The reading is ON SNOW HIL on 7700, HILL on 7035-6, 7693, 7695-6; ON SNOWHIL on 7698, SNOWHILL on 7699; SNOW HILL on 7694, 7697; cf. 7701-2

7693a	1.07	16.5	Br	180°	*Bonner,* Gabriel. nd. 5.14 Grocers; B|GD. BW 2901. Nott. E of surname double-entered. ?Gabriel Bonner, Weaver; children b. 1631-54; will, PCC, 1663, St Sepulchre (Boyd 27332)
7693b	1.03	15.9	Br	180°	Same dies. [Nott ex Taffs]
7694	1.35	20.9	Br	270°	*?C—,* A—, apothecary. nd. 5.76.160; 5.2.40. BW 2902 but weathercock not on a spire. Nott [ex Spink]. Rev. legend starts at 2 o'clock. The monogram is quite uncertain: the larger C (or G?) could represent a forename (cf. Holme 1905, p. 412) and be followed by A M or M N or W...; the other letters may include I, N, V, W. Whittet 1983, pp. 133-4, offers six identities for an apothecary A. C.
7695	0.83	12.8	Br	0°	*Sartan,* Alan (ALLEN). nd. 5.82.1; S|AE. BW 2910 but a roll of tobacco. Nott [ex Spink]. Allan Sartan of St Sepulchre, b. 1643, Grocer; md. Elizabeth Harmond 1668 (Boyd 17564)
Named signs					
7696a	1.70	26.2	Br	180°	*Ball* (AT Y^E^): Pulteney, Tho—. [16]57. 1.40.3; P|TM. BW 2908 but THO:. [Baldwin]. Edge a little hammered and filed
7696b	1.44	22.3	Br	180°	Same dies. Nott [ex Taffs]

Named signs (*cont.*)

	Weight g	gr		Die axis	
7697a	1.11	17.2	M	120°	*Black Lion:* Stamar, Fran—. nd. 3.11 (•FRAN•STAMAR•BLACK around); S|FM (•S•|F•M; •LION•SNOW•HILL around). BW —; Dickinson 2910A. Nott. Obv. legend starts at 2 o'clock
7697b	0.80	12.4	M	120°	Same dies. [Baldwin ex Macfadyen, lot 157]
7698	0.96	14.7	Br	0°	*Lion & Lamb* (AT THE LION AND LAMBE): ?W—, L—. nd. 3.39.7; L W. BW 2911. Nott
7699	1.31	20.2	M	180°	*Star* (AT STARR): Hitchcock, Tho—. nd. 2.4.3; H|TE. BW 2905 but SNOWHILL. Nott [ex Taffs]. John Bunyan (ODNB: Last works) d. 1688 at the home on Snow Hill of the grocer John Strudwick; his billhead *at the Sign of The Star* illustrates the building, with a star on the fascia (Cockett 1928, p. [30]). See also 7128
7700a	0.95	14.6	Br	150°	*Talbot* (AT THE): Lawrance, Thomas. nd. 3.67.4 (•THOMAS•LAWRANCE•AT around); 5.76.161 (T L) (•L•; •THE•TALBOT•ON•SNOW•HIL around). BW —; Dickinson 2905A. [Nott]. Thomas Lawrence of St Sepulchre, Tallow Chandler, 1651; will, PCC, 1674 (Boyd 46657). A Thomas Lawrence bound apprentices 1637-75; Thomas Lawrence, son of Thomas, appr. to his father 1656 (Webb 1996-, xxxix. 64, 131)
7700b	0.88	13.6	Br	150°	Same dies. Baldwin [or Nott]

SNOW HILL neighbourhood

The reading is AT SNOW HILL on both

Named signs

7701	0.94	14.5	M	180°	*Cock* (AT THE COK): ?B—, E—. 1649. 3.101.1; B|EE. BW 2900 but SNOW•HILL. Baldwin. Same obv. die as 7702
7702	0.85	13.0	Cu	0°	*Cock* (AT THE COK): ?N—, R—. 1656. 3.101.1; N|RE. BW 2906 but I656 = .N.|RE; Dickinson 2905B. Baldwin. Reading of rev. completed from BM specimen; it is possible to read the date as 1660 and the wife's initial as T on the present specimen, which was probably the source for BW 2906. Same obv. die as 7701

SOMAR'S KEY neighbourhood *subsequently* NICHOLSON'S WHARF *etc. see* BOSS ALLEY (Billingsgate ward); LITTLE SOMER'S KEY

SOPER'S LANE *subsequently* QUEEN STREET (part) *see* QUEEN STREET

STAINING LANE (Aldersgate ward & Cripplegate ward Within) [25-F10]

The reading is STENINGE LANE

7703	0.68 (chipped)	10.5	Br	90°	*Marefeild,* Jonathan. nd. 4.1.1; M|IM. BW 2941 but tree not charged with three royal crowns. Nott [ex Taffs]

STAR COURT (Bread Street ward, Bread Street) [25-H10, i49]

The reading is STARR COVRT BREADSTREET

Named signs

7704	7.93	122.4	Br	0°	[*Star*] *coffee-house* (AT THE): [anonymous]. nd. 3.6.51; 2.4.3. BW 408 but BREADSTREET. Nott [ex Spink]. Sign name from Lillywhite 1972, nos. 13698, 13700 (c.1667-72). The 25 mm diameter suggests a penny

STEELYARD (Dowgate ward). The Hall [36-K12]

The Queen took possession of the Hall 1598 for the purposes of a Navy Office; destroyed in the Fire (Harben 1918, p. 550). The reading is STILLYARD HALL

7705	1.08	16.6	Br	0°	*Dernelly,* Richard. 1661. Date; D|RS. BW 2949 but STILLYARD. Nott [ex Taffs]. Legends start between 10 and 11 o'clock both sides. Reading completed from MoL specimen. Richard Darnelly of St Mary Abchurch and St Stephen Walbrook (1613-67), Haberdasher, oilman; md. Sarah Nicols who d. 1679 (Boyd 24927). No evidence that he kept the wine house, cf. Rogers 1937, p. 30, Berry 1978, pp. 101-2

[*continued overleaf*]

7697a 7698 7699 7700b 7701 7702

7703 7704 7705 7706a 7707a 7708

7709 7710 7711 7712a 7713 7714a

7715a 7716a 7717 7718a 7719 7720b

Plate 54 (*cont.*)

STOCKS MARKET *otherwise* WOOLCHURCH MARKET *subsequently* MANSION HOUSE (Walbrook ward) [26-H12]

The reading is WOLL|CHVRCH MARKET on 7708; WOLLCHV|RCH MARKETT on 7706; WOOLCHVRCH MARKET on 7707

	Weight *g*	*gr*		*Die axis*	
7706a	3.24	50.0	Br	0°	*Lumbard,* Hugh. 1670. 3.107.4 (ICH DIEN); 5.77 (L|HI). BW 3535 but WOLLCHV|RCH:. Baldwin. Reading confirmed from MoL specimen A7722 and Greenall 1997, pl. 5.136. Diameter 26.5-27 mm, suggesting a penny. See also 6712
7706b	2.07	31.9	Br	0°	Same dies. [Nott ex Taffs]. Diameter 26.5 mm
7707a	3.16	48.7	Br	0°	*Wybert,* Henry, poulterer. 1671 1d. W|HS; 5.77. BW 3536 but I^{D}. Nott. Henry Wibert of St Mary Woolnoth, Poulterer; wife Sarah; children b. 1676-8 (Boyd 2474). An apprentice turned over to Mr Wiburd 1692 (Webb 1996-, xviii. 1)
7707b	2.63	40.6	Br	270°	Same dies. [Nott]
7707c	2.11	32.6	Br	270°	Same dies. [Nott]

STOCKS MARKET neighbourhood

The reading is AT Y^{E}VPPER END OF WALBROOKE IVST A GAINST WOLL|CHVRCH MARKET

7708	2.60	40.1	Br	270°	*Aynscombe,* Hen—. nd 1d. 5.77 (•|•I^{D}•; •HEN:AYNSCOMBE•AT•Y^{E}VPPER•END around); 5.77 (A|HE) (WOLL|CHVRCH|MARKET|•A•|•H.E•; •OF•WALBROOKE:IVST• A•GAINST around). BW —; Dickinson 3270A but A GAINST. Nott [ex Spink]. Henry Aynscombe of St Mary Woolnoth, Merchant Taylor, Distiller of Woolchurch, Haberdasher, d. 1697; md. Martha Bish 1669; children of [second] wife Elizabeth Chew bap. St Mary Woolchurch from 1671 (Boyd 17567)

SWAN ALLEY *subsequently* GREAT SWAN ALLEY (Coleman Street ward, Coleman Street) [26-F12]

The reading is SWAN ALY IN COLEMAN STREET

7709	2.95	45.5	Br	270°	*Sheldon,* John. 1668 ½d. 5.32.7; 5.77. BW 713 but three candlesticks. Nott. ?John Sheldon of St Margaret Lothbury, Founder; md. Susan Pool 1656 (Boyd 39543). For the obv. type cf. 7420, AT THE 3 CANDLESTICKS

SWEETING'S RENTS *subsequently* ROYAL EXCHANGE BUILDINGS (Broad Street ward, Threadneedle Street) [27-G14, h45: Swithins Alley]

The reading is SWEETINGS RENTS on 7710; SWEETINGSRENTSCORNHIL on 7711

7710	0.94	14.5	Br	90°	*Chubbe,* Tho—, cook (COOKE). nd. 3.11; C|TM. BW 3028 but THO:CHVBBE•COOKE. Nott [ex Taffs]. Overstruck on what was probably an earlier issue by Chubbe when at Abchurch Lane: dies as 6428, so also Dickinson 1989, p. 325, fig. 3, from which reading confirmed. Thomas Chubb bound apprentices 1657 (Webb 1996-, xxvi. 2, 43)

Named signs

7711	1.92	29.7	Cu	0°	*Sultaness* (THE), 'a coffee (ACOFFEE) house': [Garraway, Thomas]. nd. 3.5.66; 5.14.191. BW 3029 but THE[no stop]SVLTANESS, ACOFFEE, IN[no stop] SWEETINGSRENTSCORNHIL. Nott [ex Baldwin]. Description confirmed from MoL specimen 96.66/1131 (see Frontispiece). Rogers 1935, pp. 75-6, finds the issuer was almost certainly Thomas Garraway, in Sweeting's Rents 1658-68, who first retailed tea here. The arms confirm the issuer, see Introduction

TEMPLE BAR neighbourhood (Farringdon ward Without, Fleet Street *and* Middlesex: Westminster) [31-I2]

See also ST CLEMENT DANES neighbourhood, The Strand; TEMPLE BAR without (both Middlesex I: Westminster). The reading is AT TEMPLE BARR on both; cf. 6545-51 and 7714-17

7712a	1.24	19.1	M	180°	*Gover,* Jam—, apothecar[y]. 1657. 5.17.23; G|IK. BW 3041. Nott. James Gover, apothecary, at the Black Dog, Temple Bar, 1675 (Whittet 1983, p. 134)
7712b	1.03	15.9	M	180°	Same dies. [Nott ex Carthew]
					Laurence, Tho— *see* 6547 (Bell Yard: *Lawrance*)

Named signs

7713	0.86	13.3	Br	0°	*Cock ale-house* (THE): ?C—, H—. 1655 [¼d.]. 3.101.1; C|HM. BW 3037. [Nott ex Carthew]. Reading completed from Rogers 1928c, fig. 6 facing p. 156. According to record and envelope, ex Baldwin, whose ticket has 'Ex|Hodgkin|coll^{n} lot 198 £6'; but Nott and Carthew tickets are taken to represent the true pedigree since Hodgkin 1914, pl. iv, is clearly a different specimen. Hearth Tax lists suggest issued by Henry Crosse (Leeds 1933). See Introduction under 1665

TEMPLE BAR within (Farringdon ward Without)

The reading is WITHIN TEMPLE BAR on 7714, BARR on 7716-17, BARRE on 7715; cf. 7712-13

	Weight			*Die*	
	g	*gr*		*axis*	
7714a	1.10	16.9	M	180°	*?R—,* R—, the tallow-chandler (CAHANDLER). nd. 3.3.13; R|RS. BW 3063 but CAHANDLER. Nott [ex Taffs]
7714b	1.06	16.4	M	180°	Same dies. [Nott]
7714c	0.89	13.7	M	180°	Same dies. Baldwin
Named signs					
7715a	0.90	13.9	M	180°	*D[evil] & St Dunstan* (AT THE D AND DVNSTANS): W[adlow], J[ohn]. nd. 3.1.89; W|IS. BW 3071 but WITHIN[stop]TEMPLE. Nott [ex Carthew]. Issuer John Wadlow, Vintner, fl. here 1646-60 (Burn 1855, pp. 104-5); bound apprentices (Webb 1996-, xliii. 389); son of Simon Wadlow, who in 1608 was required by the Vintners' Company 'to put the Divell Cleane out' of his sign (Rogers 1928c, pp. 146-7)
7715b	0.89	13.7	Br	0°	Same dies. [Baldwin]
7716a	1.07	16.5	M	180°	*Dolphin* (AT THE): ?W—, W—. nd. 3.109.1; W|WM. BW 3072. Nott. Same rev. die as 7717
7716b	0.81	12.5	M	180°	Same dies. [?Baldwin]
7717	0.89	13.8	M	180°	*Dolphin* (AT THE): ?W—, W—. nd. 3.109.1; W|WM. BW 3072. Nott. Same rev. die as 7716

TEMPLE GATES *see* INNER TEMPLE GATE *and* MIDDLE TEMPLE GATE neighbourhood

THAMES STREET *subsequently* LOWER THAMES STREET *and* UPPER THAMES STREET (Tower & Billingsgate wards & Bridge ward Within & Dowgate & Vintry & Queenhithe & Castle Baynard wards) [34-J8]

See also ANGEL ALLEY (Dowgate ward); BLACK SWAN ALLEY; BREAD STREET HILL neighbourhood; COLDHARBOUR; COUSIN LANE; CUSTOM HOUSE neighbourhood; DOWGATE neighbourhood; DYERS' HALL; LION QUAY neighbourhood; PUDDLE DOCK neighbourhood; QUEENHITHE 'GATE' neighbourhood; RALPH'S QUAY. The reading is THAM STR on 7527; THAMES STREET on 6501, 6814, 6868, 6877, 7494 (THAMẸṢ), 7516, 7718, 7720, 7725-6, 7734, 7739, 7743, STREET on 7733, *Thames Street* on 6852; THAMES STREETE on 7719, 7722, 7724 (THẠMES), 7727, 7732, 7736, 7740, 7744; THAMESSTREE^{T} on 7526; THAMS STREET on 6657, 7742, STRET on 6795; THEAMES STREET on 7741, STRET on 7735; THEAMS STREET on 7721, 7745, [THEA]M[S STR] on 6700; THEMBS STREEṬ on 7723; THEMES STREET on 7730, STREETE on 7243, 7729, 7738, STREET^{E} on 7746, STRET on 7737; THEMS STREETE on 7728, STRETE on 7731; THEMSTRET on 7242

7718a	1.52	23.4	Br	0°	*Baynes,* Robert. 1668 ½d. 5.77 (B|RS); 3.65.3. BW 3080. Brand
7718b	1.39	21.5	Br	180°	Same dies. [Nott]
7718c	1.37	21.2	Br	180°	Same dies. [Baldwin]
7718d	1.05	16.2	Br	180°	Same dies. [Nott ex Seaby]. There is evidence of slight rusting on the rev. die on the specimens struck in a 180° axis
7718e	1.02	15.8	Br	0°	Same dies. [Nott ex Spink]
7719	0.96	14.8	Br	240°	*Blake,* Edward. nd. 5.8.1; B|EH. BW 3083 but obv. the Royal Exchange; Thompson 1993, p. 78, 1997b, pp. 241-2. Nott [ex Taffs]
7720a	2.03	31.3	Cu	0°	*Elkin,* Thomas. 1667 ½d. 3.101.11; 5.77 (E|TE). BW 3091 but Cock and magpie. [Baldwin]. 'In Thames Street at the south-west corner of Suffolk lane . . . on which before the Fire stood two messuages, one called "the Cock and Pye", occupied by Thomas Elken, cooke' 1668 (Rogers 1928a, p. 93)
7720b	1.47	22.6	Cu	0°	Same dies. Nott [ex Seaby]
7720c	1.25	19.3	Cu	0°	Same dies. [Nott ex Seaby]

THAMES STREET *(cont.)*

	Weight			*Die*	
	g	*gr*		*axis*	
7721	0.84	13.0	Br	0°	*Heming,* John. nd. 3.67.6; H|IR. BW 3101. Nott [ex Carthew]
7722a	2.02	31.1	Cu	0°	*Maslin,* William. 1663 ½d. 3.49.2; 5.77. BW 3109. [Baldwin]. A foundation set out for William Marslin in Thames Street 1668, for William Masline at corner of Bread Street Hill 1669 (Mills 1962-7, i. 6, 75, iv. 160)
7722b	1.88	29.0	Cu	0°	Same dies. Nott [ex Spink]
7723	1.07	16.5	Cu	270°	*Morton* (MO– –[?–]ON), Henry. nd. 5.42.30; M|HV. *BW 3111 (MORTON). Nott. Rev. legend starts at 6 o'clock. Reading partly completed from MoL specimen
					Noris, Robert *see* Middlesex I: Westminster: St James Street
7724	0.81 (chipped)	12.5	Br	210°	*Spire,* Richard. nd. 1.41.5 (S|RI); S|RI. *BW 3122 but obv. initials within a hoop. Nott. Reading largely completed from MoL specimen. A tavern called the Golden Hoope in Thames Street leased 1662 to Richard Spyre, Haberdasher (Fire Court 1966-, ii. 190-1). Richard and Judith Spire had children bap. 1653-62; he paid for the entry or doore of his Taverne the Hoope 1672 (Rogers 1937, pp. 70-2)
7725	1.78	27.4	Br	270°	*Wood,* Sarah. 1669 ½d. 3.5.51; 5.77 (S W). BW 3130 but STREET. Nott [ex Carthew]. Reading confirmed from BM and MoL specimens. A foundation set out 1668 for Sarah Wood, widow, 'neer ye ould Swan' (Mills 1962-7, i. 74). The headwear is taken to be a cardinal's hat
7726	2.00	30.9	Br	0°	*Worwood,* Joseph. 1669 ½d. 5.16.1; 5.77. BW 3131; BW Southwark 399 but THAMES. Nott [ex Taffs]. Horwood, Devon, occurs as *Horwood al. Worewood* 1692 (Watts 2004, p. 318)
Named signs					
7727	0.98	15.1	M	180°	*Adam & Eve* (AT THE): ?B—, I/J—. nd. 4.2.1; B|IS. BW 3078. Nott. Reading completed from MoL specimen
7728a	1.39	21.5	M	180°	*Black Bell* (AT THE): Nuce, P—. 1652. 5.70.1; 5.77 (P N|NVCE|date). BW 3114. [Nott]. It is unclear whether initial N stands for surname or for a wife's forename
7728b	1.20	18.6	M	180°	Same dies. Baldwin
7728c	1.05	16.1	M	180°	Same dies. [Baldwin]
7728d	0.77	11.8	M	180°	Same dies. [Nott]
7728e	0.63	9.8	M	180°	Same dies. [Nott ex Taffs]
7729	1.06	16.3	M	180°	*Black Swan* (AT THE BLACKE SWAN): ?W—, R—. nd. 3.102.10; W|RM. BW 3129 but BLACKE. Nott [ex Taffs]
7730	0.93 (pierced)	14.3	Br	180°	*Blue Anchor* (AT THE BLEW ANCOR): ?M—, M—. nd. 5.38.1; M|MP. BW 3108. Nott [ex Taffs]. Reading confirmed from BM and MoL specimens
7731a	0.97	15.0	M	180°	*Bull's Head* (AT THE BVLL HEAD): ?H—, W—. nd. 3.52.25; 2.1.6 (H|WK). BW 3098 but AT•THE, sun and a small charge. Nott [ex Spink]. The small charge may be a hare, suggesting the surname Harrison
7731b	0.85	13.2	M	180°	Same dies. [?Baldwin]
7732a	1.27	19.6	Cu	180°	*Cross Bullets* (AT THE CROSE BVLETS): ?W—, B—. nd. 1.50.4; W|BE. BW 3126. [Nott ex Carthew]. The term 'cross bullets' has not been found, but cf. *Cross-bar shott* in Holme 1905, 3.18.55 and 3.19.2 (pp. 140, 148). The device resembles double-headed shot between two pieces of round shot (Lavery 1984, p. 159)
7732b	0.99	15.3	Br	180°	Same dies. Nott [ex Taffs]
7732c	0.97 (pierced)	15.0	M	180°	Same dies. [Nott]
7733a	2.43	37.5	Cu	180°	*Golden Ball* (AT): Yeeles, Will—. nd. 1.40.3; W Y. BW 3132 but GOLDEN, STREET. [?Baldwin]. Legends start between 10 and 11 o'clock both sides
7733b	2.29	35.3	Cu	180°	Same dies. Nott
7734a	0.87	13.4	Cu	270°	*Golden [?Horseshoe]*: Baynes, Roger. nd. 5.68.10; B|RI. BW 3081. Nott [ex Taffs]
7734b	0.71 (chipped)	11.0	Cu	270°	Same dies. [Nott]
7735	0.72	11.2	M	180°	*Mermaid* (AT THE MAREMADE): ?C—, R—. 1653. 3.10.17 (•AT•THE•MAREMADE•IN around); C|RA (•C•|R•A; •THEAMES•STRET•I653 around). BW —; Dickinson 3084A but MAREMADE. Baldwin, on whose ticket initials read as R.A.G. See also 6552
7736	1.24	19.2	Cu	0°	*Nag's Head tavern* (THE NAGGS HEAD TAVERNE): ?B—, T—. nd. 3.60.30; B|TE. BW 3079. Nott. Reading completed from MoL specimen
7737	1.08	16.7	M	180°	*Pink* (AT THE PINKE): Sewell, Rich—. nd. 5.13.15; S|RS. BW 3121 but STRET. Nott
7738	1.04	16.0	M	180°	*Prince's Arms* (AT THE PRINCES ARMES): ?W—, I/J—. nd. 3.107.6 (P C); W|IE. BW 3127 but ARMES = P[feathers]C. Nott [ex Carthew]. Reading THEMES confirmed from Wetton 1989, pl. 9.246
7739a	0.91	14.1	M	180°	*Queen's Head* (THE): ?S—, S—. 1657. 3.5.90; S|SD. BW 3119. Baldwin
7739b	0.81 (pierced)	12.4	M	180°	Same dies. [Nott]

[*continued overleaf*]

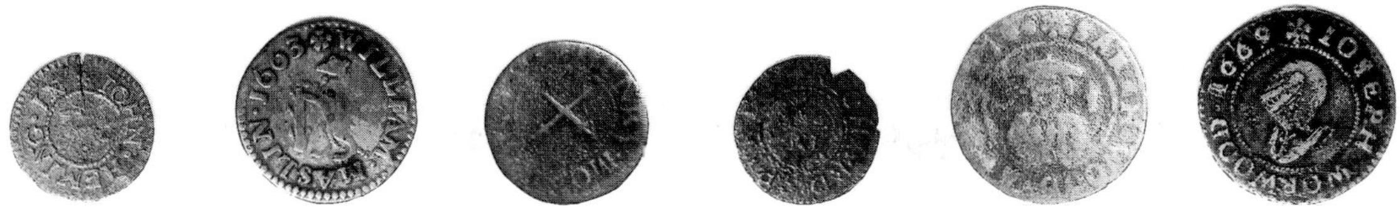

7721 7722b 7723 7724 7725 7726

7727 7728c 7729 7730 7731a 7732b

7733b 7734a 7735 7736 7737 7738

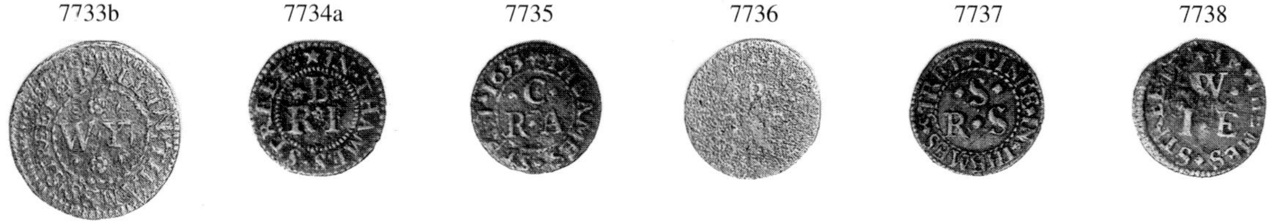

7739a 7740a 7741 7742 7743 7744

Plate 55 (*cont.*)

	Weight			Die	
	g	*gr*		*axis*	
7740a	0.89	13.7	M	180°	*Sugarloaf* (AT THE SHVGERLOFE): ?B—, G—. nd. 5.14 Grocers; B|GK. BW 3077 but SHVGERLOFE. Nott
7740b	0.59 (chipped)	9.2	M	180°	Same dies. [?Baldwin]
7741	0.81	12.5	M	180°	*Sugarloaf* (AT THE SVGGAR LOFE): ?K—, A—. nd. K|AE; 5.64.1. Burn 1855, 1146; BW 3107 but .K.|A·E. Nott [ex Carthew]. Description confirmed from MoL specimens. The present specimen was probably the source for Akerman 1849, 2148; Boyne 1858, London 2467; and BW
7742	1.12	17.2	M	0°	*Three Goats' Heads* (AT THE 3 GOATS HEAD): ?A—, H—. nd. 3.57.5; 3.67.2 (H A). BW 3076. Nott. Reading confirmed from MoL specimens. ?Herbert Akehurst of St James Garlickhithe, Cordwainer, d. 1653 (Boyd 44671)
7743	2.90	44.7	Cu	270°	*Three Queens* (THREE QVƎENES): Browne, Richard. 1659. 3.4.21; B|RR [and either side of the B in chief] I6 [and in base] 59. BW 3084. Nott [ex Carthew]. Reading confirmed from MoL specimen and Greenall 1997, lot 131. Cf. Mills 1962-7, i. 74 (Richard Browne esq. 1668)?
7744	0.87	13.4	M	90°	*Three Tuns tavern* (THE 3 TVNNES TAVERN): ?P—, W—. nd. 5.64.40 (•THE•3•TVNNES•TAVERN around); P|WM (•P•|W•M; •IN•THAMES•STREETE around). BW —; Dickinson 3116A. Nott. Obv. legend starts at 3 o'clock. Attribution to William Page, free 1659 (Fleet 2000, p. 152), is unsafe: see Dickinson forthcoming

THAMES STREET (*cont.*)

Named signs (*cont.*)

	Weight g	gr		Die axis	
7745a	1.16	17.8	Br	0°	*White Bear* (AT THE WHITE BARE): ?A—, G—, grocer. nd. 3.49.5; G A. BW 3075. Nott [ex Carthew]. Stop in chief of rev. field, in base stop i.m.
7745b	0.84	13.0	Br	180°	Same dies. [Nott ex Taffs]

THAMES STREET. Old Swan neighbourhood (Dowgate ward) [37-K13: Old Swan Lane]

The area and traffic point served by the Old Swan landing stairs, including a lane and a notable tavern (Pepys 1970-83, x. 305-6). See also ST MICHAEL'S LANE. The reading is NEARE OVLD SWAN IN THEMES STREET^{E}

7746	1.16	17.9	Br	180°	*?H—*, H—. nd. 5.76.157 (HH) ([heart]NEARE•OVLD•SWAN: around); 5.54 ([heart]IN•THEMES•STREET^{E} around). BW —; Dickinson 3085A (this specimen); Oddie 2001-4, p. 433. Baldwin [ex Hodgkin 1914, lot 193]. BW 3085 likewise reads NEARE|Y^{E} OLD SWAN IN THAMES STREET, with plough on reverse

THAVIE'S INN neighbourhood (Farringdon ward Without) [22-F4, A86: Thavy's Inn]

The reading is NEXT THAVIS INN HOLBORNE

7747	2.15	33.2	Br	180°	*Cartwright,* Robert. nd ½d. 3.5.125; 5.77. BW 1385. Nott. C of surname cancels [–?]. Obv. bust holds in her arms a small quadruped; if a lamb, she may be St Agnes, though its right ear seems attached to its forehead. A small unicorn is possible, as in Raphael's *Lady with a Unicorn* (Rome: Museo Borghese)

THREADNEEDLE STREET (Broad Street ward) [27-H13]

See also FRENCH CHURCH. The reading is THRED NEDLE ST^{E} on 7748; THRED:\|NEDLE STREET on 6995-7; THREDNEEDLE STREET on 7753; TḤṚEẸDNEDLE STREET^{E} on 7750; THREEDNEEDLE on 7749

7748	0.74	11.4	Br	0°	*Pearsone,* George. nd. 5.14 Merchant Taylors (•GEORGE:PEARSONE: around); P|GM (.P.|G M|•; •IN•THRED[?stop]NEDLE•ST^{E} around). BW —. Baldwin. H and second E of NEDLE double-entered; the superscript E, perhaps from a broken punch, resembles F

Named signs

7749a	1.84	28.3	Br	180°	[*Crown*] *tavern* (AT Y^{E}): Blagrave, Tho[mas]. nd ½d. 5.60.1; 5.77. BW 3135 but THO:. [?Baldwin]. Obv. struck off-centre. Thomas Blagrave appr. Vintner, 1642 (Webb 1996-, xliii. 31, see also 340); of St Christopher le Stocks, took a lease of the Crown Tavern 1663, which he agreed to surrender 1667 (Fire Court 1966-, i. 36-7, ii. 8-9); a foundation to be set out for Thomas Blagrave 1668 (Mills 1962-7, i. 72); Captain; d. 1693 (Rogers 1935, pp. 55-7; Boyd 14024)
7749b	1.80	27.8	Br	0°	Same dies. Nott
7749c	1.79	27.6	Br	0°	Same dies. [Baldwin]
7750	1.06	16.4	Br	180°	*King's Arms tavern* (AT Y^{E}KINGS ARMES ṬAVE^{R}): ?P[ywell], B[artholomew]. nd. B P; B P. *BW 3137 but ARMES, STREET^{E}. Nott [ex Taffs]. Issuer probably Bartholomew Pywell, appr. Vintner 1649 (Webb 1996-, xliii. 242, see also 377); of St Benet Fink 1662 (Rogers 1935, pp. 71-2); and 1657, but children bap. St Michael Cornhill 1662-5 (Boyd 2293)

THREE COLTS ALLEY (Bishopsgate ward Without, Angel Alley) (*lost*) [18-C16, cf. c9: Angel Alley] *see* Uncertain I

THREE CRANES WHARF neighbourhood (Vintry ward) [36-K11, cf. m55: Three Crane Lane]

The reading is AT 3 CRANE WHARFE, yet Harben 1918, p. 578, found the first mention in Rocque 1747, 13Ab: Three Cranes (wharf)

Named signs

7751	0.84	12.9	Br	0°	*Red* [*?Portcullis*] (AT Y^{E}): Jackson, Rob—. nd. 5.17.5; I|RI. BW 3140 but ROB:. Nott [ex Taffs]. Reading confirmed from MoL specimen. Obv. legend starts at 6 o'clock, rev. at 3 o'clock. The sign-name might have been the Red Lattice, 'enemy to the sign-post' (Lillywhite 1972, p. 439)

[*continued overleaf*]

7745a 7746 7747 7748 7749b 7750

7751 7752b 7753 7754 7755 7756

7757 7758b 7759a 7760b 7761a 7762a

7763c 7764 7765 7766 7767 7768b

Plate 56 (*cont.*)

THREE FOX COURT (Farringdon ward Without *and* Middlesex: Finsbury: Long Lane) (*lost*) [14-D7, c65]

The reading is 3 FOX COVRT IN LONG LANE

	Weight g	gr		Die axis	
7752a	2.32	35.9	Br	0°	*Drew,* Rich—. nd ½d. 3.66.10 (•RICH:DREW•IN•3•FOX•COVRT around); 2.2 (•IN•LONG•LANE•HIS•HALPENY around). BW —; Dickinson 3142A. [Nott ex Taffs]. Flaw on both sides
7752b	2.23	34.4	Br	90°	Same (flawed) dies. Nott (envelope), Baldwin (record and ticket)
7752c	1.94	30.0	Br	0°	Same dies. [Nott]. Flaw either side less pronounced on this specimen

THREE NUN ALLEY (Broad Street ward, Threadneedle Street) (*lost*) [27-H13, i62]

The reading is 3 NVN ALY on 7753, 7755, with IN THREDNEEDLE STREET on 7753; 3 NVNN ALLY on 7754

7753	1.08	16.7	Br	0°	*Ken,* Richard. nd ½d. 3.4.22; 5.77 (K|RE). BW 3146 but THREDNEEDLE. Nott [ex Spink]. Richard Ken fl. 1670 (Rogers 1935, p. 54)
7754	0.89	13.7	Br	180°	*Lowe,* Thomas. nd. 3.4.22; L|TM. BW 3147. Nott [ex Taffs]. Obv. legend starts between 10 and 11 o'clock, rev. legend at 11 o'clock. Thomas Low of St Christopher le Stocks, Merchant Taylor, d. 1662; wife Mary, children bap. from 1647 (Boyd 834)

THREE NUN ALLEY. Post House neighbourhood

The Post House was at the junction of Threadneedle Street and Cornhill (Harben 1918, p. 483). The reading is 3 NVN ALY NEAR Y^{E}OLD POST HOVS

7755	7.83	120.8	Cu	0°	*Glover,* Cornelius, truss-maker. nd 1d. 3.1.66; 3.2.3. BW 3145 but I^{D}, copper with plug of brass. Nott [ex Taffs]. Cornelius Glover fl. 1670 (Rogers 1935, p. 54)

THROGMORTON STREET (Broad Street ward) [27-G13]

The reading is THROCKMORTON STREET

7756	1.38	21.2	Br	90°	*Charles,* Robert. nd. 3.60.30; C|RI. BW 3148. Nott [ex Spink]

TOWER HILL *i.e.* GREAT TOWER HILL/LITTLE TOWER HILL (*liberty, and* Middlesex: Stepney) *see* Middlesex I: Stepney

TOWER ROYAL *subsequently* COLLEGE HILL (Cordwainer & Vintry wards) [36-J11]

See also COLLEGE HILL; The WARDROBE. The reading is IN TOORE ROYALL on 7757; THE TOWER ROYALL on 7758

Named signs

7757	0.99	15.3	Cu	0°	[*Shaw's*] *coffee-house* (AT –HE): Shaw, W—. nd. 3.6.51; S|WE. *BW 3228 (THE) but TOORE•ROYAL^{L} = •S•|W:E. Nott. Restruck after turning over. Description largely completed from BM and MoL specimens. Sign-name from Lillywhite 1972, no. 1195

TOWER ROYAL neighbourhood

The reading is NEERE THE TOWER ROYALL

7758a	3.73	57.5	Br	[?]	*Scarlett (Scarlett),* Tho—. nd 1d. (*his Coffee|Penny*). 5.77.1; 3.5.40. *BW 3227 but *Tho:, Penny.* [Nott ex Carthew]. Obv. worn flat. 'Scarletts Coffee House' (Lillywhite 1972, no. 1175)
7758b	3.05	47.0	Br	0°	Same rev. die. Nott [ex Taffs]. Reading largely confirmed from MoL specimen

TOWER STREET *subsequently* GREAT TOWER STREET (Tower ward) [39-J17]

See also WHITE LION COURT. The reading is TOVR STREETE on 7761; TOVRSTREET (S retrograde) on 7759; TOWER S^{T} on 7773, STREET on 7762-4, 7767-8, 7772, STREETE on 7760, 7765-6, 7769, 7774-5; TOWERSTREET on 7776; TOWR STREET on 7770, STREETE on 7771

7759a	1.09	16.7	Br	180°	*Barefoote,* Benedict (BENEDICK). nd. 5.66.30; B|BA. BW 3205 but TOVRSTREET, S retrograde. Nott. Benedick Barfoot of St Dunstan in the East, Merchant Taylor; wife Anne; children bap. 1647-51 (Boyd 6545). There is some evidence for an English form *Benedick* (Withycombe 1977, p. 46)
7759b	1.05	16.1	Br	180°	Same dies. [Nott ex Taffs]

	Weight			*Die*	
	g	*gr*		*axis*	
7760a	0.99	15.3	Cu	180°	*Butcher,* Ralph. 1664. 5.64.22; B|RA. BW 3206. [Nott ex Carthew]. ?This issuer in Bishopsgate Without after the Fire (6609). Diameter 16-17.5 mm
7760b	0.71	11.0	Br	0°	Same dies. Nott [ex Taffs]. Diameter 16 mm
7760c	0.47 (corroded, chipped)	7.3	Br	0°	Same dies. [Baldwin]. Diameter reduced to 15 mm through corrosion
7761a	1.24	19.1	Br	180°	*Finch,* Richard. nd. 4.10.1; F|RI. BW 3211. Nott [ex Taffs]
7761b	0.89	13.8	Br	180°	Same dies. [Nott ex Daniels]
7762a	0.92	14.1	Br	180°	*Gosling,* John. 1658. 3.102.33; I G. BW 3212 but three goslings. Nott [ex Taffs]
7762b	0.87	13.4	Br	180°	Same dies. [Nott]
7763a	1.58	24.4	Cu	180°	*Remnant,* Samuel (*Samuell*). 1666. 5.77.1; 3.102.10. BW 3219. Nott [ex Taffs]
7763b	1.31	20.1	Cu	270°	Same dies. [Baldwin]
7763c	1.01	15.5	Cu	0°	Same dies. [Nott ex Carthew]. Struck off-centre
7764	0.81	12.4	Cu	270°	*Samworth,* Chri—. nd. 5.59.20 (•CHRI:SAMWORTH•AT•Y^{E} around); S|CR (:S:|C•R|•••; ••IN•TOWER•STREET• around). BW —; Dickinson 3220B but CHRI. Baldwin. Description confirmed from Baldwin's Auction 38, lot 803 (illus.)
7765	1.18	18.2	Br	180°	*Steele,* Tho—, chandler. nd. 3.3.13; S|TM. BW 3223. Nott [ex Carthew]. Reading confirmed from MoL specimen
Named signs					
7766	0.90	13.9	M	0°	*Blue Helmet* (AT THE BLEW HELMET): ?H—, A—. nd. H|AE; 5.16.1. BW 3213 but •H•|A•E. Nott [ex Carthew]. Description confirmed from MoL specimen
7767	2.06	31.7	Cu	270°	[*Tower*] *coffee-house* (AT THE COFFE HOVSE): Harison, Richard. 1666 ½d. 5.77 (THE|COFFE|HOVSE|•••; •RICHARD•HARISON•AT• around); 5.77 (HIS|HALF|PENY|•••; •IN•TOWER•STREET•1666 around). BW —; Dickinson 3213A. Baldwin. The Tower Coffee-house (Lillywhite 1963 and 1972, no. 1376). ?Richard Harrison, b. 1608, Draper, free 1634; tailor, Fleet Street, 1641; will 1668, All Hallows Barking (Boyd 38028). Two foundations to be set out for Richard Harrison 1668 (Mills 1962-7, i. 71)
7768a	2.83 (pierced)	43.7	Br	90°	[*?Crown*] *tavern* (AT THE TAVERNE): Uthwat, Richard. nd ½d. 5.60.2 (C R) (•RIÇHARD•VTHWAT•AT•THE: around); 5.77 (V|RL) (•V•|R L|•½•; •TAVERNE•IN•TOWER•STREET around). BW —; Dickinson 3224A but VTHWAT. Baldwin. Surname presumably from Outhwaite, Lancs.
7768b	1.04	16.0	Br	270°	Same dies. [Nott (whose ticket reads VTHWAY) ex Carthew] ex Baldwin 1905. Struck off-centre

TOWER STREET (*cont.*)

Named signs (*cont.*)

	Weight *g*	*gr*		*Die axis*	
7769	0.81	12.5	M	180°	*Dolphin tavern* (THE): W[eedon], R[ichard]. 1650. 3.109.1 (•THE•DOLPHIN•TAVERN around); W|RE (•W•|R•E; •IN•TOWER•STREETE•I650 around). BW —, cf. 3225 (device a dolphin and bear) and Berry 1978, p. 114. Nott. Description completed from Greenall 1997, pl. 4.134: this type, without bear, is of later style (c.1656). Richard Weedon (1619-1696), appr. 1636 (Webb 1996-, xliii. 313, see also 391); of St Dunstan in the East, Innholder then Vintner, at the Dolphin until at least 1670; wife Elizabeth (Rogers 1937, pp. 62-7; Woodhead 1966, p. 173)
7770a	1.12	17.3	M	180°	*King's Head* (AT THE KINGES HEAD): ?S—, P—. 1648. 3.5.77; S|PM. BW 3220. Baldwin. Cf. 7771. 'This is the first ever coined' (Milne 1951, p. 334); see Introduction
7770b	0.78	12.0	M	180°	Same dies. [Nott ex Spink]
7771a	1.44	22.3	M	180°	*King's Head* (AT THE): ?S—, P—. 1648. 3.5.77 (•AT•THE•KINGS•HEAD around); S|PM (•S•|P•M; •IN•TOWR•STREETE•I648 around). BW —, cf. 3220 (KINGES, STREET). Nott [ex Taffs]. Cf. 7770
7771b	0.94	14.5	M	180°	Same dies. [?Baldwin]
7772	1.08	16.7	Br	180°	*Rose tavern* (AT THE): W[ormwell], W[alter]. nd. 4.12.1; W|WM. BW 3226. Nott. Walter Wormell (etc.) bound apprentices (Webb 1996-, xliii. 393). 'The house of Mr Wa[l]ter Wormewell, Vintner, at the sign of the Rose in Tower Street' was one of five blown up by the firing of gunpowder, 1649; 'of his owne family were slain (the Master of the house himselfe being absent about business) his wife…' (Rogers 1937, p. 59). Mr Walter Wormwel was in All Hallows Barking 1638, whereas William Wormell (identified as the issuer in Rogers 1928a, p. 96) was in St Mildred, Poultry (Dale 1931, p. 159)
7773a	0.91	14.0	M	180°	*Salutation tavern* (AT THE SALVT•ATION TAVERNE): B[rockett], T[homas]. nd. 3.4.2; B|TE. BW 3204 but SALVT•ATION [*sic*]. Nott [ex Carthew]. T of ST positioned lower than S: it either cancels another T, positioned in line with S, or has a tittle above it. Issuer Thomas Brockett (Rogers 1928a, p. 95); appr. Vintner 1634 (Webb 1996-, xliii. 42, see also 342); of St Dunstan in the East, Clothworker; will, PCC, 1671; wife Ellen d. 1652 (Boyd 6626); his wife Ellinor mentioned 1657 (Rogers 1937, p. 58)
7773b	0.71	10.9	M	180°	Same dies. Baldwin
7774	0.65	10.1	Cu	0°	*Swan* (AT): Hiett, Will. nd. 5.14 Grocers (•WILL•HIETT•AT•SWAN around); H|WP (H|WP; •IN•TOWER•STREETE•:• around). BW —; Dickinson 3213B but HIETT. Baldwin, on whose ticket surname read as HUETT
7775	1.10	17.0	Br	120°	*White Lion tavern* (THE WHITE LYON TAVERNE): ?M—, T—. nd. 3.11; M|TA. BW 3215. Nott [ex Carthew]. Obv. legend starts at 2 o'clock
7776 (pierced and plugged)	1.10	16.9	Br	90°	*White Swan* (AT Y^{E}WHIT SWAN): Peake, William. 1668 ½d. 5.77 (P|WM); 3.102.11. BW 3218 but TOWERSTREET•I668. Nott [ex Taffs]. Reading largely confirmed from BM and MoL specimens. Two foundations to be set out for William Peake 1668 (Mills 1962-7, i. 71)

TRINITY LANE *i.e.* GREAT TRINITY LANE/LITTLE TRINITY LANE (Vintry & Cordwainer & Bread Street & Queenhithe wards) [35-I10]

See also GREAT TRINITY LANE; LITTLE TRINITY LANE. The reading is TRENETY LANE on 7778; TRINITY LANE on 7777

7777	1.51	23.4	Br	240°	*Clayton,* Thomas. 1668 ½d. 3.107.1; 5.77. BW 3230 but AT•Y^{E}. Seaby, [*SCMB* April 1967]. E of Y^{E} same size as Y but raised, touching outer circle
7778	0.85	13.2	M	180°	*Millist,* John, baker. nd. 4.10.1; M|IE. BW 3233. Nott [ex Spink]. Reading confirmed from MoL specimen. John Millist, brown baker; paid rent £20 in Holy Trinity the Less 1638, poll tax 1641 (Boyd 55898). John Millest appr. 1622; bound apprentices 1633-45 (Webb 1996-, xxxi. 22, 40)

TRUMP ALLEY *subsequently* FREEMAN'S COURT (Cheap ward) [25-H10: north out of Cheapside to Honey Lane Market]

The reading is TRVMP ALEY CHEAP SIDE

7779	1.21	18.6	Cu	90°	*Sharpe,* William. nd ½d. 3.2.2; 5.77. BW 598. Nott. Reading confirmed from BM specimens. ?William Sharp of All Hallows Honey Lane, Founder, d. 1677; children bap. 1663-8 (Boyd 25983). William Sharpe appr. 1652 (Webb 1996-, xxi. 47, 68). A foundation set out for Mr Will Sharpe 1669 (Mills 1962-7, i. 28, iv. 182)

TURNAGAIN LANE (Farringdon ward Without, Snow Hill) [23-G5]

The reading is TVRNAGEN LANE

7780a	0.85	13.1	Br	180°	*Dunmore,* John. nd. 3.53.32; D|IR. BW 3236 but rev. IN•TVRNAGEN•LANE = D|I R. [Nott ex Taffs]. Description confirmed from MoL specimen
7780b	0.84	12.9	Br	180°	Same dies. Nott [ex Carthew]

[*continued overleaf*]

7769 7770a 7771a 7772 7773a 7774

7775 7776 7777 7778 7779 7780b

7781 7782b 7783a 7784 7785 7786

7787 7788b 7789 7790 7791 7792

WALBROOK (*street*) (Walbrook ward) [36-I12]

See also STOCKS MARKET neighbourhood. The reading is WALLBROOCK on 7782; WALLBROOKE on 7781

Weight (*g*, *gr*) — *Die axis*

7781 1.06 16.4 Br 0° *Smith,* Jonathan, oilman (OYLEMAN). 1669 ½d. 5.64.158 (•IONATHAN•SMITH•OYLEMAN around); 5.77 (HIS|HALFE|PENNY|•••; •IN•WALLBROOKE•I669 around). BW —; Dickinson 3271A. Seaby, [*SCMB* May 1971]. For a 1667 halfpenny of this issuer, from the same obv. die, see Middlesex I: Finsbury: Chiswell Street

Named signs

7782a 4.70 72.5 Br 180° *Globe* (AT THE GLOVB): Frost, William. nd 1d. 5.77 (W F); 5.49.1. BW 3271 but $\mathrm{I^D}$. [?Baldwin]

7782b 3.41 52.6 Br 180° Same dies. Nott

7782c 3.31 51.1 Br 180° Same dies. [Nott ex Taffs]

7782d 3.29 50.7 Br 180° Same dies. [Nott]

7782e 2.61 40.3 (corroded) Br 180° Same dies. Baldwin, on whose ticket identified as '738A (unpub), WILLIAM [FROSLAND], COVENT GARDEN'

The WARDROBE *otherwise* The QUEEN'S WARDROBE (Cordwainer & Vintry wards, Tower Royal) [36-J11: College Hill]

Tower Royal was given by Edward III for a wardrobe to Queen Philippa, 1331 (Stow 1603, i. 243-4, ii. 324); in 1649 this was presented by Parliament to the City Corporation of the Poor (Pepys 1970-83, i. 180n.). The reading is AT THE WARDROBE

7783a 1.07 16.5 M 180° [*London,* Corporation of the Poor], hemp, flax-work (WORKE) for the poor (POORE). 1653. 5.77 (W H); 5.77 (W H) (R). BW 3357. Nott [ex Taffs]. Although this was a workhouse, W H would make better sense as the initials of William Haslope, who signed a 1655 broadside as Clerk to the Corporation of the Poor (Pearl 1978, esp. pp. 223-5). The R is the initial of David Ramage

7783b 0.81 12.5 M 180° Same dies. [Nott ex Carthew]

WARWICK LANE (Castle Baynard ward & Farringdon ward Within) [24-G7]

The reading is WARWICK LANE on 7784, 7787; . . .ẈICK LAN- on 7786; [?–]–IRWICK LANE on 7785

7784 1.75 26.9 Cu 0° *Butterfeild,* Hen—. 1663̣ ½d. 5.77 (ḤỊS|HALḶFE|PENY|•••; •HEN:BVTTERFEILD•I663̣ around); 5.64.19 (•IN•WARWICK•LANE around). BW —. Baldwin. Date also read as I665

7785 1.77 27.4 Cu 270° *Jones,* Edward (– –WARD). [16]63 ½d. 5.77 (HIS|HALFE|PENY; – –WARD•IONES•AT•THE around); 3.2.9 (•IN [?–]–IRWICK•LANE•63 around). BW —, cf. 3362; Dickinson 3362A, from a report of this specimen. Nott. Overstruck, or possibly double-struck

Named signs

7786 0.42 6.5 (chipped) M 315° *Black Swan* (AT THE): ?H—, W—. nd. 3.102.1 (AT•THE•BLACK•SWAN•IN around); W H (W•H; . . .ẈICK•LAN . . . around). BW —; cf. Dickinson 3363A and Gilbert 1987, 20 (rev. initials H•W). Nott. Obv. legend starts between 1 and 2 o'clock; reading completed from Gilbert 1987, 20, probably the original die-pairing, on which rev. location is WARWICK LANE ALS STR, i.e. *alias* STREET; on streets and lanes see Ekwall 1954, pp. 1-7. Below the swan a rosette countermark (?)

7787 0.42 6.5 (chipped) Br 180° *Crown* (AT THE CROWNE): George, Matthew (MATHEW). nd ½d. 5.60.1; 5.77. BW 3361. Nott [ex Taffs]. Reading confirmed from BM specimen

WATER LANE (Tower ward, Tower Street) *see also* CUSTOM HOUSE neighbourhood

WATERMAN'S LANE (Farringdon ward Without, Whitefriars) (*lost*) [32-J4: Water Lane, confirmed from Stow 1720, Farringdon ward Without, map, no. 74]

The reading is WATER|MANS LANE IN WHITFRYER^{S}

7788a 1.62 25.0 Br 90° *Gurden,* Isaac. nd. 4.12.2; G|II. BW 3477 but GVRDEN•IN•WATER, WHITFRYER^{S}. [Baldwin]

7788b 1.60 24.6 Br 90° Same dies. Nott [ex Taffs]

WATLING STREET (Bread Street & Cordwainer wards & Farringdon ward Within) [25-H9]

The reading is WATLIN ST on 7790; WATLING STREET on 7789; WATLING STRET on 7791

	Weight g	gr		Die axis	
7789	1.46	22.5	Cu	90°	*Cooper,* Thomas. 1668 ½d. 3.5.37; 5.77. BW 3369. Nott [ex Carthew]. ?Thomas Cooper of St Mary Aldermary, Cordwainer, d. 1687; children bap. 1678-84 (Boyd 50584)
Named signs					
7790	1.37	21.2	Br	180°	*Bell* (BELL): Webb, Will (WILL) & Webb, Sam—. nd. W W|S W (•|WW|•••|S•W|•; •WILL•&•SAM;•WEBB around); 5.70.1 (•BELL•IN;WATLIN•ST around). BW —; *Dickinson 3371A (this specimen). Nott [ex Carthew]. ?William Webb of All Hallows Bread Street, Tallow Chandler; md. Sarah Walcot 1662; will, PCC, 1679 (Boyd 26066). William Webb appr. 1645, bound apprentices 1657-73; Samuel Webb, not obviously related, appr. 1658 (Webb 1996-, xxxix. 109, 142)
7791	1.24 (pierced)	19.1	Br	180°	*Guildhall* (AT THE GVILD HALL): Kitchinman, Thomas. nd ½d. 5.8.12; 5.77 (K|TA). *BW 3371 but IN•WATLING•STRET. Nott [ex Taffs]. Reading largely confirmed from BM specimen and Greenall 1997, pl. 4.135

WEST HARDING STREET (Farringdon ward Without) [22-G4]

See also NEW STREET (Uncertain I). The reading is WEST HARDING STREET on 7792; WESTHARDEN STREE^{T} on 7793

7792	0.56	8.7	Br	0°	*?G—,* S—, chandler. nd. 5.14 Tallow Chandlers (•IN•WEST•HARDING around); S G (•|SG|•; •STREET•CHANDLER around). BW —; Dickinson 3376B, from Seaby 1949, p. 85, Uncertain 116D. Baldwin. Obv. legend starts at 10 o'clock

WEST HARDING STREET (*cont.*)

	Weight g	Weight gr		Die axis	
7793	1.26	19.5	Br	180°	*Hadley,* Isaac. nd. 5.70.16 (•ISAAC•HADLEY•IN around); H|IA (.H.|I•A|•; :WESTHARDEN•STREE^{T} around). BW —; Dickinson 3376C. Nott [ex Carthew]. Tinned. Overstruck on a token of Robart Wildbore of Long Lane (BW 1829), from the same dies in the same axis (0°) as a specimen in MoL, the rev. with legend starting between 10 and 11 o'clock. The reading WESTHARDEN confirmed from BM specimen, also tinned, which is overstruck on a token of Nevell Harwar of Moorfields: 'New Cheapside'

WEST SMITHFIELD (Farringdon ward Without) [13-E6: Smith-field]

See also PYE CORNER; SMITHFIELD BARS neighbourhood; SMITHFIELD PENS neighbourhood; 'SMITHFIELD ROUNDS'. The reading is SMITH FEILD on 7798; SMITHFEILD on 7799, 7803, 7812; SMITHFIELD on 7815; WEST SMITH FEILD on 7798 (FEILD), 7800, 7808, 7813, FILD on 7807; WEST SMITHFEILD on 7794-5, 7802, 7804-6, 7810-11, 7814, SMITHFEILDE on 7801, SMITHFLD on 7505; WESTSMITHFEILD on 7796, 7809; WESTSMITHFIELD on 7797

7794	0.86	13.3	Br	270°	*Conaway,* Robert. nd. 5.3.30; C|RE. BW 2850. Nott [ex Carthew]. ?Robert Conway, Skinner; will, PCC, 1660, St Bartholomew the Great; md. Elizabeth Morton 1647 (Boyd 24896). There is a flaw between H and F of SMITHFEILD
7795	1.12	17.3	Br	180°	*Constable,* Rich[ard]. nd. 3.9.1; C|RF. BW 2852 but WEST[no stop]SMITHFEILD. Nott. 'Mr Richard Constable at the Golden Hart in Smith-field' 1661 (BW 2852 n.). See also 7796
7796	2.45	37.8	Br	270°	*Constable* (CVNSTABLE), Richard. 1667 ½d. 3.9.1; 5.77 (C|RE). BW 2851 but WESTSMITHFEILD, the W cancelling ?M. Nott [ex Carthew]. Form of surname from 7795, q.v. ?Richard Constable, Stationer; md. Elizabeth Elmes 1666; will, PCC, 1669, St Sepulchre (Boyd 24895)
7797	1.09	16.9	Br	0°	*Graves,* Samuel (SAMVELL). 1669 ½d. 5.14 Tallow Chandlers; 5.77. BW 2856 but WESTSMITHFIELD. Nott
7798	0.77 (pierced)	11.9	Br	0°	*Hothersale* (HOTHERSALE), Theo—. nd. 3.53.15; H|TE. *BW 2860 but probably an antelope, THEO:, SMITH[stop]FEILD. Nott [ex Taffs]. Reading partly confirmed from MoL specimen. Cf. Tho. Hatton, ANTILOP, 1664 (BW 2861)
7799	2.70	41.7	Br	330°	*Izatt,* Edward. 1668 ½d. 3.67.20; 5.77 (I|EI). BW 2863. Nott [ex Spink]. E of YE no smaller than the other letters, and not raised
7800	1.89	29.1	Br	180°	*Page,* William. 1666 ½d. 5.77 (HIS|HALFE|PENY; •WILLIAM•PAGE•IN•WEST around); 3.3.13 (•SMITH•FEILD•I666 around). BW —; Dickinson 2870A. Baldwin [ex Macfadyen, lot 157]
7801	1.06	16.3	Br	270°	*Pemble,* Richard. nd. 5.50.40; P|RE. BW 2871 but SMITHFEILDE. Nott
7802	2.73	42.2	Br	180°	*Taylor,* Thomas. [16]67 ½d. 5.53.4; 5.77 (T|TA). BW 2879. Nott. Reading confirmed from MoL specimen
7803	2.87	44.3	Br	0°	*Woodward,* Edward. nd ½d. 5.42.30 (•EDWARD•WOODWARD•IN• around); W|EA (W|E[flowerknot]A; •SMITHFEILD•HIS•HALF•PENY around). BW —; Dickinson 2885A. [Nott]. Reading completed from Gilbert 1927, pl. xv.18. For the sign cf. the Cross Daggers 'next to Millers Droll Booth in West Smithfield', 1699-1714 (Lillywhite 1972, no. 5271)
Named signs					
7804	1.32	20.4	Br	270°	*Black [?Bear]* (AT Y^{E}): Burton, Francis. 1668 ½d. (PENNY). 3.49.5; 5.77 (B|FC). *BW 2845. Nott. Reading largely completed from BM specimen
7805a	1.88	29.1	Br	210°	*Blackamoor's Head* (AT Y^{E}BLACKMORES HEAD): White, Tho[mas]. nd ½d. (HIS OB, tittle above). 3.5.39; W|TE. BW 2884 but THO:, tittle above OB. [Nott]. 'Mr Thomas White at the Blackamores-head in Smithfield' 1662 (BW 2884 n.)
7805b	1.88	29.0	Br	210°	Same dies. Nott [ex Taffs]
7806a	2.33	35.9	Br	90°	*Catherine Wheel* (AT THE CATOR^{N} WHEEL): Alldridge, Tho—. nd ½d. 5.51.20; 5.77 (A|TM). BW 2839 but THO:, CATOR^{N}. [Nott]
7806b	1.97	30.4	Br	90°	Same dies. Nott [ex Taffs]
7806c	1.75	27.0	Br	90°	Same dies. [Nott ex Daniels]
7806d	1.22	18.8	Br	90°	Same dies. [Baldwin]
7807	0.76	11.7	M	180°	*Crown tavern* (AT THE CROVN TAVERN): C[lark], I/J—. nd. 5.60.1; C|IA. BW 2848 but SMITH[stop]FILD. Nott [ex Taffs]. Reading completed from BM specimen. 'Captain Clark at the Crown Tavern in West-Smithfield' 1665 (BW 2848 n.). ?John Clarke (Clark, etc.), Vintner, who bound apprentices (Webb 1996-, xliii. 346, see also 61-2)
7808	2.46 (pierced)	37.9	Br	90°	*[?Goat] tavern* (AT THE): Blechinden, Francis. 1666 ½d. 3.54.1; 5.77. BW 2841 but BLECHINDEN, rev. TAVERN•IN, PENEY. Nott [ex Spink]. Appr. Vintner 1657 (Webb 1996-, xliii. 32, see also 340)
7809a	1.10	17.0	Br	180°	*Harp* (AT THE): Harper, Ric—. nd. 5.71.1; H|RA. BW 2859 but WESTSMITHFEILD. Nott [ex Taffs]
7809b	0.87	13.5	Br	180°	Same dies. Nott

[*continued overleaf*]

7793 7794 7795 7796 7797 7798

7799 7800 7801 7802 7803 7804

7805a 7806b 7807 7808 7809b 7810

7811 7812c 7813 7814a 7815a 7816b

Plate 58 (*cont.*)

	Weight g	gr		Die axis	
7810	1.86	28.7	Cu	90°	*Hart's Horns* (AT THE HARTS HORNS): C[harteris], C[hristopher], coffee-house (THE COFFE HOVS). 1664 ½d. token. 3.5.40; 5.77 (C|CM). BW 2847. Nott [ex Carthew]. Reading confirmed from MoL specimen. 'Mr Christopher Charteris, at the sign of the Hart's Horns, in West Smithfield' 1658, and similarly 1661, a hirer of horses (BW 2847 n.); 'and Post-Master there...' 1658 (Lillywhite 1963 and 1972, no. 549). Christopher Charteris, St Sepulchre, innholder (PCC 1671). See also 7814
7811	1.50	23.1	Br	90°	*King's Arms* (AT THE KINGS ARMES): Sherly, James. nd ½d. 5.14.5; 5.77. BW 2878 but SHERLY. Nott [ex Taffs]. Reading completed from BM specimen
					New Queen's Head: ?P—, G— *see* Middlesex I: Stepney: East Smithfield
7812a	2.37	36.5	Cu	0°	*Three* [*?Sugarloaves*] (AT THE 3): Byard, James. 1666 ½d. 5.64.22; 5.77 (B|IE). BW 2846 but SMITHFEILD. [Baldwin]. Diameter 21-22 mm
7812b	2.19	33.8	Cu	0°	Same dies. [Nott ex Taffs]. Diameter 19.5 mm
7812c	1.82	28.0	Cu	0°	Same dies. Nott [ex Carthew]. Diameter 19.5-20 mm
7812d	1.36 (corroded)	20.9	Cu	0°	Same dies. [Nott]. Diameter 19-19.5 mm
7813	1.14	17.6	Br	180°	*White Hart tavern* (THE WHIT HART TAVERN): D[ermer], R[ichard]. nd. 3.53.1; D|RI. BW 2853. Nott. Reading confirmed from MoL specimen. 'Mr Richard Darmar Vintner at the White Hart in Smithfield' 1661 (BW 2853 n.). Richard Dermer (Dearmer, Deermer) bound apprentices; ?cf. Richard Dearman appr. 1632 (Webb 1996-, xliii. 85, 351)

WEST SMITHFIELD. Hart's Horns neighbourhood [24-F7, A96: Harts Horn Inn]

For the Hart's Horns see 7810. The reading is NEAR Y^E HARTS HORNES IN WEST SMITHFEILD

7814a	3.02	46.7	Br	330°	*Coggs,* Jo[seph], chandler. 1668 ½d. 5.77 (HIS|[rule]|HALFE|[rule]|PENY|[rule]|1668; •IO:COGGS•NEAR•Y^E•HARTS around); 5.77 (C|IS) (•••|CHA|NDLER|•C•|I•S; •HORNES• IN•WEST•SMITHFEILD around). BW —; Dickinson 2849B. Nott. Joseph Coggs appr. 1633 to William Wiggins (cf. 5563 Wickins); bound apprentices 1651-79 (Webb 1996-, xxxix. 23, 122)
7814b	1.52 (corroded, pierced)	23.5	Br	330°	Same dies. Baldwin [ex Macfadyen, lot 157]

WEST SMITHFIELD. Ram neighbourhood [13-E6, A37: Ram Inn]

The reading is NEXT THE RAM IN SMITHFIELD

7815a	2.45	37.8	Br	180°	*Kem,* Tho—, grocer. nd ½d. 5.14 Grocers (•THO:KEM•NEXT•THE•RAM around); 5.77 (HIS|HALFE|PENNY|•:•:•; •IN•SMITHFIELD•GROCER•:• around). BW —; Dickinson 2863B. Baldwin
7815b	2.33	35.9	Br	180°	Same dies. [Nott]

WHITE HORSE YARD (Broad Street ward, London Wall) (*lost*) [17-E13, A68: White Horse Inn]

The reading is WHIT HORS YRD LONDON WALL NEER MORGAT

7816a	1.54	23.8	Br	0°	*Benion,* Jo[hn]. nd ½d. 3.60.1; 5.77. BW 1764 but IO:. [Nott]. 'Mr John Benion, at the White-Horse London-Wall' 1664 (BW 1764 n.)
7816b	1.26	19.5	Br	0°	Same dies. Nott

WHITE LION COURT (*several*). Possible locations are in Aldersgate ward, Barbican (*subsequently* New Zealand Avenue) [14-C8, b60 (confirmed from Ogilby 1677, p. 2)]; Coleman Street ward, Coleman Street [26-F12, f68] *or* London Wall [16-E12, e41]; Farringdon ward Without, Fleet Street (*lost*) [33-I5, k48]; and Tower ward, Tower Street (*subsequently* Barking Court) [39-J17: not identified]

The reading is WHITE LION COVRT

	Weight			*Die*	
	g	*gr*		*axis*	
7817	0.69	10.7	Br	180°	*Sommers,* William. nd. 3.53.20 (•WILLIAM•SOMMERS• around); S|WK (.S.|WK; •WHITE•LION•COVRT• around). BW —; Dickinson 1097B. Nott [ex Taffs]

WHITECROSS STREET (Cripplegate ward Without *and* Middlesex: Finsbury) [5-A10]

See also CHEQUER ALLEY and RED LION COURT (Middlesex I: Finsbury). The reading is WHIT CROS STREET on 7830, 7834, STRET on 7827, 7833; WHIT CROSE STREET on 7818; WHIT CROSS STREETE on 7837; WHITCRASSTREET on 7819-20; WHITCROSSTRET on 7835; WHITE CROS STREẸT on 7831, CROSS STREET on 7821-6, 7828, 7841-2, CRO–S SṬREET on 7838, CROSS STREETE on 7840; WHITE\|CROSS STREET on 7832; WHITE CROSṢTREET on 7829; WHITECROS STRET on 7843; WHITECROSSTREET on 7839; WITCROSSTRET on 7836

7818	1.01	15.6	Br	180°	*Altham,* John, b[odice]-maker. nd. 3.1.96; A|I1. BW 3432 but MAKER, CROSE[stop]STREET. Nott. Device and trade identified from the description THE STOMACHER & BODDYS MAKER (Heal 1928, p. 17). For a stomacher see Cunnington 1972, esp. pl. 40(a)
7819	0.79	12.2	Br	180°	*?B—,* G—, a chan[d]ler. nd. B|GM; B|GM. BW 3435 but WHITCRASSTREET. [Nott]. Reading confirmed from MoL specimens
7820a	1.84	28.3	Br	180°	*?B—,* G—, a chan[d]ler. nd. B|GM; B|GM. BW 3435 but WHITCRASSTREET. Nott. Diameter 17 mm
7820b	0.84	12.9	Br	180°	Same dies. [Nott ex Taffs]. Diameter 15.5-16 mm
7821	1.89	29.2	Br	270°	*Clement,* John. 1666 ½d. 5.77 (HIS|HALF|PENY|••:••; •IOHN•CLEMENT•1666: around); C|IO (C|I[flowerknot]O; •IN•WHITE•CROSS•STREET. BW —; Dickinson 3440A. Nott. Reading completed from MoL specimen NN19590
7822a	1.77	27.4	Br	0°	*Dove,* Francis, tallow-chandler (CHAND|LER). 1669. 5.77; F D|date. BW 3443. Nott
7822b	1.34 (chipped)	20.7	Br	0°	Same dies. [Nott]
7823	2.01	31.1	Br	0°	*Gray,* John, wine cooper (WINECOOPER). nd ½d. 5.60.1; 5.77. BW 3451 but WINECOOPER, PENY. Nott [ex Taffs]
7824a	1.23	19.0	Cu	0°	*Harrison,* John. nd. 3.7.25; H|IM. BW 3454 but a boot, WHITE•CROSS. Baldwin
7824b	0.76	11.7	Cu	0°	Same dies. [Nott]
7825a	1.21	18.7	Cu	0°	*Harrison,* John. 1665 ½d. 5.77 (H|IM); 3.7.25. BW 3453 but IOHN|[rule]|HARRISON|[rule]|HIS HALF|[rule]|PENNY•:•|[rule]|•H•I•M, rev. a boot. [Nott]
7825b	1.12	17.3	Cu	0°	Same dies. Nott [ex Seaby]
7826	2.27	35.0	Br	0°	*James,* Samuel (SAMVELL). [16]67 ½d. 5.64.174 (I|SE); 5.32.11. BW 3455 but rev. :67:|[stick of candles]|HIS HALF|PENNY|• •:• •. Nott [ex Carthew]. Description confirmed from BM specimen. First E of STREET cancels ?R
7827	0.95	14.6	Br	0°	*Millen,* Robert. nd. 5.77; M. BW 3462. Baldwin [ex Pridmore]. Reading confirmed from BM and MoL specimens
7828	0.83	12.8	Br	0°	*Sayer,* Michael (MICHAELL). nd. 3.113.7; S|ME. BW 3470 but MICHAELL, WHITE[no stop]CROSS[no stop]STREET, device a serpent? Nott
7829	0.78	12.0	Br	270°	*Smith,* Richard. 1661. Date (.•.|I66I|•.•; •RICHARD•SMIṬH•IN around); R S (•|R•S|•; •WHITE•CROSSṬREET around). BW —; *Dickinson 3471A. Baldwin. Evidence of die-clashing on obv.
7830	0.77	11.9	Br	180°	*?W—,* I/J—, tallow (TALLOE) chandler. nd. 5.3.41; W|IA. BW 3473 but CROS, and only the charges from the Merchant Taylors' arms. Baldwin [or Nott ex Carthew]. Reading confirmed from MoL specimen
7831	2.21 (chipped)	34.1	Cu	270°	*Webley* (WẸBLEY), Richard, chees[e]monger. nd ½d. 3.1.25 (•RICHARD• WẸBLEY•IN•WHITE around); 5.77 (HIS|HALFE|PENNY|•:•:•; •CROS•STREẸT• CHEESMONGER around). BW —; Dickinson 3473B but WẸBLEY; Dickinson 3473C (this specimen). Baldwin [ex Hodgkin 1914, lot 197]. Surname from Weobley, Herefs.
7832	4.07	62.8	Cu	0°	*Webster,* Edward, brewer. 1666 ½d. 5.77; 5.77. BW 3474. Seaby, [*SCMB* May 1971]. Reading completed from MoL specimen

[*continued overleaf*]

7817 7818 7819 7820a 7821 7822a

7823 7824a 7825a 7826 7827 7828

7829 7830 7831 7832 7833 7834b

7835a 7836 7837 7838 7839a 7840b

Plate 59 (*cont.*)

Named signs

	Weight			Die	
	g	*gr*		*axis*	
7833	1.11	17.2	Br	180°	*Bear & Ragged Staff* (THE BEARE AND RAGET STAF): ?B—, R—. nd. 3.49.2; B|RI. BW 3436. Nott [ex Taffs]
7834a	1.00	15.4	Br	180°	*Child's Coat* (AT THE CHILDS COATE): ?S—, I/J—. nd. 3.1.90; S|IS. BW 3467. Nott [ex Taffs]
7834b	0.86	13.2	Br	180°	Same dies. Nott
7835a	1.03	15.9	Br	0°	*George* (AT Ỵ^{E}G̣ORGE): Frith, Tho—. nd. 3.2.14 (•THO•FRITH•AT•Ỵ^{E}G̣ORGE around); F|TD (.F.|T•D; •IN•WHITCROSSTRET around). BW —; *Dickinson 3448A (this specimen). Nott [ex Taffs]
7835b	0.79	12.1	Br	0°	Same dies. Nott [ex Carthew]
7836	0.98	15.2	Br	180°	*George* (AT Y^{E} GORGE): Frith, Tho—. nd. 3.2.14 (•THO•FRITH•AT•Y^{E}•GORGE around); F|TD (.F.|T.D; •:IN:WITCROSSTRET: around). BW —; Dickinson 3448A. [Baldwin]. Description largely confirmed from BM specimen. E of Y^{E} above Y
7837	0.75	11.6	Br	0°	*Glovers' Arms* (AT THE GLOVERS ARMES): ?D—, I/J—. nd. 5.14 Leathersellers; D|II. BW 3442. Nott. Reading confirmed from MoL specimen
7838	1.18	18.2	Br	0°	*Grasshopper* (AT Y^{E}G̣RASHOP^{R}): Byat (BỴẠṬ), Thomas (THOMAṢ). nd ½d. 3.116.1 (•THOMAṢ•BỴẠṬ•AT•Y^{E}G̣RASHOP^{R} around); 5.77 (B|TM) (HIS|HALF|PENY|B|T.M; •IN•WHITE•CRO–S•ṢṬREET around). BW —; Dickinson 3439A (BVRT), from reports of this specimen. Nott [ex Carthew]
7839a	2.17	33.5	Br	180°	*Lion's Head* (AT Y^{E}): Ware, Nicholas (NICHOLVS). [16]67 ½d. 5.77 (.HIS.|HALFE|PENY|•6•7•; •NICHOLVS•WARE•AT•Y^{E}•LIONS around); 3.35.2 (W|NM; •HEAD•IN•WHITECROSSTREET around). BW —; cf. Gilbert 1927, 286, Dickinson 3473A (undated). Nott. Date apparently added subsequently to die between ornamental stops
7839b	1.60	24.7	Br	180°	Same dies. [Baldwin]
7840a	1.15	17.7	Br	270°	*White Cross tavern:* ?S—, T—. nd. S|TI; 1.60. BW 3468. [Nott]
7840b	1.13	17.4	Br	270°	Same dies. Nott

WHITECROSS STREET (*cont.*)

Named signs (*cont.*)

No.	Weight g	gr		Die axis	
7841a	1.25	19.3	Cu	180°	*White* [*?Rose*] (THE): Doughty, Will—. nd. 4.12.1 (•WILL:DOVGHTY•THE WHITE around); D|WC (•D•|WC|•; •IN•WHITE•CROSS•STREET around). BW —; Dickinson 3443A. [Nott ex Carthew]. Description completed from MoL specimen
7841b	0.69	10.6	Cu	180°	Same dies. Baldwin
7842	0.74 (chipped)	11.5	Br	270°	*White* [*?Swan*] (AT): Page, Daniel (DANIELL). nd ½d. 3.102.0 (•DANIELL•PAGE• AT•WHITE around); 5.77 (P̣|DA) (HALF|PENY|••P̣[•?]•|D.A; •IN•WHITE•CROSS• STREET: around). BW —, cf. 3465 (no denomination). Baldwin. An example of BW 3465 in BM, from the same obv. die as the present halfpenny, is probably the original die-pairing
7843	0.74	11.4	Br	270°	*Yarn shop* (AT Y^{E} YEARNE SHOP̣E): ?G—, I/J—. 1657. 3.7.7 (I6[stocking]57; •AT•Y^{E}•YEARNE•SHOP̣E around); I G (•|I•G|•; •IN WHITECROS•STRET around). BW —; Dickinson 3448B but I.G., YEARNE SHOP̣E, stocking. Baldwin [ex Macfadyen, lot 159]. Initial I confirmed from MoL specimen NN19597

WHITEFRIARS (*precinct*) (Farringdon ward Without) [32-I4]

See also WATERMAN'S LANE. The reading is AT WHITE FRYERS on 7846; IN WHIT FRIRS on 7845; IN WHITE FRIERS on 7848, FRYARS on 7844, FRYERS on 7847; IN WHITFRYER^{S} on 7788; cf. 7849

No.	g	gr		Die axis	
7844a	2.23	34.4	Cu	90°	*Clay,* John, woodmonger. 1667 ½d. 5.53.15; 5.77. BW 3475. Baldwin [or Spink 1973+]
7844b	2.04	31.4	Cu	90°	Same dies. [Nott ex Taffs]
7845a	1.28	19.7	M	180°	*Gouldegay,* Gawain (GOVIN), woodmonger (WOOD|MONGER). nd. 5.14 Woodmongers 2; G|GA. BW 3478 but •G•|G•A. Nott. Gawain occurs as *Gauvain, Gawein, Gawan* etc. (Gerritsen 1998, p. 113), and *Gawin* 1530 (Withycombe 1977, p. 127). See Welch 1914, p. 32, for this other coat for the Woodmongers
7845b	1.10	16.9	M	180°	Same dies. [Baldwin]
7845c	0.55	8.5	M	180°	Same dies. [Nott ex Taffs]
7846a	0.98	15.1	M	180°	*Hancock,* Robert. nd. 3.6.9; H|RI. BW 3479. [Nott ex Taffs]. Robert Hancock (1620-1667), Woodmonger, of St Brides; md. (2) Mary Barrow 1662; will, PCC, 1667 (Boyd 20972; Woodhead 1966, p. 83). Style of the token indicates issue within c.1651-3 (Dickinson forthcoming)
7846b	0.89	13.8	M	180°	Same dies. Baldwin [or Nott ex Spink]
7846c	0.80 (corroded)	12.4	M	180°	Same dies. [Nott]
7846d	0.75 (corroded)	11.5	M	180°	Same dies. [?Baldwin]
7847	2.57	39.7	Cu	0°	*Horne,* Jeremiah. 1664 ½d. 4.10.1; 5.77. BW 3480. Nott [ex Taffs]
7848	1.07	16.4	Br	180°	*Stotesbery,* Thomas. nd. 3.2.8; S|TA. BW 3485. Nott [ex Taffs]. Surname from Stuchbury or Stutsbury, Northants., *Stotesbur* c.1230 (Ekwall 1960, p. 451)

WHITEFRIARS (*precinct*). 'The Gate' neighbourhood

Waters, James *see* 7045a (Grey Friars. The Gate neighbourhood)

WHITEFRIARS DOCK neighbourhood (Farringdon ward Without) (*lost*) [33-J5: 'Wharfe']

At the south end of Water Lane (Harben 1918, p. 625). The reading is AT WHITE FRIERS DOCK

No.	g	gr		Die axis	
7849	2.21	34.2	Br	180°	*White,* William, brewer. nd ½d. token (HSI, *sic*). 5.77; W|WI. BW 3486 but WHITE•FRIERS. Nott [or Baldwin]. William White appr. 1642 (Webb 1996-, xxxvi. 103). Foundations set out for William White at Whitefriars Dock 1669, and in Whitefriars 1670 (Mills 1962-7, i. 81, 82, iii. 58v, 158v)

WHITE'S ALLEY *see* Middlesex I: Westminster

WINDMILL COURT (Farringdon ward Without, Snow Hill) [23-G6, g64: Wind Mill Court]

The reading is AT WINDE MILL COVRT. Documentation of the issuer permits other locations of the name to be disregarded

No.	g	gr		Die axis	
7850a	1.10	17.0	M	180°	*Burt,* Nathaniel (NATHANILL). nd. 5.9.10; B|NA. BW 3500. Baldwin. Reading WINDE confirmed from Greenall 1997, pl. 5.135. Nathaniel Burt of St Sepulchre, Saddler, Master 1632, Senior 1637; md. Anne Soloman 1607; he or another of same name and occupation fl. 1651 (Boyd 43284)
7850b	0.91 (edge cut)	14.1	M	180°	Same dies. [Nott ex Taffs]

[*continued overleaf*]

7841b 7842 7843 7844a 7845b 7846b

7847 7848 7849 7850a 7851 7852

7853 7854 7855 7856a 7857 7858

7859 7860 7861b 7862 7863c 7864

WOOD STREET, southern part *otherwise* GREAT WOOD STREET (Farringdon and Cripplegate wards Within) [25-F10, south of Addle Street]

See also LITTLE WOOD STREET. The reading is GREAT WOOD STREET on 7859, 7861, 7863-5 (STREET on 7865), STREETE on 7860, 7862; GREAT WOODSTREET on 7851-2, 7855, 7866, WOODSTREETE on 7853, WOODSTREETE on 7854; VPER END GREAT WOODSTREET on 7857 (both Ds inverted). 7858 (D in WOODSTREET inverted); WOOD STRET on 7155; WOODSTREETE on 7856

	Weight			Die	
	g	*gr*		*axis*	
7851	1.18	18.2	Br	180°	*Cooper,* Edmund. [16]64. 5.69.1; C|EM. BW 3514 but WOODSTREET. Nott
7852	1.82	28.0	Cu	0°	*Cooper,* Thomas. 1670 ½d. 5.77 (•••|[dotted rule]|THOMAS|[dotted rule]|COOPER|[dotted rule]|HIS•HALF|[dotted rule]|PENY); 5.47.11 (•IN•GREAT•WOODSTREET•1670 around). BW —; Dickinson 3514A. Nott [ex Taffs]. See also 7853
7853	0.98	15.1	Cu	0°	*Cowper,* Tho—, ironmonger. nd. 5.47.20 (•THO:COWPER•IRONMONGER around); C|TH (•C•|T•H; •IN•GREAT•WOODSTREETE around). BW —. Baldwin. See also 7852. Thomas Cooper bound an apprentice 1660; another not bound 1664 (Webb 1996-, xxiv. 6, 9)
7854	2.16	33.4	Br	90°	*Drafgate,* Samuel (SAMVELL). nd ½d. 5.53.21 (•SAMVELL•DRAFGATE•AT•THE around); 5.77 (S D) (HIS|HALF|PENY|S•D; •IN•GREAT•WOODSTREETE• around). BW —; Dickinson 3517A but DRAFGATE. Baldwin. Cf. John & Elizabeth Draftgate (Draughtgate) in Wood Street 1668 (Rogers 1928c, p. 169; Mills 1962-7, i. 79)
7855	1.85 (chipped)	28.5	Br	0°	*Ferrers,* Philip (PHILLIP). nd ½d. 2.4.7; 5.77. BW 3518 but WOODSTREET. Nott [ex Carthew]. Reading confirmed from MoL specimen
7856a	3.49	53.9	Cu	0°	*Hayes,* William, ironmonger (IRONMVNGER). [16]64 ½d. 5.50.40; 5.77. BW 3524 but WOODSTREETE; Woodhead 1966, p. 87. Nott [ex Carthew]. William Hayes bound apprentices 1655-82 (Webb 1996-, xxiv. 60). In accordance with a 1667 decree a foundation was set out for William Hayes in Great Wood Street 1668 (Fire Court 1966-, i. 190; Mills 1962-7, i. 79, iv. 5)
7856b	2.71	41.8	Cu	0°	Same dies. Nott [ex Taffs]
7857	0.89	13.7	Br	0°	*Ragdall,* Jos[iah]. nd. 3.3.13; I R. BW 3529 but IOS:, WOODSTREET, all Ds inverted. Nott. Legends start between 10 and 11 o'clock both sides. Josiah Ragdale of St Peter Westcheap, Tallow Chandler; md. 1659; fl. 1700 (Boyd 30240). Same rev. die as 7858. Joshua Ragdall [*sic*] appr. 1651; Josiah Rag(s)dale bound apprentices 1659-1703 (Webb 1996-, xxxix. 84, 136)
7858	0.64 (chipped)	9.9	Br	0°	*Ragdall,* Jos[iah]. nd. 3.3.13; I R. BW 3529 but IOS;, WOODSTREET (D inverted). Nott [ex Daniels]. Obv. legend, with normal Ds, starts at 11 o'clock; same rev. die as 7857, q.v.
7859	0.82	12.6	Cu	180°	*Wells,* John. nd. 5.14.5; W|II. BW 3532. Nott [ex Taffs]. Struck off-centre. Reading completed from BM specimen and Greenall 1997, lot 136
					Woodward, Thomas *see* Uncertain I
Named signs					
7860	0.98	15.2	Br	180°	*Cock* (AT THE): ?C—, I/J—. 1651. 3.101.1; C|IH. BW 3509. Nott [ex Taffs]. Reading completed from BM specimen
7861a	1.00	15.5	Br	180°	*Eagle & Child* (AT THE): ?F—, M—. nd. 3.82.1; F|MA. BW 3519. [Nott ex Taffs]
7861b	0.89	13.7	Br	0°	Same dies. Nott. From rev. die in flawed state
7862	1.10	16.9	M	180°	*Hen & Chickens* (THE HENN AND CHICKENS): ?M—, R—. nd. 3.101.21; M|RT. BW 3526 but obv. THE•HENN etc. Nott [ex Carthew]
7863a	0.90	13.9	Br	180°	*Mitre tavern* (AT THE MIYTER TAVERNE): P[rocter], W[illiam]. nd. 5.59.20; P|WE. BW 3528 but AT•THE•MIYTER•TAVERNE; Rogers 1928c, pp. 165-72; Woodhead 1966, pp. 133-4. Baldwin [or Nott]. Reading confirmed from MoL specimen NN19646. William Procter, appr. Vintner ?1628 (Webb 1996-, xliii. 241, see also 377); at the Mitre Tavern c.1641 till he died 1665 of the plague, leaving a considerable estate (Pepys 1970-83, vi. 175-6, x. 347, *pace* Smyth 1849, p. 64); md. Elizabeth Foster 1629 (Boyd 41470)
7863b	0.84	13.0	Br	180°	Same dies. Baldwin
7863c	0.79	12.3	Br	180°	Same dies. [Nott]
7864	0.84	12.9	Br	270°	*Mitre tavern* (AT Y^E MITER TAVERNE): P[rocter], W[illiam]. nd. 5.59.20; P|WE. *BW 3527. [Nott ex Carthew]. Description largely confirmed from MoL specimen. For issuer see 7863. Same obv. die as 7865

WOOD STREET, southern part (*cont.*)

Named signs (*cont.*)

	Weight *g*	*gr*		Die axis	
7865	0.52	8.1	Br	270°	*Mitre tavern* (AT Y^E MITER TAVERNE): P[rocter], W[illiam]. nd. 5.59.20; P|WE. *BW 3527 but IN[no stop]GREAT. Baldwin. Description largely confirmed from BM specimen. Same obv. die as 7864, q.v.
7866	1.00	15.4	Br	0°	*Shears* (AT Y^E): Combs, Ralph. [16]68 ½d. 5.43.31 (R C); 5.77 (C|RE). BW 3513 but no stop below or after E of Y^E, WOODSTREET. Nott [ex Carthew]

WOOLCHURCH MARKET *see* STOCKS MARKET

ADDENDUM

MOORGATE without (Coleman Street ward) [16-E12]

The reading is WITHOVT MORE GATE

Named signs

7867	2.40	37.0	Br	180°	*White Swan* (AT Y^E): Baker, John. 1667 ½d. 3.102.1; 5.77. BW 1965 but MORE•GATE. [Nott ex Carthew]. Description completed from MoL specimen

7865 7866 7867

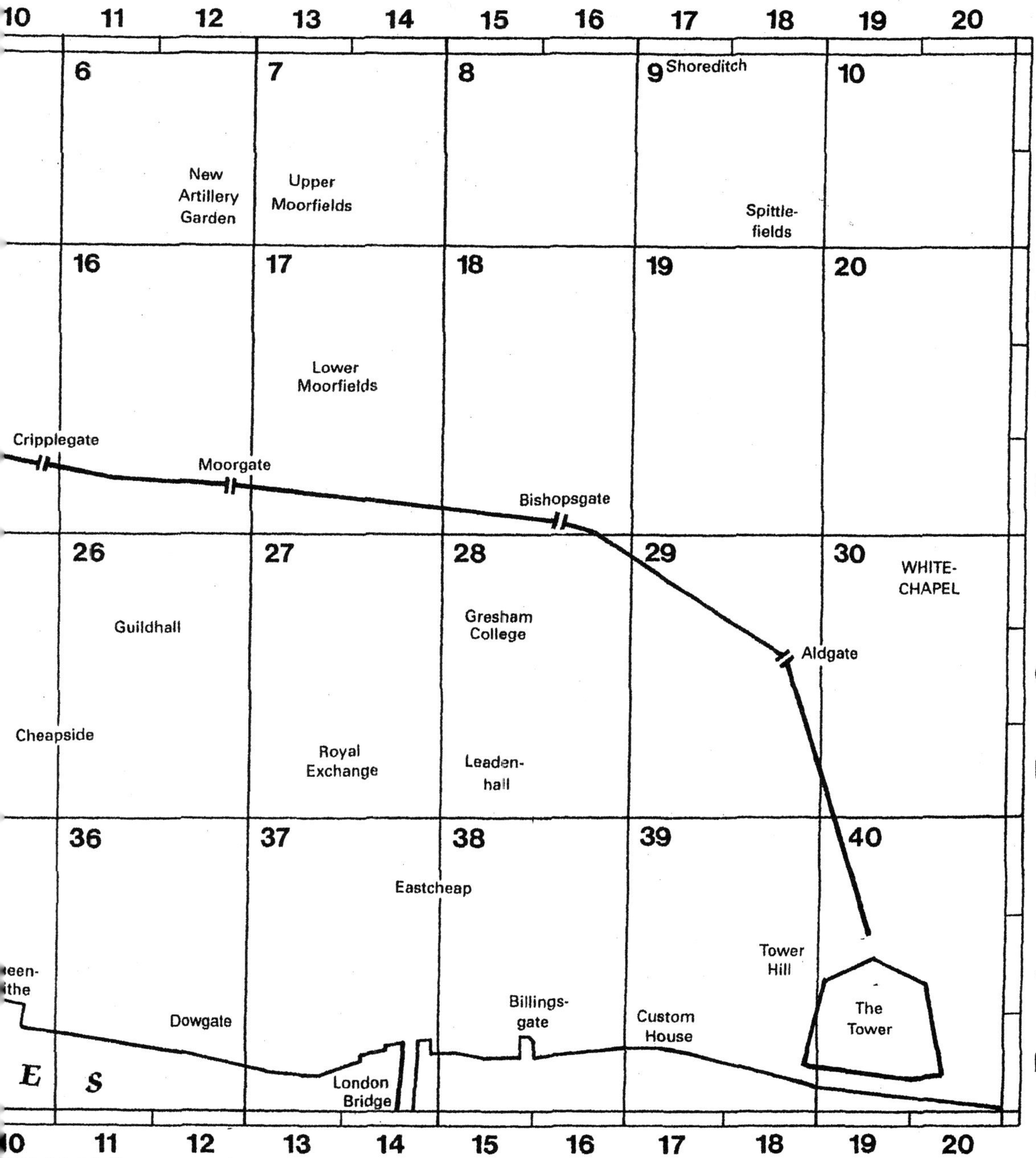

10
11
12
13
14
15
16
17
18
19
20
A
B
C
D
E
F
G
H
I
J
K
6
7
8
9
10
Shoreditch
New
Artillery
Garden
Upper
Moorfields
Spittle-
fields
16
17
18
19
20
Lower
Moorfields
Cripplegate
Moorgate
Bishopsgate
26
27
28
29
30
WHITE-
CHAPEL
Guildhall
Gresham
College
Aldgate
Cheapside
Royal
Exchange
Leaden-
hall
36
37
38
39
40
Eastcheap
Tower
Hill
The
Tower
Dowgate
Billings-
gate
Custom
House
London
Bridge
E
S

ΚEY MAP

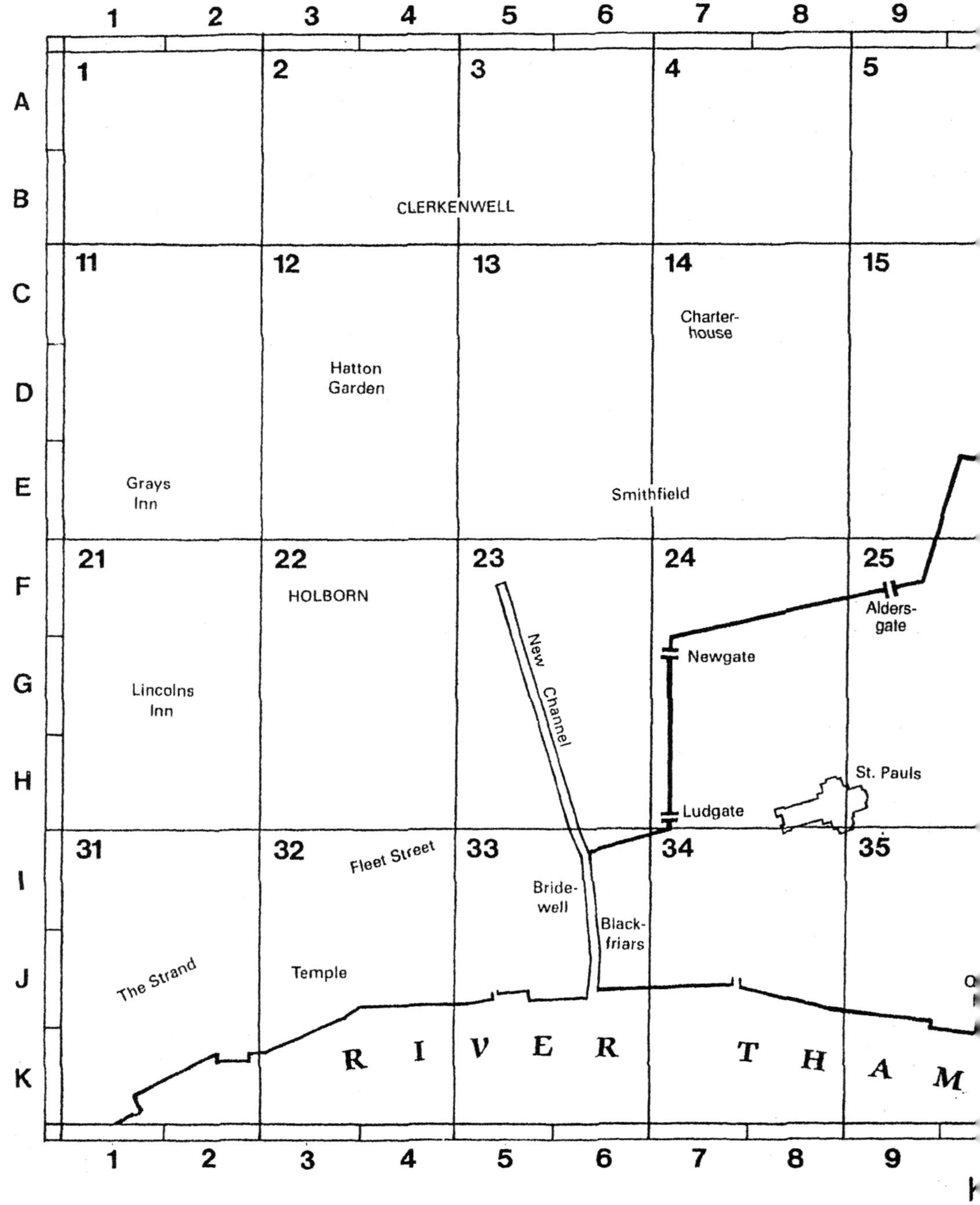
1 2 3 4 5 6 7 8 9
A
B
C
D
E
F
G
H
I
J
K
1
2
3
4
5
CLERKENWELL
11
12
13
14
15
Charter-
house
Hatton
Garden
Grays
Inn
Smithfield
21
22
23
24
25
HOLBORN
Alders-
gate
Newgate
New Channel
Lincolns
Inn
St. Pauls
Ludgate
31
32
Fleet Street
33
34
35
Bride-
well
Black-
friars
The Strand
Temple
R I V E R T H A M
1 2 3 4 5 6 7 8 9

INDEX OF PLACES OF ISSUE

This index includes streets and other localities occurring in Part VII, with bridges, buildings, conduits, and other structures mentioned on the tokens. The named signs of taverns, coffee-houses and other establishments are also covered, as are references to places outside the City. Streets etc. are grouped by the name of each City ward.

INDEX OF TRADES AND OTHER DESCRIPTIONS

Only trades or descriptions named on the tokens or in the notes are indexed; other trades may be identified through the Classified Index of Types

INDEX OF ISSUERS

Personal issuers are indexed by a standardized form of surname, normally the commonest London form as counted by Bardsley 1901, although Cottle 1978, Hanks 1988, and a London telephone directory have been consulted also; reliance has been placed on Reaney 1995 for the etymology of different spellings. Some surnames nevertheless have not been identified, in particular BICKCEM, CLARVEATO, KIFTELL, and KILDERMORE. Others of local origin have been identified with the help of Bardsley 1901 (TORSHELL), Ekwall 1960 (STOTESBERY), Bartholomew 1972, and Ordnance Survey 1989. The Latham rules (Hunnisett 1972, pp. 40-4) provide guiding principles for the early modern period, viz:

(i) Surnames derived from occupations under the standard modern form of the corresponding noun, e,g, Kitchenman, Harrower, Stonehewer;
(ii) Descriptive surnames likewise, e.g. Paramour; but Tyus is from Old French *tieis*;
(iii) Patronymics;
(iv) Surnames derived from clearly recognizable British place names under the modern form, e.g. Carlisle, Coleshill, Gelsthorpe, Goldingay, Horwood (there is no WORWOOD), Outhwaite, Pickford, Sleightholme, Weobley.

Names in Fitz- have been agglutinated, with an intermediate capital, as recommended by Elrington 1970, para. 80. Numbers 6866, 7022, 7164, 7192, 7217, 7296, 7525, 7672 and 7704 are anonymous, and on 6578 and 7623 there is probably a monogram of the issuer's name if it could be deciphered. The actual readings when different from the chosen form are added within brackets, in capitals or italics according to the token, or in lower case (after an initial capital), if from documentary sources. References from these readings are provided unless they would be immediately adjacent.

Abbreviated forenames are silently extended where there is no ambiguity. Indexed also are the following rare forenames (absent from Withycombe 1977): Allanson, the classical Ascanius, Avery, the biblical Euodias, Farnelius, Lowe, Partridge, Pelham, Pharaoh, Thomason, and Grace used as a masculine name.

The Corporation of the Poor, the Parish of St Lawrence Jewry, and Bridewell Hospital, are the corporate issuers listed. Another collective heading is 'Yeomen of the Waterside'. In addition there are entries for the exceptional legends BEST INK FOR RECORDS, FORGET NOT, HIS FARTHINGE WORTH OF COPPER, IN LIEV OF THIS TO Y^{E} BEARER A PENY IS DVE, IN SHOE LANE BY PROVIDENCE, and WORKE FOR THE POORE; in Latin AD SVPEROS, FECIT LON, IN HORAS AD ARMA SVM PARATVS, NISI DOMINVS; and in German ICH DIEN.

INDEX OF LETTERS IN OBVERSE AND REVERSE TYPES

Groups of two or three letters are alphabetized according to the first, i.e. the forename initial. Triangles of letters are read in the order $_{1}{}^{2}{}_{3}$, viz. forename of husband – surname – forename of wife, which was probably the contemporary way of reading them. On 7728 it is unclear whether the initial N stands for the surname Nuce or for a wife's forename.

SYLLOGE OF COINS OF THE BRITISH ISLES

1. FITZWILLIAM MUSEUM, CAMBRIDGE. Ancient British and Anglo-Saxon Coins. By P. GRIERSON. 32 plates, 1958.
2. HUNTERIAN MUSEUM, GLASGOW. Anglo-Saxon Coins. By A. S. ROBERTSON. 42 plates, 1961.
3. COINS OF THE CORITANI. By D. F. ALLEN. 8 plates, 1963.
4. ROYAL COLLECTION, COPENHAGEN. Part I. Ancient British and Anglo-Saxon Coins. By G. GALSTER. 30 plates, 1964.
5. GROSVENOR MUSEUM, CHESTER. Coins with the Chester Mint-Signature. By E. J. E. PIRIE. 16 plates, 1964.
6. NATIONAL MUSEUM OF ANTIQUITIES OF SCOTLAND, EDINBURGH. Anglo-Saxon Coins. By R. B. K. STEVENSON. 29 plates, 1966.
7. ROYAL COLLECTION, COPENHAGEN. Part II. Anglo-Saxon Coins: Æthelræd II. By G. GALSTER. (Publ. jointly with the Carlsberg Foundation.) 71 plates, 1966.
8. BRITISH MUSEUM. Hiberno-Norse Coins. By R. H. M. DOLLEY. 8 plates, 1966.
9. ASHMOLEAN MUSEUM, OXFORD. Part I. Anglo-Saxon Pennies. By J. D. A. THOMPSON. 42 plates, 1967.
10. ULSTER MUSEUM, BELFAST. Part I. Anglo-Irish Coins, John-Edward III. By M. DOLLEY and W. SEABY. (Publ. jointly with the Trustees of the Ulster Museum.) 20 plates, 1968.
11. READING UNIVERSITY. Anglo-Saxon and Norman Coins; ROYAL COIN CABINET, STOCKHOLM. [Part VI.] Anglo-Norman Pennies. By C. E. BLUNT and M. DOLLEY. (Publ. jointly with the Swedish Royal Academy.) 20 plates, 1969.
12. ASHMOLEAN MUSEUM, OXFORD. Part II. English Coins 1066-1279. By D. M. METCALF. 36 plates, 1969.

13-15. ROYAL COLLECTION, COPENHAGEN. Parts IIIA, B and C. Anglo-Saxon Coins: Cnut. By G. GALSTER. (Publ. jointly with the Carlsberg Foundation.) 158 plates, 1970. (3 vols.)

16. NORWEB COLLECTION. Ancient British and English Coins to 1180. By C. E. BLUNT, F. ELMORE JONES and R. P. MACK. 17 plates, 1971.
17. MIDLAND MUSEUMS, Ancient British, Anglo-Saxon, and Norman Coins. By A. J. H. GUNSTONE. 30 plates, 1971.
18. ROYAL COLLECTION, COPENHAGEN. Part IV. Anglo-Saxon Coins from Harold I and Anglo-Norman Coins. By G. GALSTER. (Publ. jointly with the Carlsberg Foundation.) 54 plates, 1972.
19. BRISTOL AND GLOUCESTER MUSEUMS. Ancient British Coins and Coins of the Bristol and Gloucestershire Mints. By L. V. GRINSELL, C. E. BLUNT and M. DOLLEY. 27 plates, 1972.
20. MACK COLLECTION. Ancient British, Anglo-Saxon, and Norman Coins. By R. P. MACK. 56 plates, 1973.
21. YORKSHIRE COLLECTIONS. Coins from Northumbrian Mints c. 895-1279; Ancient British and later coins from other mints to 1279. By E. J. E. PIRIE. 54 plates, 1975.
22. ROYAL COLLECTION, COPENHAGEN. Part V. Hiberno-Norse and Anglo-Irish Coins. By G. GALSTER with M. DOLLEY and J. STEEN JENSEN. 22 Plates, 1975.
23. ASHMOLEAN MUSEUM, OXFORD. Part III. Coins of Henry VII. By D. M. METCALF. 53 plates, 1976.
24. WEST COUNTRY MUSEUMS. Ancient British, Anglo-Saxon and Anglo-Norman Coins. By A. J. H. GUNSTONE. 35 plates, 1977.
25. NATIONAL MUSEUM, HELSINKI. Anglo-Saxon and Anglo-Norman Coins. By T. TALVIO. 41 plates, 1978.
26. MUSEUMS IN EAST ANGLIA. Morley St Peter Hoard and Anglo-Saxon, Norman, and Angevin Coins, and later coins of the Norwich Mint. By T. H. MCK. CLOUGH. 52 plates, 1980.

27. LINCOLNSHIRE COLLECTIONS. Coins from Lincolnshire Mints and Ancient British and later coins to 1272. By A. J. H. GUNSTONE. 68 plates, 1981.
28. CUMULATIVE INDEX OF VOLS. 1-20. By V. SMART. 1981.
29. MERSEYSIDE COUNTY MUSEUMS. Ancient British and later coins to 1279. By M. WARHURST. 39 plates, 1982.
30. AMERICAN COLLECTIONS. Ancient British, Anglo-Saxon and Norman Coins. By J. D. BRADY. 30 plates, 1982.
31. NORWEB COLLECTION. Tokens of the British Isles 1575-1750. Part I. Bedfordshire to Devon. By R. H. THOMPSON. 35 plates, 1984.
32. ULSTER MUSEUM, BELFAST. Part II. Hiberno-Norse Coins. By W. SEABY. (Publ. jointly with the Trustees of the Ulster Museum.) 16 plates, 1984.
33. BROOKER COLLECTION. Coins of Charles I. By J. J. NORTH and P. J. PRESTON-MORLEY. 130 plates, 1984.
34. BRITISH MUSEUM. Anglo-Saxon Coins. Part V. Athelstan to Edgar's Reform. By M. M. ARCHIBALD and C. E. BLUNT. 56 plates, 1986.
35. ASHMOLEAN AND HUNTERIAN MUSEUMS. Scottish Coins. By J. D. BATESON and N. J. MAYHEW, 116 plates, 1987.
36. STATE MUSEUM BERLIN. Anglo-Saxon, Anglo-Norman and Hiberno-Norse Coins. By B. KLUGE. (Publ. jointly with the State Museum Berlin.) 41 plates, 1987.
37. POLISH MUSEUMS. Anglo-Saxon and later medieval British coins. By A. MIKOŁAJCZYK. (Publ. jointly with the Archaeological and Ethnographical Museum in Łódź.) 20 plates, 1987.
38. NORWEB COLLECTION. Tokens of the British Isles 1575-1750. Part II. Dorset to Gloucestershire. By R. H. THOMPSON. 41 plates, 1988.
39. NORTH COLLECTION. Edwardian English Silver Coins, 1279-1351. By J. J. NORTH. 46 plates, 1989.
40. ROYAL COIN CABINET, STOCKHOLM. Part IV. Anglo-Saxon Coins: Harold I and Harthacnut. By T. TALVIO. 74 plates, 1991.
41. CUMULATIVE INDEX OF VOLS. 21-40. By V. J. SMART. 1992.
42. SOUTH-EASTERN MUSEUMS. Ancient British, Anglo-Saxon and later coins to 1279. By A. J. H. GUNSTONE with V. SMART and others. 78 plates, 1992.
43. NORWEB COLLECTION. Tokens of the British Isles 1575-1750. Part III. Hampshire to Lincolnshire. By R. H. THOMPSON and M. J. DICKINSON. 51 plates, 1993.
44. NORWEB COLLECTION. Tokens of the British Isles 1575-1750. Part IV. Norfolk to Somerset. By R. H. THOMPSON and M. J. DICKINSON. 50 plates, 1993.
45. LATVIAN COLLECTIONS. Anglo-Saxon and later British Coins. By T. BERGA. 12 plates, 1996.
46. NORWEB COLLECTION. Tokens of the British Isles 1575-1750. Part V. Staffordshire to Westmorland. By R. H. THOMPSON and M. J. DICKINSON. 51 plates, 1996.
47. SCHNEIDER COLLECTION. Part I. English Gold Coins and their Imitations, 1257-1603. By P. WOODHEAD. 83 plates, 1996.
48. NORTHERN MUSEUMS. Ancient British, Anglo-Saxon, Norman and Plantagenet Coins to 1279. By J. BOOTH. 64 plates, 1997.
49. NORWEB COLLECTION. Tokens of the British Isles 1575-1750. Part VI. Wiltshire to Yorkshire, Ireland to Wales. By R. H. THOMPSON and M. J. DICKINSON. 43 plates, 1999.
50. HERMITAGE MUSEUM, ST PETERSBURG. Part I. Anglo-Saxon Coins to 1016. By V. M. POTIN. 54 plates, 1999.
51. ESTONIAN COLLECTIONS. Anglo-Saxon, Anglo-Norman and later British Coins. By I. LEIMUS and A. MOLVÕGIN. 54 plates, 2001.

52. UPPSALA UNIVERSITY COIN CABINET. Anglo-Saxon and Anglo-Norman Coins. By E. LINDBERGER. (Publ. jointly with the University of Uppsala.) 37 plates, 2006.
53. SCOTTISH MUSEUMS. English Coins, 1066-1279. By J. D. BATESON. 38 plates, 2001.
54. ROYAL COIN CABINET, STOCKHOLM. Part V. Anglo-Saxon Coins: Edward the Confessor and Harold II, 1042-1066. By F. COLMAN. Part VI supplement. Anglo-Norman Pennies. By M. BLACKBURN and K. JONSSON. 57 plates, forthcoming.
55. HERMITAGE MUSEUM, ST PETERSBURG. Part IV. English, Irish and Scottish Coins, 1066-1485. By M. MUCHA. 23 plates, 2005.
56. MASS COLLECTION. English Short Cross Coins, 1180-1247. By J. P. MASS. 82 plates, 2001.
57. SCHNEIDER COLLECTION. Part II. English Gold Coins, 1603 to the 20th Century. By P. WOODHEAD. 58 plates, 2001.
58. NATIONAL MUSEUMS OF SCOTLAND, EDINBURGH. Scottish Coins Part I. 1526-1603. By N. M. MCQ. HOLMES. 99 plates, 2006.
59. NORWEB COLLECTION. Tokens of the British Isles 1575-1750. Part VII. City of London. By R. H. THOMPSON and M. J. DICKINSON. 61 plates, 2007.

Published by the British Academy, except Nos. 8 and 34 published by the Trustees of the British Museum, and Nos. 16,31,33,38,43-4,46-7, 49, 57 and 59 published by Spink & Son Ltd.